A First Course in Rail Transport Planning

Steven Boldeman

© Dolans Publishing

Copyright Notice
All rights reserved. This work is copyright. No part of this work may be reproduced, stored in a retrieval system, or transmitted in any form or by any means with the prior written permission of the publisher. Except as permitted under the Copyright Act 1968, for example, any fair dealing for the purposes of private study, research, criticism, or review, subject to certain limitations. These limitations include restricting the copying to a maximum of one chapter or 10% of this book, whichever is greater.

National Library of Australia Cataloguing-in-Publication Data
Creator: Boldeman, Steven Author
Title: A First Course in Rail Transport Planning
ISBN: 978-0-648093-1-4

Subjects – Railroads – Planning
Transportation – Planning
Transportation - Australia

Dolans Publishing

For Bianca and Sam

Foreword

This book is the culmination of many years of effort and research. This book is meant to be a complete first course for those wishing to learn about rail transport planning in one semester. The book is divided into weeks, with 12 weeks in total. This is the standard university semester in Australia.

The book has been pitched at students of engineering and economics. It is not meant to be a book on managing rail operations, which is a different topic and different to the one presented in this book.

I've written a number of books on topics around rail transport planning, and this is the seventh in that series. The first was a very large book called "An Introduction to Rail Transport Planning", but actually the coverage of the topic in that book was very extensive. I then wrote several other books, each specialising on a specific topic for rail transport planning. These books used material mostly drawn from my first book.

This book is intended to be a complete reference for the topic, but limited to the easier and more digestible topics. Some of the topics in rail transport planning are pretty challenging, and so for this book I have excluded them. This is a shame, but I may write another book on the advanced design of passenger rail systems, in which case these topics will be again included. The topics are in "Introduction to Rail Transport Planning", which is a big book and very long.

One again I am confronted by the challenge of choosing which topics to include. Some topics, such as station design is not covered as thoroughly as my book on station design, but it's not too bad and there is some good stuff in there. Much of the material from my book on rail economics is also there, but I really couldn't include all of it as this would make the book too long. I really hope the reader appreciates the topics I have chosen to include.

Table of Contents

WEEK 1 2

An overview of the rail industry 2

Describing a Rail System 18
    Number of passengers per day 18
    Route Length 19
    Number of Stations 20
    Traffic Type 21
    Power Supply 22
    Gauge 23
    Number of Lines 24

WEEK 2 27

Types of Passenger Rail Systems 27
    Light Rail Systems 30
    Heavy Rail 45
    Other Rail Systems 62

Overview of Rail Infrastructure 73
    Track 73
    Signalling 82
    Electrical (Traction systems) 88
    Tunnels 94
    Bridges 97
    Road and Pedestrian Level Crossings 99
    Control Systems 101

WEEK 3 106

Basic Station Types 106
    Styles and Configurations of Stations 106
    Terminal Stations 113
    Major Components of a Station 114
    Access in and out of Stations 118

Customer Support on Stations 122
    Passenger information systems 123
    Maps 127
    Timetable Information 127
    Tickets and Ticketing 129

Vending Machines and Advertising	132
Souvenir Shops	135
Other Infrastructure	136
Other Aspects of Station Design	**139**
Introduction	139
Exits and Entrances	139
Concourses	142
Interchange Stations	147
Short Platforms	151
Cover for Passengers from the Elements	153
Straight and Curved Platforms	154
Light Rail Station Design	157

WEEK 4   163

Rollingstock, Capacity and Seating	**163**
Capacity	164
Helping People with Disabilities	168
Seating Layout	171
Getting People On and Off	174
Grades	177
Stabling	**183**
The Tidal Nature of Commuter Services	189
Well designed stabling	190
Different Configurations of Stabling	191
Stabling of Freight	195

WEEK 5   197

Rail System Drawing and Configuration	**197**
Passenger Orientated Rail Drawings	198
Geographically Correct Maps	203
Detailed Drawing of Rail Systems	204
Approaches to Network Design	**215**
Introduction	215
Avoiding Mistakes with Network Design	217
A Standard Rail System for Large Cities	219
Some Examples of Network Design – Multiple Lines	233
Rail Systems and Connections to HSR	247

WEEK 6 — 251

Structure/Loading Gauge and Platform Heights — 251
- Loading and Structure Gauge — 251
- Platform Heights — 258

The Kinematics of Train Movement and other useful equations — 262

Getting People through Stations — 275
- Introduction — 275
- Passenger Flow Modelling — 277
- Designing better Platforms — 287

WEEK 7 — 295

Emissions and Rail Systems — 295
- Introduction — 295
- Formulas and Calculations for Energy Consumption — 298
- CO_2 Emissions per Kilowatt hour per Country — 301
- Typical Emissions per Rail Mode — 302
- Diesel Vs Electric — 307

Power Consumption — 314
- Introduction — 314
- Typical Values for Power Consumption — 314
- Driving Trains Efficiency — 322
- Power Consumed in Stations and other Facilities — 325
- Being more efficient with Power Consumption — 328
- Power Consumption, the Environment and the Population Density of Cities — 332

WEEK 8 — 339

Supply and Demand — 339
- Introduction — 339
- The Supply Demand Curve/Model — 341
- Elasticity of Demand — 348
- Fixed/Variable Cost, and Marginal Costs — 350
- Financial Comparison of Train Travel to Automobiles — 352

Externalities — 356
- Introduction — 356
- Changes in Asset Values from Building Rail Lines — 358
- The Pricing of Road Congestion — 360
- The Economics of Safety Benefits — 365
- The Relationship between Property Values and Freight Systems — 368

WEEK 9 — 370

Demand Estimation — 370
- Introduction — 370
- Different Techniques — 371
- Demand Elasticises — 375

Financing Large Projects — 380
- Introduction — 380
- Public Private Partnerships — 385
- Gifts and Aid — 386
- Success and Failure — 388

Tourism and Rail Systems — 390
- Introduction — 390
- Economic Benefits of Tourist Railways — 395

WEEK 10 — 404

Freight — 404
- Introduction — 404
- Overview of Freight Systems — 406
- Rail Freight Lines — 416
- Rail Freight and Government Policy — 419
- Different Types of Freight — 425
- Terminal Design — 438

WEEK 11 — 445

Timetabling — 445
- Introduction — 445
- Express, Limited Services and All Stoppers — 453
- Increasing Trip Speed as Much as Possible (Using Timetables) — 458
- Structuring a Timetable — 461
- Managing Dwell Times — 463
- Adding more trains into a Timetable — 465
- Making Changes to a Complex Timetable — 467
- The Process of Creating a Timetable — 468
- Managing a Bad Timetable — 471
- Timetabling Freight — 472

Choosing Frequencies of Trains and Service Hours — 475
- Choosing a train frequency (and headway) — 477
- Choosing Service Hours — 484

Week 1

An overview of the rail industry

The rail industry worldwide is very large, and employs large numbers of people. There are 130,000 people directly employed by rail infrastructure companies in continental Western Europe alone, not including all the people indirectly employed and rail operators. The rail industry is very large and generally speaking, fairly well funded.

Railways are common on all continents of the world except Antarctica. Large railway companies exist on every continent, and worldwide there are millions of kilometres of track in place. At any one time there are hundreds of construction projects progressing, and billions of dollars being spent on new rail lines. This frenzy of activity is not expected to really end any time soon, the rail industry will provide a home and continued employment for many years to come.

The rail industry can be divided into a number of key industry participants, companies and government departments. These include:
- Rail operators, who run trains and passenger services
- . This also includes freight operators. Rail operators are often split into the company that maintains the fixed infrastructure, and so are free for focus on maintaining and operating trains. This type of organisation often contains people with many years of operational rail experience.
- Infrastructure maintainers, who maintain the infrastructure needed to move trains around. These companies can be very large, and almost always rely heavily on government support for money. Mostly these organisations have many engineers, and tend to hire a lot of electrical and civil engineers. A common profession within this company is the "fettler", who maintains track. Since 1996 the EU has required infrastructure companies to be separate from operating companies
- A combined company that manages all rail operations and maintenance of equipment. This company may also run other transport services in the area, such as buses. This type of company is common for metros, which are operationally simpler than commuter or regional railways. One rail company in Singapore is called SMRT, and operates buses, trains and taxis.

- Manufacturers of railway equipment, companies that can be very large. Bombardier, one of the largest companies, reputedly has almost 35,000 people worldwide, and manufacturers almost all the components needed for a railway. Other companies are Alstom, Siemans, Kawaski, and Ansaldo, but there are many others. Smaller companies may specialise on particular engineering items. Overall the competence of these companies seems high.
- Government departments supervising rail companies, and there is obviously at least one of these in each country. A government dep
- artment will usually monitor, and report on the performance of each rail company, for both infrastructure companies and operators. There may be more than one department involved, or one may predominantly manage the rail industry whilst the others have a smaller role. Often this department will make recommendations on large rail projects, and be involved in long term rail planning.
- Professional consulting companies, who provide specialist advice on the management of rail companies and services. There are many of these, and one well known example, especially in the US, is Parsons Brinkerhoff (now WSP). These companies may specialise in the rail industry, or provide more generalised advice to many different heavy industries. The rail industry is very large and has many niche engineering areas, and even the larger rail consulting companies struggle to provide a complete range of services to rail projects.
- Universities, especially ones with specialised departments researching in rail technology and planning. These departments can be very large, hundreds of people, and can be very influential in the development and approval of large rail projects. These departments are often very strong in economic analysis of rail and large infrastructure projects.
- Construction companies, which project manage the construction in any major project. These companies specialise in project management of construction projects, and often have large numbers of civil engineers. These companies will often manage large projects for rail companies or governments, and subcontract out many different parts of the construction project.

- Companies that provide management of transport within cities or sometimes even countries. Some companies specialise in management of transport systems, and this can be useful when a government wants to "franchise" out the management of the rail sector or a part of a rail system. Perhaps the best known of these companies is Veolia, a French company, which manages transport for buses and trains.
- Specialist maintainers of equipment, who maintain equipment for a fee. This type of company will maintain almost anything, and several in Australia have grown to be very large, both in revenues and number of employees. There has been an upsurge of activity in this sector, where private companies are now maintaining more and more of the assets in a railway. The experience in Australia with this type of company has been mixed. This type of company may be involved in the bid for any project that is design-build-maintain.

There are of course other participants, but these are the main ones.

Another organisation that should be mentioned is Comet Nova. This organisation benchmarks the performance of many different railways across the world, and writes reports on rail related topics. This organisation is managed from Imperial College in London, and they collate a lot of the information and write a lot of the reports. This information can be useful should the reader obtain access to the reports produced by them, but this is challenging. Even for a rail employee to get access to this information is very difficult, and access is limited to a small number. Often rail companies publish graphs and other items from Comet Nova reports, and those with an understanding or have seen other complete reports can reconstruct what these reports actually mean. Someone on the outside without any prior exposure would have difficulty in using the reports effectively.

A large railway will be dealing constantly with all of the different organisations listed above. The interface between each of these organisations is often managed by specialised liaison managers, who provide information, create and monitor contracts, and report to their respective departments on the goings on in the other organisations. The author's experience has been that many of these interfaces are difficult, but not unmanageably so. The relationship with government departments often depends on the history of the rail organisation in that country, where there have been accidents and poor operating performance, then the relationship is poor. Where the rail system is widely respected, the relationship is better.

The writing of contracts is key to the management of some of these interfaces. In not all cases will a contract be appropriate, and between two government departments a contract has relatively little meaning. A contract should be precise and clear as to the responsibilities on both sides. A poorly written contract can have a large impact on the financial performance of the respective organisations that signed it. Interface contracts are created in substantial numbers, and usually contain key performance indicators that are relevant to the management of the rail business. The success of each company is measured against these KPI's.

Within a rail operator, typically there are a number of key business units, who deliver services to customers. Depending on the nature of the business, there will be the following business units:
- An operating division, that contains train crews, i.e., drivers, guards, ticket inspectors, passenger attendants, and any staff that serve food in bistros or other serving outlets
- Station staff, who sell tickets, clean stations (sometimes), provide information to customers, refund money, etc
- Signalling staff, who set signal routes, and control the movement of trains. In some railways this function is fully automated, or a very small number of people perform this function.
- The control centre, from which the network is operated. This is usually a large room with a large central control panel or view screen in the middle of the room, which displays the position and status of trains. There are varying levels of automation for this type of system.
- A business unit that deals with liaison with external parties, such as government, other companies, infrastructure companies, and customers. This unit is sometimes referred to as media relations.
- A department that contains cleaners, both for trains and stations. Rail companies, especially ones that move people, need a lot of cleaners. This type of work may or may not be outsourced.
- Support services, such as Human Resource Management, payroll, Information Technology, legal, finance and the like.

- Auditing and business reform, and this group often contains project people, who are responsible for implementing some types of business improvements. This group may also perform audits to standards and other quality like documentation.
- A safety department, who are responsible for some parts of safety. This group may perform audits, and investigate incidents that potentially may have become accidents. This group is also responsible for publishing a list of rules for how trains are managed and driven.

There may be other departments, and each rail operator is different.

The other type of rail organisation that will be discussed in detail here are rail infrastructure companies. There are lots of these as the EU requires member countries to separate out these functions from rail operators. A lot of information is available on the internet on the details of these companies, and many of them are very large. These companies can be split into operational groups that include:

- Minor maintenance, where the workers perform routine maintenance, and inspection equipment. This is a large part of the overall company in terms of numbers of staff.
- A group that performs larger maintenance, which requires heavy and specialised equipment. This group may also complete projects. This department often has a large part of the overall maintenance budget.
- A safety assurance group, which inspects and assures maintenance is performed to the standard expected.
- An engineering group, which maintains corporate knowledge of new engineering systems that are available for rail technology. This department will often publish the network statement, which details under what conditions trains can travel through the network.
- A planning group, which decides what projects and major work to perform. This group will also often liaise with external parties and other companies.
- A procurement group, that either organises or supervises the purchase of major materials and equipment
- Support functions, such as finance, HR, legal, and others.

Rail infrastructure maintainers have large budgets, and are often unable to recoup their costs through access charges. Governments usually provide a substantial subsidy to these companies to keep them solvent. As a rough rule of thumb, maybe 25 -50% of their costs may be recovered from fees and other charges to rail operators. The rest usually comes from government, although in some cases may come from land or other taxes in the area around the railways. The author has seen many company reports for this type of company, and they often feel the need to have a long complex annual report with much financial information. They always report a profit, which is a bit strange as most of their funds come from subsidies or taxation.

All large industrialised countries have extensive rail systems, although the purpose to which these railways are put varies widely. Almost all Western countries have sophisticated rail systems (even the Vatican has a small railway!). Andorra has no railway. Most of the European railways are very extensive and have been in existence for at least 100 years. Europe is cris-crossed with large numbers of rails and tracks. Rail is a central part of the lives of most Europeans.

The situation is the United States is rather different from Europe. The rail system in the US is dominated by freight, and passenger networks whilst large are rather small when compared to size of the population. There is almost no high speed rail, and commuter rail systems are mostly limited to the New England area. Light rail is common in the US, and there are some large systems, for example Los Angeles. For a country that has displayed a high degree of technical leadership in many fields, it is surprising to many that the rail industry in the US is so quiet, or at least this is how it seems in Australia. Countries that are active in the rail sphere are France, the UK, Italy, China, Germany and Japan.

The rail industry in Japan is an interesting one, and there is much to learn from that country. Japan has a number of large rail companies who manufacture rail equipment, such as Mitsubishi. The Japanese have invested heavily in research and development in rail technology, and their understanding of rail concepts is generally good. Their high speed rail systems are well run and well maintained, and their technology, especially for tilting trains is excellent. The Japanese rail industry is however very fragmented, and there are numerous rail companies in Japan. In cities such as Osaka there may be 4 or 5 smaller commuter railways, in addition to the subway, that move passengers from the city centre to the suburbs. The high degree of fragmentation, in the author's view, robs them of the ability to demonstrate their ability in rail systems. Their rail companies do not seem to have the critical mass to create a persona in the larger rail industry, which means that their excellent rail technology and systems seem to go unnoticed.

Japan was the first country to implement high speed rail. Their high speed rail system is very good, and has operated for almost 50 years without any fatalities from train collisions or derailments (but other deaths have occurred, and they are difficult to prevent entirely). Japan has a very large number of rail systems, much of which is narrow gauge. The high speed rail system between Tokyo and Osaka is the busiest in the world, and operates profitably.

Japan itself has a large number of rail lines, but limited rail freight. Metro systems in Japan are common, and can be very large. Tokyo has a very large commuter system as well, and the high speed rail system that is so well known. Japan also has the busiest monorail system in the world, as well as the world's busiest metro system. The Tokyo metro system is extremely large, and moves the most people per day of any rail system in the world.

Within Europe the French seem to be the most advanced for rail technology. They too invest heavily in developing it, and their high speed trains are very good. In Paris the metro system is operated by the RATP, and this company manages transportation systems in dozens of countries. France is home to the International Union of Railways, the UIC, which publishes standards and other documentation on rail technology and the management of rail systems.

Canada has some interesting rail systems. There are two old metro systems in Canada, located in Montreal and Toronto, and some large light rail systems in Calgary and Vancouver, and some others. There are two very large freight companies in Canada, who run large operations. There are also significant commuter railways operating in Toronto, as well as Montreal. Perhaps the most interesting railway in Canada is the Vancouver Skytrain, which is a fully automated light rail system.

The Calgary C-train is an interesting rail system because its costs of operation are so low. Railways often benchmark the cost for each passenger journey, and this is an important number. Calgary has a cost of operation at about 30c per trip (Canadian 2005), a very low amount.

They set the standard for reducing costs to a lower level, and have written interesting documents on how to reduce costs.

It is possible to do a lot of benchmarking with Canadian railways. They have every different type of system, and publish interesting articles on rail planning and the management of railways. The author recommends in any rail planning work, to make a quick comparison with one or more Canadian railways, as there is usually some good information to draw upon. The Canadians also have a good understanding of the operation and management of railways, and can be trusted to produce good quality materials.

South East Asia has very good rail systems. The rail system in Hong Kong is truly outstanding, and this railway is considered by many in the region to be the best in Asia, if not the world. This sometimes provides some amusing situations, as rail professionals from Europe know little of the system in Hong Kong, whereas in Australia and Asia the rail system there is held in the highest regard.

Hong Kong's rail company is called MTR, short for Mass Transit Railway. It operates a very impressive railway, and is one of the few profitable railways in the world today. The MTR network is a professionally run efficient operation, and there is much to be learned from travelling through their system. In this book many examples are used from Hong Kong. The main system in Hong Kong is a metro system, although there is a moderate size light rail feeder system in Tuen Mun. Some of the things that make Hong Kong's system so good are:
- A simple ticketing system
- Well laid out stations with good passenger information
- Cheap tickets
- Stations placed in useful and convenient places
- Extensive shopping centres and other facilities placed over the top and near stations
- Shops within the stations themselves, usually bakeries, banks and convenience stores
- It's clean, tidy and safe
- Extremely impressive station design, allowing for very efficient transfers from one line to another
- Easy to use ticketing machines, in multiple languages
- Obvious help points, with staff empowered to offer refunds

- Fast travel times
- Large number of interconnections with surrounding buildings and facilities
- Good cost control

Hong Kong is an example of a rail system that has been improved through constant innovation and attention to detail. There are a large number of innovations installed throughout their system, and in many of the chapters in this book there is some discussion of these, and how they work. Perhaps the greatest advantage of the MTR system is its simplicity, and ease of use.

Whilst there are some railways that produce profits, most are financially very poor performers. Many railways require constant financial support from government, although there are some railways where support is not needed. It is possible to operate a profitable railway, but it's not easy. The vast majority of railways are loss making, and require substantial subsidies to remain in operation. Railways that are profitable are usually drawn from the following list:

- Metros that have very high numbers of passengers, or have some level of property development that supplements their income
- High speed rail services that are well designed and operate between two very large cities (such as Tokyo to Osaka)
- Tourist railways that can charge large amounts for the pleasure of the ride
- Some freight railways, especially ones that move coal or other bulk materials. In Australia these railways are so profitable that they can even support the entire cost of the infrastructure in addition to the cost of rollingstock
- Train services where the cost of the infrastructure is not paid for or the government provides the use of the infrastructure at a greatly reduced rate
- Rail cruises, where very high prices are charged for long distance travel on trains, usually over several days or even more

The key to operating a rail system that generates a profit is a well designed system, and the movement of lots of people or freight. Both are required.

Rail cruises are a very interesting new type of rail company and service. Whilst they do seem to be a relatively new innovation, the Orient Express is one type of rail line that is often seen as being very similar to a rail cruise. Rail cruise trains are often very luxurious and richly furnished. Australia has a small number of these, and there are some in Malaysia and India. They provide high quality food and accommodation to guests. This type of service is almost always privately operated for a profit.

The kinds of systems that operate at a substantial loss are:
- Most metros
- Almost all light rail systems
- Tram systems
- Most commuter systems
- Train systems operating in airports, which don't charge money for the trip, but are paid for by the airport
- Some high speed rail systems
- Monorails with low levels of patronage (which is many of them)

Light rail systems are particularly poor in terms of returning their costs of operation, although there are always exceptions. The problem is that the light rail as a system is characterised by low capacity, and struggles to move enough people to recover its costs. Some light systems were very expensive to build, and the Vancouver Skytrain, an automated people mover, being a good example. Intermediate capacity metros also sometimes suffer from the same problem.

Another particularly interesting light rail system is Metro de Porto, in the Portuguese city of Porto. This system is really a light rail system, but has many of the features of a metro system. Built at substantial cost, and always losing money, this system is very pretty and looks visually very impressive. This system has also won awards for energy efficiency, which makes it useful for benchmarking and comparative purposes.

Combining rail systems with property development and management can be a very successful way to raise revenue. Hong Kong MTR has really pioneered this type of rail planning and construction, and it seems to be relatively uncommon in Europe and the US. This is sometimes called Transport Orientated Development, or TOD. In the construction of the New Delhi metro, this model was closely followed. There is a lot to be said about how to go about this/

The list of metro systems that produce a profit is interesting. The author is aware of at least the following:
- Tokyo metro
- Taipei metro
- Hong Kong MTR
- Singapore SMRT
- New Delhi metro
- Moscow metro
- Osaka metro

Hong Kong MTR has shares listed on the stock exchange, and is easily the best known profitable railway. Their annual reports make for very interesting reading, as the focus is clearly on property management, and not on moving people. The first part of their annual report is entirely devoted to various statistics on property management.

Singapore SMRT and the Tokyo metro are also listed on stock exchanges. Taipei metro is interesting because it operates at an extremely low cost per passenger kilometre, and is able to generate a profit because its costs are just so low. Moscow metro moves huge numbers of people very efficiently.

A number of rail systems exist in airports. Some airports are so big that a train system is needed to get around within the airport. Both Hong Kong and Singapore airports have rail systems which are surprisingly large given they are entirely contained within the airport. Other cities that have these systems include Osaka, and Taipei. All fully automated, these systems operate without drivers. JKF airport in the US also has one of these systems. The rail system typically used in airports is an Automated People Mover (APM), which is a type of rail system where the rail vehicles are very small, and the trains are driverless.

A small number of rail systems code share with airlines. This unusual situation allows customers to buy a combined ticket with an airline that includes travel on a train. This type of arrangement is used in Germany and Switzerland. It is important for the railway, if it is participating in this type of alliance, to have good quality services that are reliable and efficient. Also, a code share agreement would be unlikely with a rail service without reserved seats, such as a metro, but much more likely with a regional service or an intercity connection.

Swiss airways has a code share agreement with Swiss Railways for any trips from Basel through Zurich and then on to any destination as served by Swiss Air. Two tickets are issued for the trip, one for the train trip and the other for the airline. Whilst there is a lot of information on code sharing on the internet, the author has struggled to find information on combined rail/air services. One suspects that this arrangement works only with difficulty, and should be only reserved for cities with no airports, with reserved seating on trains to a city with a large airport.

In general the relationship between rail and air transport seems to be improving. It is becoming more common for rail companies to provide check-in facilities at very major stations for air travel. The way this works is that passengers buy a ticket to the airport on the rail system, and the price of the ticket includes the ability to check-in luggage at the station, for a journey on a plane. Check-in is performed at the station away from the airport, and luggage is transferred by the rail system to the airport.

Checkin for Airlines at a Station

The photo above shows the air check-in counters at KL Sentral in Kuala Lumpur in Malaysia. The ticket barriers stop passengers for using the service without buying a rail ticket in addition to the plane ticket. Once through the barriers, passengers go to the check-in counters to check-in their baggage.

REFERENCES

1. Zhang, Y & Yan, X & Comtois, C *Some Measures of Increasing Rail Transit Riderships: Case Studies*, Chinese Geographical Science, Volume 10, Number 1, pp 80 – 88, 2000

2. BTS Group, Annual Report 2009/2010 (the Bangkok Skytrain)

3. DG-TREN, *Final Report BOB Railway Case – Benchmarking Passenger Transport in Railways*, Aug 2003

4. Ang-Olson, J. & Mahendra, A. *Cost Benefit Analysis of Converting a Lane for Bus Rapid Transit – Phase II Evaluation and Methodology*, National Cooperative Highway Research Program, Research Results Digest 352.

5. Taipei Rapid Transit Corporation *2013 Annual Report*, http://english.metro.taipei/ct.asp?xItem=1056448&ctNode=70219&mp=122036

6. banedanmark, *Profile brochure*, http://uk.bane.dk/publikationer_eng.asp?artikelID=915

7. Infrabel, *Network Statement*, Version of 9/12/2011

8. banedanmark, *Network Statement,* 2012, Jan 2011

9. Infrabel, *Annual Financial Statements 2010*

10. CFL, *Rapport Annuel*, 2011 (In French)

11. Metro de Porto, *Annual Report*, 2009

12. Jernbaneverket, *On Track 2010*

13. Koppenjan, J. & Leijten, M. *How to Sell Railways: Lessons on the privatisation of Three Dutch Railway Projects*, European Journal of Transport and Infrastructure Research, Sept 2007

14. Prorail, *Network Statement 2013*

15. Andersonn, M. *Marginal cost of railway infrastructure wear and tear for freight and passenger trains in Sweden*, Swedish National Road and Transport Research Institute (VTI), Department of Transport Economics, 2011

16. Fabian, J. *The Exceptional Service of Driverless Metros*, Journal of Advanced Transportation, Vol 33, No 1, pp 5-16

17. Kimijima, N. et al New Urban Transport for Middle East Monorail System for Dubai Palm Jumeirah Transit System, Hitachi Review Vol 59, (2010), No 1

18. Cheng, HY. *High Speed Rail in Taiwan: New experience and issues for future development*, Transport Policy 17 (2010) 51-63, Nov 2009

19. MTR, *Annual Report 2012*, https://www.mtr.com.hk/en/corporate/investor/financialinfo.html#02

20. Cervero, R. & Murakami, J. *Rail and Property Development in Hong Kong: Experiences and Extensions*, Urban Studies, 2009 46:2019 Aug 2009

21. Scarsi, G.C. & Smith, G. *Different Approaches and Responsibilities for Investment Sustainability in EU Railway Infrastructure: Four Case Studies*, EUI Working Papers, RSCAS 2010/88

22. BSL Management Consultants *The Cost of Railway Infrastructure Status-Quo and Ways Ahead*, Presentation to the ProMain Council of Decision Makers, Brussels Nov 2001

23. Metro de Porto *Annual Report 2011*, http://www.metrodoporto.pt/en/

24. SMRT Corporation Ltd *Annual Report 2013*, http://www.smrt.com.sg/Investor-Relations/Annual-Reports

25. Gaylord, MS. & Lester, D *Suicide in the Hong Kong subway*, Soc Sci Med, 1994 Feb; 38 (3): 427-30

26. The Government of Western Australia Public Transport Authority, *Annual Report 2010-11*,

http://www.pta.wa.gov.au/PublicationsandPolicies/AnnualReports/tabid/106/Default.aspx

27. International Union of Railways *Line Comparison Study*, Project Report of the UIC Asset Management Working Group, Jan 2011

28. South Coast British Columbia Transportation Authority Translink 2009 Annual Report, http://www.translink.ca/site-info/search-results.aspx

29. Transportation Research Board National Research Council *TCRP Report 2 Applicability of Low-Floor Light Rail Vehicles in North America*, 1995

Describing a Rail System

There are several commonly used parameters that can be used to almost completely describe a rail system and many of these are described below. Some of them are related to the size of the network, the number of people that use the system, how the system is used by its passengers, and some other useful information.

Number of passengers per day

The size of any rail system is often judged in terms of the number of trips per day. A rail system that moves 10,000 per day is dramatically different to one that moves 1 million per day. Small rail systems can have a lot less infrastructure, compared to a large system that might move 3 million per day.

An alternative name for trips is boardings.

Sizes of rail systems – Number of Passengers		
Trips per day	**Description**	**Comments**
<10,000	Very small	Tourist trains, some tram systems, a small light rail system, an APM in an airport
10,000 to 100,000	Small	High speed rail, most commuter rail systems, small to medium light rail systems
100,000 to 1,000,000	Medium sized	Metros with 2 or 3 lines, large light rail systems, large commuter systems
> 1,000,000	Large	Very large commuter systems, some metros in big cities. No light rail or high speed rail systems move this number of people, nor monorails

Rail as a transport system is capable of moving very large numbers of people. Buses may only move small numbers in comparison, as a reasonable sized bus may move 60 to 100 people, and a commuter train may move a thousand. One of the great advantages or rail systems is the ability to move large numbers of people. A BRT (Bus Rapid Transit) system that has 20 buses per hour, will only move between 1200 to 2000 people per hour for one line in any one direction, and for rail transport this would be considered a very low number. Even the largest BRT systems are small in comparison to a moderately sized rail system.

Route Length

The route length of a rail system is an important metric. Rail systems can be very small, but can also be very effective. A short length system can move very large numbers of people, especially if it is a metro, even it is quite small. Tram and light rail systems often have a very low number of kilometres of route length, whereas a regional rail system can be extremely large.

Route length is normally measured in kilometres, unless it's in North America or the UK. Care needs to be taken in not confusing route length with track length. The route is the rail corridor where the tracks pass through, and there can be more than one track in any rail corridor. Some rail corridors have many tracks, and up to six is quite common, and some places there are more. There are also some places where trains are stored, and this is called stabling. When counting track length, stabling and marshalling yards can add a lot of kilometres, but for route length add very little.

The table below shows how many route kilometres constitute a large or small system. Again, these numbers are just a guide, and are included to give the reader some sense of what a large or small system looks like.

Route kilometres		
Length	**Size**	**Comments**
< 10 kms	Tiny	One metro line, tourist railway, monorail, airport syste

Route kilometres		
Length	**Size**	**Comments**
	m	
10 – 30 kms	Very small	One or two metro lines, mostly removed legacy tram systems
30 – 100 kms	Small	Many metro systems, many light rail systems, small commuter rail systems, no high speed rail
100 – 500 kms	Medium	Very large tram or light rail systems, commuter rail systems, smaller high speed rail systems
500 – 5000 kms	Large	Large commuter or high speed rail systems, no metros, light rail, monorails nor trams in this category
> 5000 kms	Extremely large	National rail systems, extensive regional train system

What is large for one system can be small for another. High speed rail systems tend to be large, hundreds of kilometres at least, whereas metros are far smaller.

Number of Stations

The number of stations is a key measure for any rail system. The number can vary enormously, as high speed rail systems may have only a tiny number of stations, for example the high speed rail system in Taiwan only has 8 stations. On the other hand, even small tram or light rail systems can have very large numbers of stations, as every street corner can serve as a station. Tram stops are often only 500 metres apart, and a stop on one side in one direction does not mean that there is a matching tram stop on the other side/direction. A tram system of 10 kilometres may have 20 stations. In a tram system there can be large number of stops.

Even for heavy rail, it is not always clear what constitutes a station for counting purposes. Some stations are only opened at certain times of the year, or for special events. Others, especially ones for horse racing or stadia, are only opened when an event is on. There are also small stations where trains do not ordinarily stop, and sometimes these are called halts. A halt is a stop where passengers need to ask rail staff for the train to stop, otherwise the train does not stop. Passengers who need to board a train from a halt need to signal to the driver to stop, and with some luck, this will happen.

Despite the problems with counting the number of stations in a rail system, most of the time it is a very good measure of the size of a system. In most situations a station can be clearly identified from the surrounding track.

Traffic Type

Many, or maybe most, rail systems move only one type of rail traffic. For example, a tram system moves only trams, and does not move commuter or high speed rail traffic. There are always exceptions to this, and some tram systems used to move freight, and there are still a very small number that still do. The different categories of rail traffic types are:

- Light rail
- Trams
- Freight
- Metros (heavy rail)
- Commuter (heavy rail)
- High speed rail
- Others

It should be noted that a rail system that has both passenger and freight traffic is often described as a "mixed" system.

Power Supply

The source of power for any rail system is a very important parameter for any railway. The choice of power source has a large influence on the type of infrastructure that needs to be built to support rail operations. As a rough guide, electricity is provided for rail services where there are large numbers of train movements per day, or for high speed rail. Freight, regional, overnight and commuter systems often use diesel power.

Many rail systems are powered through electricity. Steam power was once extremely common as a source of power, but has fallen out of favour with its high maintenance and running costs. The trend away from steam and to diesel and electric power took decades, and by the mid 70s most of the steam locomotives had been removed, although in some parts of the world continued to be used for another 10 years or so. Steam locomotives now are only used on tourist lines.

There are other methods of propulsion other than steam, electricity and diesel power. An extremely small number of rail systems still use cables, where the rail vehicle grabs onto the cable and is pulled along. This type of system was once common, and cables run underneath city streets, pulled from a central point called a powerhouse. One of the last remaining cable car systems is in San Francisco, and this system is still manual, so a tram employee (called the gripman) needs to apply a clamp to the cable to get the street car to move.

Most trains are diesel or electric, although there are some tourist trains that are steam powered. Diesel systems use diesel fuel to move trains, and electric systems use power generated far away at a power generator to move. Electric systems can be divided into a number of smaller categories, and these are based on the type of electrical power provided. Each rail system can be identified as using one or more power systems that are typically used in a rail system. Power systems are either AC (alternating current) or DC (direct current). AC is now the standard for new rail systems, although the voltages need to be higher, and in some cases this can present a safety risk, so for light rail and trams DC is still preferred. DC is the older power system that previously was commonly used, but now is being slowly replaced with more cost efficient AC power.

Also with the power system almost always a voltage is specified. Common voltages are:
- 750 volts
- 1500 volts
- 3000 volts
- 25,000 volts

The first three voltages are used for DC, and the last one for AC. There are other more unusual ones, but these are the more commonly used voltages. Specifying the power supply for an electric railway requires stating the voltage, followed by whether the power is AC or DC. So specifying a power system would be something like; 1500 Volts DC, or 25,000 Volts AC. The type of power system in use will further influence the choice of trains that are used on the system, and also may increase or decrease the costs and structure of any tunnels constructed.

Where a system has no electricity supply for traction, and there are many of these, then often the system is described as unwired. Power is needed for stations and lighting, but this may be unconnected to traction power.

Many rail systems deliver power through wires suspended over the train, and power is delivered through to the train through a structure on top of the train called a pantograph. However, another structure is also possible called a "third rail", and for this system power is delivered near the ground. This information is also included in any description of a rail system.

Gauge

The gauge of a railway is the distance between the insides of each rail. Most railways have only one gauge, although there are exceptions, such the Tokyo metro. The most common gauge, the one used in the US and for almost all high speed rail, is standard gauge, which is 1435 mm. This corresponds to 4 foot 8.5 inches. Gauges wider than this are normally described as broad gauge, and narrower than this are described as narrow gauge. Common sizes are 1067 mm (cape gauge), and 1520 mm (Russian gauge).

Gauge Distance

The gauge distance is measured from the inside of each rail to the other. This measure can change a little when the rail is worn, but for reference purposes the gauge is set for one railway (or line as the case may be).

Almost all high speed rail systems use standard gauge. Most modern installations, except where interoperability with older systems is needed, use standard gauge. Standard gauge is the most commonly used gauge, and more than 50% of the world's railways, in terms of track length, use standard gauge. The use of non-standard gauges will impact upon rollingstock purchases and decisions.

Number of Lines

The number of lines is a useful measure for any railway. A line is a continuous length of track along which passengers can travel without alighting from a train or breaking their journey. In a metro system or a light rail system it mostly very clear how many lines exist, and where lines start and end.

Typically a system with over 6 lines would be considered large, and one with 1 or 2 lines is a small system. Some systems have over a dozen lines.

A commuter system may or may not be described in terms of the number of lines. Commuter lines can converge to a single large station, and there is often shared track where trains from different destinations share the one track. In this situation it can be very difficult to determine how many unique lines there are. In Sydney it is almost impossible to determine how many lines there are as many of the lines meet each other a large distance from the city. Alternatively, in the Go Transit system in Toronto Canada it is very clear how many lines there are because each is mostly separate from each other, and can be easily counted. Again, for a commuter system, more than 6 or 7 lines would be considered a large system.

REFERENCES

1. Zhang, Y & Yan, X & Comtois, C *Some Measures of Increasing Rail Transit Riderships: Case Studies*, Chinese Geographical Science, Volume 10, Number 1, pp 80 – 88, 2000

2. CFL, *Rapport Annuel*, 2011 (In French)

3. Metro de Porto, *Annual Report*, 2009

4. Jernbaneverket, *On Track 2010*

5. State of Florida Department of Transportation, *Central Florida Commuter Rail Transit Design Criteria*, October 2008

6. DB Netze *AG Network Statement 2014,* April 2013

7. Cheng, HY. *High Speed Rail in Taiwan: New experience and issues for future development*, Transport Policy 17 (2010) 51-63, Nov 2009

8. Chun-Hwan, K. *Transportation Revolution: The Korean High-speed Railway*, Japan Railway & Transport Review 40, March 2005

9. Texas Department of Transportation *Austin San Antonio Commuter Rail Study*, 1999

10. Metro de Porto *Annual Report 2011*, http://www.metrodoporto.pt/en/

11. Burge, P. et al Modelling Demand for Long-Distance Travel in Great Britain, www.rand.org, 2011

12. Cataldi, O. & Alexander , R. *Train control for light rail systems on shared tracks*, Railroad Conference 2001

13. Transport for London *Rail and Underground Annual Benchmarking Report* June 2012

14. Prescott, T. *A Practical Scheme for Light Rail Extensions in Inner Sydney*, Transit Australia, vol 63 no 11, 323 – 330 Nov 2008

Week 2

Types of Passenger Rail Systems

There are many different types of rail systems, and each has advantages and disadvantages. When one thinks of rail images come to mind maybe of high speed trains or of metros running underneath major cities. The range of different types of rail systems is actually quite large, and the reader might be surprised as to the variety and large differences between them all.

The distinctions between the different types of rail systems is not always clear. Whilst it is easy to distinguish between a freight system, and a commuter one, things are not always so easy. For example, the distinction between a light rail system and tram systems is particularly difficult, as the different types of systems in many cases are quite different, but in others extremely similar. Whilst some tram systems, especially historical ones, appear different to light rail, more modern trams are almost indistinguishable. As such separating out the different types is not an easy task, and an attempt is made here to classify the different rail systems, and it is not possible to consider all the different variations, but nonetheless an attempt must be made.

Rail systems fall under larger headings, and one of those is light rail. This is particularly problematic, as light rail is both a heading and a rail type. This makes things extremely confusing, as the term can refer to either a whole group of different systems, or one particular type of system. The convention that has been adopted to manage this crazy and almost impossible situation in this book is to describe the group of rail systems that fall under the heading of light rail as "light rail systems" and the specific system referred to as light rail as just "light rail".

The choice has been made in this book to separate all the smaller rail systems into the heading of "light rail system". There is no real definition of what this means, especially as a heading, but it is a term commonly used in Australia. It seems clear when looking at the different systems which is a light one, and which heavy, but it is difficult to provide a clear definition. Some of the characteristics of a light rail system include:
- Trains are narrower
- Trains are shorter

- Trains move at slower speeds
- The capacity of any rail lines is lower
- They are physically lighter, and the maximum axle loads can be quite low
- Stations are smaller
- They tend not to have large complex junctions
- They are often much cheaper to construct
- Each individual rail line is quite short, and a maximum line length would be about 30 to 40 kilometres. In contrast high speed rail lines can be hundreds or even thousands of kilometres long.

Alternatively, some light rail systems can be quite expensive to build, especially where the frequency of trains is very high, and the system is driverless. Light rail systems with high capacities can resemble much larger rail systems, and the number of people moved can be reasonably large, ie, one hundred or two hundred thousand per day. The platform heights for light rail systems can also be very low, but in some systems platform height is the same as a heavy rail system.

It is also possible to operate two separate rail systems over the same tracks. Freight trains often share their tracks with regional or commuter trains, and more rarely light rail. Light rail trains can share tracks with heavy rail, so that the infrastructure supports two or potentially more rail systems at the same time. This situation would typically be described as a "mixed system", with at least two different rail systems.

Freight systems can be described as either light rail system or heavy rail classification, and particularly serious rail freight systems, with high axle loads are called "heavy haul".

To the casual observer the type of rollingstock is often the best way to determine which type of rail system is which. Rollingstock has been designed for each different system, and they look different, so this is quite a good way to start. There are however lots of other system parameters that are also relevant, and the top speed is one, and the number of passengers moved is another.

One of the key distinctions between railways is whether they are "at grade" or "grade separated". Grade separation refers to putting different types of transport modes, or even the same ones, at different heights so that traffic on each can pass one another easily, without having to wait for the traffic to clear an intersection before proceeding. The development of light rail, where trains are often at the same grade as road traffic, has changed the perception that grade separation is always necessary for a rail system.

The photo below shows two grade separated metro lines. This design allows one train to pass over another. For high frequency rail services grade separation is the key to ensuring that trains move smoothly. Where one of the lines crosses another at a junction, the junction may be described as a "flying junction" (as it is in this case in Singapore).

Elevated Metros

Another important distinction between rail systems is the ability of some rail vehicles to have articulation. Articulation is the presence of a joint in a vehicle, so that the vehicle can "bend" around corners and curves. Trucks and buses can be articulated, and rail vehicles also. Light rail vehicles may be articulated, to allow them to turn around very sharp curves. Whilst in the past the lack of articulation in trams was an easy way to separate these vehicles from light rail vehicles, some modern trams are articulated as well.

It is sometimes possible to blend two different types of system together. There is no rule that dictates that a rail system must have characteristics from only one type of system, and hybrid systems have been created. Possibly the best known hybrid is the tram-train system that was pioneered in Karlsruhe city in Germany, where trams were re-designed to operate with higher speeds on main line tracks.

Light Rail Systems

Trams

Trams are a very old form of rail transportation. They evolved from the horse drawn carriages that were common in large cities in the mid nineteenth centuries, and were initially steam powered (or pulled by cables). Almost all remaining tram systems in the world are now powered through overhead power lines, where power is supplied from a remote generator to the tram.

Trams are called streetcars in the US and Canada. They are still used in parts of North America, including San Francisco, and Toronto. Trams can be used as simple tourist railways, as they are slow, but a good way of seeing different parts of the centre of a city. Trams may be free in some parts of the centre of large cities, and can be a very pleasing experience to travel on.

Trams were an extremely common system in the Western world until the 1950's, when governments started to remove them. Before their removal they were a central part of the transport for the public for many cities, and some of the tram systems removed were extremely large. The tram system in London was particularly large, and was dismantled with surprising haste in the late 40's and early 50's. Now tram systems are something of a rarity, and very few cities have any kind of remaining tram system. This was particularly the case in the US and Canada, where almost all the old tram systems were removed. Only Toronto and New Orleans operate trams systems that resemble what they were 70 years ago.

In Australia, and the Asia Pacific, the only significant remaining tram system is the one in Melbourne, although there is a much smaller system in Hong Kong that continues to operate for over 100 years. By route kilometres it is the largest remaining tram system in the world, although in the past there were systems that were much larger. The now dismantled system in Sydney was much larger than the one in Melbourne.

Tram systems are rarely double decker (or bi-level) Trams are usually quite narrow, and it is challenging to construct a double decker tram that is both stable and comfortable to use. The trams in Hong Kong are a very rare example of bi-level tram, and offer a quite rough ride.

Trams owe their popularity, and demise, to where they operate. They operate down the centre of streets in the middle of major cities, in what in Australia we would call the CBD, but in the US would be described as downtown. They are very slow, but are often filled to capacity. This should be contrasted to the situation with light rail, where trains often run on grade separated tracks, or in the middle or roads where road traffic cannot intrude with their separate right of way.

Loading and unloading times (or dwell time) on trams can be very long. As there are only a small number of entrances and exists, overcrowded trams can be very slow in moving off from one stop to the next. Trams are not a very effective mass transit system, for moving large numbers of passengers. They are really too small to move millions of people per day, and are better suited for applications where the number of people moved is modest.

Trams are at the same grade as road traffic, and so collisions between trams and cars are possible, and even common. In one year in Melbourne there were over 1000 collisions between trams and road vehicles. Trams need to be strong enough to withstand a collision with a road vehicle from almost any direction. Whilst the collision between any train and road vehicle is serious, the collision of a heavy rail train and a road vehicle can be catastrophic.

The main differences between light rail and trams are:
- Trams are much shorter than light rail vehicles
- Trams travel down the middle of roads in the centre of cities, something that is often described as being "at-grade", and do not have a separate right of way
- Trams are not connected together
- Trams make a large number of very frequent stops
- Trams are often 2.45 metres wide, whereas light rail is often 2.65 metres wide

Very old trams often look like this one below. This is a W class heritage tram from Melbourne. Note the shape and structure, and that passengers need to step up from the ground to get into the tram. It is also very short, and is only 14 metres in length. It is also rigid, so that there is no articulated section where the tram can bend around corners.

Melbourne W Class tram

Notice that the tram stop has protection for passengers. Passengers wait alongside the fencing, protecting them from road traffic. The gap between the tram and the fence is quite narrow, but this situation is far preferable than having people wait on the side of the road and cross in front of traffic to reach the tram.

The tram shown below is also in Melbourne and was built in the 80's and 90's. It is not single body like the W class, and is articulated to allow it to pass through tight curves. This tram still has high floors, but looks more like a conventional light rail vehicle than older trams. In Melbourne this type of tram is known as a B class tram.

Melbourne B Class Tram

This is a tram stopped on Brunswick St in Melbourne. Notice that there is no dedicated tram stop in the middle of the road, and passengers must cross the road from the kerb to reach the tram. Cars are expected to stop before the end of the tram to allow people to board the tram. This situation, very common in a large legacy tram system like Melbourne, is probably mostly unacceptable in any modern tram system.

It was a common feature of trams that passengers had to step up into the tram and this was a major problem for people with disabilities. There has been a major design effort since the 90's to reduce the height of the floor on trams to make them more accessible for wheelchair bound passengers and others who might struggle to climb the stairs. Trams, and light rail, can be classified as ultra low floor, low floor, or high floor. Whilst the low floor design is popular with passengers, maintenance costs are higher. Ultra-low floor trams and light rail vehicles have been plagued with numerous engineering problems, cracked structures and shells, although things do seem to be getting better for this technology.

High Floor Tram

Passengers boarding this tram will need to climb from the lowest step to the highest. The tram above is considered to be high floor, as for the purposes of determining if this vehicle is low or high floor, it's high floor because this calculation is made from the ground to the floor of the tram where people are sitting, not to the first step.

Low floor trams and light rail vehicles are typically 300 to 350 mm from the ground to the floor of the tram. Ultra low floor trams that distance can be even lower, even as low as 180 mm. High floor trams the distance is often 550 mm or even more. This distance can be reduced by elevating the surface of the road or sidewalk.

It should be noted that many trams and light rail vehicles which are low floor are not consistent height throughout the entire vehicle. The floor above the bogies may be raised, so that passengers moving through the tram will need to walk up and down steps to get from one end to another. This is undesirable from the perspective of passengers with disabilities, but better than having a high floor where disabled passengers can't get on at all. Where the tram is only partly low floor, passengers with limited mobility will need to stay near the doors, as they can't move up and down throughout the steps that are in the vehicle.

The percentage of floor area that is low floor is an important percentage for any tram or light rail vehicle. A typical number seems to be about 70%, although the number can be lower than 50% or up to 100%. This figure is important in purchasing any tram or light rail vehicle.

Given the obvious convenience of low floor trams, why was anything built with a higher floor? Surely it made more sense to design all the trams and light rail vehicles with a low floor? The answer to this is that it was only recently that the technology was available to build a successful a low floor tram. High floor rail vehicles structurally stronger, and trains with higher floors are stronger than those with lower floors. So very long trains, and definitely those over 100 metres in length, will need to have high floors. Even comparatively short trains, such as the DLR or the Bangkok Skytrain, which are only 60 to 80 metres in length have quite high platforms, as it is easier to design trains with higher floors. Rollingstock manufacturers are designing stronger and stronger vehicles, which can combine low floors with longer trains, but there are still limits on the length of these trains.

Note the significant differences between the above tram, and the one above, it has a much lower floor, is articulated in several places, and looks a bit "space age". This particular tram had very few seats, and most of the space inside was for standing passengers. It is also 100% low floor, and there were no steps other than the one into the tram.

Low Floor Tram

The vehicle in the photo above is a good example of rail vehicles that can lie between light rail and trams. Given where the vehicle operates, and its width, and the average speed, it's probably best to consider this vehicle operating as a tram, even though there are signs and advertisements throughout Melbourne describing this vehicle as light rail.

Most trams are only one level, but there are a small number of systems with double decker trams. Trams in Hong Kong are double deckers. This system is a very old system, and operates wooden double decker trams with two sets of stairs at either end of the tram. There is not much suspension, and it's a very bumpy ride. The cost of a ride is very low, somewhere around 40 US cents (as of 2012), and it's extremely heavily used. These trams operate at amazingly frequent intervals, and there are hundreds of trams in use at any one time.

Double Decker Tram in Hong Kong

A modern trend has been to install computer control over traffic lights so that trams get priority. Infrastructure is installed to detect the presence of any tram, and then change the lights to allow the tram to proceed sooner than the normal sequencing of the lights would allow. This situation is particularly common for light rail, where the number of road crossings is much lower than for trams, and the intention is to get the train moving as fast as possible. So doing can substantially increase the average speed of trams, and this is a good way to improve the quality of the system.

An interesting feature of tram systems, and this is especially true for Melbourne, is that often tram stops are marked only with sign, and nothing more. Tram stops are not really stations, and are very low key, and those new to an area with trams may not even notice that the tram stop is there. Stations for other types of rail systems, even light rail, are much larger and more expensive to build.

(Classic) Light rail

Light rail is seen by many as the next evolutionary step in the development of tram systems. Light rail vehicles are usually larger and longer than trams, and several vehicles can be combined into one longer train, something that is unusual for trams. Whilst there does not seem to be any formal definition anywhere that supports this rule, it seems that light rail vehicles are normally 2.65 metres in width, which is larger than the 2.4 metres common for trams.

Light rail vehicles are designed to travel along city streets. They can climb steep grades, and turn through very tight curves, much like trams. They are a very versatile train type, and can go almost anywhere. Light rail vehicles can climb grades of 10%, and almost unthinkable grade, and far more than any other rail system other than a ratchet and pinion rail line. Light rail vehicles can also negotiate around very tight curves, and curve radii of as low as 20 or 30 metres is possible. Heavy rail is often limited in the size of the curve, and a typical lower value for the tightest curve is 200 metres.

The picture below shows the light rail vehicle moving through central Sydney. Notice that it is a larger and wider vehicle than the trams pictured above. Whilst trams are often only 25 to 40 metres in length, light rail vehicles can be much longer than that, up to 60 metres, and can be coupled together to form even longer trains. This particular light rail vehicle is not designed to be coupled with other light rail vehicles.

Light Rail in Sydney

Once again we note that light rail vehicles can operate on city streets, and building a rail line with a shared right of way with road traffic can be a very effective way to save money on construction costs. As always it is better if the rail line is separated from road traffic as this allows average speeds to be higher, as there is no need for light rail trains to stop for road traffic, although achieving this is sometimes very expensive and not economic.

It is important to distinguish between classic light rail, and an intermediate capacity metro. The DLR (Docklands Light Rail) is often classified as light rail, and it is a light rail system, but it is much more like an intermediate capacity metro, and has many of the features of one. It is not considered to be classic light rail within this book. The DLR is fully automated and there are no drivers, and it does not operate down city streets, but is fully grade separated. The DLR is a very good system, re-classifying it as an intermediate capacity metro is no insult. This type of system will be discussed further below, under the correct heading.

Light rail vehicles traditionally have drivers, important because light rail vehicles need to avoid street traffic, and collisions. At the time of writing it is not possible to design a light rail system that is able to avoid street traffic and pedestrians in all situations, so drivers are needed. Light rail vehicles are designed to be able to withstand an impact from a road vehicle, and are toughened up to resist collisions and not allow any injury to the passengers inside. This toughening can add a lot of weight to the vehicle.

Light Rail in Hong Kong

Light rail has become very popular in the US, and in Germany, although it exists in many different countries. The pictures above and below show a light rail system in Hong Kong. Note that the system used there has high platforms and vehicles are not joined (amalgamated) together to make longer trains.

One of the main attractions of light rail systems is the relatively low construction cost. Costs are lower because the light rail trains travel along city streets, and expensive tunnelling can be avoided. Light rail is also a solution where the number of passengers is not that high, and there is a need or desire to install a rail system. Heavy rail systems are excessive in many situations, and a light rail system can be a more appropriate solution. Aside from the lower construction cost, light rail is seen as a sexy and attractive looking system, and this type of rail system has proved very popular with passengers throughout the world.

An added advantage of the light rail system is its simplicity. Unlike heavy rail, which is technically very complicated, light rail is a lot simpler and easier to install and manage. Lower speeds, and the lower loads associated with smaller trains, means that the system is relatively simple to install, and the complexity associated with speed calculations and vertical curves for example is avoided.

Automated People Mover

Automated people movers (APMs) are automatic trains that are driverless, and operate on separate right of way with grade separation. They are often very small and often installed in airports, theme parks, and other large facilities. These vehicles fall within the family of light rail systems, and are common in airports in Asia. Also sometimes included in this category are larger automatic trains such as the Docklands Light Rail (DLR), which is driverless, and technically speaking an automated people mover. Larger APMs are very similar to light metros, or intermediate capacity systems, and are also discussed under that category.

The picture below shows an APM in Singapore. The vehicle is very short, and it runs on rubber tyres. It is also driverless, and moves around the small network by itself picking up and dropping off passengers. This particular system is a contained within an airport. The capacity of this system is not large, and the distances travelled are short.

An APM Vehicle in Singapore Airport (Changi)

Airports often have trains that move travellers from one terminal to another. A particular large airport may need such a system, as the distances between terminals are so large that transport is needed. These rail systems can be quite significant, and the system in Hong Kong Airport contains two short lines. The APM in Changi airport has several lines, all of them quite short. APM systems in airports are provided as a convenience for passengers, and add to the value of the airport. APMs also exist in theme parks, particular large ones such as the different Disneyland parks.

Intermediate Capacity Metros

Intermediate capacity metros are a system that is designed much like a metro system, with few seats, low headways, and many doors to allow fast and easy boarding and alighting, but much lower capacity and smaller trains. Some intermediate capacity metros are also Automated People Movers, some are not. As a group these rail lines are sometimes described as a "light metro".

What distinguishes an intermediate capacity system from a full metro is:
- Trains are equal to or less than 60-70 metres in length
- The trains narrower than full metros
- Stations are much shorter in length, therefore cheaper to build
- In some cases built with rubber tyres rather than metal wheels, although there are some full sized metros with this technology too

Intermediate capacity metros seem to be increasing in popularity, and their numbers are slowly increasing. There are a few rail systems of this type of system in Asia, and the Bangkok Skytrain is probably the best example. The picture below shows a train in the Bangkok Skytrain.

Bangkok Skytrain

There is much to recommend these systems. They are often extremely cheap to build, and well below the cost of a metro system. The Bangkok Skytrain was constructed at a cost of only $20 million per route kilometre, and amazingly low price, and this cost was achieved 2009 to 2011, relatively recently. Trains in an intermediate capacity metro are also very short, 50 to 60 metres is common, and costs are kept down so purchasing rollingstock is very cheap. Stations in an intermediate capacity metro are also short, and an 80 metre station would be considered large. As such it is easy to place stations in convenient places, as they are so short. Stations are also cheap to build.

Intermediate capacity metros would normally be classified as light rail systems. Recall with light rail systems, the lower capacity of this type of system means that the total capacity in people per hour is lower than a metro. A medium capacity system will usually have less than half the capacity of a metro, maybe even a third, and so there is a significant risk of severe overcrowding. Intermediate capacity metros often operate full, even late at night and on weekends. This type of system is attractive to use because of its cost and versatility, but is frequently overcrowded, a trade-off that is sometimes worth making.

Intermediate capacity metros are commonly installed on concrete viaducts, which makes them cheaper than tunnelled full size metros or at least in South East Asia that seems to be the case. It seems common to install this type of system in elevated viaducts, and this also reduces the cost compared to tunnelling. Intermediate capacity systems can operate at very low headways, similar to metros.

Freight Systems (Light Rail)

Freight trains are rarely small enough to be considered light rail, but in a small number of cases they do exist. Sugarcane railways are where sugarcane is transported from the farm to a sugar mill, and these freight systems are often, but not always, operated on 2 foot gauge (61 cm). This is the smallest gauge in operation in a rail system in any significant way at the time of writing of this book. The locomotives and freight wagons are much smaller than traditional freight trains, and their signalling systems are very simple indeed.

The photo below shows some wagons transporting sugar cane in Northern Queensland. Notice that the wagons are very small, and maybe only 3 to 4 metres in length. The ones in the photo below are fully loaded and on their way to the mill.

Sugar Cane Wagons

Small rail freight trains in some mines were also common, but the author is not aware of any that have continued in operation, although they were once common in Australia.

Heavy Rail

Heavy rail systems have much longer trains, move more people faster, and longer distances. It would be very surprising for a light rail system to move passengers one hundred kilometres from one large city to another. Heavy rail systems are more expensive to build, and ordinarily require a larger space (structure and loading gauge).

Metros

Metros are the mainstay of many transport systems. There are hundreds of metro systems installed around the world, and they have been installed in places such as Algiers and San Juan in Puerto Rico. Many more systems are currently being built.

The metro has become the standard for transport around large cities. The metro system forms the backbone of any transport system in many large cities, and bus lines and other forms of public transportation integrate into the rail system. The key to the success of the metro is its ability to move large numbers of people quickly and efficiently from one place to another, as well as its engineering simplicity, and relatively low cost of operation.

Metros almost always have very few seats. People need to stand most of the trip, and consequently many people can be packed into a metro. More people stand than sit, as seating takes up a lot of space. The number of people that can be moved by a large metro is extremely large, over 70 thousand pph (people per hour) in one direction, and this can be done at relatively low cost per person. The ability of a metro system to move such large numbers of people quickly is one of the key reasons why this system has become so successful. The cost of operating a metro system can also be low when compared to the number of people moved, and in very busy cities it may be possible to operate a passenger service at a profit, without any kind of government subsidy.

Metro trains also have a large number of doors. Metro rail carriages are never double decker (bi-level) and so can have large numbers of doors. Dwell time is an important parameter for many rail systems, and it is defined as the time a train spends at any one station waiting for passengers to alight and board. The minimisation of dwell time is critical to getting trains through a rail system quickly, and on many different types of system, especially commuter systems, the dwell time can be very long. Metros have very low dwell times because doors are numerous and people can move into the train quickly as most people stand. The low dwell time of metros is another contributor to their success.

Inside a Metro

The picture above shows a metro train in Hong Kong. As with many metro trains, there are seats along the side of the train, and none in the middle. This allows a very high concentration of people in the train.

Metro trains mostly move along a single line, starting at one end, finishing at another, and then returning along the same path. More unusually, the metro line may bifurcate, and split into two, with maybe half the trains going to one terminus, and the other half to the other. This is different from a commuter system, or a light rail system, which often has a main station where many of the services converge, and passengers can make their way from one service to another quickly and easily. Metro lines do not converge to a central terminus, and so passengers that need to use more than one line must change trains at a large interchange station. These interchange stations usually have the metro lines passing over and under one another, so that passengers need to use stairs or escalators to move up and down to get to the right platform. This is one of the main disadvantages of metro systems, but can be managed quite effectively with good station design.

Metros have high service reliabilities. Metro trains are almost always on time, mostly due to the simplicity of the system, and that metros operate grade separated from other road and rail traffic. As metros run backwards and forwards all day, from point A to B and then back again, there is very little track infrastructure needed and so there are very few engineering failures. A metro can be compared extremely favourably with commuter rail systems which are often plagued with problems and are frequently late. An on-time-running (OTR) figure of over 99% is the minimum for a properly maintained and operated metro.

Metro trains are not physically very high nor very large. Commonly 3.5 metres in height from the bottom of the wheels to the top of the roof would be considered normal for a metro train. This allows tunnelling costs to be significantly reduced, as the size of the tunnel that needs to be excavated is smaller than for commuter trains, especially double decker commuter trains.

Metros can move immense numbers of people. Most rail systems can only move 10 to 15 thousand people per hour (pph) in one direction, but metros can move 60 to 80 thousand in an hour. Some metro lines in Asia and other countries can move over 1 million passengers per day, a truly enormous figure.

Metro systems can have a powerful effect on transport within a city. A good quality metro can clear the roads and allow cars to move through cities very effectively. Even a small number of metro lines can have this effect, and 3 or 4 metro lines is usually enough for cities with even 5 to 6 million people. Hong Kong, which has 4 metro lines (as of 2017) and some other lines that are basically commuter lines, is well served. The same can be said for Taipei, where the city has effectively 3 metro lines and one medium capacity line (although they claim there are many more lines than that, essentially there are three main ones). The utility of metro lines is often very high, and even a small number can transform transport within a city.

Metros are not as suited for long distance travel. As most passengers stand, a journey that takes hours would require passengers to stand for hours, and many people can't or won't do this. High speed and regional trains are never metro trains. So the question arises as to how far passengers will be able to stand when travelling on a metro line, and whilst no one seems to have written or researched this topic, perhaps the answer should be about 1 hour.

Metro lines seem to be getting longer and longer. Traditionally metro lines were quite short in length, and lengths of 10 to 15 kilometres were common. For example, the longest line in the Paris metro is only 24 kilometres long. The author used to believe that one of the lines in Shenzhen was far too long, at 41 kilometres in length, and then another line was constructed in New Delhi that was 49 kilometres long, and another line is under construction in Malaysia that is 51 kilometres long. There is even a line being extended in Shanghai, which was completed in 2010, which is over 61 kilometres long.

The reader should remember at this point that metros typically average 35 kms/hr as an average travel speed, which can be higher or lower depending on the spacing of stations. A metro line that is 60 kilometres in length may require someone to stand for 2 hours to get from one end of the other, and even more if they need to change trains and use another rail line. Older people and those with disabilities will have difficulty in completing this type of journey, as standing for hours may be difficult or even impossible.

The picture below is of a metro station in Taipei. This type of open layout for a metro station is a little unusual. Note the platform screen doors.

A Busy Metro Station in Taiwan

Metro systems may or may not have drivers. Older systems will have drivers, but a more modern approach has been to build systems that are entirely automatic and require no drivers. As metro trains are usually captive along one line, and underground, it is relatively easy to program a computer to drive the train. Often rail staff are on board the train, and may control some aspects of the train operation such as opening and closing doors and making announcements. In this case rail staff are described as "operators" rather than drivers.

The design of stations in a metro system is very important. The large number of people present in the system, and on each train, means that it is very important to get people on and off trains quickly. The key to designing a good metro station is to allow people to move freely to and from platforms, and this often involves separating passengers walking through the station in different directions. The correct design of stations is very important for metro systems, as most stations are underground, and so there is a risk of fire. Also the large number of people using the system means that dwell times can be very large is the station is not designed with care.

Metros can operate at very short headways, 2 ½ minutes is common. Another common headway between successive trains is 5 minutes. This extremely high frequency of trains contributes much to the popularity and convenience of metro systems.

Commuter/Suburban rail

Commuter rail is a rail system where passengers are moved from an outlying area into the centre of a city, and then back out again. Commuter rail is often considered a rail system for working people, as most trips occur on weekdays. Commuter trips are often from suburban stations far from the centre of the city, to the business centre, and then back out again at the end of the working business day.

Commuter trips are often 1 hour or more in length. Commuter trains have lots of seats, and are not metros, so most people are not expected to stand. It is often the case that people stand on a commuter train, but often this is only for the last few stops before the train reaches the centre of the city.

Commuter trains differ significantly from metros. Commuter trains often travel at higher speeds than metros, a common maximum speed for a metro is 90 kms/hr, whereas commuter trains often reach speeds of 130 kms/hr or even faster. Commuter trains are larger, heavier, and longer and often longer than metro trains. The additional speed requires a heavier and more powerful train. Commuter trains also have extensive seating.

The train below is a commuter train in Brisbane (in Australia). This one is on an elevated concrete viaduct, and at Brisbane airport.

Commuter Train on a Viaduct in Brisbane

Commuter trains can be either single or double deck. Double deck trains are common for commuter trains, especially in Europe, and also the US and Canada. Double deck trains can be an effective way of increasing the capacity of a rail line, as more passengers can be seated for one carriage. Double deck trains are used extensively in the Sydney rail system as well.

The photo below is of a double decker train in Paris.

Parisian Double Decker Train

Commuter trains may operate on a large number of different stopping patterns. The stations at which a service stops at is called the stopping pattern, and there are many different possible combinations of stopping patterns even on quite simple lines. For a metro system, and light rail, trains almost always stop at every station. With any commuter line there are sometimes stations where very few people board and alight from, and so not every train needs to stop there. Commuter trains, because of the large distances they travel, will need to travel as quickly as possible, and not stopping at smaller stations can reduce the travel time. This is common with commuter systems.

The need for up to date information on a commuter line is very important. Again, as commuter services may not stop at every station, passenger information systems need to display where the train will stop, and when it will arrive at the station. As commuter systems can be very complex, and therefore difficult to understand for passenger, and trains can move in many different directions, providing prompt and accurate passenger information is very important in a commuter system, as it is in any rail system.

The photo below shows the inside of a commuter train in Brisbane. This configuration is 2 x 2, and most of the space inside the train is taken up by seating.

Inside a Single Deck Commuter Train

Commuter systems often have a large central station where all the commuter rail services converge. Easily the most famous of these is Grand Central Station in New York, which has the largest number of platforms of any station in the world (but not the largest number of passengers). Metro systems do not converge to a single station, and this is a good way of distinguishing the difference between the two different types of rail system.

Commuter rail systems often have much more rail infrastructure than metros and light rail. At the commuter main station there are many tracks that carry trains to the station, and many points to move trains to the right platforms. The infrastructure at a main station can often be very expensive to install and costly to maintain.

In a small number of commuter systems, trains carriages are split between 1st and 2nd class. Different fares are charged for each, and more comfortable seating is provided in 1st class. Hong Kong has such a commuter rail line (it's not really a commuter line, as it goes to the border with mainland China, but close enough) with two classes. Passengers in 2nd class get metro style seating, which is very limited and not comfortable at all, and in 1st there are quite "standard" fabric seating in a 2 x 2 arrangement. The fare for 1st class is double that for 2nd class.

Again, comparing commuter systems to metros, most commuter rail systems operate above ground. In the centre of the city, there are sometimes some commuter stations below ground, but most stations away from the centre of town are above ground. Commuter systems are longer and larger compared to metros, and can be over 500 routes kilometres in length. The commuter system in Sydney is over 800 route kilometres in length.

Commuter systems almost always have drivers. The long distances commuter trains travel makes automation difficult, and drivers are almost always used. There may be other staff on the train as well, for example a guard who opens and closes doors, or a ticket conductor that goes through the train and sells tickets of checks passengers have paid for tickets. Commuter trains are more difficult to drive than metros, within the rail corridor many things can happen that require intervention by a driver. There can be landslips, or animals on the track, or trespassers. Trees may fall over onto the track when winds are high.

Commuter systems may share rail tracks with freight, commuter trains operate at low frequencies and over long distances, and so it is often not economical to separate commuter lines from freight ones. Commuter lines that share tracks with freight trains as well typically have a lower capacity.

Commuter trains mostly do not have toilets, unlike regional services. Commuter trips are typically about 1 to 1.5 hours and this is considered short enough that toilets do not need to be provided.

Commuter systems can have a very low service frequency, and one train every 20 or 30 minutes or is quite common. In some systems one train every hour is considered acceptable. Passenger information becomes very important in this environment, as passengers need to plan to meet the train they need.

Regional rail

Regional rail services are those that move from a large city or town to remote or rural towns or villages. They can be, but often are not, commuter services, and regional services can have travel time of up to 3 or 4 hours. Regional services can be very infrequent, from one every half an hour to one per day. Regional services always have a driver, and maybe other staff on the train. Some regional services may have toilets, or even a buffet car where light refreshments can be ordered.

In Australia regional services often pass through areas of national park and wilderness, where there are large numbers of animals and very few people. Collisions with animals are frequent. There is often no mobile phone reception for large parts of the trip for regional services.

Sydney Regional Train

The photo above is a regional train. Note the clear differences with the other doubler decker trains displayed earlier, the much smaller doors, and the greater overall length of the carriage. Loading and unloading of passengers can be very slow for a regional train, but that doesn't necessarily matter because regional services move only moderate numbers of passengers, and the trip length is commonly 3 to 4 hours. It is preferable to design small doors because this increases the structural strength of the train. Carriages in a train designed for regional services can be very long because this reduces the overall cost of procuring the train.

Regional services can be powered by either electric power, or propelled by diesel motors. Many regional services are diesel powered, as there is relatively little rail traffic on many regional lines, and the cost of installing overhead power cannot be justified. Where trains are powered by diesel, then a refuelling depot is needed to top up trains when they run low on fuel.

The photo below was taken at Southern Cross station in Melbourne. This regional train was destined for Albury. Non-driven carriages, drawn behind a locomotive, are referred to as coaches. This configuration is often used for regional services as it is cheaper then electric multiple units (EMUs), or diesel multiple units (DMUs)

Melbourne Diesel Hauled Regional Train

Regional services may operate with very few passengers, and as such don't generate a lot of revenue. Many regional services are provided as a community service, and so are not profitable, and need government subsidies to continue to operate. The regional services that the author has seen in Asia, such as in Thailand, Taiwan China and Malaysia, and in Australia are often dirty and not really very pleasant at all, but provide a basic service to those living in remote places with small numbers of people.

High Speed rail

High speed rail (HSR) is a flashy, sleek and sexy system that is the glamorous side of rail transport. High speed rail is often defined as being any rail system where the train reaches 200 kms/hr, or 125 miles per hour.

High speed rail can be divided into two broad categories; trains/systems where trains travel at less than 250 kms/hr but over 200 kms/hr, and those that travel above that. Below 250 kms/hr, HSR trains are sometimes diesel powered, and do not have the extreme aerodynamic streamlining that gives high speed trains their futuristic look. The more sophisticated high speed rail systems all have top speeds in excess of 250 kms/hr, alternatively HSR rail vehicles that use existing lines have top speeds mostly below 250 kms/hr. Some high speed trains are designed to tilt, although most are not. At high speeds tilting as a strategy is not effective for high speed trains.

Below is a high speed train in Taiwan. High speed trains in Taiwan are based upon a Japanese design (as of 2012) and based on the 700 series Shinkansen.

Taiwan High Speed Train

High speed rail can offer a very high level of service. Its speed and convenience often contribute to this perception. The installation of high speed rail often refreshes and renews the rail system in a country or region. High speed rail sometimes codeshares with airlines, so that passengers can buy a ticket that combined flights and rail trips.

While most high speed trains are single deck, there are a small number of double deck high speed trains. The Japanese have the E4 Shinkansen, and the French have the TGV duplex, but other than those specific trains, all other high speed trains are single deck. Double deck trains have higher capacity, which can be important where route capacity is limited.

High speed trains are almost always powered through overhead power, at 25 kV AC. DC power cannot propel trains at high speeds, as high voltages are needed, and diesel trains can only reach about 250 kms/hr, with difficulty. The higher voltages are needed to drive trains to higher speeds.

High speed trains can be very comfortable. The rail infrastructure that supports the train, such as the track, sleepers and ballast, needs to be very strong and in very good condition so that trains can operate smoothly. This results in a very smooth ride quality that provides very little sensation of movement to passengers. Walking around the train is easy, because the ride is so smooth, and some high speed trains have buffet or dining cars where passengers can get meals.

It is a great achievement for a country to install a high speed rail system. Despite the volume of discussion in Australia and other countries concerning high speed rail, very few systems have been installed. There is only one small high speed line in the US, and it operates at around the 200 kms/hr mark, and so does not have the glamour of the French or Japanese systems. Even in the UK there is only one dedicated high speed rail line, which links the Chunnel to London.

Countries where there are significant high speed rail systems, in 2012, include:
- France
- Germany
- Spain
- China
- Japan
- South Korea
- Taiwan

Other countries have smaller parts of a high speed rail system, one such country is Sweden, where a lot of research has been conducted into high speed rail, despite the small size of their high speed system. The line between Moscow and St Petersburg also has some high speed trains, but the line is shared with freight, and this reduces the average speed and the route capacity.

High speed rail systems face many technical challenges. High speed trains are moving too quickly to move through curves quickly, and can only move through very high radius curves. This often means that high speed rail systems cannot move around mountains and other obstacles, so the rail line often passes through mountains and over other natural obstructions. The alignment of a high speed rail line is very inflexible, and the line can only be designed around any kind of natural barrier with great difficulty.

Tunnels present all sorts of problems for high speed trains. Tunnel design requires the consideration of air movement caused by the train as it moves through the tunnel. The pressure of the air in front of the train is higher than behind the train, and the faster the train moves the worse this problem gets. The pressure drop can cause discomfort to passengers, as the pressure inside the train will equalise with the pressure alongside the train. Rapid changes in air pressures will cause passengers to experience pain in their ears. What is commonly done is to seal the train as much as possible, but even so the seals are not perfect, so the pressure will drop in the train as it passes through a tunnel. Sealing the train can reduce the impact of pressure changes to passengers, but in particularly long tunnels the pressure drop will be significant, even in a well designed train.

High speed trains moving through tunnels can cause an effect often described as similar to sonic boom, and the boom is generated at the exit of the rail tunnel. A high speed train entering the tunnel will generate a pressure wave, which creates the sonic boom. A number of design features can be installed into tunnels to attempt to mitigate this problem, but the most effective strategy is to reduce the speed or the increase the cross-sectional area of the tunnel through which the train is moving. In many cases neither of the strategies will be available.

High speed trains in Taiwan and Japan have very interesting ticketing systems. One feature of these systems is that passengers can buy either first or second class tickets, and first class is more comfortable than second class. But the major difference with "normal" ticketing is the difference between a reserved seat and a non-reserved seat. Reserved seats are those where a seat number is allocated, and these are more expensive that non-reserved. The risk with a non-reserved ticket is that a seat is not available, and it is possible that a passenger may have to stand for part or all of their trip.

High speed rail systems may have services with different stopping patterns. All stops trains alternate with express services, and passengers will want to take the service that takes the minimum time to get to their destination. Prices can be different between HSR services with different stopping patterns, those trains with more stops are cheaper.

Given the appeal and popularity of high speed rail, it is surprising that more of these systems have not been installed. High speed rail competes effectively where the total travel time between one major city and another is 3 hours or less. High speed rail is particularly effective where the travel time is 2 hours or less. When this is so, high speed rail can be so dominant that air services between the two cities is discontinued, for example, Paris and Brussels. Where the travel time is less than 3 hours but more than 2 between cities, then air services will continue but will have a small percentage of the overall market.

Where the travel time is over 4 hours, high speed rail is no longer competitive with air travel. The trip time is simply too long. Many (or most, depending on the type of engine) planes travel at approx 850 kms/hr, less for turboprop planes, and at that speed a trip of 1000 kms is slightly over an hour. For a high speed train, for a top speed of 300 kms/hr, longer journey distances can. High speed rail will only have a small percentage of the market for trips of this length.

Long Distance Rail

One type of rail system that is often forgotten is the long distance rail system. This book uses this title for this type of rail system, but in truth there is no universally accepted definition for this type of system. This category applies for trains that travel over 5 or 6 hours to get to their destination, or even longer. In Australia the train trip from Sydney to Perth takes 3.5 days.

Long distance services are often overnight, and passengers sleep on them. More expensive tickets offer passengers a sleeper berth, and they may sleep in comfort on the train. In some cases a full bed is provided. The experience in Australia has been that sleeper berths are easily the most popular option for long distance rail, despite their additional cost, and are always booked out before other ticket classes.

Below is a photo of a travel compartment in a sleeper carriage in the long distance train that travels from Kuala Lumpur to Singapore. Long distance travel is still somewhat common in Malaysia, and sleepers are available on many night time trains. In a private room there are two bunk beds, as well as a toilet and shower.

Sleeper Compartment in Malaysia

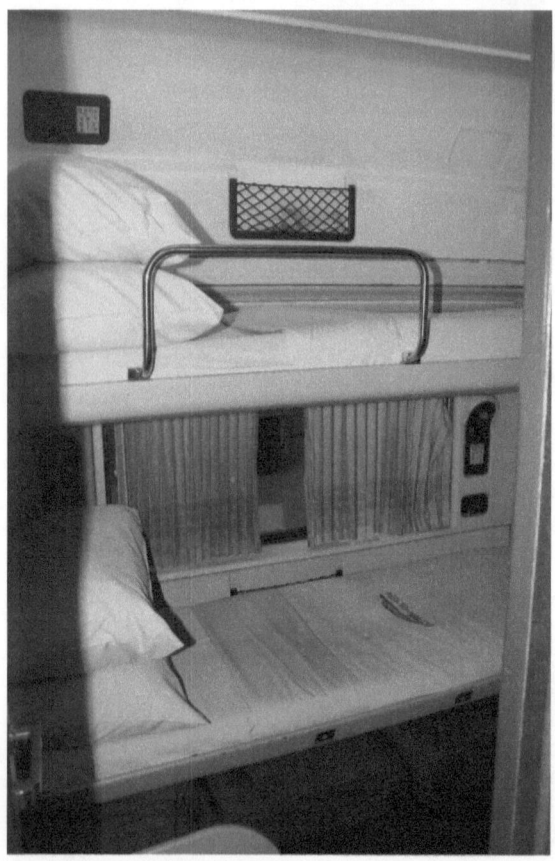

Long distance services are common in Australia, as the distances are so large. There are a number of train services where travel takes well over a day, and these trips can get very boring. The author's experience of these trips is that many of them are rather dull.

Where a rail line has not been upgraded to HSR, or even to a reasonable speed, then overnight distance trains are common. For passengers sleeping on the train makes the trip appear to pass faster, even though it is still a long trip. To justify having sleeper berths on trains, the travel time needs to be at least 7 hours, but preferably 9. Otherwise passengers will have an interrupted sleep, and arrive at their destination at an early time in the morning. For example, a train that leaves at 9pm, and takes 6 hours to reach its destination, will arrive at 3am in the morning. Unless passengers are allowed to stay and sleep in their beds then many will be unwilling to wake at this time in the morning.

Where the train trip is especially long, and the rail operator has made an attempt to upgrade the service, then sometimes the long distance trip is referred to as a rail cruise. A rail cruise can be extremely expensive, thousands of US dollars, and can be over 10 thousand US dollars for 2 people. A rail cruise is often slower than a normal long distance service, and may stop for a time in different cities, and provide tours to places of interest in the city. This kind of service is rare in Australia, but the small number of services provided are profitable, and it's a rare example of a rail company operator generating a healthy profit. In Australia a company called Great Southern Railways provides rail cruises that are very long, in some cases 21 days, and their trains travel all over Australia. These cruises are very expensive, and are more similar to ocean cruises than rail a service.

Long distance overnight trains that offer sleeper berths seem to be disappearing, especially from Europe. Only a very small number of people can be moved in a sleeper carriage, in one sleeper carriage in Malaysia, the capacity of the carriage was 12 people, a very small number. Sleeper carriages are rarely economical to operate, and the cost to passengers to have a separate cabin with beds can be very high. The role and significance of overnight travel seems to be shrinking.

Other Rail Systems

Monorails

Monorails are normally classified as a type of rail system even though monorails systems are significantly different to almost all other rail systems. Monorails were a popular transport system in the 80's but have since fallen out of favour. There are many monorail systems installed in the world, and possibly the most significant is the commuter monorail system in Tokyo, which connects Haneda airport with the rest of Tokyo city. This monorail moves more people than any other monorail in the world per day. Kuala Lumpur also has a monorail line, which is very heavily used.

Maglev systems are a type of monorail, but are discussed separately below. Maglevs differ from monorails in the way the rail vehicle is propelled.

Mumbai in India has constructed a new monorail line, although their enthusiasm for monorails seems to have waned.. Whilst monorail systems are still being built, they are mostly installed in airports, theme parks and other entertainment related venues, such as casinos and hotels. Serious commuter monorails are rare, and there may be only 20 in the entire world. Overall the experience with monorails has not been a happy one, and several monorails have been installed, only to be removed later. Bankruptcies and failed companies are common with monorail systems.

Monorails can perform very similarly to any other rail system. Rubber tyred monorails can climb grades of up to 6% and top speeds of 80 to 90 kms/hr seem common. Monorails are most comparable to intermediate capacity metros, as they travel at about the same speeds, and carry similar number of people. They also cost about the same amount of money per route kilometre. The system under construction in Mumbai has an estimated cost of only US $22 million per kilometre (2012 dollars), which is a good price, but similar to what was paid for the Skytrain in Bangkok.

The picture below is of the Kuala Lumpur monorail. The vehicle length is rather low, but it is a very effective rail system and moves large numbers of people, despite its short length.

A Monorail in Kuala Lumpur

One criticism of monorails is that the monorail itself, what the monorail vehicle runs on, is unsightly. Another way of saying the same thing is to describe the monorail as visually intrusive. This is true, although not as visually intrusive as an intermediate capacity metro, built on an elevated system.

Monorails are for all practical purposes intermediate capacity systems. The capacity of a single monorail is unlikely to be more than 500 people, which is about the limit for light rail and intermediate capacity metros. A small number of monorails are able to carry thousands of people in one train, as a full metro can.

The high frequency of failure of monorails as a system is somewhat baffling. As a transport system they are safe, and cheap to build, and operate at reasonable speeds. It is surprisingly that monorails have been so unsuccessful in so many cases. Perhaps some reasons for the many failures of monorails are:
- Monorails compete with light rail and intermediate capacity metros, such as the DLR, or the Bangkok Skytrain, and do not quite perform as well
- Monorails cannot be expanded to have the same capacity as full metros
- Monorails cannot travel large distances, as most passengers stand when travelling on a monorail
- The ride quality in a monorail is not quite as good as light rail or metros
- Many monorail systems suffered from excessive political interference, especially during the planning stage
- Many monorails had a very low design capacity, and so were unlikely to ever generate a profit
- Transport orientated development is more difficult with elevated monorail stations, as they are smaller, reducing revenue
- Monorails have no real cost advantage compared to intermediate capacity metros
- Most importantly, a power failure for a monorail can have terrible consequences, as cranes need to be employed to remove trapped passengers, unlike intermediate capacity metros, where passengers can walk to the next station

On the other hand, some of the advantages of monorails are:
- Quick to build
- Cheap

- Monorails can accept sharp curves, down to as low as 50 metres (that said, light rail vehicles can accept 15 to 25 metre curves)
- The airspace needed for monorails is smaller than for light metros

Overall, one could easily say that monorails offer no real advantages over a light metro system, and have only disadvantages, the most important of which is the inability to get passengers off a train that breaks down. It would seem reasonable to recommend that monorail systems should only be used where light rail or an intermediate capacity metro is impossible, and this would generally be rare.

Maglevs

Perhaps one of the most interesting rail systems is a technology called the "Maglev". This has been in existence since the 80's and there is constant talk of the installation of new maglev systems. At the time of writing of this book only one commercial Maglev system is in operation, and this connects Pudong airport to the Shanghai metro system. A picture of this system is below:

Shanghai Maglev

Maglev is a contraction for magnetic levitation, and the train itself does not have any wheels and does not even contact the monorail. The train floats above the monorail and, as it has no contact with any surface, can reach speeds of over 400 kms/hr.

Despite the promise of Maglev technology, in practise only one commercial system has ever been installed. There also exists a low speed Maglev system in Japan, but its top speed is very low, so the full potential of the technology has not been achieved.

The author is not convinced by the arguments for a maglev train. The major problem to be overcome is economics, and central to this is the cost of accelerating trains to speeds over 400 kms/hr. A number of high speed trains have been developed, using conventional tracks, where speeds of over 350 kms/hr have been achieved. These trains rarely operate over 300 kms/hr as the power consumption required to drive trains at any speed faster than that is very high. Power consumption seems to increase exponentially with speed, and at 400 kms/hr power consumption must be very large indeed. This problem cannot really be resolved, other than constructing a vacuum tunnel for the maglev, something that seems rather improbable.

Tilt Trains

Tilt trains are an interesting type of technology used on intercity and regional services. The train tilts so that it can go around sharp curves at a higher speed. The speed increase can be considerable, and this technology, and the equations to calculate maximum speeds.

The greater the degree of tilt, the better the train can accept sharp curves. Tilt trains have revolutionised rail travel between many different centres, and can dramatically increase higher average speeds on existing rail lines, especially where those lines contain a lot of curves.

Tilt trains are normally only single deck, and passengers must be seated. The tilting action makes standing on a tilt train a little difficult.

The photo below is of a tilt train in Taiwan and from the outside it does not really appear any different to any other trains, although the outer shape is slightly different from other trains.

A Tilt Train in Taiwan

Tilting trains are usually regional or intercity trains, that travel from one city to another. It would be strange to use a tilt train within one large city, as a substitute for a metro or commuter system.

Tourist Trains

A tourist train is a train which provides an enjoyable experience to passengers, and may or may not connect important destinations that passengers may want to go. Many tourist railways go nowhere important, and the experience is the reason why the service is popular. Alternatively, a tourist railway may connect tourist destinations to the main rail system.

Tourist railways often use old rollingstock, which is custom made for that particular application. The structure of the rollingstock may be very unusual, and may not even afford protection from rain or wind. Some tourist railways connect hard to reach places, and the rollingstock required to achieve this can be very distinctive.

The picture below shows two different types of tourist tram in the town of Christchurch in New Zealand. On the left is the tourist tram that runs around the city, which is an old style tram that is rigid and very short. On the right is a tram that has been converted to be used as a restaurant.

Tourist Trams in Christchurch

Tourist railways can be divided into several categories:
- Railways through parklands, mountains, and other areas which are very scenic and the entire trip might last 1 to 2 hours. The Kuranda railway form Cairns in Australia up into the nearby mountains is probably the best known example of this type of train in Australia, but there are several others.
- Rail cruises, where the rail trip might take weeks, or in some cases, months. The cost of the ticket is extremely high, potentially thousands or tens of thousands of US dollars, for one ticket. Food is provided, and the quality can be very high. Passengers will sleep on the train. The Indian Pacific in Australia is an example of this type of rail service.
- Trains that are mostly "normal", but are richly decorated, and connect the rail system to an area which tourists commonly visit. The commuter train in Paris to the palace at Versailles is a good example of this kind of train, other examples include the Disneyland train in Hong Kong, or the Xinbeitou train in Taipei to the hots springs resorts. These trains are often visually impressive and richly appointed. There are no trains like this in Australia
- Old heritage trams that move throughout cities. These trams are often 100 years old, and have a lot of charm. The distance

moved might be quite small. The best known example of this type of tram is the San Francisco heritage tram.
- Trains, that are more like trolleys, that climb steep inclines, and connect major destinations to carparks or other access points to a high value destination. This type of tourist railway is relatively common, and Perhaps the best known of these is the Peak Tram in Hong Kong, which connects the Peak on Hong Kong Island with the rest of the island. This type of tourist railway is sometimes used to connect mountains and ski fields to access points.
- Small railways, sometimes monorails, contained entirely in amusement parks, and are paid for an operated by the amusement park owner.

As can be seen from the list above, tourist railways are actually quite common and varied.

Tourist trains have high ticket prices, and so can operate at a profit. Passengers rarely would use a tourist railway for daily transportation.

REFERENCES

1. Zhang, Y & Yan, X & Comtois, C *Some Measures of Increasing Rail Transit Riderships: Case Studies*, Chinese Geographical Science, Volume 10, Number 1, pp 80 – 88, 2000

2. Smith K. *Alstom puts weight behind Citadis Dualis, International Railway Journal*, Feb 2010

3. ALSTOM, *AGV Full Speed Ahead into the 21st Century*, 2009, www.transport.alstom.com

4. BTS Group, *Annual Report 2009/2010* (the Bangkok Skytrain)

5. Kemp, R. *T618 – Traction Energy Metrics*, Rail Safety and Standards Board, Interfleet Technology, Dec 2007

6. Taipei Rapid Transit Corporation *2013 Annual Report*, http://english.metro.taipei/ct.asp?xItem=1056448&ctNode=70219&mp=122036

7. Dearien, J. *Ultralight Rail and Energy Use*, Encyclopaedia of Energy, Elsevier Publishing, March 2004

8. Siemens, *Siemens Velaro datasheet*, www.siemens.com/mobility

9. Fabian, J. *The Exceptional Service of Driverless Metros*, Journal of Advanced Transportation, Vol 33, No 1, pp 5-16

10. Kimijima, N. et al *New Urban Transport for Middle East Monorail System for Dubai Palm Jumeirah Transit System*, Hitachi Review Vol 59, (2010), No 1

11. IBI Group, E&N Railway Corridor Study: Analysis of Tourist Train Potential, (Date Unknown)

12. Hassan A The Role of Light Railway in Sugarcane Transport in Egypt, Infrastructure Design, Signalling and Security in Railway, Chapter 1

13. Parsons Brinkerhoff *High Speed Rail*, Network, Issue No 73, Sept 2011, http://www.pbworld.com/news/publications.aspx

14. Chun-Hwan, K. Transportation Revolution: The Korean High-speed Railway, Japan Railway & Transport Review 40, March 2005

15. Alstom Metropolis 21 st Century Metro Train Technology, http://www.alstom.com/turkey/products-and-services/-alstom-transport-turkey/rolling-stock/

16. Scomi Rail, *Monorail The Revolution of Urban Transit*, http://www.scomirail.com.my/

17. Duncan, B *The Hunter Rail Car: A versatile design solution for regional rail transport*, Australian Journal of Multi-disciplinary Engineering, Vol 7, No 2

18. Burge, P. et al Modelling Demand for Long-Distance Travel in Great Britain, www.rand.org, 2011

19. Railway Gazette *Commissioning the world's heaviest automated metro*, Metro Report 2003

20. Stadler *Electric Double-Deck train KISS*, www.stadlerrail.com

21. Transportation Research Board *Integration of Light Rail Transit into City Streets*, 1996

22. Turnbull, G. *The development and retention of Melbourne's trams and the influence of Sir Robert Risson*, ISSN 1038-7448, Working Paper No. 01/2002, Aug 2002

23. Transportation Research Board *Track Design Handbook for Light Rail Transit*, Second Edition, TCRP Report 155, 2012

24. Mora, J. *A Streetcar named Light Rail*, IEEE Spectrum Feb 1991

25. Sarunac, R. & Zeolla, N. *Structural and Crashworthiness Requirements of Light Rail Vehicles with Low-Floor Extension*, Transportation Research Circular E-C058: 9th National Light Rail Conference

26. Schroeder, M. *Developing CEM Design Standards to Improve Light Rail Vehicle Crashworthiness*, Proceedings of JRC2006 Joint Rail Conference April 2006 Atlanta

27. Daniel, L. *Light Rail Systems – Assessing Technical Feasibility*, Conference on Railway Engineering Melbourne May 2006

28. Swanson, J. & Thomes, C. *Light-Rail Transit Systems*, IEEE Vehicular Technology Magazine, June 2010

29. Transportation Research Board National Research Council *TCRP Report 2 Applicability of Low-Floor Light Rail Vehicles in North America*, 1995

30. Coifman, B. *IVHS protection at light rail grade crossings*, Proceedings of the 1995 IEEE/ASME Joint Railroad Conference, 1995

31. Swanson, J. *Light Rail Systems Without Wires*, Proceedings of the 2003 IEEE/ASME Joint Rail Conference April 2003

32. Maunsell Australia Pty Ltd, *Perth Light Rail Study*, 0284/05, August 2007

Overview of Rail Infrastructure

Track

Track is the system that provides a running surface for rail wheels, and supports the rail vehicle. Track is easily one of the most important engineering systems for a railway, and is a central part of the design of any new rail system. Track is mostly standard in its design and configuration from many different railways, although there are some different types used for light rail systems.

Most rail systems use a fairly standard track system, with the exception of trams, monorails, and some light rail. For trams the rails are often embedded into the road, so as to allow road vehicles to pass over the rails as well as trams. Rails for trams have a separate and quite different design to normal rail. The shape of the rail, as well as the system by which the rail is held in place, is quite different.

Rails are made of steel. Some smaller rail systems run on concrete viaducts, but the vast majority of rail systems use steel rails. Train wheels are also often made of steel, and the behaviour of this steel to steel physical interface is very important. Surprisingly, the steel wheels of the train can often slide over the steel top surface, and when this happens the top of the rail and the wheel can be badly damaged. Care must be taken in ensuring that the wheel never slides over the rail, but rolls instead, and this requirement is central to the design of any rail system. One way to avoid this problem is to use rubber tyred trains, and this is occasionally done, such as the Montreal metro, but so doing adds a lot of cost as rubber tyres need to be constantly replaced as they wear.

Much of the track around the world is ballasted, which means the sleepers and rails sit on ballast. Ballast is made up of crushed rock, and major railways use substantial quantities of it. Sleepers sit within the ballast, and the ballast holds them in place. The major alternative to ballasted track is slab track, where the sleepers and rail sit directly on concrete. The track structure for ballasted track is shown below.

Figure 2.1 Track System

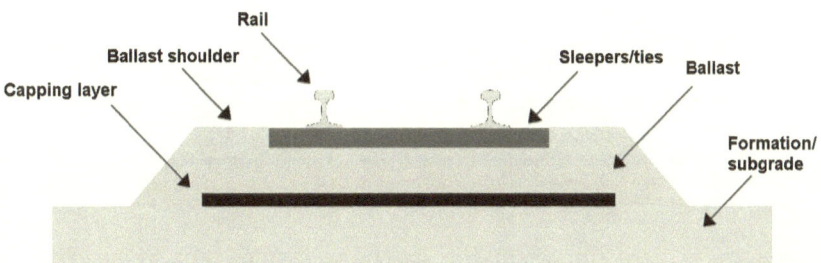

The function of each of the components of the track system is:
- The rail; supports the train, provides a running surface for the wheels of each train.
- Sleepers; which support the rails, hold the rails at a fixed distance from each other, and transfer the weight and load of the train into the ballast. Sleepers are often made of wood or concrete, although other materials such as steel or polymer are also used
- Ballast, which sits under the rails, and is made of hard crushed rock. Ballast distributes the load from trains, reducing wear, so that many trains can pass without causing serious damage to the track system. Ballast is a sacrificial item, which means it is designed to degrade over time. The degradation of ballast, and managing its replacement, is one of the key maintenance activities of any railway.
- The capping layer; which provides separation between the ballast and the subgrade. The capping layer maintains the separation between the ballast and the formation. The capping layer is sometimes replaced with geosynthetics, which is a type of textile matting, keeping the formation and ballast separate.
- Formation: which is usually the compacted ground underneath the track structure. The formation supports the track, and the condition of the formation is one of the key parameters for determining the maintenance of track.

Tracks are normally in pairs. Away from the track the ground normally has a fall to it, this is to allow for the water to run away from the track.

Figure 2.2 The Double Track System

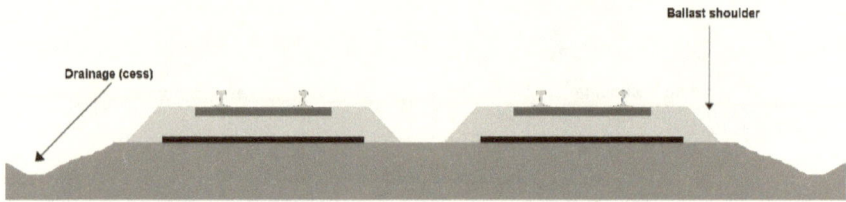

Drainage is very important for any track system. Drains need to be provided so that water can be removed when the track is rained on. Drainage, or the lack of it, can cause substantial problems in any rail system.

The rails are fastened to the sleepers with specially designed fasteners. The picture below shows the clips holding the rails to the sleepers.

Rail Track

If the reader looks carefully, notice that most of the rail is rusty, but on top of the rail there is part of it where train wheels sit when travelling over the rail. This patch of worn shiny rail is called the wear band, or the contact band, and it's important for a rail system to maintain this clear band of clean steel for signalling equipment to operate. The picture below shows it better.

Rail Fastenings

Rails are quite standard, and come in a number of sizes. Rail sizes are usually expressed in weight per unit of length, and in metric countries this is often 53 or 60 kgs per metre. Other sizes are also possible, with 40 and 50 also being common. In the large heavy haul freight networks in northern Australia, 74 kg/metre is now being used (as of 2012), which is a very large size and suitable for very heavily loaded trains with a high frequency. The imperial unit of measurement is pounds per yard, and 40 to 100 pounds per yard is common.

Increasing the size of the rail increases the size of train that can pass over the rails. For a light rail system, only a small rail is needed, and where small trains operate only small rails are needed. For larger trains, and especially freight lines, the rails need to be large to accommodate the higher weight.

Figure 2.3 The Rail Profile

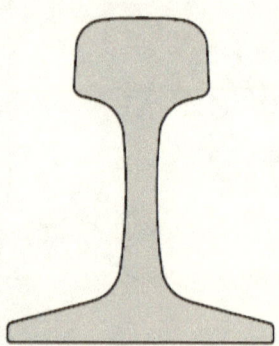

Above is a very standard profile for rails. The top is called the head of the rail. Different sizes of rail have slightly different shapes, but overall they mostly look similar to the rail shape above. Tram rails look significantly different, and monorails do not have rails, but just the one beam. The image below shows the profile of a tram rail, and it is designed to allow trains to run on it and allow road vehicles to drive over it as well.

Figure 2.4 Tram Rail Profile

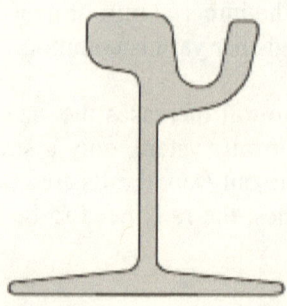

The ballast underneath the track plays an important role. The main purpose of ballast is to maintain and support the track, which is generally does well, but also to suppress vibration. Trains moving over tracks generate a lot of noise and vibration, and the ballast, surprisingly enough, suppresses this. Ballast is even used in tunnels, to suppress noise, again which is does quite well. It seems strange that ballast does this, but it does.

Ballast is made up of many small hard rocks. The amount of ballast placed under the track is not fixed, and more is usually better. Putting more ballast is expensive, as the stuff is unexpectedly expensive, and actually quite heavy. The best ballast if tough and rough, and locks together to form a tight bed for the sleepers and rails. Generally the harder the better, and quartz and granite are often considered the best materials, but many different types of rock are used. Railways often use materials that are found locally, to reduce costs and ensure the ballast does not need to be shipped very far.

Achieving the great noise reduction that ballast achieves is done through breaking down the ballast. Each time a train passes over the ballast, a small amount of it breaks into smaller pieces. Over a long period of time, such as decades, the ballast breaks down into such small pieces that most of it becomes powder. The powder intermixed with the rocky ballast is often described as fines. Once the ballast is full of fines it needs to be either cleaned, or entirely replaced, and both of these options are not cheap. Also, the track will be unable to hold track geometry, and this can be a real problem for high speed track where maintaining good track geometry is quite important.

So in summary ballast is a sacrificial item. This means that it is designed to be destroyed, which on most tracks it will be sooner or later. As ballast degrades, it gets smaller, and so the track starts to sink. Over a period of time the track can sink up to 200 mm, and if this occurs at a platform, train floors will be lower than the platform. For maintenance, railways often top up ballast as it degrades.

The photo below is of tram tracks in Hong Kong that have been uncovered during maintenance work. Rarely is there any ballast for tram tracks, and as can be seen from the photo below the tracks are embedded into the road, and surrounded in bitumen. This type of systems does not allow the noise suppression that normally comes with using ballast, especially at joins, ie, where two rails are joined together.

Uncovered Tram Tracks in Hong Kong

So why is more slab track not used? Slab track, or putting the rails and sleepers onto concrete, seems to eliminate many of the problems associated with ballast. Ballast is expensive, and needs to be replaced after it has degraded. When it sinks it creates all sorts of track geometry problems, which can only be fixed with expensive track maintenance vehicles.

Slab track in Bangkok is shown below, on the Bangkok Skytrain. Note that on this track a third rail is also used, and it is located in between both running tracks.

Slab Track in Bangkok

Slab track is technically more complex to install. Problems with vibration usually mean that the concrete base can be damaged, and so vibration damping is needed. Whilst this function is normally provided by ballast, this is not possible with slab track, so some complicated vibration dampening scheme is needed. Different types of these have been designed and are in use, and quality control when they are installed is very important.

In some cases track may be designed for two gauges. Dual gauge track is sometimes needed in boundaries between areas with different gauges. Below is dual gauge track, this one is located in Brisbane, the inside rails are narrow gauge, and the outside are standard gauge. As Queensland uses narrow gauge, the inside rails are used more often than the outside ones.

Double Gauge Track

Superelevation (Cant)

Superelevation is the difference in level between the two rails. It is common for the two rails to be at different heights, and it is a very useful thing to do in many different situations. The height different between the two rails is show below.

Figure 2.5 Superelevation (Cant)

Superelevation is also called cant. Superelevation is installed in track to allow trains to be able to move through curves faster, and so reduce travel times. It is a cheap and effective way of improving the efficiency of track.

Signalling

The signalling system plays a critical role in any railway. Train movements are constrained by the signalling system. Trains are not like cars where they can travel along, and then stop when reaching an intersection. Almost all railways (excluding trams and light rail) operate on the principle that all rail tracks are divided up into sections, or blocks, and to enter each section trains need authorisation. For the most part trains are authorised to enter track sections using signals.

The signalling system is more than just signals, although this is the most obvious part of the signalling system. The purpose of the signalling system is to authorise the movement of trains, communicate this to drivers, and to keep trains separate so that one does not collide with another. The signalling system is composed of many different parts, including:
- Signals
- Track circuits and axle counters (train detection)
- Points installed over turnouts
- Signal boxes, and the control panel that display where trains are
- Interlockings

Signalling, like track design and the design of electrical power systems, is a huge area that has specialist people working in for decades, and there are courses and textbooks written on this asset system. Again, it is not possible here to provide anything here but the simplest explanation of how this system operates.

Signals provide information to drivers of trains; the driver sees the signal, and then knows what to do. The driver has control over the motor of the train, and the brakes, and can instruct the motor to drive harder, or slower, or brake the train. He/she does this in response to what the signal displays. The driver almost always cannot determine the direction of the train, and so his control of the train is limited to setting the speed.

Some signalling systems do not have signals by the side of the track, but instead replicate signals in the driver's cabin. The driver can see the relevant indications on his control panel, and this is called "in-cab signalling". This style of signalling system is becoming more and more common, as it eliminates the need for lineside signalling, which is expensive to install and maintain. For the purposes of explaining how the signalling system works, it is helpful to examine how lineside signals work, as this can effectively explain how signals control the movement of trains.

The purpose of the signalling system is to prevent trains colliding with each other, as well as managing the passage of trains through the rail system. Trains stop by braking, and this means that the wheels use the rail to stop the train. As trains have steel wheels, and the rails are made of steel, then trains need to stop by braking through their wheels onto the rail. Steel normally slides quite well over steel, so trains need to stop slowly, and a typical trains moving at 70 kms/hr might need 200 metres to stop. Trains moving at higher speeds may need greater distances to stop, and the signalling system needs to inform the driver well ahead of time that there is a stop signal ahead, and then the train needs to be slowed so that it can stop.

Many rail systems require the signalling system to provide something called a "movement authority". This is the permission to move through a rail system, and to perform any movement. Many signalling systems grant movement authority for trains to move, often through the use of signals. More advanced signalling systems also use movement authorities.

Light rail and trams often use road signals for movement authorities. Trams may use traffic signals like road vehicles, although sometimes they have rail like signals that direct their movements. Signals on light rail and trams systems, where they exist, tend to be very simple. Light rail and trams also run on steel rails, and have steel wheels, so their ability to stop will be similar to that of any other rail vehicle. The steel on steel sliding problem, mentioned above, applies equally to trams and light rail vehicles but trams do not move very fast, and so can slow down in time to stop at red traffic lights. Modern light rail vehicles are equipped with magnets that latch onto the rail and provide additional deceleration. It's this new braking system that allows light rail vehicles to brake hard, and so use traffic lights as signals.

What colours are used on the signals, and how the lights are arranged, varies substantially from railway to railway, and from country to country. There is very little standardisation between countries, even within the same country. Even in Australia, which has only a rail system moderate in size, the style and structure of signals varies from railway to railway. This makes explaining signalling in a book of this type extremely difficult, as it's impossible to explain all the different scenarios, the US is different to French signalling, and so on. The method used here is to use NSW signalling, as the author is familiar with it, and it looks like traffic lights, so it's a bit easier to explain. Again, this situation is a difficult one, and there is no real best answer as to how to explain signalling systems in general.

The picture below is of a signal is the Sydney rail system. This one has two red lights illuminated, with a black background. This signal is described as a double light signal, as there are basically two signals, one of top of the other. The use of two heads for a signal allows the provision of additional information.

A Double Light Signal

The signalling system was designed to give drivers the warning time they need to stop the train, otherwise a collision could result. The most common way to do this is to put "signals" alongside the track to tell the driver what to do. As the driver drives his train he sees the signals, and based on what colours are displayed he knows what to do. It is the signalling system that determines the number of trains that can pass through a section per hour, and this is called the train frequency. The minimum time between trains is another important measure, and this is called the headway.

So who controls the signals? Signals can display many different meanings, and there needs to be some sort of decision making process to determine what is displayed. For road traffic lights many of these are controlled by computer, or sometimes by controllers at a control centre somewhere. Rail signals can be computer controlled, and many are, but many are also controlled by a person with a job description of "signaller", or in the USA and Canada a "dispatcher". The signaller sets the signals, and so controls the movements of trains. Signallers are physically located in signal boxes.

Signalling systems around the world can be divided into two broad categories; speed signalling, where the driver of the train is told the maximum permitted speed, and route signalling, where the driver is told the direction he will go, and not the actual speed. It might seem strange that the driver may not know where he is going, but in complex junction there might be many points lying in many different directions, and it may not be clear to him which track is the one that he will take. In a complex junction there may be ten or even more different possible directions, and the driver will need to know which one his train will take. Of course almost always the driver is not free to choose the path his train will take, but will need to follow the path chosen for him by the signaller.

Below are some lights and signals for the trams system in Hong Kong. At this turnout trams can go either to the left or the right, and the traffic light shows either a white line perpendicular up, or sloping to the left. This traffic light is operating as a route indicator. Trams can possible go two ways, to the left and right, to the tram stop ahead. The traffic light gives the tram permission to proceed, and in the middle of the picture is the route indicator, that displays how the points are set, so the tram driver knows where the tram will go. Route indicators such as the one below are more common in rail systems in commonwealth countries.

Hong Kong Route Indicator

There is absolutely no standard for signalling systems around the world. There are a very large number of different ways of constructing signalling systems, and signals can vary even within the same country. The enormous variety of different ways of building signalling systems makes it difficult in a book like this one to explain how this kind of system works, and it is necessary to find a common thread between the many different signalling systems. An attempt has been made below to do this, but the reader must remember that is impossible to explain anything more than the very basics of a signalling system.

What is described below is the British method of signalling. It is used in most of Australia, and places like Hong Kong and Singapore. It is obviously also used in the UK. The structure of the signalling is common to many countries, and has the basic rule of red/yellow/green, also used for traffic lights. This basic structure is also used in France and the US, but this is really the only commonality. For this reason these basic signals are described, and nothing more complex than this is explained.

The schematic below shows a very basic signal. The top part of the signal is called the signal head, and signals may have one or more of these. There are lights installed in the head of the signal, and there may be only one, or multiple of these. Remember that many railways do no structure their signal this way, but some do, and for the purposes of explaining how signalling works, this signal design is clear and easy to understand.

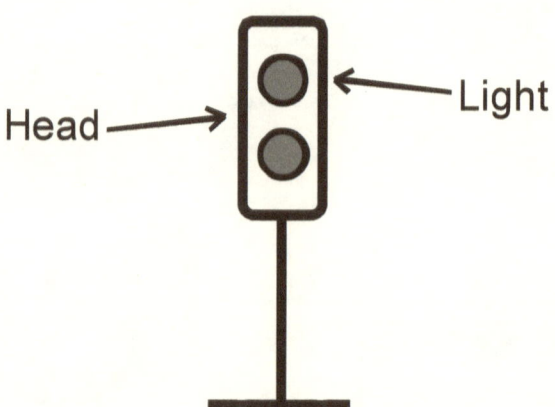

Notice that the green is on top, and the red is below the green. Whilst this is not always how signals are structured, this layout seems to be common. Normally only one signal light would be lit at any one time.

The "*aspect*" of a signal is its appearance, so if the green light is on we say that the signal is showing a green aspect. The "*indication*" of the signal is the meaning of the signal to the driver, and for a green aspect this will be a proceed indication.

So what do the colours mean? Well green means "Proceed", which is go at full line speed, at the place where the rail signal is located. The red means "Stop", which obviously means stop. These two colours are the minimum for any signal that can display different indications, but a signal can also be a single red light.

The signalling system includes more than just the signals that control the actions of train drivers. Another important component of the signalling system is the method of detecting the presence and location of trains, and this is commonly done with two pieces of engineering equipment; the track circuit and the axle counter. These items are able to sense when trains enter and exit fixed blocks of track, and provide this information back to the signalling system. The signalling system uses this information to make decisions about what signals should display, as well as provide this information to the signaller.

The heart of all signalling systems is the interlocking. An interlocking is the key device that prevents trains from running into another. In a junction, or a crossover, one trains passes in front of another, and it is possible for the two trains to collide. The interlocking checks that there are no trains in the way when a train is sent through a crossover or a junction. The interlocking takes information from the train detection system and makes some calculations, and then decides if trains can be allowed through junctions. Interlockings are very safety critical, and they must be designed with great care to ensure that there is no possibility that trains will collide with each other.

Signals are very important to calculating the capacity or headway of a rail system. This topic is extremely important for calculating how many people can be moved by a rail system.

Electrical (Traction systems)

Electrical power is often supplied to power them. Electricity is generated at a power station, or possibly locally and closer to the railway, and is then transmitted through transmission lines, to the railway. Once the power has reached the railway it is transformed down to the appropriate voltage, and then delivered to the trains.

Connecting an electricity network all this distance is expensive, and there needs to be a good reason to build the infrastructure that allows this to happen. Whilst it is true that the emissions from electrical power is mostly lower than from diesel locomotives, there are other reasons why electric power is preferred over diesel engines. These include:
- Electric trains are quieter than diesel trains
- Electric energy is mostly much cheaper than diesel fuel
- Diesel engines produce a lot of smoke from combustion, and in tunnels the smoke is quite unpleasant for passengers
- Diesel engines require fuel, which in certain circumstances can ignite, and this is a fire risk which requires additional mitigations in tunnels
- And as mentioned previously, normally CO_2 emissions are often higher from diesel fuel than from electrical energy supplied from a generator

- For high speed trains diesel trains are limited on the top speed to 250 kms/hr, which is too slow for many high speed rail services

Almost all rail services in major cities are electric, although there are some exceptions. Freight services are mostly diesel, although as with many things in rail, there are some more exceptions. In Australia the Mount Black railway line is entirely electrified, and very large amounts of coal are moved on that rail line, so it certainly is possible to electrify freight lines.

There are two main ways to supply power to a train, using overhead wiring, or a third rail. Overhead wiring is generally preferred, although it makes the rail line look messy. For overhead wiring the wires hang down from above the train, and then the train has a matching system that allows it to reach up and touch the wires. This part of the train is called the pantograph. As a general observation, overhead wiring is preferred as the live electrical wires are far above the track, so that track workers can walk along the track without the need to isolate power. Also trespassers are not in any danger when entering the rail corridor as the wires are too high.

The alternative to overhead wiring is a third rail system. Third rail systems are often used because they are cheap to install, and tunnels with third rail systems are smaller and so are cheaper. Many urban rail systems have third rails installed. One challenge with third rails is that anyone that touches them will be instantly killed, and they are at ground level and so easy to reach.

The schematic below shows how overhead wiring is often configured.

Figure 2.6 Overhead Wiring and Structure

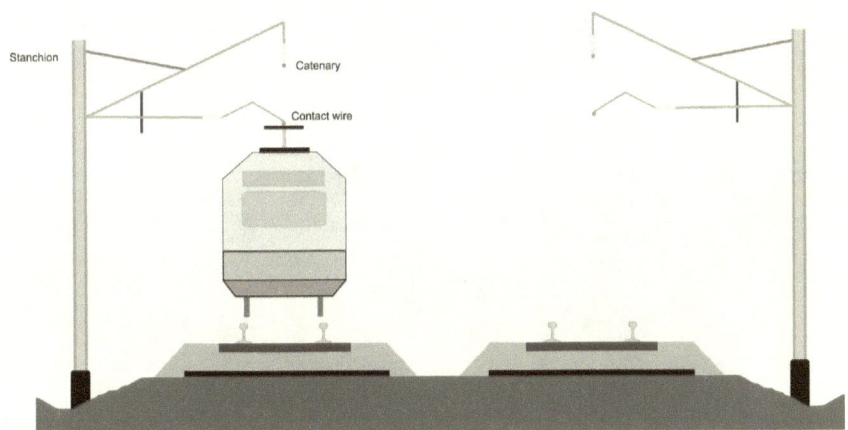

Overhead wiring needs to be supported and usually strong beams are concreted into the ground to hold the entire structure up. These beams in Australia are called stanchions, and are visually unappealing. Rail lines with no electric power are definitely visually more appealing than those with electric power. Recently there have been attempts to smarten up the appearance of rail lines with overhead wiring, with colours that are similar to the colours of the surroundings, with some success.

Overhead wiring structures come in many different shapes and sizes. The one below is for 25 kV, and is bolted onto a tunnel wall.

Registration and Contact Wire Support

Below is a pantograph that conducts electricity from the contact wire into the traction systems in the train. The top of the pantograph has a strip of carbon, and this wears as it rubs along the contact wire. The pantograph is pushed up hard against the contact wire with springs, and so if the contact wire is removed then the pantograph will spring up high into the air.

A Pantograph

Below is a substation in Perth for converting power. A substation is a truly ugly thing, but it is needed to convert and use the power successfully. Substations also contain electrical power equipment, much of which is fatal to the touch. Preventing trespassers from coming into contact with any of the equipment in a substation is a key requirement.

A Substation

The photo below shows a number of third rails in and around a couple of crossovers. Trains need to maintain contact with the third rail, and if contact is lost then the train will come to a stop, not immediately, but relatively quickly. Notice how much cleaner and nicer the track looks, and the appearance of the tracks is really much better.

Ballasted Track in a Viaduct with Third Rails

Installing power onto railways comes with many problems. Electricity in a DC (Direct Current) system can leak away, and if the leak is large enough, passengers or the public can be injured or even killed. The leaking electricity can do damage through a chemical process called electrolysis, which can result in metals near to the track being reduced to a soup of unpleasant chemicals.

For AC powered systems, there are other different problems to a DC system. The power moving through the overhead can induce currents in nearby metal objects, which means that there is now electricity in something that should not have it. For example, pipes along a tunnel in a system with AC power can now have currents passing through them. Again, this problem needs to be managed, and specialist technical people are needed who understand the problem.

A problem often encountered in Australia is that providing power to rail lines requires high voltage power lines running from generators to the rail line. In Australia generators are often located in remote areas next to coal supplies, and transmission lines need to run through national parks. Providing maintenance to transmission lines is raises some issues, as trees may need to be cut down. This is especially difficult where the trees are protected or endangered. Running power lines through a national park is a real problem, as access roads will need to be cut, and no one wants to do that. Even for a very conscientious and diligent railway, managing transmission lines through environmentally sensitive areas is difficult and constant problems emerge.

Overall providing electrical power to trains can be quite technically complicated. Specialist technical people are needed, and their salaries are not low. From the perspective of rail system design, only when the case for electric power is clearly overwhelming should electric power be used. Electric power provides many benefits and is the correct solution in many cases.

Tunnels

Tunnels are a long thin space underground often set aside for a specific purpose. Tunnels are an enclosed space through which trains can pass. Tunnels can be used for many different purposes.

Tunnels provide many benefits, the main one being the ability of a rail line to avoid obstructions and other immovable objects, and still provide a transport service. Tunnels require large amounts of specialised infrastructure, and so are costly to construct and maintain.

Tunnelling is a challenging area of engineering. The soil conditions are important to the costs and challenges associated with tunnelling, and there is no real way to know what the soil conditions will be like without actually tunnelling. To get an appreciation of the ground conditions, a project may organise for test bores to be drilled to sample what the ground is like, and this will provide some information on what the ground conditions are like. Whilst test bores provide some information, the actual ground conditions won't be known until digging actually commences.

Tunnels, and the management of fire in a tunnel, will impact upon station design. A "standard" tunnel will have ventilation, although many do not. All the ventilation equipment will normally be located at a station. An underground station can have a large amount of equipment, located in several large rooms within the station, including ventilation. The need to ventilate a tunnel significantly adds to the cost of constructing an underground station.

The picture below shows a rail tunnel, with the photo taken from one end of an underground station. Rail tunnels are commonly black or very dark with not much lighting. In this case this tunnel is single bore, and the track is ballasted, rather that being slab track. Note that the lighting is very close to the floor of the tunnel, so that drivers won't experience flashing lights when passing them, something that in rare instances can cause epileptic seizures.

A Tunnel and Portal

Whilst underground stations are also strictly speaking tunnels, they are not referred to as such, and the tunnels connect two underground stations. The transition from station to tunnel is shown below, with the station being light coloured and well-lit, and the tunnel dark and black. The transition from station into a tunnel is called a portal.

Rail tunnels can be described in terms of the following:
- The length of the tunnel
- What type of traffic is permitted to move through the tunnel
- The diameter of the tunnel, or if not round, the cross-sectional area
- The type of ventilation
- If the tunnel is single bore or double bore, and the configuration.

So let's discuss each of these in turn.

The length of the tunnel is probably the most important parameter for any rail tunnel. Usually measured in metres, it is measured as a distance that a person following the rail track would walk, rather than a linear distance from one portal to another. A long tunnel would be over 1 km in length, although there are many tunnels over 10kms, these are a small percentage of the total number of tunnels worldwide. In the US tunnels less than 160 metres are not described as tunnels, and are not normally classified as tunnels (at least under NFPA 130).

The risk and challenge with rail tunnels is fires. As tunnels are confined spaces, any fires can quickly incapacitate any passengers in the train. The heat itself is not the danger, but the smoke produced from the fire. Small fires are often started through vandalism in trains, but large fires are rare. The hazard of a large fire has a very low probability of occurrence, but when they occur the number of deaths can be very large. Preventing fires, or providing some method of escape for a tunnel can greatly add to the cost of the construction of a rail.

The diameter of the tunnel is an important parameter. Most tunnels are roughly circular in shape, so it's possible to customary the cross-sectional area of the tunnel from the diameter, using the very simple formula $Area = \dfrac{\pi D^2}{4}$. A typical diameter for a rail tunnel is about 7 metres, and a typical cross-sectional area about 40 to 60 metres. Larger cross sectional areas make ventilation and management of the movement of air in the tunnel easier, and overall a larger tunnel is better than a smaller one. Trains need to push the air out of the way when moving through a tunnel, and where there is little room between the walls of the tunnel and the train then the power needed to move the train is significantly greater. Also very narrow tunnels will make the air hotter as trains pass through, and the heat can become very great.

The type of ventilation is also relevant, and there are a number of different types. Many tunnels have no ventilation at all, but for new tunnels ventilation is often installed. Ventilation is required based on the length of the tunnel, the frequency of traffic, and the cross-sectional area of the tunnel. Ventilation can be described as either transverse, or longitudinal. For transverse ventilation, air is pushed into the tunnel from the walls towards the middle of the tunnel, whereas longitudinal the air is pushed in from the end of the tunnel, from one end to another.

Below is the layout of a twin bore tunnel in plan view. The key features are shown.

Figure 2.7 Rail Track through Tunnels

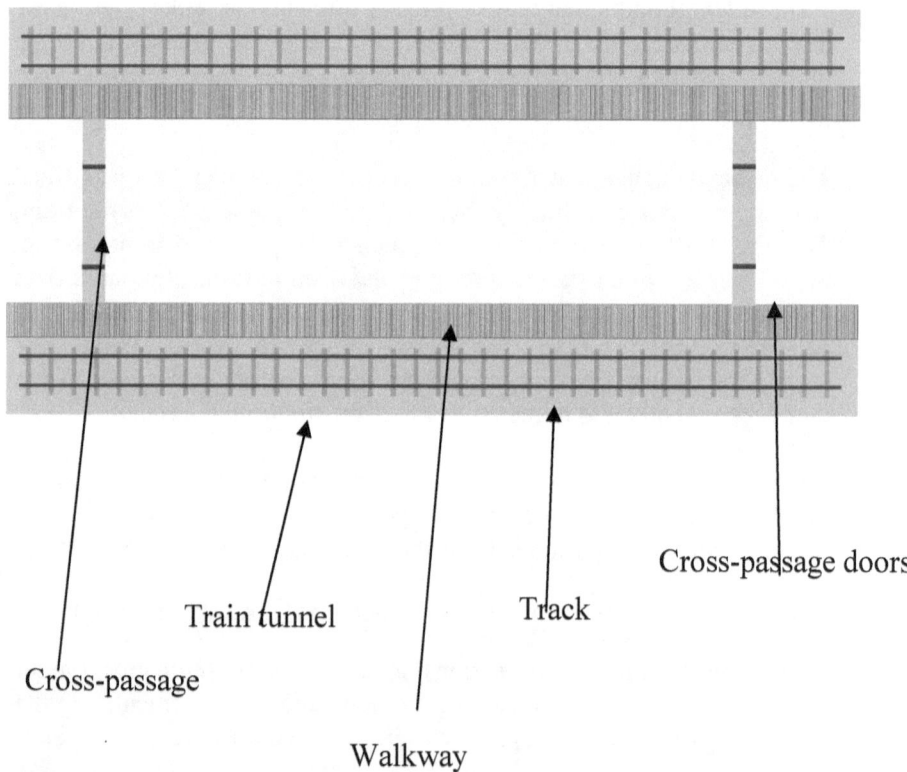

The main components of this tunnel system are:
1/ the tunnels
2/ the tracks
3/ the walkway next to the tracks
4/ the cross-passages
5/ the doors in the cross-passages.

Bridges

Everyone knows what bridges are and what they do. Any large rail system will have dozens, if not hundreds of bridges. Bridges are used to get the rail system across natural obstacles such as rivers, roads, valleys, and other natural obstacles.

Bridges are an attractive asset for any rail system. They are usually low maintenance, and they rarely contain any moving parts. In some cases rail lines pass over draw or swing bridge, but generally this is uncommon. The Skelton viaduct in Yorkshire is one rare example of a rail system using a swing bridge, and the El Ferdan bridge in Egypt over the Nile is another.

Bridges need to be very strong, but constructed properly they are can last hundreds of years. The one below is over the Cooks River in Sydney.

A Rail Bridge

Bridges that move, such as swing bridges and drawbridges, have some safety issues. There have been a number of fatal accidents in the US on swing bridges. Bridges that need to be opened and closed can be a problem, and these are usually situated over bodies of water, and are installed to allow large boats to pass underneath them. Care needs to be taken that the train does not enter over the bridge when it is open, otherwise the train can plunge into the water, and that's not good.

One problem with rail bridges, especially where the railway passes over a highway, is that occasionally trucks with high loads will strike the bridge. When this happens care must be taken that the bridge has not been damaged, and sometimes it is damaged, and trains need to slowly pass over the bridge just in case it has suffered some damage. Raising rail bridges is an important part of investing into rail infrastructure, as the higher the bridge over the highway, the smaller the chance that there will be a collision. Where a truck does hit a bridge, it can make a terrible mess and the damage to the truck can be considerable.

A more complicated version of a bridge is a viaduct. A viaduct is a long section of bridges that are all connected together. Viaducts are often used over marshy or swampy terrain, or for high speed rail.

The Viaduct connecting Italy with Venice

The picture above is of the viaduct that connects Venice to mainland Italy. This viaduct is needed because the ocean separates the historical city from Italy, and so the viaduct is quite long.

Road and Pedestrian Level Crossings

Level crossings are places where road vehicles are able to cross rail tracks. The picture below shows a level crossing outside of Paris, and it has lights and bells installed. Level crossings are sometimes described as being an "at-grade" crossing.

A Level Crossing in Paris

Level crossings can have a boom or booms installed, which descend when a train is approaching the level crossing. The boom provides an additional visual aid to drivers that the road level crossing is alarming, and that a train is coming.

Level crossings are installed in huge numbers around the world. The majority of level crossings in Australia do not have any form of protection or warning system installed over them, and they are just a place where road vehicles can cross the track. Many level crossings only have lights and bells and no boom.

Level crossings can pose some serious risks to trains and users. Every year there are fatal accidents at level crossings, and people are killed. In almost all cases the driver of the road vehicle has crossed the level crossing without looking, and there has been a collision. There have also been accidents involving buses and can result in the deaths of dozens of people.

Level crossings are places of high risk for any rail system. The construction of bridges is a viable alternative, and bridges pose almost no safety risk to trains. The cost of bridges is not small, and replacing hundreds of level crossings with bridges is simply not possible for many railways operating on limited budgets.

Tram systems operate at road level, and so effectively the entire system is one giant level crossing. There are rarely fatal accidents involving trams, as the operational speed is rather low, and the drivers know to look out for cars. Low speed collisions between road vehicles and trams are however very common, and in one year there were over one thousand collisions such as this in Melbourne. Fatal accidents with trains seem to occur when the train is moving fairly fast, and the impact to the road vehicle has the energy to cause substantial mechanical damage.

Level crossings can be a part of the signalling system, because if the level crossing has bells and lights then the signalling system needs to tell the level crossing when to activate. A level crossing with no protection other than a sign has no connection to the signalling system. Complex level crossings can be expensive to maintain.

Sometimes there are pedestrian level crossings attached to road crossings. A pedestrian crossing is designed purely for passengers, and it operates in a very similar way to a road crossing. Pedestrian crossings are much smaller than road crossings, and have lights and booms. Pedestrian crossings in Australia at least are less common than road crossings.

There are also other types of rail crossings, but they are fairly unusual. There are sometimes crossings provided for animals, and in Sydney there is a horse crossing next to Rosehill Racecourse. Crossings for animals needs to be designed differently than for people, and more space needs to be provided, depending on the size of the animal. Given the rarity of level crossings designed for animals, they won't be discussed any further.

Control Systems

A control system for a railway is an engineering system that displays the position of trains and the status of signals. Control systems normally have a computer screen where trains and their position are displayed. Large rail systems have particularly large control system displays, and these can cover the wall of a large room.

Control systems display tracks as divided up into sections, and each section is displayed as either empty or occupied. Trains are often identified with some sort of alphanumeric code, such as 111A, which identified which run it is. Alternatively, the set number (ie the train identifier) can be displayed.

Control systems also allow the signaller to set trains to routes. This means that the signaller can set the direction of turnouts, and can direct the movement of trains. Remember that drivers mostly cannot set turnout directions themselves (although there are exceptions to this rule, once again), and this function is performed either by the signaller, or in modern times, a computer program.

Tram systems and light rail systems can also have control systems, but they operate differently, partly because of the simpler network design. There is often no track detection system for trams, or almost never, so trams need to be detected and found using a different system. GPS, or some system that effectively operates the same as GPS, can be used to locate where the trams are. On the control system the screen will show the location of the trams, but unlike a control system the trams can't be directed with points and track infrastructure to different routes. The control system for a tram system is much more passive.

A control system links in closely with the signalling system, but is not the same thing. The purpose of the signalling system is to prevent the collision of trains, and the purpose of control systems is to manage the movement of trains. If the control system is directed to allow two trains to collide with one another, then the signalling system will prevent it and send an alarm to the control system.

It is also common to refer to other systems that manage rail infrastructure as control systems. For example, a system that displays information on lifts and escalators may be called a control system. It is important to distinguish between the train control system, and a system that manages other rail infrastructure.

REFERENCES

1. Zhang, C. & Li, L. Zhang, D. & Zhang, S. *Types and Characteristics of Safety Accidents Induced by Metro Construction*, 2009 International Conference on Information Management, Innovation Management and Industrial Engineering, 209

2. Kimijima, N. et al *New Urban Transport for Middle East Monorail System for Dubai Palm Jumeirah Transit System*, Hitachi Review Vol 59, (2010), No 1

3. Murphy, E. *The Application of ERTMS/ETCS Systems*, IRSE Technical Convention Melbourne, Oct 2007

4. State of Florida Department of Transportation, *Central Florida Commuter Rail Transit Design Criteria*, October 2008

5. DB Netze *AG Network Statement 2014*, April 2013

6. Parsons Brinkerhoff *High Speed Rail*, Network, Issue No 73, Sept 2011, http://www.pbworld.com/news/publications.aspx

7. Lindahl, M. *Track geometry for high-speed railways*, Department of Vehicle Engineering Royal Institute of Technology, Stockholm 2001

8. Oura, Y. *Railway Electric Power Feeding Systems*, Japan Railway & Transport Review 16, June 1998

9. BSL Management Consultants *The Cost of Railway Infrastructure Status-Quo and Ways Ahead*, Presentation to the ProMain Council of Decision Makers, Brussels Nov 2001

10. Tateishi, Y. *Broadband Radio Transmissions in Railways*, JR EAST Technical Review-No 20

11. Zhang, W. et al *Pantograph and catenary system with double pantographs for high-speed trains at 350 km/hr or higher*, Journal of Modern Transportation, Volume 19, Number 1, March 2011

12. Eyre, P. *Signalling of the Southern Suburbs Railway*, IRSE Technical Convention – Perth, July 2007

13. Rail Industry Safety and Standards Board, *ROA Manual Section 01 Civil*

14. Kohel, J. *Optimised catenary maintenance measures on Austrian Federal Railways, Rail Engineering International Edition*, 2002 Number 1

15. Huth, P. *Overview of QR Signalling Principles*, IRSE Technical Meeting, Brisbane, July 2008

16. Kerr, D. Rail Signal Aspects and Indications, http://dougkerr.net/Pumpkin/articles/Rail_signal_aspects.pdf

17. Broderick, E. & Lemon, S. *Case Study: Application of CBTC on DLR*, IRSE Australasia Technical Meeting, March 2011

18. Thales *SelTrac CBTC Communications-Based Train Control for Urban Rail*, www.thalesgroup.com/security-services

19. Siemens Transportation Systems *GSM-R Terminals Flexible GSM-R Dispatcher Systems, Terminals and Cab Radio Solutions*, http://www.siemens.com.au/files/Mobility/RI/Documents/mob_gsm-r_terminals.pdf

20. Railway Gazette *Commissioning the world's heaviest automated metro*, Metro Report 2003

21. Thales *Netrac 6613 Aramis*, www.thalesgroup.com

22. Victorian Rail Industry Operators Group Standards Track Circuit Types Characteristics and Applications, Nov 2009 http://ptv.vic.gov.au/assets/PTV/PTV%20docs/VRIOGS/VRIOGS-012.7.4-RevA.pdf

23. Davey, E. *Rail Traffic Management Systems, IET Railway Signalling and Control Systems Course*, May 2012

24. Ancarani, G. et al *Mobile radio for Railway Networks in Europe*, June 1999

25. Hillenbrand, W. *GSM-R The Railways Integrated Mobile Communications System*, Dec 1999, http://www.tsd.org/

26. Mok, S. & Savage, I. *Why Has Safety Improved at Rail-Highway Grade Crossings?*, Risk Analysis, Vol 25, No 4, 2005

27. Klinger, R. *Radio Coverage for Road and Rail Tunnels in Tunnels in the Frequency Range 75 to 1000 MHz*, Vehicular Technology Conference, 1991.

28. Ahren, T. & Parida, A. *Overall railway infrastructure effectiveness (ORIE)*, Journal of Quality in Maintenance Engineering Vol 15 No 1 2009, pp 17 – 30

Week 3

Basic Station Types

Styles and Configurations of Stations

Stations come in a large array of different configurations. Stations can be described in terms of a number of simple parameters, which are commonly understood throughout the rail industry. Some of these are:

- Platform length. Typically platforms are raised and higher than both the ground and the track running alongside it, and the length of the platform is same as the length of the train that can sit alongside it, and passengers can board and disembark safely. Not all platforms however are the same length as the trains that stop there.
- Height of the platform. This measurement is taken from the top of the running surface of the rail to the place where passengers stand to board a train.
- Number of platforms. Each platform typically will have a separate track alongside it, although in some cases a very long platform may be classified as two separate platforms.
- Number of passengers through the station each day. Almost always the number of passengers is counted through the ticketing system, and the number of barrier/gate entries and exits is counted per day.
- The role the station plays in the operation of the network. Stations may be very large and play an important role in the network or small and trains may stop there only rarely. Some stations are used only for special events. Alternatively, a station can be a terminus, where services terminate and do not continue, or am interchangestation, where passengers can alight from one service on one rail line, and then board a service on another line.
- If the station is underground, at the same grade as the ground, or elevated. These differences are important for the design and use of the station.

Some stations may have disused platforms, and these are not normally counted as part of the total number of platforms. Old stations may have a substantial number of disused platforms, and the numbering or identification of platforms may reflect this. At Rockdale station in Sydney platform numbering runs from 2 to 5, as platform 1 is no longer used, and the platform numbers have not changed since that platform was built over 50 years ago.

The station below is typical of stations in remote areas, and there is only one track at this platform. Trains moving in both directions stop at the same platform. There is no track on the other side. Also note that the station has no roofing, although there is a small area provided, a bit like a shed, where passengers can stand to get out of the rain. Stations of this kind are rarely manned with staff, as there is no booking office for staff to sell tickets at, or store cleaning implements, or any of the other accessories of an office.

A Simple Regional Station

This station has only one track, which has some advantages and disadvantages. A carpark on the side of the station without a track may be accessed without crossing any tracks, which for disabled passengers is a real benefit. Alternatively, the number of trains that can pass through this station will be limited to a small number per hour, as trains moving in both directions will need to pass over the same track. Another configuration possible with thinly used stations is that there is a loop around the station, allowing trains top stop at both platforms to pass one another.

We can see the facilities provided on this station, which is in outer Sydney. There is no booking office, so no staff will ordinarily be present to help passengers and sell tickets. Seating and lighting is provided, as well as a covered waiting area. The covered area will provide some protection from rain, but given its small size will provide shelter for only maybe 20 passengers, and no more. There are no vending machines, nor any screens providing information on when the next train is due. There are no barriers to restrict entry to the station, and passengers can move around freely. The reader may notice a small yellow box under the orange sign attached to the waiting area, which is a help point for any passengers who feel their safety is threatened. There are no lifts or escalators of any kind.

Whilst this particular station is in a remote area of Sydney, this configuration of station is very common in Australia. There are hundreds of this type of basic yet functional station across the country, and these exist in all states of Australia. They are cheap to construct, and maintain, and perform an important function whilst being relatively immune to damage from vandalism and weather. It may be that some transport planners feel that this type of station is somehow inadequate, but it is an efficient design that performs its function well.

The picture below is of a regional station outside of Paris. We may observe that this station has a clock, covered waiting areas, and is very long indeed. The platform height is also quite low, consistent with the platform heights across Europe and France especially. On the right hand side is a booking office, where tickets are sold, station staff work, and there is an air-conditioned office. Notice that the station has roofing over part of its length. Also notice that the two platforms are on the side of the track, and this configuration is called a side platform station. There is no obvious platform numbering on the station. Given that there is a waiting area and booking office on one side of the station, and not the other, this station is likely to be a commuter station, which passengers waiting to go to the city centre on one side, and using the other platform to only alight when returning from the nearby city (in this case Paris). This configuration is very common.

A Regional Station in Paris, Side Platforms

The station below is in urban Sydney, and is an island platform station. For this type of station the platforms are in the centre of the tracks, and trains move around the platforms. Passengers wait in the middle of the platform, and can wait in the same place for trains in either direction. Notice on this station there is a vending machine for Coke Cola drinks next to the wall of the old building in the middle of the platform. Express services bypass this station, and local all stopping services, which are slower, stop here with a low frequency.

A Suburban Station in Sydney, Island Platform

Island platforms are often considered superior to side platform stations. This is because:
- Rail staff can be placed in the middle of the island platform, to provide customer information, assistance, and sell tickets
- Toilets, if provided, need only to be located in the middle of the island platform
- In underground systems, island platforms are generally bigger, so there is more room for passengers to wait. For above ground stations with side platforms can be any size based on the nearby available land
- It obvious where passengers should wait, but with side platforms passengers need to make a decision.

There are also some disadvantages to island platforms, and some of these are:
- Island platforms often need more space, and this can particularly be a problem with elevated railways where space is quite limited
- Island platforms require tracks to move in a curve around the station. Notice in the pictures above that the tracks for the side platforms are very straight, whereas one of the tracks for the island platform needs to curve around the platform. If there are

high speed trains not stopping at the station this could be a real problem.
- Side platforms can be convenient for passengers with disabilities, as they can enter one platform directly from the carpark. This can be very handy as there is no need to use a lift, assuming that the platform is on the side for trains going in the desired direction
- Island platforms are more expensive than smaller side platforms, especially in underground stations

Another type of station is one where passengers need to request the train to stop, to either board or alight. For heavy rail these stations are relatively uncommon, but for light rail are extremely common. For tram systems this is normal, and the waiting passenger would signal the driver to stop, usually with a movement of a hand. In the US this kind of station is called a halt. There are also a small number of stations like this in Sydney. The stations above are not halts, which are never installed in busy city railways, but are always located in remote areas with very limited numbers of passengers.

Stations for tram systems tend to be very simple, likewise for classical "light rail" systems. Tram stations are mostly called stops, and are in most cases not really stations. Many of the stops are so small that that are almost invisible, and are can only be detected by a small street sign indicating that trams stop there. In some cases passengers may even need to board and alight from the side of the road to the waiting tram.

The photo below is a tram stop in Zurich. It is very basic, and there is an oval building alongside the tram tracks, which has a small number of shops in it. Note that the tram stop is just a flat space with no cover, no obvious lighting, and very little by way of facilities. This is common for tram stops, even in very busy cities.

A Tram Stop in Zurich

The photo below is a light rail station in Hong Kong. Light rail vehicles use this station to move passengers from the main metro line to apartment buildings in outer Hong Kong. From this photo we note that the platforms are quite high from the passenger walking surface to the top of the rail. Older light rail systems had this design, but this is now uncommon. Also note that the entire station is covered, but very poorly lit, and the platforms are very short. The photo was taken when standing on the tracks, something that is allowed with light rail and trams, but not with heavy rail. This station is a blend of a heavy rail station and a tram stop.

A Light Rail Station

Terminal Stations

Large terminal stations are places where regional, high speed and commuter trains meet and sit to allow passengers to change from one train to another. This type of central city station is quite common, and in the US and Canada these stations are often called "Union" station. There are union stations in Chicago, Los Angeles, Toronto, and Montreal, and many others. The most famous terminal station in the world is Grand Central Station in New York. In large cities there might be many terminal stations, for example, in Paris there are six. In all Australian cities there is only one in each major city.

Below is an example of a small terminal station. This one is in Perth. Services leave here for some regional destinations, and almost all commuter trains pass through this station. The high ceiling provides a feeling of space. Notice the platforms are numbered, and there are text passenger information displays for each platform. As is common with terminal station, trains are waiting for their scheduled departure times at the station.

Perth Main Station

Terminal stations often have flashy designs to make them look more impressive. Open areas to give a feeling of space and to make the station look sexy and more cool. Large open areas are common in large stations, although there is no real reason why all stations should not be designed in this way.

Major Components of a Station

Platform screen doors have become increasing common around the world. They are often installed in metro stations or at stations where there is significant crowding. To work properly the doors on the station need to line up with the doors on the train, and this is usually only possible with ATO (automatic train operation), where a computer drives the train. A human driver will rarely be accurate enough to allow a rail system to use platform screen doors.

Overall platform screen doors seem to be becoming more common, especially in Asia. Below is a picture of some platform screen doors in Singapore, and as with just about everything in Singapore, it's very clean and shiny. The platform screen doors below are full height, and completely the station from the tunnel in which the train moves.

Platform Screen Doors

Platform screen doors have a number of benefits, including:
- It is very difficult for people to commit suicide at stations with platform screen doors
- No one will be pushed under a train from overcrowding with platform screen doors
- The air-conditioning load for the station will be lower, as the air from the station will not mix with outside air
- The station looks better, as passengers cannot see the dirty tracks and tunnel, but instead see the clean shiny platform screen doors.

Of course no discussion of any asset in a rail system would be complete without mentioning the disadvantages:
- They are expensive
- They can fail, and this can delay trains
- Their use is limited to trains that are at least partially computer controlled, as drivers cannot stop their trains with the accuracy needed to position the train next to the platform doors.

Notice on the floors the lines painted to direct passengers. These are common in major metro lines where the number of passengers is very large. Passengers alighting move through the middle of the doors, and on the outsides wait for passengers to alight before boarding the train.

The doors above are full height doors, but it is not necessary to do that. Below is a picture of some half height doors in Tokyo, which provides many of the benefits of full length doors. In terms of passenger flow and safety the half height doors work quite well, but do not assist with air conditioning. Also note the advertising screens on the walls across from the platform.

Platform Edge Barriers

Concourses are the area above or near a station where many of the entrances and exists are connected. Passengers move throughout a station from the concourse, and it is often above the station. The photo below is of a metro station in Hong Kong. Long concourses like this are common in underground metro stations, where the station has the additional purpose of allowing people to move around the city without catching a train. In the front of the picture are the barriers that provide entry into the station proper, and on the left is a walkway to the other end of the station. The concourse here is above the platforms where the metro stations stop, and as the metro trains are quite long, the concourse also is quite long. The area behind the barriers is often referred to as the "paid area", where passengers need to buy a ticket to enter.

A Metro Station Concourse

Some of the stations in Hong Kong serve as major thoroughfares without the need for passengers to catch a train. Stations may be connected through overpasses, and passengers can walk along these to get to the next station without riding a train. In some cases pedestrian overpasses or shopping centres can extend for several kilometres, connecting several stations together.

The picture below is of a station in Osaka where the platforms are on both sides of the train, and doors are opened simultaneously on both sides of the train. In practice passengers enter form one side and exit from the other. This type of station is sometimes called the Spanish solution, because it is commonly used in the Barcelona metro. Passengers get on through one side of the train, and alight from the other. This structure of station is able to move more people quickly.

Barcelona Style Platforms for a Terminus Station in Osaka

The station structure above is sometimes used in terminus stations, and in stations with very high numbers of passengers. This station structure can be very effective in reducing dwell times.

Access in and out of Stations

Trains are large, and in many cases there are two or more tracks making up any rail line. Passengers need to be able to get from outside the rail corridor to the platform to catch a train. This means that need in many cases to either go over the top of below where a train might go, and where the train is quite large then going over the train requires passenger to climb quite a height.

The raised section over a station is called the concourse. For a station on flat ground, a concourse is quite common, and often stairs lead to the concourse from both outside the station, and from platforms.

The design below is a very good one, and there is no need for a concourse. For a side platform, where there are no barriers, this solution is quite acceptable, and there are only two ramps at this station, one in view and the other to the left. The ramp allows passengers to get across the tracks without getting in the path of trains. Also the ramp allows wheelchair passengers access across the tracks, without the need for a ramp.

A Station Ramp

Ramps are a cheap solution to providing access to stations for those with disabilities. Ramps also are very unlikely to fail, and require very little maintenance, unlike lifts and escalators.

There are international and national standards on ramp design. Normally ramps must be design to be below a certain grade, and a steep ramp will be difficult to those with disabilities to use. Also, long ramps need to have landings, which is a flat space where people with wheelchairs can rest during the ascent of a ramp.

Lifts can be used to get passengers from one platform to another, and from one side of the station to the other. Lifts are very popular with passengers, and will be extensively used where installed. Lifts will be unable to move large numbers of passengers, as they are too slow, but can be very effective in moving passengers with prams, disabilities, and those with luggage. Whilst expensive, the installation of lifts has become commonplace across Australia, even for regional stations.

A Station Lift

Adding mechanical aids to a station will help disabled people use the station more effectively, but they can be very expensive to install. On the left is a lift which can move people from the concourse to the platform. This type of free standing structure is extremely expensive to install as there is no other structure upon which the lift well can use for support, and so it needs to be a free standing structure.

Escalators are often also used to move people from and to the platform. Escalators are very popular because the speed up the departure of people from the platform once passengers have alighted. Escalators can be provided individually, in pairs, or even in groups of three or more.

A Station Escalator

Customer Support on Stations

Many of the ancillary services provided to passengers during their rail trip are provided at stations. Stations are also the entry point for passengers into the rail system and where money changes hands, support services are provided, and information passed on to passengers about the operation of the rail system.

The trend in recent years has been an increase in the volume of services provided to passengers. Mobile phone reception is now more common in underground stations. Free wifi may be provided. Passenger information is more comprehensive than it was in the past. What services are provided in stations has improved significantly.

Many of the services that can potentially be provided on a station require space for them to be located. The structural design of the station is important, for many reasons, but also to allow the installation of different services to passengers. Small stations may not be able to accommodate the installation of escalators or lifts, as there is no space to put them. Small concourses may limit the number of ticketing machines that can be installed. In general it is best if stations are large to accommodate the installation of additional services should the need arise later in the life of the station.

Some of the customer facilities that can be provided on a station include:
- Toilets
- Covered waiting areas
- Air-conditioning
- Vending machines and food stalls
- Information of all sorts, including tourist information
- Television screens showing news and other information
- First aid
- Internet kiosks
- Wifi
- Free water
- Mobile phone reception
- Prayer rooms
- Breast feeding rooms
- Lockers

- Services with baggage (such as long term storage)
- Sale of rail related souvenirs
- Shops selling all sorts of products
- Banking facilities
- Library facilities for long journeys

In any one station it is unlikely that all of these facilities would be installed simultaneously.

Toilets may or may not be installed at stations, although of course they are popular with passengers. The problem with toilets is that they are expensive to maintain, and are focal points for crime. They can also attract the homeless, and drug deals and other crimes can be committed there. Toilets are not always installed, even in the most heavily used systems, and Hong Kong MTR has toilets only in a small number of stations.

Passenger information systems

Passengers need information on when trains are arriving and on which platform. Passenger information systems (PIS) provide this information to passengers, and this can be provided through a variety of different media, such as display boards, telephones, announcements, or through the internet. Recently many railways have set up systems so that apps on smart phones can be installed so that real time information can be obtained for trains and their movements.

Below is a picture of passenger information screens in Central station in Brisbane. This system provides information on when trains are arriving and leaving, and what platform they are on. This system is a good one, and passenger information is clear.

Passenger Information Display

Information other than train running can also be provided to passengers. For example, where train lines are removed for service for major maintenance or upgrading, then information can be provided to passengers on when and where this is happening. Alternatively, when trains are delayed, information should be provided to passengers so that they know where to go to get buses, or what the forecast is for the resumption of services.

The photo below shows an old style timetable display. The older style was able to present a lot of information, and this one has a clock above and the stopping pattern below. In red are the interchange stations. At this station there are two platforms. The name of each station is painted onto a block of wood, which can be turned to display the relevant information for the next train. Whilst this system looks primitive, and it is, in practice it worked quite well. Clearly the station needs to be manned so that staff could come out and change what is displayed after the passage of each train. This type of system has become uncommon, and computerisation has resulted in the removal of many of the timetable displays like the one below.

Wooden Timetable Passenger Display

Information on the next available train is also very useful. Often located on station, screens are provided overhead on station platforms where passengers can look up and see the next train. The picture below shows a simple rail passenger information screen in a metro station in Paris. The information is very basic, but provides what passengers need.

Passenger Information Sign in Paris

The photo below is of a different type of passenger information. Very long trains, in particular regional and HSR trains, have numbered carriages and can be very long. Their length, and use of reserved seating on HSR trains, means that passengers need to know where their carriage is located. For HSR services where a stop is only a couple of minutes at any one station, passengers need to know where their carriage is located along the platform, and so these signs are provided along the platform to provide this information.

Passenger Carriage Information

Maps

Information about the local area can also be provided to passengers. This includes exits, where important landmarks are located, and how to get there from where passengers are standing.

Maps should be provided and easy to read. Network maps in particular should be very common. Below in the two smaller photos are geographical maps provided in two different stations. The one on the left is of the metro network in Tokyo. The one on the right is the regional rail system of Taiwan.

Geographically Correct Maps in Stations

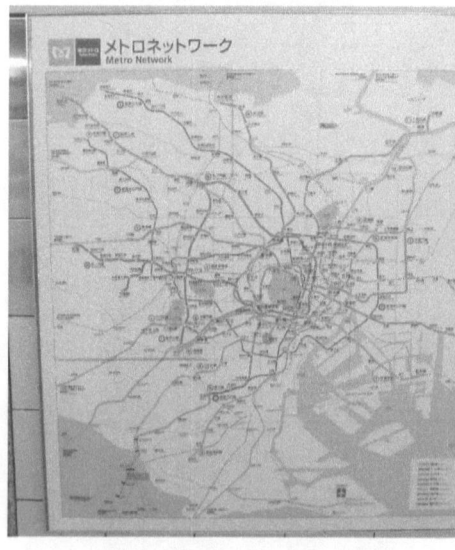
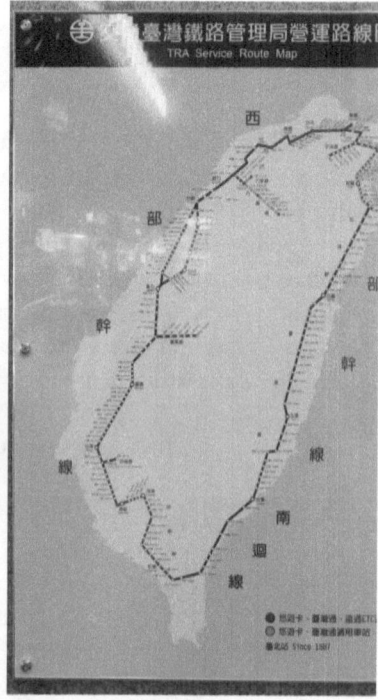

Timetable Information

Not all rail systems have passenger timetables, in fact many do not. Metros operate with a frequency that means that timetabling of trains is not really necessary. People arrive at a station and catch the next train, which is only a few minutes away because the frequency of train services is so high. Intermediate capacity rail systems also do not have passenger timetables, for the same reasons as metros, and monorails may or may not have passenger timetables, depending on the frequency of service, but commonly do not have one. Of course the rail operator keeps a working timetable.

For all other train systems timetables are the norm. Timetables provide a time and a stopping pattern for services, and a timetable may either describe the services on the entire rail system, or one part. Timetables when created, and when appropriate, need to be made available to the public. Timetable information can be made available through a variety of different media.

A distinction needs to be made between passenger timetables, and railway working timetables. A railway will usually need to move trains around to get them ready for the next revenue service. Many train trips during the night are made with no passengers, and these services are timetabled, just like trains that carry passengers. Sometimes the timetable that describes all the train trips, including empty trains is called the working timetable. Timetables for complicated systems can be very large and run to hundreds of pages.

Trains in a timetable may or may not be given a train number. Train numbers can be used for ticketing, and when seats can be reserved on a train. A train ticket will need to specify the train number and the seat. There are however, many rail systems where trains are not numbered.

Timetables also need to provide information on the stopping pattern. Trains do not need to stop at every station, and often do not. Express trains will stop at only a small number of stations, and for all other they will pass without stopping. This needs to be clearly indicated in any timetable.

Timetables are often available from information counters in railways, as a brochure or a pamphlet. Often it is a small document that easily fits into people's hands. Timetables can also be distributed to customers through small cards that fit into the palm of one's hand, or plastic laminated sheets of paper. Large timetables may take the form of a printed book.

Timetables can also be presented in the form of large boards or posters in stations and at key locations. These boards can be posted up against a wall, or free standing.

Much more commonly now timetables are on websites where passengers can access them. This is a very good way of presenting timetable information to passengers, and web portals with timetable information can be heavily used. Another solution to providing customers with timetable information is to create custom purpose apps, which can be easily searched to find trains arrival and departure times.

Tickets and Ticketing

Passengers on many rail systems need to provide proof of payment to rail staff, or conductors. Passengers may need to retain a paper ticket to show to that payment has been made for the trip that the passenger is making, or where passengers board a train using a smart card, some rail systems have staff that check tickets using a smart card reader. Other rail systems use a barrier system, where passengers gain access to the station by passing through barriers. Ticket prices may be calculated when passengers exit from the station. Any type of ticket fare calculation system can be used, such as a zonal or point to point system which is checked with barriers.

Some rail system use an honour system, where passengers are required to pay without any form of compulsion to do so. There is no one to check their tickets or payments, and the rail system simply trusts that the money has been paid. This has been tried in Australia, and the experience was not a happy one, with very few passengers paying anything. In Hong Kong typically a barrier system is used to gain access to stations, but on one line an honour system is used when passengers gain access to first class (that's the train to the border with mainland China). This system seems to work quite well. Overall honour systems for rail ticketing do seem to be rare.

A common system used in Australia for enforcing payment is a little different from the systems mentioned above. In many of the large commuter systems that exist in Australia, there are a small number of city stations, with barriers and staff checking tickets, and large numbers of small suburban stations where very few people get on or off. Typically there might be 5 to 8 inner city stations, and over 150 to 300 other stations. Tickets are checked at the major stations, but not at the small ones. Any passengers that travels from one small station to another essentially travels for free, and everyone else has their ticket checked at the major stations. This system works quite well in most cases.

The old style proof of payment system used printed paper tickets. Old style tickets were often made of paper, with information printed onto them. Before this tickets were often pre-printed, with small writing, and made of fairly hard cardboard. Some of these old tickets were quite pretty to look and, and had a satisfying feel to them. In modern times paper tickets have become rarer, with smart card becoming more common, at least for rail systems that involve short trips within major urban centres. For long distance rail paper tickets are here to stay, at least for the time being.

Below are some ticket machines in Western Australia. On the right is an add value machine, which is used to add money on to their smart card. In the middle are the machines for selling old style paper tickets.

Ticketing Machines in Perth

Below is a picture of some paper tickets from the Perth rail system.

Paper Tickets from Perth Western Australia

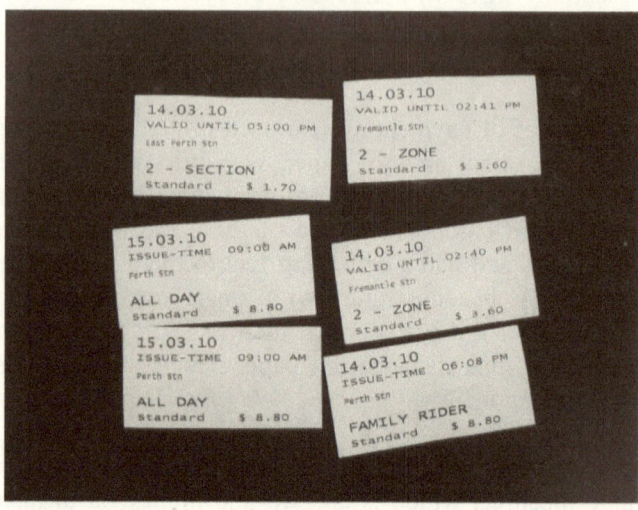

Smart cards have become much more common in rail systems around the world. A smart card is a card like a credit card where passengers put money and then use the card to enter and exit stations. As passengers pass through station barriers money is deducted from the smart card. There are usually many machines located at stations through which passengers can deposit more money, check transaction history, and see their card balance. Smart cards are extremely common in Asia, less so in Australia. Some common smart cards from Asia and Australia are shown below. The card in the top left is for Kuala Lumpur, and the bottom right is the Octopus card for Hong Kong. Normally discounts are offered on rail travel for those who have a smart card, as opposed to those who pay with cash.

Smart Cards from Various Railways

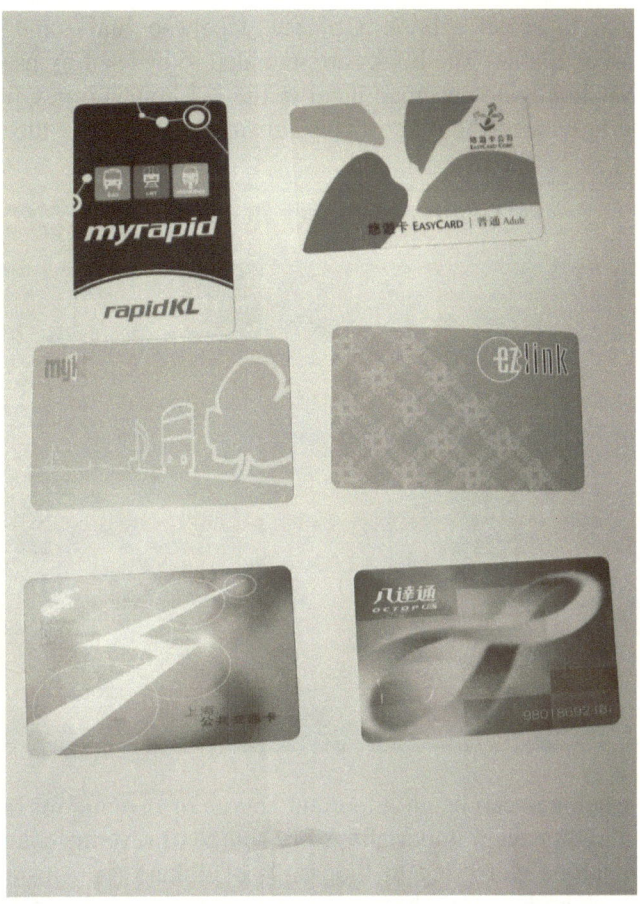

Vending Machines and Advertising

Vending machines installed into stations, especially in Asia, are amazing. An extraordinary variety of products are available for sale, including food and drinks, cosmetics, souvenirs, key rings, books, umbrellas, pens, and even clothing. These vending machines are often visually stunning for those who have not seen them before, and some of them contain very unusual items. Whilst not specifically part of the design of a station, adding vending machines that offer a variety of different items can add to the amenity of the station.

The vending machine below is the most remarkable the author has seen. Very large, several metres long, it is located in Taipei main station at the entrance to the HSR platforms. It is a library, and a passenger can buy or borrow books, and the control panel on the right hand side is to select a book. Chinese, Japanese, and some English books were available. The books are intended to be used by passengers on the HSR line, who can read them in the 2.5 hour journey from one end of the system to the other. (The Taiwanese are very educated and read a lot!)

A Lending Library in a Station

Vending machines can be an important source of revenue for railways. Whilst it may not seem important, every source of revenue counts. One vending machine can bring in thousands of dollars (in Australia) per week, and where large numbers of vending machines are installed then the revenue can be considerable.

One major problem with vending machines is vandalism. Vending machines almost always require money to sell goods (although electronic payment is becoming more common), and where there are high levels of violence and property crime then vending machines can be attacked. Whilst in theory it is possible to install CCTV cameras to watch vending machines, in practice protecting them is rather difficult. In many parts of Asia, where this kind of crime is rare, exotic and interesting vending machines are installed in many stations. In some parts of Australia, crime is frequent enough that vending machines cannot be installed due to theft and damage to the machines.

Advertising also can be an important source of revenue for a railway that can be quite cash strapped. Passenger revenue in most railways is rarely sufficient to cover operating costs, and anything that can contribute to the cost of running a railway is welcome. Advertising can bring in substantial revenues, and advertisers will pay for the right to place their advertisements in various parts of the station. MTR in Hong Kong describes a place where advertising can be placed as an "advertising point".

Stations can be designed to allow for the largest possible number of advertising points. Advertising points are places where passengers will be looking directly at, or walking by. Areas where passengers wait can also be useful for placing advertising. The insides of trains can also be good places to put advertising, and the photo below shows a metro train in Japan with banners reaching down from the ceiling.

Banners in Tokyo Metro

Advertising plays an important part in the revenue earned by Hong Kong MTR. In 2012 Hong Kong MTR earned $130 million US just from advertising. MTR has large numbers of advertising points in station, and many of the tunnels and passages leading to their stations are lined with advertising. It is important to note that the cost of installing and maintaining advertising is not high, and a very high percentage of any revenue earned from advertising can be kept as profit, or contribute towards the cost of running trains.

Advertising is not limited to signage. This display is for digital cameras, in a display cabinet in Thailand. This one is at Chit Lom station in Bangkok, and seems to contain actual digital cameras.

Promotions in stations for different products can take a variety of different forms.

An Advertising Display

Many rail companies have taken an aggressive approach to installing advertising and shops within a station. It is possible for railways to earn substantial revenue from a station, and this is particularly true for stations with high numbers of passenger movements. Careful design of a station can return substantial revenue to a rail system, and whilst many stations are not designed to maximise shop and advertising revenue, it is a very effective and powerful way to increase revenue. MTR in Hong Kong is able to generate a substantial profit from running a rail system because of the management of the shop and advertising rights within their stations.

Souvenir Shops

Souvenir shops are sometimes established for railways that are very proud of their construction and operation. These quaint little shops are located near the centre of the rail system, and are often quite small and may be overlooked by the casual passer by. There are a number of these in South East Asia.

The photo below is of the souvenir shop in Hong Kong, although this one was modified around 2015. It sells models of trains that operate on its network, as well as cup holders, pens, T shirts, stationary with MTR branding, and mouse pads. The souvenir shop also doubles as a ticket sales office.

A Rail Souvenir Shop

There is no harm in installing a souvenir shop for a railway. It promotes pride in the rail system, and generates free marketing. It's probably a good idea for a souvenir shop to be included in the design of a really good quality railway. It provides an opportunity for the citizens of the area where the railway operates to demonstrate their appreciation of the railway, and support it by using its merchandising. It also reflects well on the railway that people would want to buy its products, and can be an effective way of demonstrating that the railway is operated efficiently and in a way that suits its customers.

Other Infrastructure

Bins are often provided on stations, but with the increase in terrorism, many of the bins were removed from stations in Australia. The fear was that terrorists would place a bomb in the bin, then leave, allowing the bomb to go off and them to escape. A solution was found to this problem by having transparent bins. In theory any bomb would be seen before it would explode. The picture below shows this type of bin. The photo was taken at Tokyo high speed station.

Transparent Rubbish Bins in Tokyo

REFERENCES

1. Infrabel, *Network Statement*, Version of 9/12/2011

2. banedanmark, *Network Statement,* 2012, Jan 2011

3. Liang, H. & Ning, Z. & Yana, S *Analysis and Selection on Fare System of Urban Rail Transit*, Advanced Management Science (ICAMs), 2010

Other Aspects of Station Design

Introduction

This chapter covers many of the miscellaneous features of rail stations. For example, stations consumer power, and this is discussed below. Also passenger movements into and out of stations is important, and this includes interchange stations, where passengers move from one rail line one to another.

Many different station configurations are drawn below. Also discussed in this chapter is the design of light rail stations, which is a special case for station design. There the relationship between road and rail design is the key, as light rail stations are often designed at the same grade as roads.

Exits and Entrances

An important aspect of station design is the location and placement of exits and entrances. The quality of stations, and the customer experience, can be strongly influenced by the placement and number of entrances and exits.

For busy rail systems such as metros one important aspect of overall station design is the placement of entrances. Entrances should be placed in convenient places, which allow passengers to enter and exit the station efficiently. Poorly located entrances and exits can a string of problems, including:
- Longer journey times as passengers need more time to get to an exit
- Station crowding
- Poor passenger flows, and slow walking times
- Reduced utility of service, perhaps even affecting passenger numbers
- Large bottlenecks forming in stations

When we discuss entrances and exits it is important to note that in many cases an entrance serves as an exit as well. Entrances to many stations are sets of stairs, and passengers can move in either direction on these. Escalators move in only one direction, and so where there is only one escalator at an entrance or exit, the direction of the escalator will largely determine how the entrance or exit is used. This is especially the case where the escalator is moving in the down direction, and passenger need to walk up steps to exit the station, and they may not want to do this.

Where security is important, and everyone is checked before entering the rail system, then an entrance may require security equipment, and potentially not be usable as an exit. In China for example security scanning before entry to metro rail systems is common, so there may be entrances that are cannot be used as exits.

In practice more entrances and exits is better, especially for underground stations. Shinjuku station in Japan has over 200 entrances and exits, and there are entrances and exits scattered all around that suburb into the station. There is no real limitation on the number of entrances and exits, and more always seems to be better. Note that there are practical limits on the amount of vertical transportation that can be installed, escalators and lifts are expensive, consume lots of power, and need maintenance. It is common on large stations for only a small number of the entrances and exits to have vertical transportation, and the other exits are just stairs.

Below is a diagram of a very simple station design with two entrances and exits. They are located in the middle of the platform, and there is only one entrance/exit on either side. This cheap and efficient station design works well in many situations, and from a passenger perspective this design is very easy to understand.

Figure 3.1 Standard Station with Exits

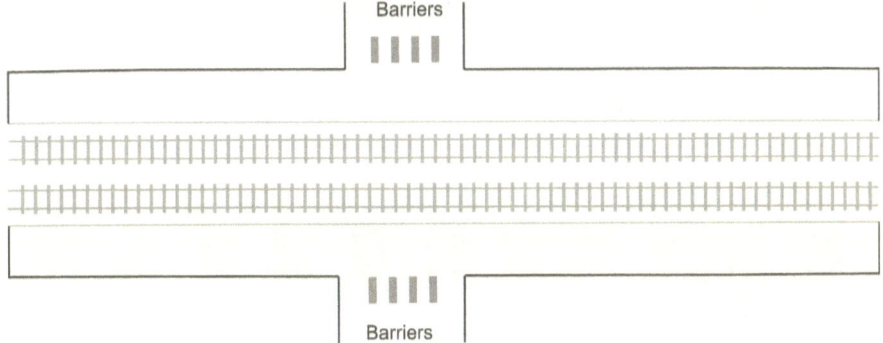

The station above shows a very common layout for station exits. There are two exits, one for either side of the station. The station is fenced, which is generally better to do, but not always done. Not drawn in 3.1 is the method for passengers to get from one side of the station to the other. There will be a way, and it may be something like a nearby bridge, a pedestrian subway, or even a pedestrian crossing. This station layout numbers in the several hundreds in Australia.

Commonly there would be parking on either side of this station, especially if it is a commuter station. A more elaborate station of this type would include a structure over the top of the station, to allow passengers to move from one side to another. This is shown below.

Figure 3.2 Standard Station with Exits through the Concourse

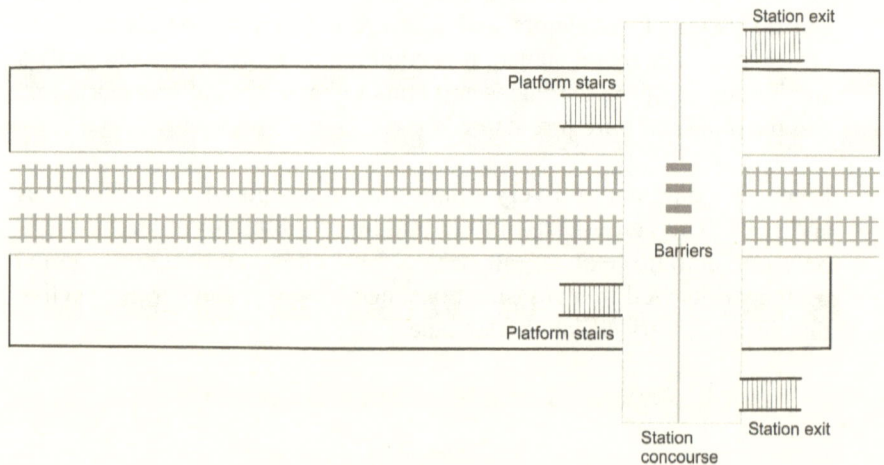

In this station the platforms are accessed through the concourse. Concourses can get very complicated, and in the next section much more complex ones are shown. The concourse is separated into two sections, with one side included in the paid area, and the other unpaid. Note that this station design allows for the public to use the station without paying, and cross from one side of the tracks to the other without entering the station paid area. This station design is superior and more complex than the simpler station design without the concourse.

Station entrances and exits will normally connect street level to the concourse.

Concourses

Concourses are large open areas where the barriers and entry to the paid area of the station is located. A concourse is where many of the facilities of a station are located, including toilets, passenger information, lifts, station staff, help points, ticketing, and potentially other facilities. Concourses come in three forms; above underground stations, above stations at ground level, and below elevated stations.

Concourses are very useful but their installation does increase the size of the station, and hence the cost. Concourses provide a place for passengers to organise themselves and ask for information or use toilets. Shops may also be located on stations as well.

In an underground station concourses are places where passengers can be evacuated to. Platform level is one level below the concourse, and there can potentially be a fire there (or really a fire anywhere). One of the objectives for fire safety for an underground station is to evacuate passengers from the platform to the concourse as quickly as possible. Another objective is getting passengers from concourses out of the station as quickly as possible. The efficient design of the concourse, to get passengers in and out quickly, is important.

The drawing below shows a typical concourse. It has 4 exits, a paid area, and stairs connecting to the platform in the middle of the paid area. This type of concourse is "standard" and represents a reasonable level of design, and has many of the features that are attractive for a concourse.

Figure 3.3 Light Rail Station on the Side of the Street

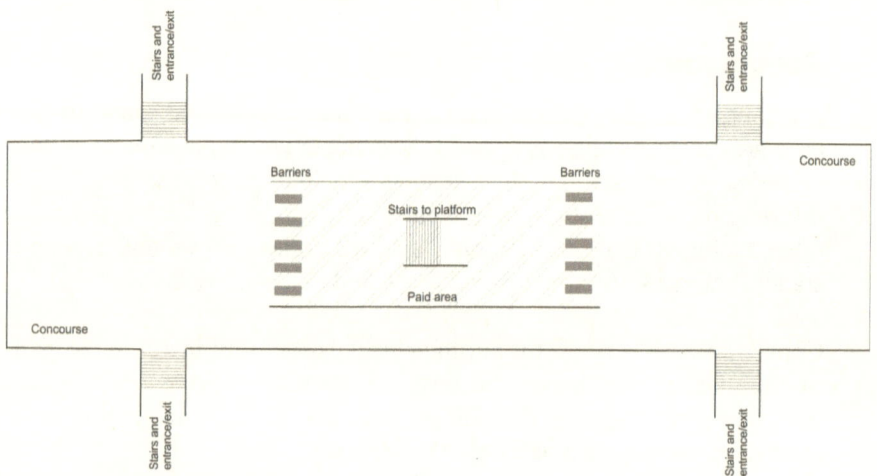

We note the above concourse has the following advantages:
- There are two sets of barriers, which allows flexibility in how they are configured to allow passengers into and out of the paid area
- There are two connections between the left hand side of the concourse and the right hand side
- There are 4 exits from the concourse to the outside, and these can be either down or up to street level.
- The concourse is large and provides ample space for passengers

So now below is an inferior design for a concourse.

Figure 3.4 Low Quality Concourse Design

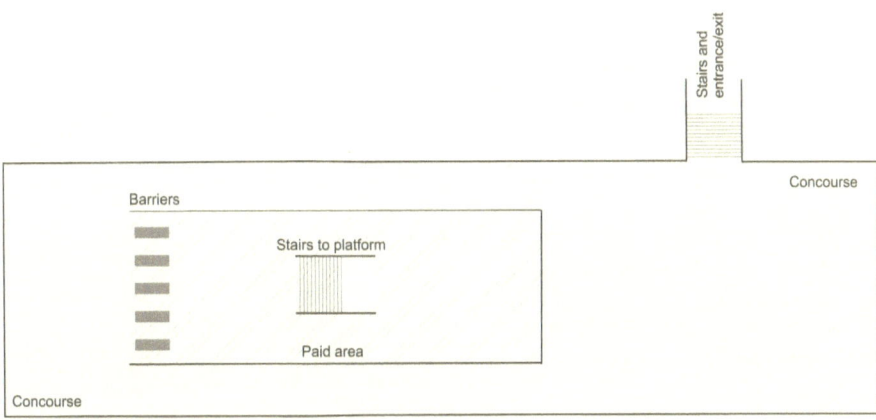

This concourse design is substantially inferior to the one above. There is only one exit, and the barriers face the opposite side of the concourse and not towards the exit. This station will have many problems with passenger flow, as passengers need to move from the stairs to the barriers and vice versa. Passenger flow will be messy and slow. Another problem is that the exit to and from street level may be extremely busy, as there is no alternative pathway. The number of problems with this kind of station abound, and the reader may think that this station design is impossible, but there are stations designed this way.

The diagram below show a common mistake with station design. The paid area fills the entire space from top to bottom, so there is no way for passengers to get from one side to another without entering the paid area. The problem here is that passengers may exit the paid area on the left, and want to exit on the right. As they are now through the barriers, normally they cannot pass through again and so will need to exit the station through the exit they don't really want.

Figure 3.5 Large Paid Area

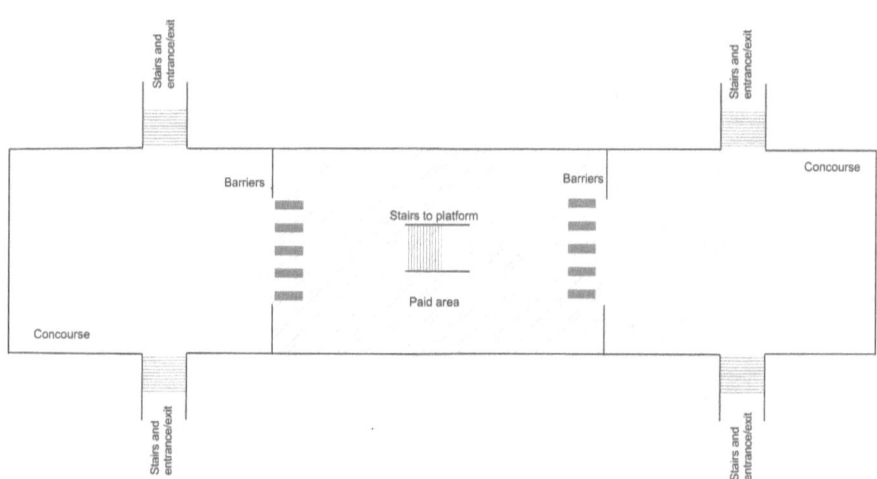

It is generally better if passengers exit from stations as close to their intended destination as possible. This reduces the time taken for the trip, and also the number of road crossings pedestrians needs to make. Where a station is busy, and passengers need to cross streets, these street crossings can become very busy, which through effective station design may have been completed unnecessary.

Stations are often underground and built under roads, Where this happens then is it best if there are multiple exits. The problem of course is cost, and constructing large concourses can make things very expensive. It's easy to say to build a large high quality concourse, but sometimes the budget simply isn't there.

Where trains are very long, such as commuter trains, what is sometimes done is to construct stations with two separate concourses. The author has seen designs proposed for stations with three separate concourses. Below is a diagram showing what this rather unusual situation would look like:

Figure 3.6 Split Concourses

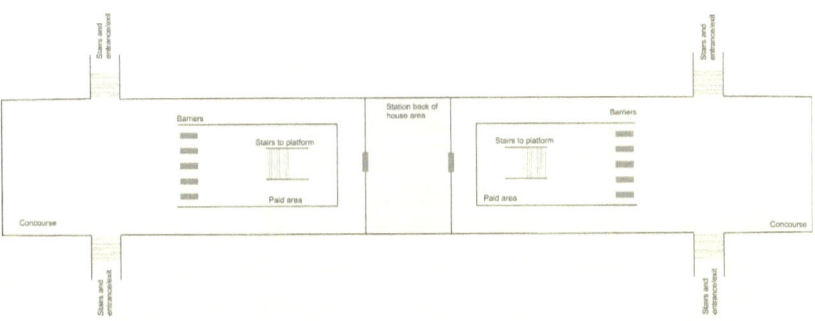

A number of stations exist in Australia with this structure. There are two concourses, and all the exits are located far away from each other. The exits from one side of the station can only be reached through the paid area, and the platform, which is a difficult path and not an attractive option. There is no access for passengers through the station back of house areas.

For a station designed as above things can be very confusing for passengers. There are two stairs connecting the station to the concourse, and depending on which they take then the choice of exits is limited.

Overall this structure of station has a number of issues which mean that it should be avoided where possible.

Figure 3.7 Station Infrastructure

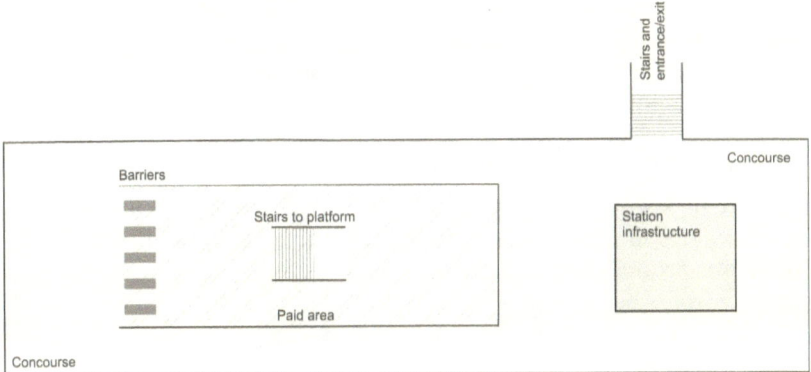

The diagram above shows the situation when station infrastructure is located in the centre of a concourse. This unusual situation should be avoided where possible, and infrastructure should be separated from public areas as much as possible. This is particularly the case for power, such as high and low voltage, or traction power. Electrical assets can catch fire, and whilst this is unusual, a substation fire occurs per substation perhaps every 500 years (as an average). Where many substations are located in station, this can become a real problem. This problem is especially serious where infrastructure is located near the only means of egress from the station, which is how the station above is constructed.

Interchange Stations

Interchange stations are places where multiple rail lines are connected through the rail station, and passengers must alight to get to other rail lines. Passengers are able to move from one line to another and board another train. Whilst many interchanges are designed well, many are not, and rail system designers face many challenges with interchange stations.

One important parameter in the design of interchange stations is the time taken for passengers to get from one set of platforms to another. The best interchange stations are constructed so that one set of platforms sits above the other, and the interchange time is almost nothing, perhaps 20 or 30 seconds. Other interchange stations are very large, and the connection between different sets of platforms may take several minutes, or in unfortunate cases even longer than that. Overall rail travel times can be badly affected when the travel times becomes very long, and so correctly designing the interchange is very important.

The most common scenario for an interchange is where there are two sets of tracks, for a total of four tracks. There are two platforms, each with two tracks, and there is connection between the two platforms. Whilst the author has not taken a poll of how many different types there are, this would be the majority of interchange stations. In rare cases there are three rail lines coming together, but typically there are two.

Interchange stations can be described through how the different sets of platforms are connected. Passengers need to walk from one platform to another, and different connection possibilities are:

- From one platform to another directly
- From the paid area (but not the platforms) to one another
- From each concourse
- Through public streets or shopping centres

The above list is in order of best to worst, and where interchange is through public streets the interchange station is not very effective. There are many of this type of interchange station.

The distance between the different sets of platforms will normally determine how to connect the two together. Connections from one platform to another requires the platforms to be extremely close together, and this can be done through a large terminus station. Paid areas are normally relatively small, so sets of platforms to be connected in an interchange station would need to be within 100 metres of each other, typically, to connect through the paid area. Where connections are several hundred metres, or even over a kilometre, then at best connections are through concourses.

Some of the more common problems with interchange stations are:
- Two or more rail lines are far apart, and their interchange stations are far apart, and passengers need to walk large distance to get from one to another
- Poor signage means that it is not clear what direction to go to get to the other rail line
- Numerous flights of stair connect different rail lines together, which is a challenge for many passengers to negotiate
- Problems with ticketing, where tickets may not work from one line to another, or passengers need to go out of the paid area to reach the other rail line and do not realise they need to do so
- Some interchange stations are extremely large, and can be difficult to get around due to their size (such as Shinjuku station in Tokyo)
- Walkways between rail lines are little more than construction sites, with poor footing, broken surfaces, barriers around construction work, and poor signage.
- In some cases there may be multiple stations to interchange with, and signage needs to identify which is the correct one for passengers to walk to, and to get to their final destination.

The ideal construction of interchange stations should allow passengers to easily and quickly move from one rail line to another. Ideally, interchange stations should have platforms close together, so that the interchange time is small. Good station design will allow passengers to interchange without going to far, and in Hong Kong it is possible to interchange between rail lines by moving from one side of an island platform to another. This is done by designing stations so that trains arrive on two sides of a platform moving in the same direction.

The photo below shows a moving walk. A moving walk is similar to an escalator, but along flat ground. Moving walks do not have stairs, and are there to assist passengers in getting quickly from one place to another. Moving walks are common in airports, and also in large interchange stations. There are a number of large moving walks installed in stations in Hong Kong at interchange stations. The moving walk shown below is located at the Domestic Airport station in Sydney, where it is used to connect the two terminals together though the underground station.

A Moving Walk

Figure 3.8 An Interchange station – connected through the concourse

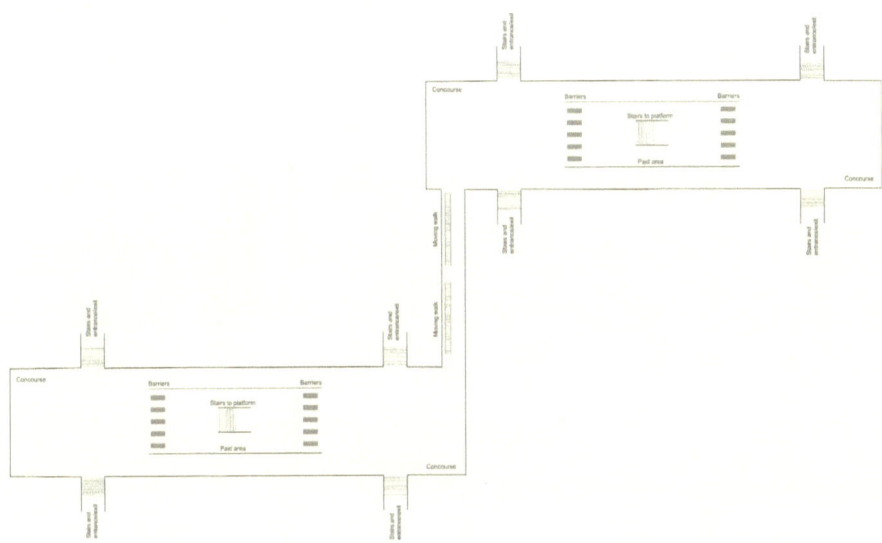

The station above is an interchange station which is connected through the concourse. The paid areas for the two connected stations are not connected. This structure of station is very common, and is really two separate stations connected through a pedestrian walkway. The way this station is drawn suggests that the station is underground, although it is possible to structure a station this way above ground as well. Note the moving walks connecting the two stations, making them one larger station.

On the rail system map this station may be identified as one station, or as two. This may depend on the distance between what are really two separate stations, although common practice seems to identify these stations as one station.

The station below is connected through the paid area.

Figure 3.9 An Interchange station – connected through the paid area

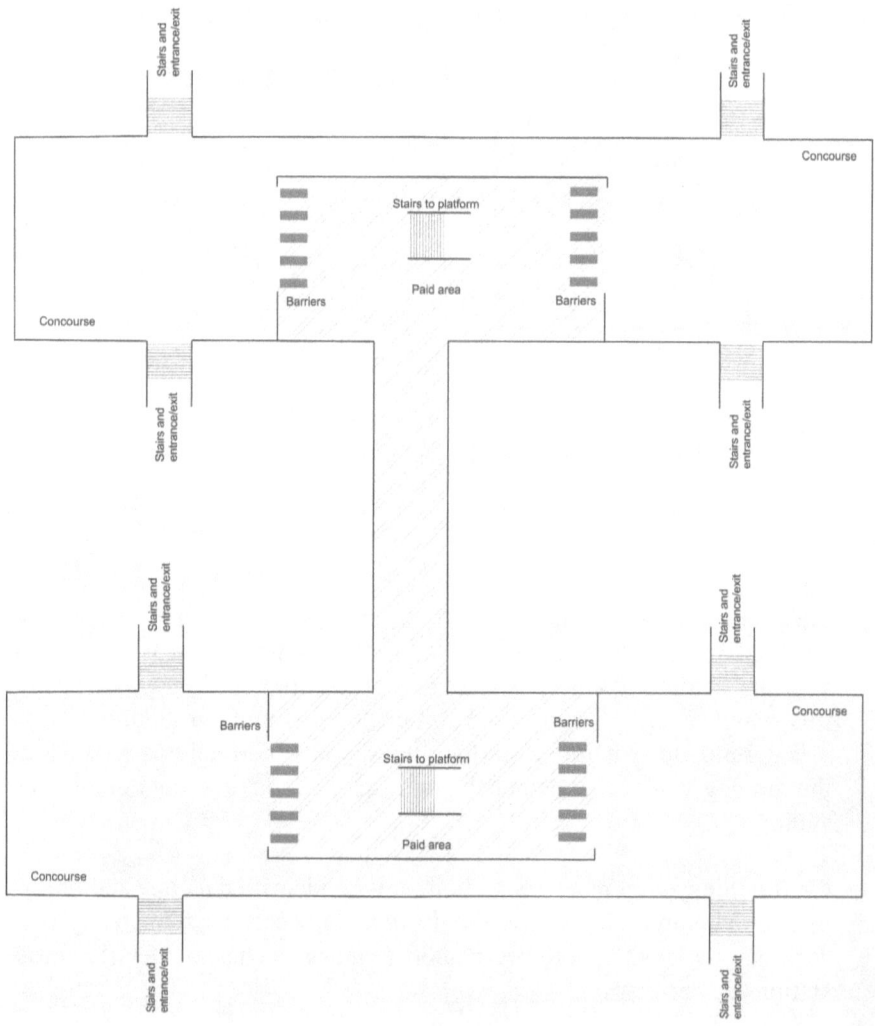

Short Platforms

In some cases the length of the platform may be shorter than trains which use the platform. Whilst this situation may seem a little silly, in some railways it is common, and passengers can only disembark from parts of the train there is a matching platform next to the door. Where there is no platform next to the train, people wanting to disembark may decide to leap from the train onto the ground below.

Where a train stops at a station that is shorter than the train, its best if the train is configured so that the doors with no matching platform don't open. This requires rollingstock of a special type, and programming to direct the doors not to open. It's better to have this technology if at all possible, but at the time of writing this book in Sydney there are still dozens of stations where the platform is too short, and no technology to stop all the doors from opening, although something is planned in this area. So it is possible for this situation to exist, even in modern times.

Regional trains can be very long because passengers need to sit down, making the passenger density rather low. In some cases platforms where the train stops are not long enough, so doors will face nothing but grass or open space. Furthermore the drop down from the train door may be quite large, and so any passengers that attempt to alight down to the ground are risking injury. In rare cases most of the train may have no matching platform, and disembarkation may be impossible from several carriages of the train.

For obvious reasons it is far better if all platforms are as long as the train itself. In a metro or any other system that operates in an urban environment, this will generally be the case. In some rail systems that operate to remote places, where the number of passengers per day can be counted in the dozens, building a full station may not be appropriate. Alternatively, and this sometimes happens where the station is located next to a river or other body of water, it may not be possible to build a station to the length needed as space is severely constrained, and so a compromise is made. In many cases the local residents may be prepared to accept a reduced length platform as long as there is some sort of rail service.

For any railway that creates this situation there are a number of factors that need to be considered:
- Where passengers jump from the train and are injured, how will medical assistance be provided?
- What happens where a passenger does not know that their carriage does not have a matching platform, and cannot alight, and so are overcarried to the next station. Will a taxi be provided? Overnight accommodation? What happens if

children are overcarried, is the railway going to allow them to find their own way home if they are overcarried at night?
- Which doors on the train are to be opened? Will it be the front doors or the back ones? Someone in the middle perhaps?
- How can passengers be informed that trains cannot provide exit to certain stations? Perhaps posters on station walls, or announcements to passengers.

Overall if at all possible stations should be constructed to at least the same length as the longest train, but in a small number of cases it may not be appropriate to do this.

Cover for Passengers from the Elements

Underground and elevated stations in major rail systems are almost always protected from the rain. There is complete coverage of the railway station, and heavy rain will not effect the movement of passengers and trains. In regional or commuter systems, almost all stations will be above ground and be exposed to the elements. The station below is common in some rail systems and the covered area is very small. This station is in Perth in Australia, and like many stations in that city has almost no coverage of the platform.

An Uncovered Station

For small stations there is no real reason why the entire platform should be covered. During rainstorms passengers can wait under the small shelter provided, and this will be adequate in most cases. For larger stations, lack of coverage can be a problem, as passengers will want to avoid getting wet, and will all wait under whatever cover is provided. Where the covered area is small, it will be come very crowded, and when boarding any trains there will be delays are the passengers will all crowd into one or two doors. This can create serious problems with dwell time, as passengers will attempt to board trains only through train doors next to covered areas.

Stations that are only partly covered will need less cleaning, as rainwater will wash away any dirt, especially where the station is designed with a slight slope on the platforms to allow rainwater to run away. Sunlight can sterilize the floor of any platform, in time, so this means that sanitising agents may not be needed to clean the platform. As a general rule, stations should only be covered if needed, and there is nothing wrong with leaving a station partly uncovered.

Straight and Curved Platforms

Many station platforms in large metro systems are straight, and when trains arrive they will sit in a straight line from one end of the train to another. Many platforms are curved, and not straight, and this is common in large commuter rail systems. In Australia many stations are curved, some dramatically so, as building straight stations was not considered to be important until relatively recently.

A curved platform is shown below. This station is in Hong Kong, and has side platforms. Notice that the platform on the left is concave, and on the other side of the two rail tracks, convex.

A Curved Platform in Hong Kong

The problem with curved platforms is demonstrated in the diagram below. Train carriages are built straight in all cases, and can only bend or articulate where there is a coupling between carriages. Light rail vehicles can be articulated, which means that there can be a number of joins, which allows the vehicle to appear to be curved, but in reality is made up of many short straight sections. Commuter and regional trains especially can have very long carriages, 26 to 30 metres in length is common, and passenger doors will often be located at each end of the carriage. Placing a straight object alongside a curved one will mean that in some places the carriage will be close to the platform edge, and in others far away. In extreme cases the door/carriage floor may be over 30 cm away from the platform, and with such a large gap passengers can fall into it. This may cause injuries, or even death.

The diagram below shows the problem. The centre of the carriage is close to the platform edge, and any doors located there will not have a large gap. Doors close to the end of the carriage, and they are commonly located there on double decker carriages (bi-level), will be further away from the platform.

Figure 3.10 Platform Gaps

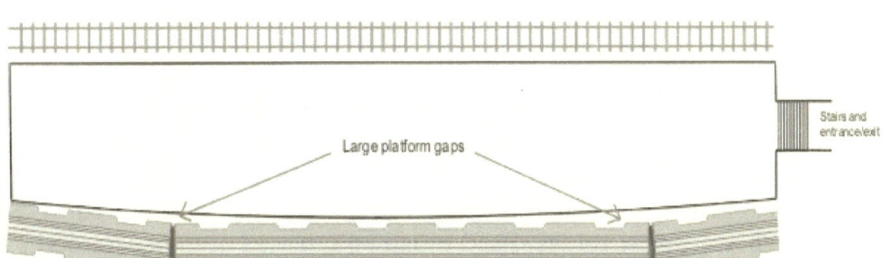

This situation is considered extremely undesirable. Passenger with disabilities, for example those with vision impairment, will struggle to contend with such a large gap, and may fall through. Passengers with wheel chairs will need some sort of mechanical assistance to cover such a large gap, and will not be able to cross this without help. Where gaps of this size exist, stations will need to be manned, and staff provided to allow wheel chair passengers to board the train. Typically a ramp is provided to wheelchair passengers to allow them to cross this gap.

Consider that where this assistance is not provided, and many regional and commuter trains are not staffed throughout the entire day, then wheelchair passengers may not be able to board a train at all. Alternatively, wheelchair passengers may not be able to alight, and may be overcarried to the next station that is staffed or where the platform and the floor of the train are close enough that the passenger can alight without assistance. Also consider that mothers with prams may also struggle to get onto and off trains. There are a large number of different passengers who are disadvantaged by this station design.

Having said all this, there are some situations where a curved platform is unavoidable. Metro stations and stations will high volumes of passengers should always be designed so that they are straight, and this is a common requirement in the standards for passenger design. However, some very small stations may only have a very small number of passengers, and it may be acceptable for a rail line and corresponding platform to be curved. Consider that there may be laws and regulations that prohibit this in many countries, as this station cannot be used by those with disabilities, even when the number of passengers using the station is very small. This is the case in Australia, and in all future construction all platforms are straight.

Light Rail Station Design

One of the advantages of light rail and tram systems is that they can be designed with little separation between the rail system and road vehicles and often operate at the same grade. This reduces the cost of construction, and makes them very accessible to public transport users, as they are at street level and usually not buried deep underground. In many cases these systems have no separate right of way. Trams often operate down the middle of roads, and in many ways are treated the same as any other road vehicle.

As light rail and trams are located in and around roads, the question arises as to the placement of track and rail corridors in comparison to where roads are located. The right of way for rail may or may not be separate from road vehicles, and a large number of different configurations are possible, and some of these are shown below:

The figure below shows a rail corridor in the middle of a street, with road vehicles on either side. This is a common design for light rail stations, and the use of a separate right of way for rail track is a good idea. For this design passengers will need to cross the road on one side or the other of the station to exit the corridor. Passengers will also need to cross the tracks to get to the other light rail station to go in the opposite direction to the one in which they came.

Figure 3.11 Light Rail Station in the Middle of the Street

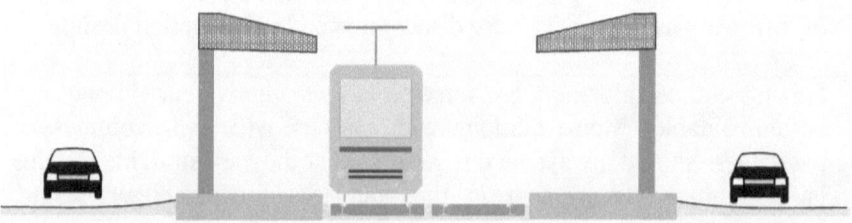

Below is another configuration for a light rail station, and the light rail station is on the left. The road is separate from the light rail station, although alongside one another. The light rail station is an island platform, so passengers will need to cross one track to get to the side of the road. This configuration is a very good one, as road and rail traffic is separated.

Figure 3.12 Light Rail Station on the Side of the Street

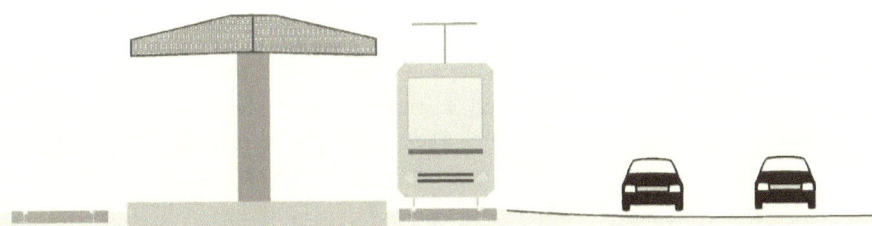

The light rail configuration below is extremely common in tram systems, but is also used in light rail systems as well. Road vehicles and rail share the same right of way, and mix freely. Whilst road vehicles can overtake trams, the converse is not true. This structure can work quite well, and is common in Melbourne with the large tram network there. One of the drawbacks with this structure is that passengers who wish to board and alight onto the tram must cross roads with fast moving vehicles on it, and the potential for an accident is quite significant. This configuration, whilst cheap and easy to implement, is not the safest, and is generally not recommended unless it cannot be avoided. There are however, many instances in a large tram network where there is no alternative, and this configuration is suitable.

Figure 3.13 Mixed Light Rail and Road Traffic with some Separation

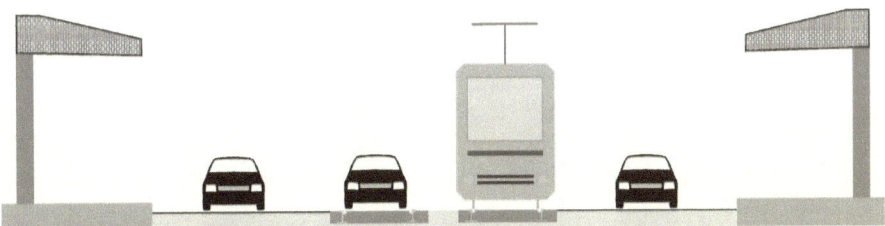

Also notice with the above configuration that road vehicles drive on the steel rails that support the light rail vehicle. Where the width of the road vehicle and rails are the same, it is possible for the road vehicle to slide along the rails, and not be able to stop when needed. This is particularly a problem in the wet, and accidents can be quite common.

The light rail configuration below is a poor one, but also somewhat common, especially in Melbourne. There is no separate right of way for rail traffic, and so road vehicles and trams/light rail share the same space. There is no way for road vehicles to pass the rail traffic, which is likely to be slow. As trams/light rail stop to allow passengers to board and alight, these vehicles will stop and wait at the tram stop. As the rail vehicle waits at the stop, road vehicles need to wait also. For a very busy street, passing through a congested shopping area, the travel speed of the tram/light rail vehicle may be very slow, to the point where there is no point in providing the service at all.

Figure 3.14 Mixed Light Rail and Road Traffic

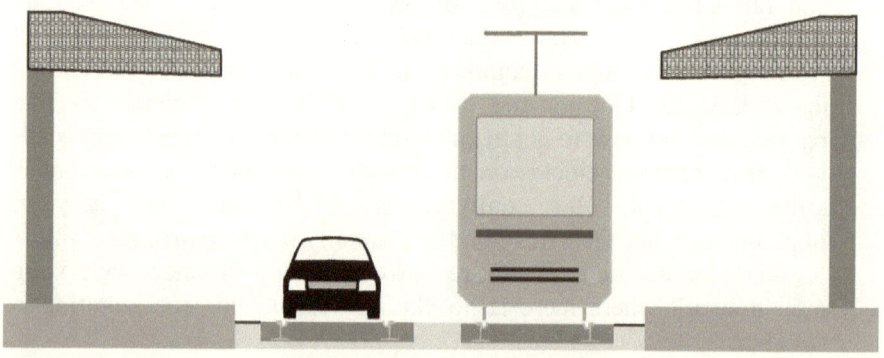

Tram systems were once very common in many parts of the world, especially Europe and North America. Almost all of them have been removed, and only a small number exist in their old form. One of the major contributing reasons for this was the use of the configuration above, which blocked road traffic and greatly contributed to congestion. The survival of the Melbourne tram network, now the world's largest, was because the configuration used above was rarely used, and so problems with congestion were avoided. The configuration above should only be used when absolutely necessary, and when there is no alternative.

REFERENCES

1. Brons, M & Givoni, M., Rietveld, P. *Access to Railway Stations and its potential in increasing rail use*, Transport Research Part A 43(2009) 136 - 149

2. Transit Cooperative Research Program, *TCRP Report 13 Rail Transit Capacity*, 1996

3. Parsons Brinkerhoff *High Speed Rail*, Network, Issue No 73, Sept 2011, http://www.pbworld.com/news/publications.aspx

4. Chengxiang, Z et al *Research on Train Dwell Time Modelling and Model Application in Metro Station*, 2009 Second International Conference on Intelligent Computation Technology and Automation

5. Kepaptsoglou, K. *A Model for Analyzing Metro Station Platform Conditions Following a Service Disruption*, Annual Conference on Intelligent Transportation Systems, Portugal Sept 2010

6. Battellino, H. *Transport for the transport disadvantaged: A review of service delivery models in New South Wales*, Transport Policy 16 (2009) 123 - 129

7. Schubert, P. *Improving Passenger Security on Urban Rail Networks*, Conference on Rail Engineering, Perth 7-10 September 2008

8. Nicol, J.F. et al, *Comfort Studies of Rail Passengers*, British Journal of Industrial Medicine, 1973, 30, 325 - 334

9. Wiggenraad, P. *Alighting and boarding times of passengers at Dutch railway stations, Trail Research School*, Delft, Dec 2001

10. Lam, W. et al *A Study of Train Dwelling Time at Hong Kong Mass Transit Railway System*, Journal of Advanced Transportation, Vol 32, No 3, pp 285 - 296

11. Chengxiang, Z et al *Research on Train Dwell Time Modelling and Model Application in Metro Station*, 2009 Second International Conference on Intelligent Computation Technology and Automation

12. Transportation Research Board *TCRP Report 13 Rail Transit Capacity*, 1996

13. Harris N G *An international comparison of urban rail boarding and alighting rates*, Proceedings of the Institute of Mechanical Engineers, Vol 221, Part F: Journal of Rail and Rapid Transit 2007

14. Transportation Research Board, *Transit Capacity and Quality of Service Manual Report 100*, 2nd edition, 2003

15. Smith, G. & Ceranic, B. *Spatial Layout Planning in Sub-Surface Rail Station Design for Effective Fire Evacuation*, Architectural Engineering and Design Management, 2008, Volume 4, Pages 99 – 120

16. Williams, R. & Chalmers, G. *Recent Developments in the Design of Cut and Cover Construction for Railway Tunnels and Stations*, Conference on Railway Engineering, Adelaide, May 2000

17. Cheong, SW. *Fire Safety Design for Rapid Transit Systems*, Proceedings of the international conference, Fire India, 2004

18. Lam, W et al *A Study of Passenger Discomfort Measures at the Hong Kong Mass Transit Railway System*, Journal of Advanced Transportation, Vol 33 No3 pp 389 – 399

19. Chen, F. et al *Smoke Control of Fires in Subway Stations*, Theoretical Computer Fluid Dynamics (2003) 16: 349 - 368

20. Kang, K. *Application of a Code Approach for Emergency Evacuation in a Rail Station*, Fire Technology, 43, 331 – 346, 2007

21. London Underground *Station planning standards and guildelines*, 2012 edition, http://www.persona.uk.com/nle/B-Core_docs/G/NLE-G1.pdf

22. Congling, S. et al Modeling and safety of passenger evacuation in a metro station in China, Safety Science(2010) doi:10.1016/j.ssci.2010.07.01

23. Liu, W et al *Modelling Passenger Flow on Stairways in Shanghai Metro Transfer Station,* 2008 International Conference on Intelligent Computation Technology and Automation

Week 4

Rollingstock, Capacity and Seating

Trains are the centre piece of any rail system. Trains, referred to as rollingstock, come in a wide variety of different styles and sizes. Many trains are very sleek and sexy, and are quite appealing to look at, and are a pleasure and joy to ride on. The choice of rollingstock is very important for any rail transport planning. High quality trains offer a smooth high quality ride, and making the travelling experience as pleasurable as possible is helpful to achieving any planning objectives. Alternatively getting the train type wrong can cause serious long term problems to any rail system.

Rollingstock needs to be the right shape and size when implemented as a transport planning solution. Rollingstock that is too small will result in a rail system that is frequently overcrowded, and the rail system will not reach its full potential. Potential passengers will tend to avoid the system, as it is crowded. Rollingstock which is too large for whatever transport problem it is applied to, will result in empty or near empty trains and too much money will be spent on acquiring the trains, and maintenance costs will be higher. In some cases these problems can be reduced with increasing or decreasing the frequency of services, but there are limits on how effective this can. It is preferable if the rollingstock is sized correctly from the beginning.

Some basic definitions are needed at this stage. Trains when purchased from manufacturers in basic units of carriages. Sometimes carriages are referred to as cars, which can be very confusing, and this usage is avoided in this book, even though it is very common. Carriages are combined together to form sets. A set of carriages is usually 3 or 4 carriages put together, and often these carriages can only operate as a combined set, and cannot move independently under their own power. Two sets can be combined together, and more rarely three sets may be combined together. However it is most common for an individual set to operate on its own.

Carriages can also be either single or double deck. A double decker train has two levels, and stairs to reach these levels. These two levels will have seating. The vestibule area, ie next to the doors, where passengers board and alight from the train can be at the same level as one of the two seated levels, or at a different level. Double decker trains are called bi-level trains in the US and Canada.

Some trains are referred to as a multiple unit. Multiple units have more than one carriage and are self-propelled. There can be two, three or even more carriages with motors. A multiple unit train does not need a locomotive, so more passengers can board a train of a given length than a train with a locomotive. The motors are often under the floor where passengers sit and stand. Adding additional motors allows for redundancy will improve the reliability, and this can be helpful. The term multiple units is widely used in the rail industry (at least in Australia).

Coaches are carriages where there is no motor or locomotive within the carriage. Coaches are used where the train is hauled by a locomotive, and are common in regional services where there is no overhead wiring. Coach services are dependent on the reliability of the locomotive pulling the train, and any problems with the locomotive and the coaches are stranded. One advantage of coaches is that without the motor and other related wiring and power, they have long operational lifetimes. Carriages in multiple units age, and the wiring and motors ages as well, and 30 years is a very long time for using a multiple unit, whereas coaches can last much longer than that. Another advantage of coaches is that they can be separated out from the other carriages without too much difficulty, for example when individual coaches are being refurbished. Despite claims to the contrary, coach carriages are still useful, and particularly so where the cost of the service needs to be kept down, and coaches often are much cheaper to operate than multiple units.

Capacity

The capacity of a train is very important metric. For any rail transport planning, it is critical to know the number of people that can travel in a train, and therefore the capacity of a rail line. The capacity of the rail line is measured in people per hour (pph), and this is one of the most important metrics of any rail line.

When calculating the number of people that can fit onto a train, we normally don't separate out men, women or children. For example, we don't normally change the capacity calculation if there are a large number of schools along the rail line, although this could be done. We assume that everyone is about the same. We do however normally estimate the number of people with disabilities who can fit onto the train, based on the special facilities that are provided for them.

The formula for the maximum number of people moved per hour on a rail line is:

Rail line people per hour (pph) = Capacity of rollingstock x frequency of trains

The capacity of the rollingstock is the total number of people that can reasonably fit into the train without serious discomfort. Trains in India and nearby countries routinely operate with extremely high numbers of passengers on one train, at a level that most countries would not accept. For the purposes of the calculations presented here, we assume that packing India type levels of people into a train is not acceptable.

Metro systems are designed so that people mostly stand. Whilst there is seating along the sides of the train, most people travelling on a metro train will stand. As a result the capacity of metros is very large. The capacity of most trains types is strongly affected by the proportion of passengers that stand and those that can sit. For long distance travel it is desirable for passengers to sit, otherwise the trip is very unpleasant for those that need to stand.

Each train has a shape that is essentially a rectangle, when looking from the top down. The area of a rectangle is given by the width multiplied by the length. The total floor area is then multiplied by a passenger loading factor to determine the capacity of the rollingstock. So for this simple formula we have:

$$Capacity = k \times length \times width$$

Where:

$k = loading\ factor.$

So what are typical values for rollingstock width? Most rollingstock comes in fairly standard sizes, and the table below provides some guidance as to what to expect for different rail modes.

Trains types and widths

Rollingstock type	Typical widths for this train type
High speed rail	2.9 - 3.4 metres
Double deck commuter	2.8 - 3.2 metres
Light rail	2.45 - 3.1 metres
Metro	2.5 – 3.1 metres
Light capacity metro	2.65 – 3.1 metres
Single deck commuter	2.8 - 3.2 metres
Trams	2.45 metres
Monorail	2.4 – 3.1 metres

Another useful detail is: how long can trains be? For most train types carriages can be amalgamated together to form much longer trains. This means that some train types can be very long and carry very large numbers of people. The numbers presented below are typical, but of course there are always some exceptions.

Trains types and lengths

Rollingstock type	Typical lengths for this train type
High speed rail	120 - 400 metres
Double deck commuter	60 - 200 metres
Light rail	25 - 75 metres
Metro	45 – 170 metres
Light capacity metro	30 – 80 metres
Single deck commuter	50 - 140 metres (although even 110 metres is large for this type of train)
Trams	13 – 50 metres
Monorail	20 – 96 metres

Increasing the length of a train normally has quite large consequences. As a train gets longer, the structural elements required within the train to keep the train together need to be larger, making the train heavier. Also the minimum height of the floor of the train increases, so that longer trains generally have higher floors, and therefore higher platforms are needed. Combining light rail vehicles together is particularly problematic, as the structure of the vehicle may not be able to accept higher forces, and trains can be damaged. This can take the form of stress cracks through the chassis, doors not opening or closing, or damage to bogies. In more unusual cases there may be electrical damage from overloading of the electrical system with the train.

For a new rail system, the rail planner is largely free to chose the width of trains. Once chosen however, it is very difficult to change. Wider trains are generally better because they can carry more people, and one train is able to move more people. Unfortunately larger trains require more money to be spent on building the system, as the space required for trains to move around is larger. The structure gauge for any rail system will increase as the width of the rollingstock increases. The cost of a rail systems is linked to the width of the trains that run on it, to a certain extent, so care must be taken in choosing a very wide train.

Long trains are also more useful for moving around passengers, but once again, the cost of building stations rises quite steeply with the length of the train. Longer trains will require longer stations, and underground this can be a problem. Extending platforms can be an expensive business, so once chosen the length of trains in the rail system is very hard to increase.

The table below shows the number of people per square metre for different train types. Again, all with all the numbers presented in this book, the values listed below are indicative only. These numbers were obtained from analysing the stated capacities for rollingstock for different manufacturers.

Train Types and Maximum Capacity per Square Metre		
Railtype	People per square metre	Mix
High speed (single deck)	1.1	All seated
High speed (double deck)	1.5	All seated
Commuter, double deck	2.05	Mostly seated
Light rail	2.65	Half-half
Metro	5	Mostly

Train Types and Maximum Capacity per Square Metre		
Railtype	People per square metre	Mix
		standing
Commuter, single deck	1.7	Half-half
Tram	2.65	Half-half

The maximum capacity for a metro is a somewhat controversial. In India metros can be loaded to up to 14 people per square metre, but in almost all other countries this would not be accepted. Some railways specify that 6 per metre is the most they will accept, and others specify a lower limit of 4. This upper limit can dramatically change the number of people that can travel on a metro.

Another problem with the estimation of capacity is that carriages at the front and end of some types of trains are less loaded than the middle of the train. This is unlikely to be too significant with trains less than about 80 metres in length, but very long trains, and especially those more than about 150 metres in length the front and rear carriages are sometimes almost completely empty, where other carriages are almost full. This problem can be compounded by poor station design, where the entrances to platforms in the middle of the platform.

A more accurate way of calculating the capacity of a train is to estimate the number of seats, and the floor area of the train. This is clearly a better way of estimating train capacity, however, this level of detail is often not needed at the early stages of rail transport planning, but can be useful once most of the details of any plan have been decided.

Helping People with Disabilities

The design of rollingstock in modern times has changed to be more accommodating of people with disabilities. Older rail systems were very difficult for a person with a disability to access, and the trend in recent years has been to improve the accessibility. This has meant a number of changes to operating railways, including station design and rollingstock. Rollingstock has changed significantly to allow better access, although not all of these changes have reached every railway. In Australia over the past 20 years facilities have improved substantially for disabled people, however there is always room for more improvement.

A disabled person can refer to many different type of people, and some of them would include:
- People in wheelchairs
- The deaf
- Pregnant women
- The elderly
- The blind
- War veterans, with injuries sustained whilst on active duty
- Other people who are movement impaired

To help those with disabilities on trains, there is often a flat area set aside those with disabilities, and almost always this is close to the doors. The picture below shows reserved seating for those with disabilities on a train in Osaka. Note the pattern on the fabric, which is to encourage able bodied people to surrender the seat when a special needs person boards the train.

Disabled Seating in Osaka

Note below the photo of the doors in a standard commuter train in Brisbane. There are help buttons and a microphone speaker next to the door to allow the disabled person to ask for help (or even an able bodied person if they need help). These features all together are sometimes described as an emergency help point. There is also a button for the door to be opened and closed

Also note that the doors have a symbol of a wheelchair towards the bottom. This indicates that there is a space provided next to the door for a wheelchair bound passenger to travel in the train. Not all doors have this space provided on this train, hence the symbol on the doors.

The colour yellow is used a lot. This is because research has been conducted that found that yellow was the easiest colour for vision impaired people to see. Consequently most of the handrails and key features for a train designed to be used by the disabled will contain a lot of yellow.

There are a number of other features provided to assist people with disabilities using trains. These include:
- Automated announcements being made on where the train is. People who are vision impaired cannot see the station signs, and need to be told which station the train is stopping at.
- The floor of the train should be at the same height as the station. Also the gap between the train floor and the station floor should be as small as possible.

Many countries have passed laws requiring a minimum level of amenity provided to disabled passengers. Meeting these requirements can sometimes be quite challenging, especially on a rail system built decades ago which was not designed with disabled people in mind.

Seating Layout

The arrangement of seats within trains is often important in the design of rail systems and rollingstock. A key decision in the purchase of any rollingstock is the number of seats in the train. Within reason, it is possible to choose the number of seats, and a small number of rail vehicles have no seats at all. Too many will mean that passengers cannot move in and out of the train quickly as the train is cluttered, as seats will slow the movement of passengers. Too few seats will mean that the travelling public will shun the rail system, as they don't want to stand for long distances.

There are a number of different configurations for seating in trains, and these are:
- No seating at all. Airport trains often have no seats. Passengers travel only very short distances, and so no seats are necessary.
- Seating alongside the walls of the train. This configuration is very common in metro style trains, and it allows many people to use the train and to board and alight quickly.
- Mixed seating, with some seats protruding from the walls of the train, but many running alongside the walls. This is a compromise seating arrangement.
- A 2 x 1 arrangement, with an aisle running down the middle of the train. This vehicle is usually a tram, as 2 x 1 requires only a small width for the rail vehicle
- A 2 x 2 arrangement, where there is an aisle between seats for two people on either side of the aisle. This is an extremely common seating arrangement.
- A 2 x 3 arrangement. This is commonly used on commuter trains, where large number of seats are needed. This type of train needs to be at least 3 metres wide.
- Other arrangements, such trains with sleeper cars.

There is always a compromise between the number of seats on a train and the available floor space. Increasing the number of seats increases the amenity of the passengers, but decreases the total number of passengers that can travel on the train. Once chosen, it is possible to exchange seats for floor space, and vice versa, at a cost. This is one of those rare decisions in a rail environment that can be relatively easily changed.

Seats that have been designed to accommodate three people are quite unpopular. Passengers that sit in the middle on these seats may have one passenger on either side, and unless they know these people, can find this situation very uncomfortable. A 2 x 2 seating arrangement is generally a little bit better, as passengers are more comfortable. Passengers will avoid sitting in the middle of a 3 person seat, and this can have the effect of reducing the amount of seating on the train. When pressed, passengers will sit in the middle seat, but only where there are no other alternatives.

Below are a series of pictures of each of the different configurations of seats. Most seats are plastic, although some are fabric. Metro style trains have seating running alongside the train.

Metro Style Seating

The photo below is for a 2 x 3 seating arrangement in a double decker train in Paris. It is common for double decker trains with three seats to have them only on one side.

3 x 2 Seating Configuration in the Parisian RER

The arrangement below is a 2 x 1 in the double decker trams in Hong Kong. This configuration is suitable for very narrow rollingstock.

2 x 1 Seating Arrangement in a Hong Kong Tram

The photos below are for a regional train in Thailand. Passengers sit facing each other. In this train there is an aisle in the middle with a matching set of seats on the other side, the same as in the photo. At night these seats convert into sleeper berths.

Inside a Regional Train 2 x 2 Configuration Ceats Facing Each Other

Getting People On and Off

So how fast can people get on and off trains? The design of rollingstock has a large impact upon the time taken to embark and disembark passengers onto trains. For almost all rail systems it is better if this time is as low as possible, as this allows trains to operate at higher average speeds, and dwell times at stations are lower. One of the major objectives of station design is to lower the dwell time as much as possible, but this can also be achieved through rollingstock design.

Where the train and the platform are at different heights then it takes longer for people to board and alight. The greater the number of steps, the longer it takes. Normally the preferred design is that people step up to the train, Stepping down into a train may on occasion result in a falls and stumbles, as passengers will lose their footing.

As a rough guide it takes about 1 second for a passenger to board or alight from a door. This number is a rough guide only and it does change depending on the size of the door and the height of the floor of the train relative to the platform. There is a large amount of variability in this number, and it is possible for passengers to board and alight much faster than this.

Doors on trains range from being very large to very small. Larger doors are better to move people faster off and onto trains, in some situations. Many trains are limited in the number of doors that can be installed, and two per carriage is a very common number. Metro trains can have more than this and up to 5 doors per carriage is possible. Of course this is per side, so a metro train can actually have 10 doors. Designers of rail systems often want to have quick boarding times, to reduce the dwell times at stations. They often want to increase the size of the door to allow more people to get on and off quickly. But does this work? Will changing the size of the door matter?

The door below is very large, and this one was installed on the intermediate capacity metro in Taipei. It's a monster, almost 3 metres wide.

A Super Large Door

It would seem likely that increasing the door size would help increase the speed at which passengers got on and off trains. Particularly narrow doors would present a real problem for people alighting and boarding. Have a look at the photo below. This is for a high speed train in Taiwan, and notice that the door is quite small. Doors on high speed rail trains are often small, because the train needs to be partially sealed so that pressure differentials from inside to outside the train do not result in rapid changes in pressure inside the train.

Taiwan High Speed Train Doors

A wider door means more room for passengers to get off, and so boarding and alighting may be quicker. However, what research there is does not really seem to support this view. A study in the US found no increase in passenger boarding times based on the size of the doors. This comprehensive study only looked at relatively large doors, but based on a reasonable range of door sizes. A Dutch study found small increases in boarding time based on smaller doors.

One possible reason for this is that in a busy crowded train only a narrow path forms between the seated area and the door. Many trains operate with many people crammed into them, and when the doors open only a fraction of the total number of passengers actually get off the train. They make their way past all the other passengers who are not getting off, and this dramatically slows down the movement of passengers. It is interesting to watch the dynamics of this situation, as a pathway needs to form from where passengers are seated, to the door. Mostly passengers are aware of the need to provide this pathway, but at other times one or more passengers need to be asked to move to allow people to either get on or off the train. In this way the door is not the bottleneck, but the other passengers in the train.

Overall, for rail transport planning purposes, it seems safe to allow for 1 sec per person per door, for both boarding and alighting. This number should be reduced maybe 20% where the platform and the floor of arriving trains is not at the same level. For interchange stations, perhaps double this rate is appropriate, especially for doors that are over 1.6 metres wide. This area, like many in rail transport planning, could really do with much more research.

Grades

The maximum acceptable grade for any rollingstock is a critical parameter in rail transport planning. A grade is a hill, and trains need to climb up hills frequently

Remember that buses, being road vehicles, can climb enormous grades. Trains run steel to steel, which is a slippery combination, so if the grade is too high then the train will either be unable to climb the grade, or seriously damage the rails when the train wheel spin freely over the rails.

The basic idea is shown below:

Figure 4.1 Grades

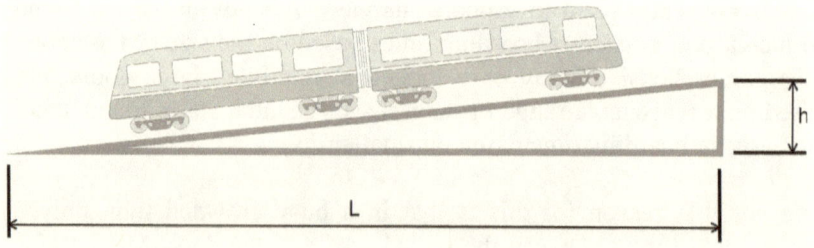

Grades, or sometimes called slopes, can be expressed as percentages, based on this simple formula:

$$Grade = \frac{height}{length} \times 100\%$$

In Australia and the UK grades can be expressed as 1 in X, where X can be found from the formula below:

$$\frac{1}{X} = \frac{height}{length}$$

Which can be re-arranged to give:

$$X = \frac{length}{height}$$

Another way of expressing grades is using this symbol (‰). This symbol is similar to a percentage, but actually means the parts out of 1000. So a 1% grade would be expressed as 10‰. This symbol is common in continental Europe, for the maximum possible grades that a particular type of train can climb. On Wikipedia the symbol is referred to a *"per mille"*, which is Latin for per one thousand.

So, the conversion tables for the grades are:

	Grades and Conversions		
%	UK/Australia	Degrees	‰
1	1 in 100	0.57°	10
2	1 in 50	1.15°	20
3	1 in 33	1.72°	30
4	1 in 25	2.29°	40
5	1 in 20	2.86°	50
6	1 in 16.6	3.43°	60
7	1 in 14.3	4.00°	70
8	1 in 12.5	4.57°	80
9	1 in 11.1	5.14°	90
10	1 in 10	5.71°	100
11	1 in 9.1	6.28°	110
12	1 in 8.3	6.84°	120
13	1 in 7.7	7.41°	130

Most rollingstock is quite limited in the grade that it can climb. Common limits for the grades that rollingstock can climb are listed below, with some comments:

Maximum Acceptable Grades

Rollingstock type	Max grade	Comments
Trams	6% or 10% with specially designed rollingstock	Some trams are specially designed to climb high grades
Light rail	6% or 10% with specially designed rollingstock	As more vehicles are combined into a consist, the total possible grade may be reduced
Commuter rail	3%	These trains are not designed to climb high grades
Regional rail	3%	
Freight	1.5%	Typically higher grades make the freight service uneconomical, as more locomotives are needed
High speed rail	1.5%	Higher grades tend to have a large speed penalty
Monorails	6%	Able to climb fairly steep grades
Metros	3%	Steel on steel metros
Metros (rubber tyred)	12%	Very large grades can be accepted

High speed rail can accept quite high grades, but the maximum speed of the train will be reduced significantly, so that it is often not acceptable to have anything other than very small grades. This is particularly true at genuinely high speeds, such as over 300 kms/hr.

The grade of a rail line often will determine what types of trains can be used. Steeper and steeper grades will require more and more specialised rollingstock. The steepest train in the world is in the Blue Mountains near Sydney, and the grade it negotiates is 55°, which is a very high grade. This train is more like an amusement ride, and is a tourist train.

REFERENCES

1. BART, ba, *Fleet of the Future, Conceptual Design Update and Community Survey Results*, March 2012

2. Ruger, B. & Tuna, D. *Influence of railway interiors on dwell time and punctuality, Institute for Railway Engineering*, Traffic Economics and Ropeways

3. Tyrell, D.C. *Rail passenger equipment accidents and the evaluation of crashworthiness strategies*, Proceedings of the Institute of Mechanical Engineers, 2002; 216; 2

4. Attorney General's Department of the Australian Government, *Disability standards for accessible public transport*, 2002

5. Fabian, J. *The Exceptional Service of Driverless Metros*, Journal of Advanced Transportation, Vol 33, No 1, pp 5-16

6. Chow, W.K. *Ventilation of enclosed train compartments in Hong Kong*, Applied Energy 71 (2002) 161-170

7. Carruthers, J.J. et al *The application of a systematic approach to material selection for the lightweighting of metro vehicles*, Proc. IMechE Vol. 223 Part F: J. Rail and Rapid Transit, May 2009

8. Alstom Metropolis 21 st Century Metro Train Technology, http://www.alstom.com/turkey/products-and-services/-alstom-transport-turkey/rolling-stock/

9. Xue, X. *Analysis of the structural characteristics of an intermediate rail vehicle and their effect on rail performance*, Proceedings of the Institute of Mechanical Engineers, Vol 221 Part F; Journal Rail and Rapid Transit

10. Duncan, B *The Hunter Rail Car: A versatile design solution for regional rail transport*, Australian Journal of Multi-disciplinary Engineering, Vol 7, No 2

11. Stadler *Electric Double-Deck train KISS*, www.stadlerrail.com

12. Battellino, H. *Transport for the transport disadvantaged: A review of service delivery models in New South Wales*, Transport Policy 16 (2009) 123 - 129

13. Railway Group Standard *Structural Requirements for Railway Vehicles*, GM/RT 2100, Issue 1, July 1994

14. Talgo *Series 8 High Speed Passenger Cars*, www.talgo.com

15. Edris, H. & Causey, R. *Light Rail Vehicle Procurement*, 0-7803-2556-7/95, 1995

16. Bombardier, *Flexity Freedom*, http://www.bombardier.com/en/transportation/products-services/rail-vehicles/light-rail-vehicles/flexity-freedom.html

17. Swanson, J. *Advanced Light Rail Vehicle Communication Systems Design*, 2004 ASME/IEEE Joint Rail Conference

Stabling

Stabling is where trains are stored, often at night, and sometimes during the day when they are not used. Passenger trains are commonly stabled during the day between peak periods. The reader will probably note the similarity between trains and horses, because the same words are used to describe both. Stabling is very important for any operational railway, as trains often need to be stabled, and the location of stabling can dramatically affect how trains are scheduled to move throughout the network.

Stabling facilities need to be distinguished from maintenance and maintenance centres, and they are quite different. Trains are not normally stabled in maintenance centres, as these have limited space, and far more space is needed for stabling of trains than is normally available in maintenance centres. Maintenance centres may be able to store a small number of trains, but ordinarily trains are stored in large stabling yards. It is also common for stabling to be co-located with maintenance centres, 20 or 30 metres away, or trains may need to pass through the stabling to get to the maintenance centre.

Stabling yards are not pretty things, and while rail transport is sexy and good to look at, stabling yards are ugly. Full of tracks, cluttered with trains, and with a very industrial look and feel, many stabling yards are very unsightly. In many cases cities with large stabling yards near the centre of the city have moved them away just to avoid having to look at them, or hide them so that no one can see them. In Melbourne much of the stabling available in the centre of the city has been removed, as it was considered a terrible eyesore. Likewise, for the tram depot in Hong Kong, it is superbly well hidden, and it's not a pretty thing, but it is well hidden. The larger the stabling yard, the worse this problem seems to be.

Given the poor visual appearance of a stabling yard, they are often hidden away as best as possible. This might be achieved by walls, or other structure that hides the yard. Alternatively, the yard may by sandwiched between two other rail lines, so that no one can see it through the other trains. Alternatively, it may be hidden in a place where there are no people to be affected by its poor appearance.

The problem is a little less serious for the various forms of light rail, such as trams, light rail proper, and Automated People Movers (APMs). These smaller trains can be tucked away in places where they cannot be seen, or buildings can be used to house all the vehicles. Larger trains, such as HSR trains, or commuter trains, will be difficult to hide, and the stabling yards will be large. Freight yards are truly enormous, and are extremely difficult to hide. Freight yards are just dreadful, and noisy, and should be put in industrial areas where no one lives nearby.

The picture below is of a tram depot in Brunswick in Melbourne. This photo was taken around lunchtime so the depot is almost empty. Tram depots are a type of stabling, and unusually for rail transport, trams can be stored inside under cover when stabled.

Tram Depot in Melbourne

Stabling yards are often a maintenance problem, and require a lot of maintenance compared to plain track. Where large numbers of trains are stabled, there needs to be a corresponding large amount of infrastructure to accommodate the trains, and this means a high concentration of infrastructure in a stabling yard. The cost of installing stabling can be substantial, especially where the number of trains to be stabled is very large. Given the quantity of infrastructure, there are constant failures of the engineering equipment, such as points and track circuits, so maintenance crews will need to be stationed very close to a stabling yard to ensure any failures are fixed quickly.

A common problem with older railways it seems is that there seems to be stabling all throughout their networks. A reasonable amount of stabling is very desirable, but too much of it can be a problem. Putting stabling everywhere is very attractive for operators of railways, because it provides all sorts of operational flexibility; if a train breaks down then it can be quietly stored in a stabling yard somewhere until it can be moved to a maintenance centre to be repaired. There are many advantages to having stabling everywhere, and operators of rail systems may ask for lots of stabling to be installed, even when there already is quite a lot. From a maintenance and cost perspective it's a real problem, and stabling yards should be installed only where needed.

Stabling needs to be properly designed and installed to allow the most efficient operation of any railway. Stabling is important, and where it is installed in the wrong place, or poorly designed, then operational railways can face some serious problems. Some of the problems with poorly designed or located stabling includes:
- Trains need to be moved large distances to start their runs in the morning, or finish at night in poor places, and again need to be moved
- Stabling can't accommodate all the trains that operate on a line, and only some can be stabled
- Infrastructure in the stabling yard is in poor condition, as the yard is so busy that important maintenance cannot be performed
- The stabling yard is too large for the number of trains stored there, and much of the equipment is not used, and is rusting away
- The stabling yard is in a place that is difficult to access, and far away from where maintenance staff are based
- Entry and exit from the stabling yard is a bottleneck, and the stabling yard cannot put trains into and receive trains from the network quickly enough
- Stabling is not long enough to accommodate the length of trains that are needed

Overall stabling yards are quite important. The author's observation is that a significant percentage of rail transport projects seem to either be about stabling, or involve changes to stabling. It is possible for a rail line to be designed to handle large numbers of trains, but the stabling is inadequate to meet the needs of the rail line.

Much consideration should be given to the placement of stabling yards. Stabling yards may be located where land is available, and this might be well away from where trains start operating and finish for the night. This can create large problems, as trains are moving around all the time, to get back to a place where they can be stabled. Moving trains from poorly placed stabling yards is expensive, staff need to staff early to get trains into position, there are the power costs and wear and tear on the train, and it makes the maintenance window for track smaller, as there are many train movements before the start of train services.

Another common problem is the entrance to and exit from stabling. It is a common problem for the capacity into and out of the stabling to be insufficient. Where this is the case, the stabling yard is limited in how many trains can be managed, regardless of its actual size. Resolving this problem can be difficult, as enlarging the entrance to the stabling can often be a difficult thing to achieve. Land, and the lack of it, can be the problem.

Freight is stabled, but it's a bit different from passenger services. Freight locomotives can be coupled to many different types of freight wagons, and when not being used these need to be stored somewhere. Some freight wagons may be very infrequently used, and spend most of their time sitting in some freight yard somewhere. The long term storage of different freight wagons is not normally called stabling, but rather just storage in the yard. Nonetheless it is a type of stabling. .

For trains with dedicated locomotives, when the train drives into any kind of stabling, or for that matter a terminus, the question arises as to how to get the locomotive out again. Locomotives can move in reverse, and entire trains can be propelled backwards if needed, but it's always better to put a locomotive at the front of the train rather than the rear. It is possible to put a second track next to the first to allow the locomotive to get out from behind the train, and sometimes this is a called a run-around road. EMU's do not have this problem, and can normally be driven from both ends of the train. Turntables were once common, and these are a way of turning locomotives around. In some situations there may be an electric locomotive pulling coaches which are unpowered, and one solution to this problem is to put an electric locomotive at each end of the train. Otherwise, just like diesel locomotives, the locomotive will need to be moved from one end of the train to the other.

So how is a stabling yard described? The key parameters for a stabling yard are:
- The number of tracks (sometimes called roads, even though it a rail track) which can be used to stable trains
- The length of the stabling tracks
- The number of trains that can be stabled. This is normally the number of tracks that can be used for stabling, but sometimes these numbers will be different
- The number of trains that can enter and exit the stabling yard per hour. It is entirely possible for a stabling yard to possess an exit through which it can take hours to get all the trains out
- The expected used capacity of the stabling yard, and this can be a number anywhere between 0 to 100%. It seems normal that for any new stabling that almost all the capacity would be used, but for old ones the percentage used might be close to zero.
- The type of train that can be stabled, electric, diesel, or even steam. Stabling for diesel trains often requires fuel pumps, where trains can be refuelled with diesel. Steam trains require water for the boiler, and often sand, and these need to be available.
- The availability of decanting. Long distance trains have toilets, and the effluent needs to be removed from the train. Old style trains did not store their effluent, but thankfully most all these trains have been removed from service around the world.
- The availability of water to add to any water tanks on trains (used for flushing toilets, drinking water for passengers, etc).

A quick point should be made here; refuelling trains and adding water is not something done only in a maintenance centre. Maintenance is performed at a frequency normally around months, ie, 3 months, and this far too long to add water only at these times. Whilst it may be possible to add water to a train at a maintenance centre, normally this would be done where trains are stabled. There is no reason why a maintenance centre should not have these facilities, but removing effluent from a train needs to be done almost daily, and this is far too frequent to be done at a maintenance centre.

The calculation of the total capacity of the yard is normally pretty easy, but the number of trains that can be moved in and out is a bit harder. Speeds in stabling yards are normally limited, and 25 kms/hr seems to be common, at least in Australia. Capacity into and out of a stabling yard is often limited when there are only two tracks in and out. Where only one track is available into and out of a yard, problems with entry and exit can be even more severe.

Tram depots are an interesting form of stabling, because of the short length of trams, tram depots are often covered. Very large numbers of trams can be stored in one place, because trams are short in length, and are narrower than most trains. As mentioned above, tram depots can be hidden because of their small size.

The photo below is of a turntable, and this is where train locomotives where turned around. Little used now, turntables were once very common. The way a turntable works is that a locomotive is driven onto the turntable, and then the turntable rotates so that the locomotive faces the opposite direction. Turntables are essentially a giant circle, with a movable section of track in the middle. In NSW at least turntables were often hand powered, and railway staff would turn a handle, and in so doing the turntable would spin around slowly.

Locomotive turntable

Most turntables were in stabling yards, so that the carriages or wagons of the steam train would be decoupled from the locomotive, and the steam engine would be turned around, and the reconnected to the carriages, and then move off in the opposite direction from whence it came. Very old staling yards may still have turntables in them, especially where old steam trains are occasionally used for heritage and tourist purposes.

The Tidal Nature of Commuter Services

Recall that commuter services are a special type of rail system, which specialise in moving people to their place of work, particularly on weekdays. The structure of commuter services is relatively standard, passengers are moved from outlying suburbs to a central location, usually where businesses are located. These businesses are often offices, and need office workers to staff them. Shift work is rare with offices, so there is little need for rail services outside of business hours. Office work is mostly day work, Monday to Friday, so many workers are needed during these times.

Commuter services are markedly different from metro style services, which operate throughout the day, and may have a higher service frequency during the day, but do not stop operation. Some of the key differences between a commuter service and a metro style service, or light rail for that matter, are:
- Some stations will close once the peak period has ended
- Trains operating in the peak are very crowded, and those that operate outside the peak are much more lightly loaded, or even almost empty
- The demand for passenger services is towards the centre of the city in the morning, and away from the centre of the city in the afternoon
- Rail services may cease away from peak periods
- There are direct services on a line to a city centre of business district in peak, but away from this passengers need to change trains to get to a city centre

In any city with a significant number of corporations operating in a large business district, there are normally rail services that cater for the employees of these businesses. Rail services start early in the morning, and then run throughout the peak period, and then resume in the afternoon when people want to go home. Commuter services have a reduced service between peak periods, or potentially no service at all. In some cases services only operate at certain times of the day. Alternatively services from the CBD to any extremely large regional centre may continue 24 hours a day, if the demand is there to justify it.

Train movements, especially for commuter and regional services are tidal. What this means is that in the morning trains move from the outskirts of a big city into the middle in the morning, and in the afternoon, when city workers finish work, trains move from the centre of the city to the outskirts or regional centres. So trains start their morning in a rural or regional stabling yard, and then move to some central point, where they are stabled again, waiting for the office workers to complete their day, and then move out again. In this situation there will be two stabling yards at least, one at the end of the line at the regional centre, and then another in centre of the large city. Train movements are tidal because they all move together in a daily pattern, much like a tide.

So how is all of this relevant to stabling? Well as there are more services into the city centre rather than out, trains accumulate in the centre of the city, and then in the afternoon these trains are needed, to move passengers from the CBD out to the suburbs again. This means that there is a requirement for stabling yards in the centre of the city, to accommodate these trains, and them some more stabling yards at the end of several rail lines to accommodate these commuter trains at night. Stabling does not necessarily need to be provided, but where it isn't there will be large numbers of empty train movements, which cost money to make.

Well designed stabling

The ease of use of any stabling yard is another important consideration. Well designed stabling, in addition to having plenty of capacity, located in the correct place, and having the ability to get trains in and out quickly, also needs to be designed so that rail employees can use it efficiently. Drivers need to be able to quickly and efficiently get into and out of trains. There should be toilets and other facilities available. There are many problems with stabling that has either been poorly designed, or has some kind of problem that makes it hard to use. Some of these problems include:

- The lighting is very poor and driver and train staff cannot see where to walk when they are getting in and out of trains
- The ground is uneven and train staff can trip or fall over when walking to or from trains
- Access is difficult into and out of the stabling yard

- The stabling has some environmental factor that impacts upon its function as a stabling yard, such as being located near the ocean and sea spray washes up onto the train
- The stabling yard is located in a high crime area and drivers and train staff get attacked going to and from their trains
- Fencing is inappropriate for the stabling yard
- Toilets are inadequate or too far away
- Other staff amenities are not available

Fencing is quite important for any stabling, as vandals commonly spray paint trains in yards. The experience in Australia has been that the location where trains are stabled needed to have substantial fencing to prevent vandalism, and 2.5 metre high fences are common, with razor wire on top of the fence. This level of security is necessary to prevent a lot of damage to trains.

Different Configurations of Stabling

One of the most important features of any stabling is the entry and exit. Stabling needs to be large enough to accommodate all the trains that are stabled there, but most passenger rail networks have a peak period in the morning, and it is necessary to get trains in and out quickly from the stabling yard onto the running lines. Many different types of entry and exit into a stabling yard exist, but most of them have severe limits on the throughput of trains in and out. The schematics below demonstrate this.

In the layout below the stabling is shown as purple, and the running lines in black. The configuration below is very common, and trains need to move from the running lines to get into the stabling yard. There is only one entrance into and out of the stabling yard, so this is a strong limitation on the number of trains that can enter and exit the stabling yard, notwithstanding the small size of the yard.

Figure 4.2 Single Entry Stabling Yard

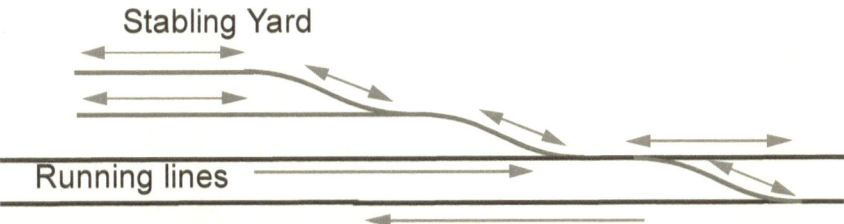

The stabling yard below is larger than the one above, and has two entrances and exits into the yard. Trains will be able to enter and leave more quickly than the one above. Also note that trains leaving the stabling yard to go to the bottom running line will need to cross one of the running lines to get there, and this movement may cause operational problems, and interfere with the passage of other trains. However, despite this, it is clear that this layout is superior to the one above.

Figure 4.3 Multiple Entry Stabling Yard

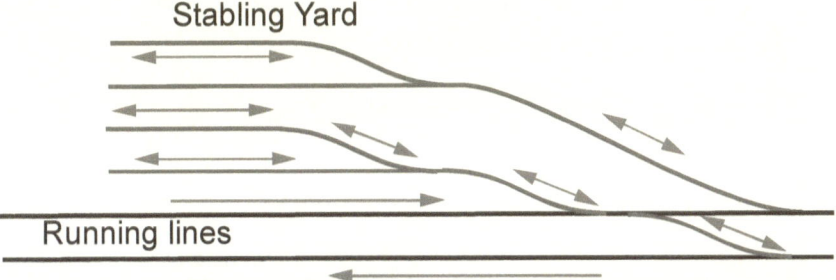

The above layout allows for something called parallel moves, where trains can move in and out of the yard at the same time. This layout is better when large numbers of trains need to be moved in and out of the yard quickly.

The layout below has stabling at the end of the running lines, and they run out and are replaced with a stabling yard. This type of layout can be very efficient, because trains can have direct access to the running lines.

Figure 4.4 Stabling at the End of the Rail Line

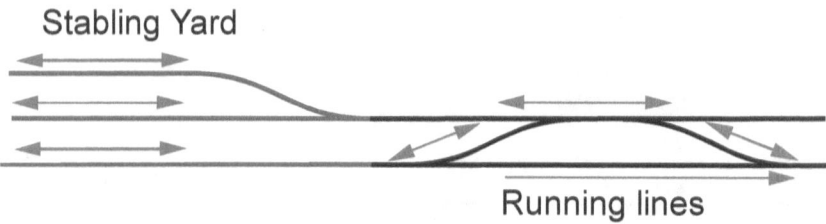

Interestingly a review of the stabling yards in and around Sydney shows that this layout, despite many advantages, is very uncommon. In practice this type of stabling can only be implemented where the rail line ends, and the stabling yard is put at the end of this line. Many rail lines, especially for regional, commuter and intercity services do not end, but continue past the terminus to another destination.

The schematic below shows how stabling is often designed in practice. In the schematic below there is a terminus on the left, where trains arrive and depart from. The terminus is the end of the rail line, and the tracks do not continue any further than this. There is often a high value location just located past the end of the rail terminus, and the railway cannot be built up or continued any further.

Figure 4.5 Terminus and Stabling

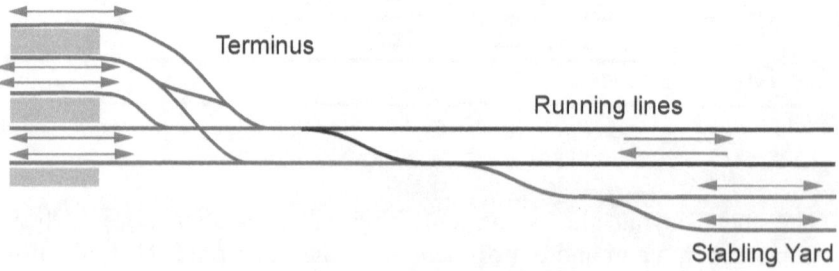

On the right hand side is the stabling, which is located further back away from the terminus. Trains arriving and departing from the terminus will pass alongside the stabling, and the number of tracks will appear, to passengers, to be quite large. This layout is quite common, as it has the advantage that trains, after completing their revenue service, can be moved back into the stabling yard to be stored, and then retrieved when needed. The presence of the stabling increases the effective capacity of the terminus, and more trains can terminate in the terminus. When the terminus becomes full, trains can be moved from the terminus to the stabling yard very quickly. Also, if there is a problem with a train, it can be brought in to the terminus, passengers taken off, and then moved into the stabling yard to await repair. The usefulness of this layout is the key reason why it's so common.

Unfortunately it is a very ugly layout, and aesthetically very unappealing. As the terminus is almost always located next to a city centre, them the stabling yard will also be located on high value land.

In some cases the running lines are so busy that stabling needs to be accessed through a dive, or possibly a flyover. What is shown in the figure below is a dive, but essentially the concept is the same for flyover. Trains need to get from either track into the stabling yard, and there is a desire to avoid an at grade crossing, so the track needs to pass either under or over the running lines.

The layout below shows a dive combined with a stabling yard. The stabling will almost always need to be on one side or the other of the running lines, so one of the lines will need to cross to the other side. In this case it is the lower line that needs to cross to the stabling yard, and it does so through a dive. A dive is a rail tunnel that dips down below the track and then comes up again on the other side.

Figure 4.6 Stabling Accessed through a Dive

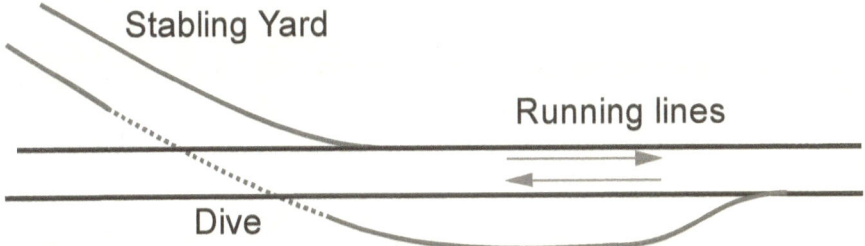

One problem with dives is that they fill up with water. Being the lowest point in the rail system, much of the water from rain and seepage makes its way into a dive. Dives, unless they are in an area that has almost no rain at all, will need a pumping station to remove all the water. Once water makes its way into a tunnel it becomes the responsibility of the railway, and this may mean cleaning and processing the water.

A flyover performs the same function as a dive but goes over the track rather than under. Both require a lot of space and are expensive to build. Once constructed the maintenance cost is quite small. Railways tend to avoid dives and flyovers, given the cost of construction, but they are very effective.

Note that flyovers and dives are used to get rail vehicles into and out of stabling, yards, and maintenance centres more efficiently. They allow trains to pass over or under the running lines without interfering with the movement of trains on the running lines. They are clearly the best way to get trains in and out of stabling yards, but are expensive.

Stabling of Freight

Freight trains need to be stabled like any other train, but freight stabling is a little different to stabling for passenger trains. Some of the differences are:
- Freight trains are very long, often over 1 km, and sometimes over 2 kms, so any stabling for freight will be very long and large
- Freight trains are rarely electric and so this large freight yard will usually have no overhead or electric traction power (although there are exceptions)
- Many freight wagons are only occasionally used, and this often sit in a freight yard waiting to be used, and may be covered in rust. In Australia milk wagons are rarely used, but milk was commonly transported by rail, so there are many surplus wagons sitting idle in various freight yards
- Freight locomotives will need to refuel, so there will often be refuelling facilities in the yard
- Very large freight yards will sometimes have other freight facilities around them, such as road freight terminals. For large freight yards with a lot of traffic, the combined road rail freight terminals can cover a very large area
- As rail freight often only generates a small profit, any freight yard are often in poor condition and covered with weeds. Coal freight yards are the exception and are almost always in good

condition because of the much higher profitability of selling coal (at least in Australia)

The diagram below shows how freight may be stabled. The running lines move around a long freight yard, and the stabling yard can be entered from either end. Note that stabling yards are often more complex than this, and the yard drawn below is a bit simplified.

Figure 4.7 Freight Stabling Yard

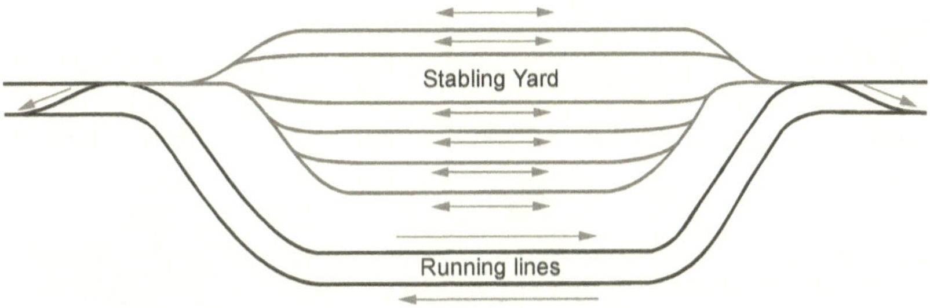

This type of stabling is suitable for long freight trains. The yard show above can be extremely large, and over 1 kilometre long. Also trains can enter from either end, have wagons added or removed, and locomotives added or removed, and then can enter or exit from either end. In many ways this layout is very suitable for freight, particularly for intermodal traffic, or any other freight where freight trains are marshalled.

Week 5

Rail System Drawing and Configuration

The creation of any new rail line or extension would not be complete without drawing it. The visual interpretation of rail systems is a very powerful way of showing how a rail system is structured. Often the creation of a rail system starts with lines on a map. This book contains a number of different ways of rail systems.

Rail systems comprise of trains moving along tracks to get from one place to another. Trains are limited to operating on tracks, and trains cannot change direction without some tracks in that direction. There are different configuration of tracks that allow trains to swap from one track to another, or turn around. In almost all railways trains, when reaching the end of the line, need to be returned back in the direction from which they came. In this chapter are ways of describing rail lines, and how they are drawn.

Many different styles exist for drawing rail systems. The level of detail can vary considerably, and maps for passengers tend to be very simple, and maps for rail operators far more complex. In some countries rail maps are more complex that the very simple lines on a map, for example, rail system may be drawn to scale, or even with some geographical features added. In some cases rail maps provided to the public may be geographically correct, rather than a simplistic representation of the rail system. Some examples are provided below of the more common methods of drawing rail systems, but the reader should bear in mind that there are many different ways, and for brevity, only the more important ones are shown here. Perhaps the most common, and the most simple, are the maps where rail lines are drawn as straight lines, with different colours for the different lines. Many examples of this style of rail map are shown below.

For rail network designers, rail maps need to be much more complicated. The basic ideas behind constructing a more complex rail map are also elucidated below, and so it may become clear as to how to construct these. Many different types of maps are useful for the purposes of rail transport planning, and the map used will depend on the situation. There is no right and wrong way, just methods with different attributes.

Passenger Orientated Rail Drawings

Passenger orientated rail network maps tend to be very simple, and show basic information related to train operations and stopping patterns. Features such as interchanges, and where trains stop, are emphasised, and more infrastructure related information such as points and turnout locations are not mentioned or shown. Rail lines made available to the public are almost often in this format, and the look and feel is quite standard between different railways. Below is an example of a rail system drawing, that does not represent any particular place, which is passenger orientated.

Figure 5.1 A Simple Rail System

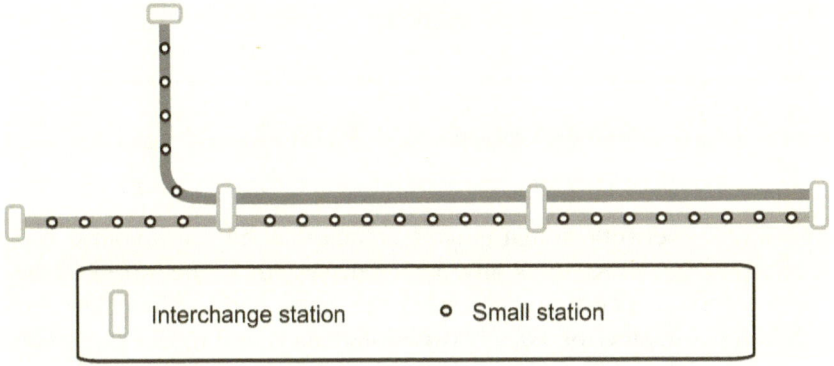

In this simple rail system, the blue and orange lines are drawn as separate lines, and there are many stations on the orange line where there is no corresponding dot on the blue line. This means that trains only stop when on the orange line, and not on the blue line. Trains on the blue line should travel faster than those on the orange, as the orange line trains are all stopping trains. Trains on both the blue and orange lines can interchange at the larger rectangular stations, of which there are only three.

A common misconception is that on a passenger rail map that lines drawn as different colours represent different tracks or different infrastructure. To the lay person this can be very confusing. Consider the rail system map below:

Figure 5.2 A Three Line Rail System

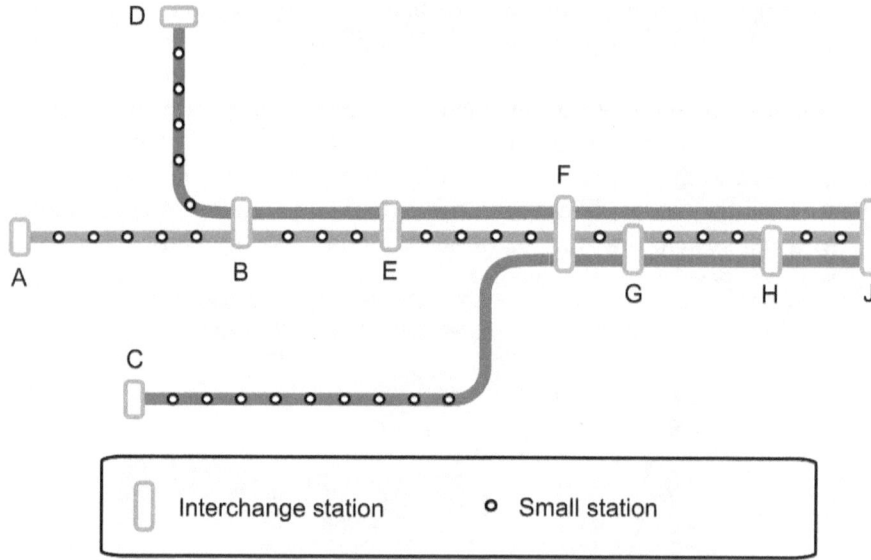

This kind of network design is quite common, although of course it is unlikely to be the same as any other rail system in the world at the present time. Notice that there are 3 rail lines, and the blue line has only a small number of stops between stations B and J. The green line has additional stops at G and H, where passengers can interchange between the orange and green lines.

This rail system map is very useful for passengers, as it clearly shows which trains stop at which stations. For example, a blue line train will stop at E & F, but no stations in between. Any passenger travelling between D & J should know where they can and cannot alight from the train.

The drawing suggests that there are at least 6 tracks between F & J, and 4 between B & F. In practice there is no reason to have this number, and a very likely scenario in the above would be to have 4 tracks between F & J, and perhaps 4 between E & F, and only two tracks between B & E. Is is also not clear how many tracks there are between B & D, there may be 1, or 2, or less likely some other number.

If we take our example a little further, and say there are only 4 tracks between F & J, then most likely local trains will operate on two tracks,

Week 5 *Page 200*

and the blue and green lines on the other two. Trains for the blue line will be able to stop at stations G & H, but won't because they are timetabled not to stop.

An interesting question arises as to when a rail line is actually a separate rail line, and not just a branch, loop, link, or rail spur. In the 3 line system drawn above the blue line is drawn separately, as the stopping pattern is quite different from the orange line. Consider the rail line below:

Figure 5.3 One Rail Line with a Branch

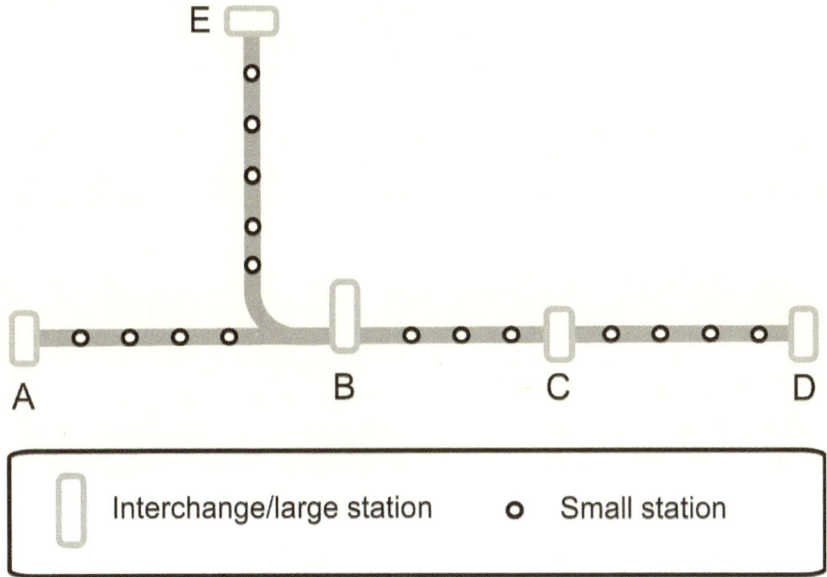

The drawing above shows a single rail line, with a branch or bifurcation. We would expect from a drawing of this type that trains do move from station D, to station E, and many stops in between. At station B passengers would need to alight if they wanted a train travelling along the other branch from the one the destination that the train they are travelling on would have.

The rail system below shows a shuttle service. A shuttle is a service that is separated from the rest of the rail system, that moves from one large station to another, typically over relatively short distances. The blue line below is a shuttle, and trains moving along B to E will not move through to any other station. This type of rail design is common.

Typically both lines will be the same type of rail system, ie, both metros, or both commuter trains.

Figure 5.4 A Rail Line with a Shuttle

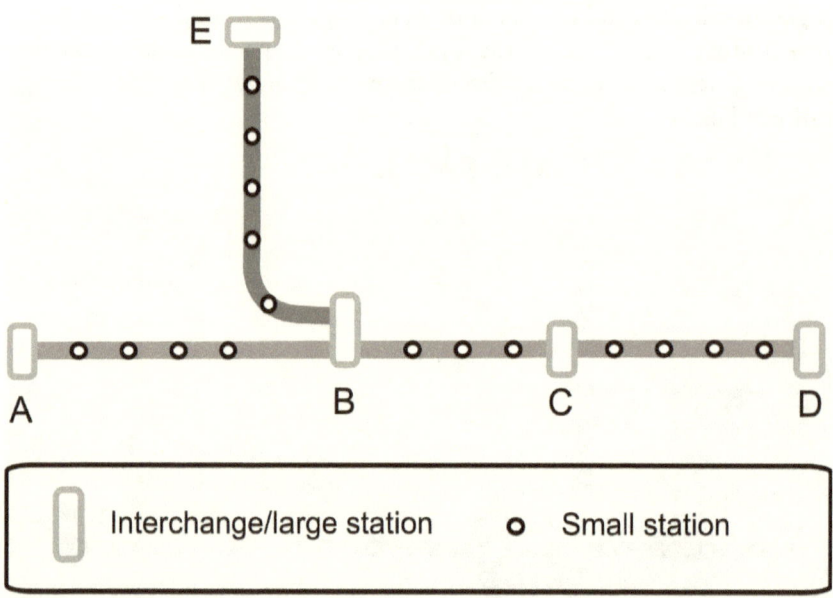

Below is another way of drawing a rail system that is sometimes used. The rail system below is made up of only 1 line, but it is drawn as 2. The top line is an express service, and the bottom an all stops.

Figure 5.5 One Rail Line with Two Stopping Patterns

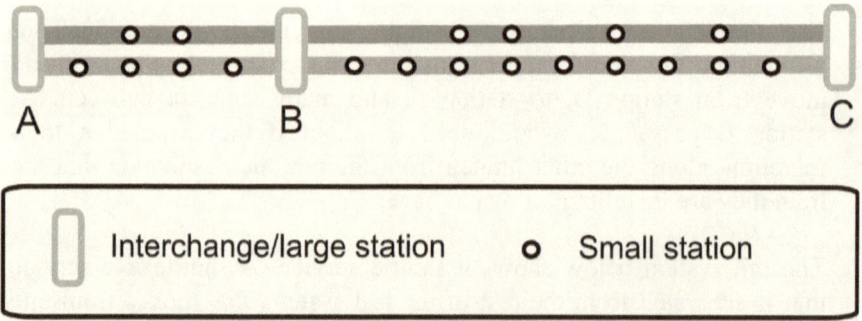

The way this system is drawn it may appear that there are three interchange stations, A, B and C, and many intermediate stations in between. This is not the case, A,B & C are larger stations, and passengers can interchange with any station where there is a dot on both the blue and orange lines.

In many cases there are other rail systems in and around the rail system being drawn. This is particularly common in Japan. The rail system in bright colours is the one being displayed, and the darker rail line with thinner lines is the one operated as a different rail mode, or by another company. The other rail system needs to be included to allow passengers to see the interchanges, but not much detail is required. This arrangement is shown below.

Figure 5.6 Two Rail Modes

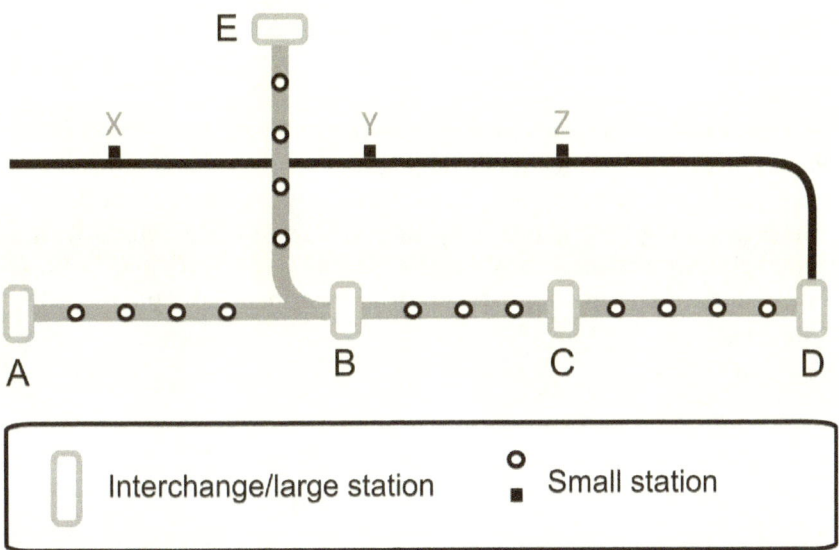

Whilst the drawings above are useful for the public, and demonstrate effectively where stations are and the services to them, this type of system drawing does not include much other useful information. Some of the pieces of information that are missing include:
- Stabling
- Turnbacks so trains can be terminated and sent back in the reverse direction
- Passing loops
- Any idea as to the number of tracks
- The number of platforms at stations
- Crossovers

For a train operator the above information, whilst not useless, is not on its own enough to fully understand the rail system and how it operates.

Geographically Correct Maps

A geographically correct map of a rail system shows the location of stations and rail lines in comparison to an underlying map. Rail lines are drawn physically where they are, and not in the idealised way that passenger rail maps are normally drawn in. This type of map can be very helpful, but is less commonly used than the idealised maps above.

Geographically correct maps show the terrain and main features of an area, and the rail system within it. For example, lakes, rivers, and oceans are shown, and urban areas can be shown. For maps of entire countries, the main features that are show would normally be the boundaries of the country.

Passengers often find geographically correct maps difficult to read. For most passenger systems they are a little unsuited, but can work well where the rail system is relatively simple. One of the problems with a geographically correct map is that the spacing between stations in a real rail system often varies greatly, and this can make the maps a little confusing.

Figure 5.7 Geographically Correct Map of the Rail System in Newcastle NSW in Australia

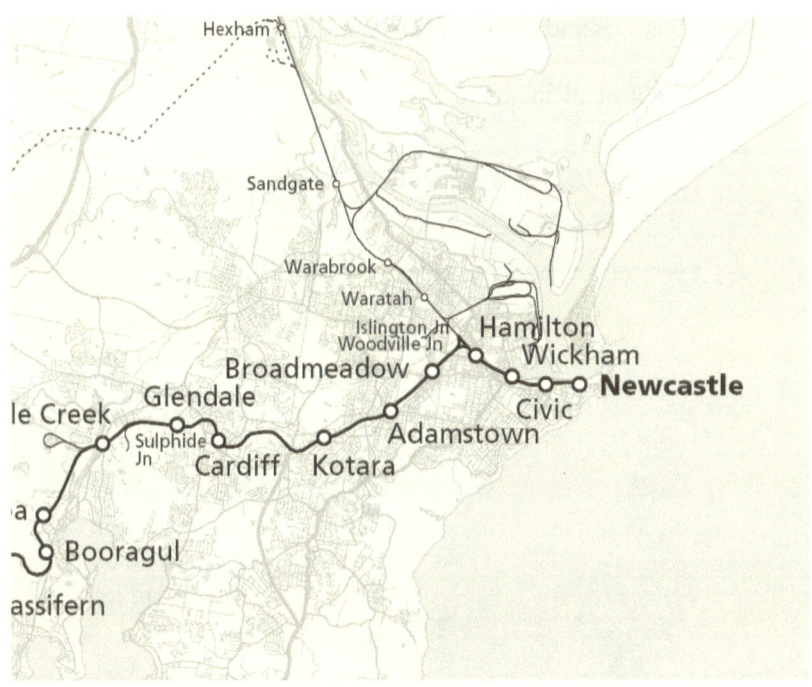

The map above also shows freight lines and the coal loader. Parts of this rail line have now closed. Bodies of water are clearly visible.

Detailed Drawing of Rail Systems

For much rail network design, detailed rail maps are essential. There are many different styles of drawing rail systems, and the one presented below is something of a compromise. Detailed design drawings of rail lines are very complex, and include all the different engineering items that are normally found in a rail system. Design drawings of rail systems are very difficult to read, and not included in this book because they are too complex for most rail transport planners to use.

The drawing method below does not include signals. As almost all signalling schemes are very complex, the signals themselves have a lot of detail and information that sometimes can make the drawing a little difficult to read.

The level of detail show below is useful to show places where trains can be stabled, and can be turned back. Many of the common features of a rail system are shown. The running direction of the rail system is also shown. Stations and platforms are also shown.

So here are the basic elements of a rail system.

	Basic Rail System Elements
————————	A rail track, with two rails, and sleepers in between. Only one train can move along this track at any one time.
←————————	Possible direction of travel of a train
▬▬▬▬▬▬	A station
(turnout diagram)	A turnout, where the track splits, and the train can take one of two paths
←————→	One track, where trains can move in either direction. This is called bi-directional track.
————→ ←————	Double track, with trains moving in one direction on both tracks.

Basic Rail System Elements

	This configuration is very standard, and could be described as the "normal" arrangement.
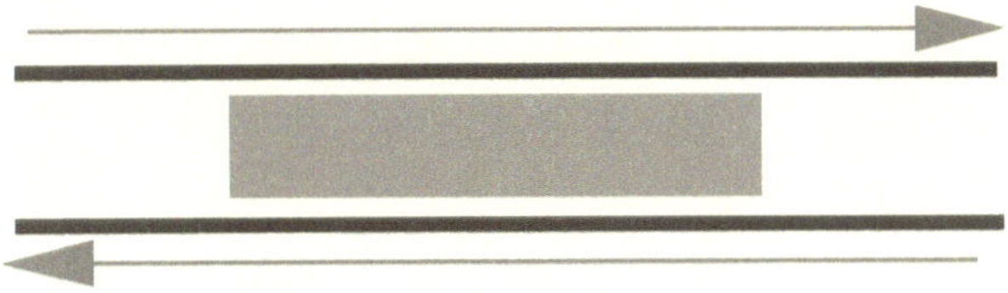	This is an island platform station, where the station is located between two tracks. This is a very common configuration.
	A station with side platforms. There is one station here, not two. Side platforms are sometimes used when space is limited or to save cost.

More complex arrangements can be built out of these basic elements. The table below shows how configurations can be built up into more complex structures.

More Complex Rail Layouts – Crossing movements

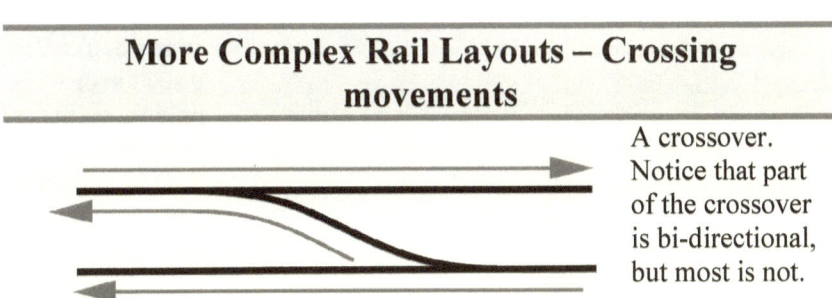

A crossover. Notice that part of the crossover is bi-directional, but most is not.

Week 5   *Page 207*

More Complex Rail Layouts – Crossing movements

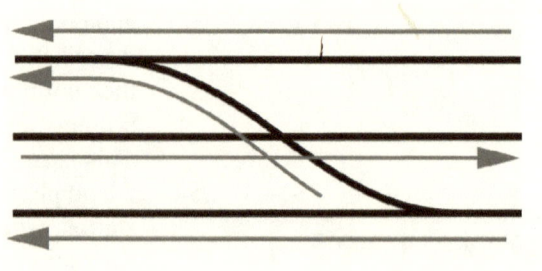

A diamond crossover. Trains crossing over would need to wait until the any trains in the middle had passed before crossing over.

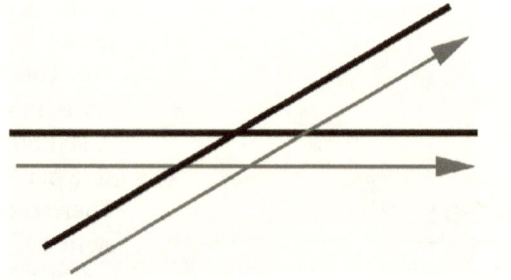

A diamond crossing, or just simply a crossing. Trains cannot change direction here, but do pass over one track to continue on their journey.

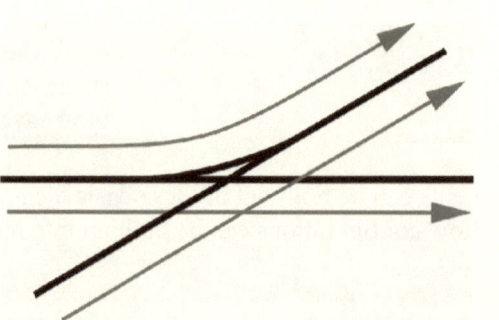

This unusual structure is called a single slip. Note that trains arriving from one direction can move in two directions, whereas arriving from another direction can only move in one direction.

This is a double slip. The addition of this infrastructure

More Complex Rail Layouts – Crossing movements

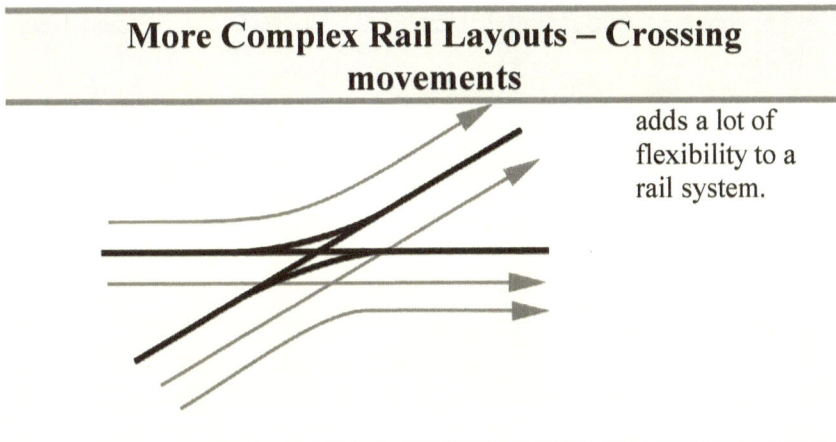

adds a lot of flexibility to a rail system.

From an infrastructure perspective, the addition of turnouts (especially in large numbers) can create a lot of additional work and expense, and additional turnouts should only be added when really needed.

Drawing Junctions and other more complex structures

The elements show above can be combined together to create more complex ones. Common examples are shown below.

A junction is a place where rail tracks either split or merge together. Below 4 tracks on the left become two tracks on the right.

Figure 5.8 A Large Junction

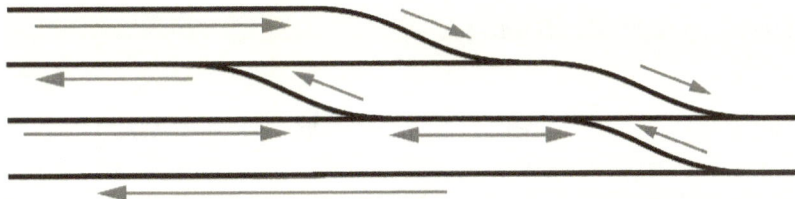

This junction is composed of 6 turnouts, of which 4 are in crossovers. Junctions can be far more complicated than the one above, and some junctions can be truly enormous.

A junction is a place where many of the above configurations have been installed, leading to quite a complex layout. Whilst the junction drawn above is quite simple, junctions get very complicated very quickly.

Crossing Loops

A crossing loop is provided for trains to pass one another, especially where there is only one track, but are sometimes used for more tracks. Crossing loops are also provided where fast moving trains need to pass slow moving ones.

The layout below best describes a crossing loop. A single track approaches the platform from either direction, and trains moving from left to right go to platform 1, and from right to left to platform 2. Thus trains are able to pass one another on the same track despite going in different directions.

Figure 5.9 Crossing Loop

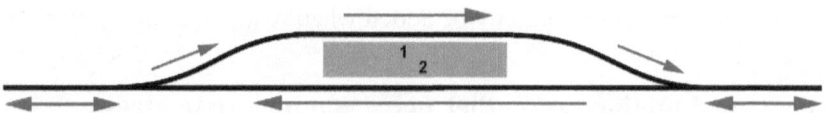

Crossing loops can be an effective way to allow trains to pass one another. Crossing loops are very common in regional and commuter networks, and also in freight networks.

Refuges

Refuges are a place where trains can be stored for hours or even days. They are almost always a loop, and do not have a platform. Refuges can be quite small.

Figure 5.10 Refuges

Refuges can be quite useful, and it is often necessary to store trains that are not in revenue service, and where no stabling is nearby. The two tracks are the ones that pass past the station. The refuge is not used for main line traffic, and the maximum permitted speed will be very low. The number of trains stored in a refuge will be small, typically only one or two.

Sidings

Sidings are used to store trains. Unlike refuges, sidings typically do not rejoin the main line. Sidings can be expanded to become very large, but the layout drawn below is not particularly large.

Figure 5.11 A Siding

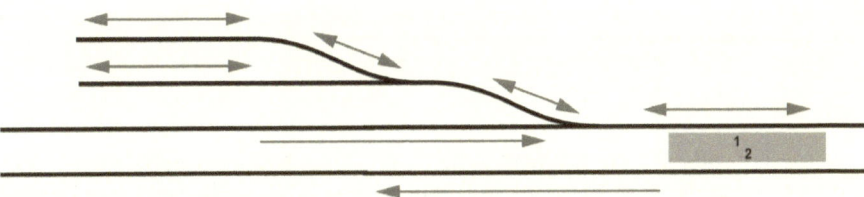

The bottom two tracks, the ones that pass the platforms, are mainline tracks. The top two are sidings. Sidings are a very important part of any rail network, and even a small network will need lots of sidings.

Termini

A terminus is where a rail line ends, and the passenger train will not continue in revenue service. A terminus may or may not have stabling, and where this is stabling then the terminus can be very complicated. Often however no stabling is provided, or very little, and the terminus is quite a simple design. Some standard designs are provided below, and there is no question some are better than others.

The termini presented here all allow trains to continue on. Most termini in a rail system will not allow trains to do this, and they must stop their journey and go back in the opposite direction. The termini presented here are common in large commuter networks, where trains frequently terminate, and express trains then pass continuing on. There can be several such termini in on one line, where trains with different stopping patterns

Goods Roads

A goods road is a track that passes round the station and other facilities, without providing for passengers to alight and board. Goods roads are provided to allow freight trains to continue their journey without disrupting passenger services. The layout below includes a centre terminating road. The goods line is drawn in green, and freight trains do not stop at the station, hence there is no platform number.

Figure 5.12 A Goods Road

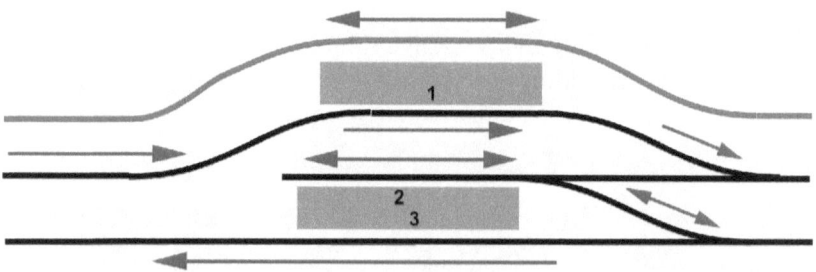

Goods roads are common in freight, regional and commuter networks, and unheard of in almost any other system. Some light rail systems, especially those constructed adjacent to a freight line, can also have goods roads around stations.

Perway Sidings

A perway siding is a place where track vehicles and other maintenance vehicles can be placed onto the track. Perway stands for permanent way, and the permanent way is the track and related components, such as rails, sleepers, and ballast. The maintenance of the permanent way requires large track machines, and there are different many of these. Sometimes, and this is especially true in large networks, it is better if track machines are put onto a truck, and craned into position. Once installed onto track, perway vehicles can then perform the maintenance that is required. Perway sidings are almost always unwired, so there is no overhead wiring, as machines vehicles are diesel powered, and cranes cannot be used where there is overhead wiring.

Figure 5.13 Perway Siding

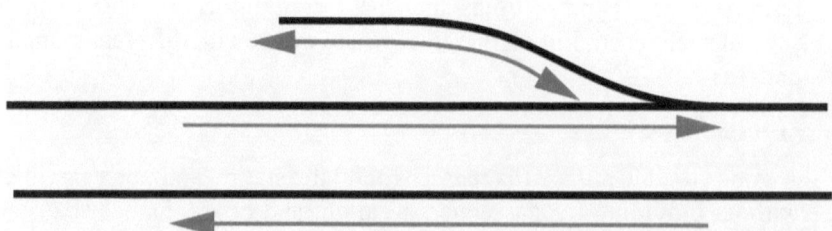

Junction for Four Tracks Becoming Two

Two track, normally with one track for each direction, can split and go in two different directions. The diagram below shows this with trains moving from right to left and there are two different ways trains can go. This type of junction is extremely common in most rail systems.

Figure 5.14 Two Track Junction

For four tracks it is important in many cases to allow trains to move between the two tracks that permit train movements in the same direction. Diamond crossovers allow this, and are shown in the diagram below. A diamond crossover is similar to a normal crossover, but crosses a track moving in the opposite direction to get to the other track. In the layout below there are 4 diamond crossovers.

Figure 5.15 Diamond Crossovers

As mentioned above, a double slip allows trains to move in 4 different directions through a single turnout. Below are two double slips. Double slips have fallen out of favour due to their complexity and maintenance challenges, and often are points of high use, so wear is high. Double slips allow substantial flexibility in the different directions trains can move.

Figure 5.16 Double Slips

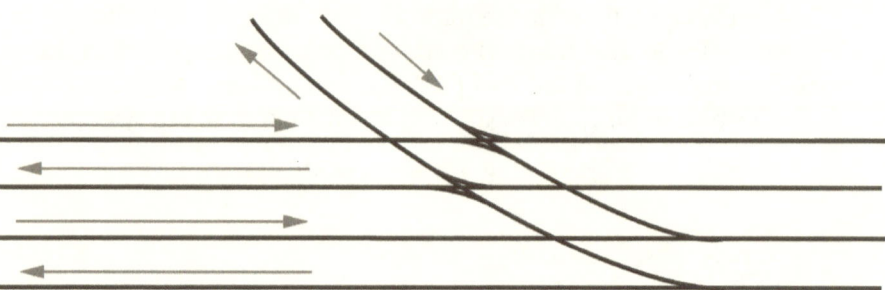

A triangle is a place where trains can move from one line to another. It is a meeting point of at least two rail lines, and sometimes three depending on the way lines are defined. Less obviously, triangles allow trains to be turned around, and face the opposite direction. The land in the middle of a triangle is entirely enclosed by rail lines, and can be used for any purpose a rail system might wish to use it for.

Figure 5.17 Triangles

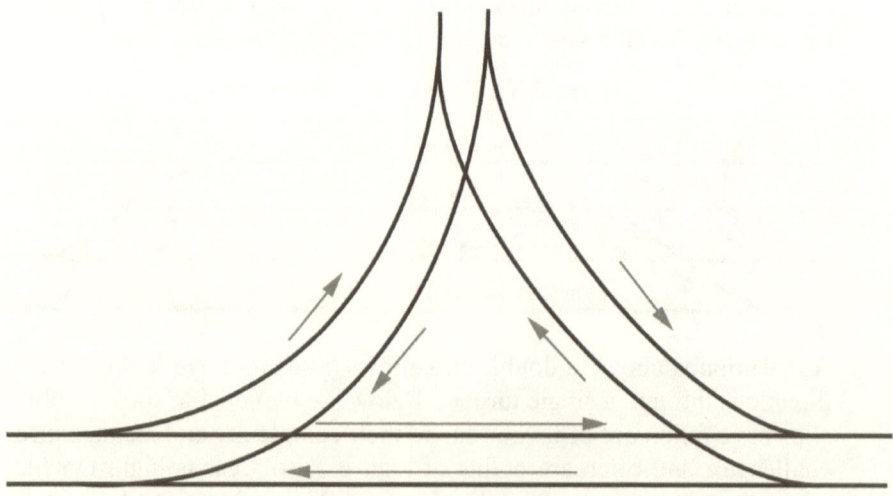

A loop is not a common feature in rail systems, but is used in some commuter rail systems in Australia, and also in Hong Kong in the tram network. A loop is very useful in allowing a train to change direction without stopping. Trains simply drive normally, and then are facing the opposite direction. Loops are difficult to deploy, but can be very effective in reducing turnaround times by removing a terminus.

Figure 5.18 Loops

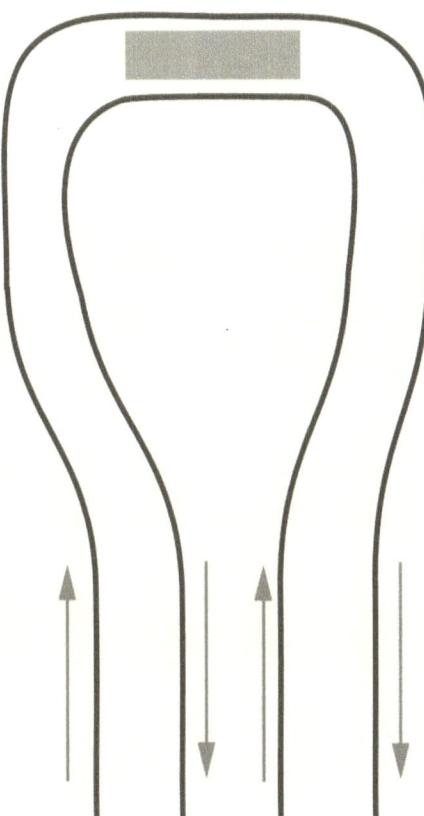

Drawing a new rail system

With all the different elements shown above, a complete rail line can now be drawn. An simple example is shown below.

As part of any new project or creating a new rail line, the new system would need to be drawn. To complete a drawing of the network, a number of key questions will need to be asked, and answers must be provided. For example:
- Where will trains be stabled?
- Where can trains be terminated from, and sent back?
- How many sidings are needed, the higher the frequency of trains, the more stabling, and hence sidings, that will be needed

How is freight going to be managed, if at all?

So below is an example of what a rail line might look like.

Figure 5.19 An Example Rail Line

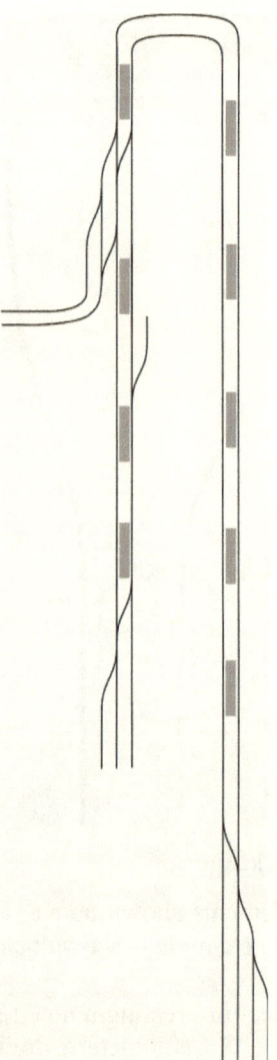

Approaches to Network Design

Introduction

The design of any network needs to allow trains to efficiently move around the network. A poorly designed network can have a powerful effect on the speed, cost and utility of the network, and the rail system will be dramatically underutilised. One of the key objectives of any rail transport design is to provide the right level of services to the right places, and one of the best ways of achieving this is through good network design.

Network design for transport networks has traditionally been somewhat mathematical. One branch of applied mathematics is Operations Research, which is concerned with applied mathematics and solving complex industrial mathematical problems. Network design for transport is often discussed in papers on Operations Research, and as a consequence this topic can be very complicated and mathematical. This is not how this topic will be discussed in this chapter, and complex mathematics will be avoided.

For any large city or country, the number of different network designs can be extremely large. There may be hundreds of different potentially feasible designs, and the large number can be very challenging to manage. Rail lines can be drawn on maps in a huge number of different ways, and filtering out all of the different options can in many cases be a near impossible task. This chapter provides examples of different network designs, and the more designs that are generated as part of the design process of a rail system, potentially the best one will be better.

Any possible network design will be limited by some practical constraints. In theory, almost any rail network design is possible, and these different designs are only limited by imagination. In practice things are not so easy, and constraints are placed on possible network designs. A constraint is a limitation placed on the network design, which must be followed. Typically rail systems are not built under oceans, but may cross between islands, for example. Some of these constraints are obvious, others less so. For example, it would be very unusual for a rail system to have a station in a cemetery, or in a garbage dump, or have entrances inside churches or temples.

For rail systems the available land, topography and ground conditions can also play a very large role in deciding where to build a new rail line. In many cases the choices are quite limited, mostly because land has been reserved in only one place and that's what needs to be used, or because land is difficult to acquire, or there is some public policy reason as to why land cannot be acquired. The availability of land is a powerful constraint, and where land is available is often where a rail line is built, even if the location of the available land is not in an ideal place.

Other constraints include the ground conditions, especially for tunnelling. Building tunnels through sand, next to seas or other bodies of water is normally a very bad idea, as the water will seep through the sand and into the rail tunnel. There are many other problems, such as large hills, immovable obstructions, heritage buildings or national monuments and other problems that will cause the rail line to have only a small number of options on where it can be placed.

Similarly with any rail tunnelling project, there are often underground obstructions that can become obstacles to any underground railway. Large buildings can have very deep car parks that can be so low that a railway line becomes too deep and cannot go under them. In many countries there are archaeological sites that can be powerful barriers to any underground excavation. Also other rail and road tunnels can be in the way of any new rail project. These limitations can be so powerful that there may be almost no design choices left for any network design.

Rail transport often involves the movement of passengers in and around large cities, or from one large city to another. Within large cities, major centres within the city may need to be connected, and this can largely drive the creation of any new rail system. Rail network design is often best optimised by connecting these centres together, and this removes many of the potential different options for network design. Major transport hubs, especially where there are large bus stations, should be connected, and so the challenge often becomes how to connect them.

Avoiding Mistakes with Network Design

Rail network design is a large area with many different possible solutions for any one planning problem. This makes the construction of general rules for network design difficult, and this entire book is about assisting with those choices. Notwithstanding the complexity of the planning problem, there are some specific problems that clearly should be avoided, and they are listed below. It is by no means an exhaustive list, and some of the key things to avoid with network design are:
- Building a rail system with lots of curves so that average speeds are low
- Building a rail system where many pieces or rail lines are unconnected to one another

- Building a rail system that misses major population centres (excluding freight systems)
- Building a rail system that is difficult to access, or located in places that take a long time to reach, such as deep in the bottom of a valley
- Connecting cities to one another that do not need to be connected, or where cities closer together should be connected first
- Building a rail line where it does not reach the centre of a city, or a place that clearly needs to be connected, such as a major regional centre
- Building an intercity rail line that does not connect to the transport network in one or both cities at either end of the line
- Placing two stations next to each other, where interchanges should be possible, but with a major obstacle in the way, so that passengers moving from one station need to make a time consuming or difficult journey
- Building a passenger rail line to pick up people in areas with low populations
- Constructing stations deep underground so that they are difficult to access
- Designing rail systems that are very wasteful of energy

Most of the list above represent major blunders, but almost all of them exist in one form or another in operational railways around the world. In some situations they may represent an acceptable solution to some localised difficult problem, but overall these situations should be avoided where possible.

So, taking the opposite of the rules above, we can identify some of the principles for good rail network design to be:
- Rail lines should be as straight as possible
- Station selection needs to be made carefully to keep the average speed high
- Lots of grades should be avoided in any rail system, especially high grades in only one position
- Underground stations should not be too deep
- Major areas of population and major commercial centres should be connected
- Good interconnections with other transport modes, and other forms of rail transportation, are very important

- Average speeds are always important
- Power and energy consumption is important and should be minimised

The ideal for any rail system is to build a cheap to maintain system that has high passenger volumes. In many cases there is a trade off between speed and connecting to major centres, and the more places that are connected the lower the average speed.

Whilst most of this chapter is directed towards passenger traffic, the ideas are the same for freight. Freight rail traffic is also time and cost sensitive, and where possible rail lines should be as straight and flat as possible.

There is a standard layout and structure for rail systems in large cities. This structure seems to be relatively consistent from country to country, and so can provide a useful template for the design of any new rail system.

A Standard Rail System for Large Cities

In large cities the configuration below is a common one. This schematic represents the "normal" situation for any large city, where most the different rail systems are represented. The city below is not based on any one city, although there are many cities with this structure, but is an idealisation of what would be considered "normal" for a theoretical city. A good example of a city with this design is Toronto in Canada.

Figure 5.20 A Standard Urban Rail System

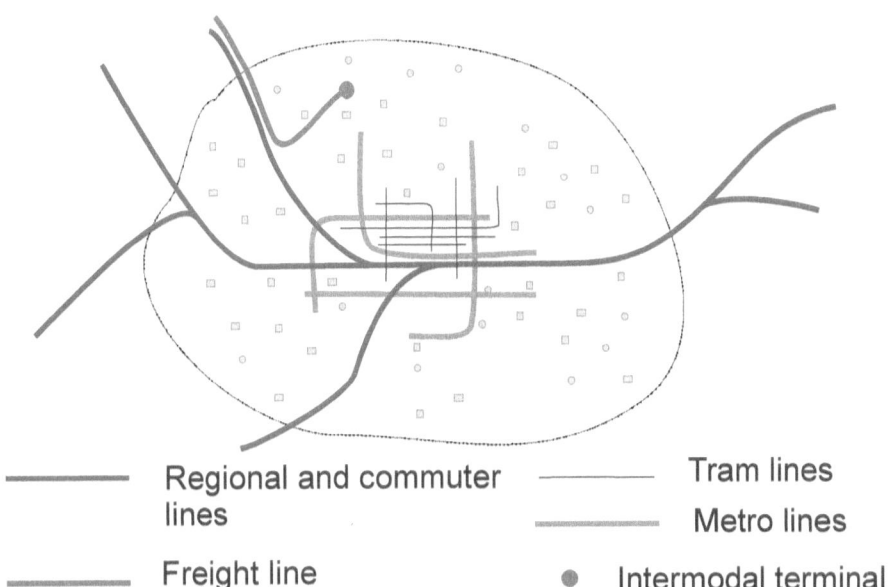

So what we see here is:
- The tram system, or possibly a light rail system, in the centre of the city, serving high value locations but at a low speed
- The metro system, which covers the centre of the city, but also the fringes of what is sometimes called the "inner city", which is suburbs located close to the centre of the city
- The regional or commuter system, which goes outside the boundary of the city. High speed rail systems may also share tracks with regional and intercity trains
- A freight line in the suburbs, which brings intermodal freight from other cities and countries into the city. The intermodal terminal is normally located in an industrial area, away from the city centre, where land is cheaper and where it won't detract from the appearance of the city.

More rarely, there are also some other rail lines present in a large city, such as a monorail, or a tourist railway. Also not shown is an automated railway connecting different terminals in an airport to one another. Some or all of the elements of the above city can be missing, but the larger the city, the more likely it is that all these elements will be there. The most common rail system to be missing is the tram/light rail system, which can only be installed if there is room or the will for it to be installed.

Larger cities tend to more closely follow the rail system structure above, although very large cities such as Tokyo can be quite different (and there's only a couple of them really). For smaller cities, such as with populations under 3 million, and especially under 2 million, many other choices are possible, and some of the rail systems in a big city can be combined together. Some of the possibilities are:
- The metro and the light rail system are combined together, forming an intermediate capacity metro, such as Porto in Portugal or in Vancouver
- There is no light rail system, and the metro is much smaller to accommodate the smaller population, such as Helsinki
- There is no or very little light rail or metro system, and the regional railway operates as the main rail system, such as Sydney
- The metro system replaces any commuter or intercity system, and is the main system, such as Singapore (excluding some very small lines, such as the rail line from Woodlands to Malaysia)
- More unusually, most of the rail system is replaced with a more uncommon rail system, such as a monorail, such as Chongqing in China

The choice as to the best system will depend on the local factors, the structure and size of the city, and the culture and vibe of the city.

The above network configuration can be used as plan for future rail construction. The above configuration has been proven to work well in many different cities and environments time and time again.

Some Examples of Network Design – Single Lines

The analysis of network design here is split into two main categories; single lines on their own, and a rail system with multiple lines. A rail system that has multiple lines can often be examined through dividing up the system into single line sections, and then characterising them as below.

To simplify things, the examples below are constructed in terms of cities or towns, and a rail connection linking them. The city at each end of the rail line could also represent a major centre within a large city. Conceptually this is the same as another city or town.

The two cities below have been connected using a rail line that is relatively direct with a minimum of curves. The rail lines get into the centre of both cities, and the line connecting them is reasonable straight.

Figure 5.21 A "Good" Intercity Connection

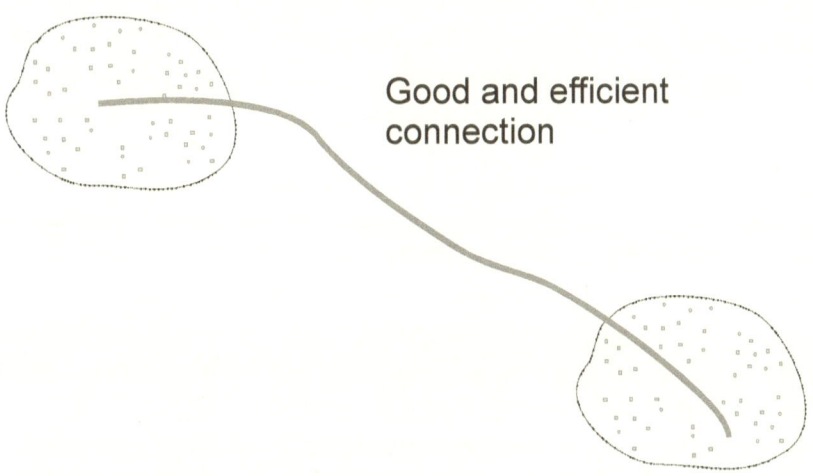

This is in contrast to the line below, which is a very poor design. The main problem with the connection below is the length of the rail line, it is long and has many curves, which will mean that trains have a longer distance to travel, and travel more slowly as curves require lower speeds to negotiate.

Figure 5.22 A Poor Intercity Connection

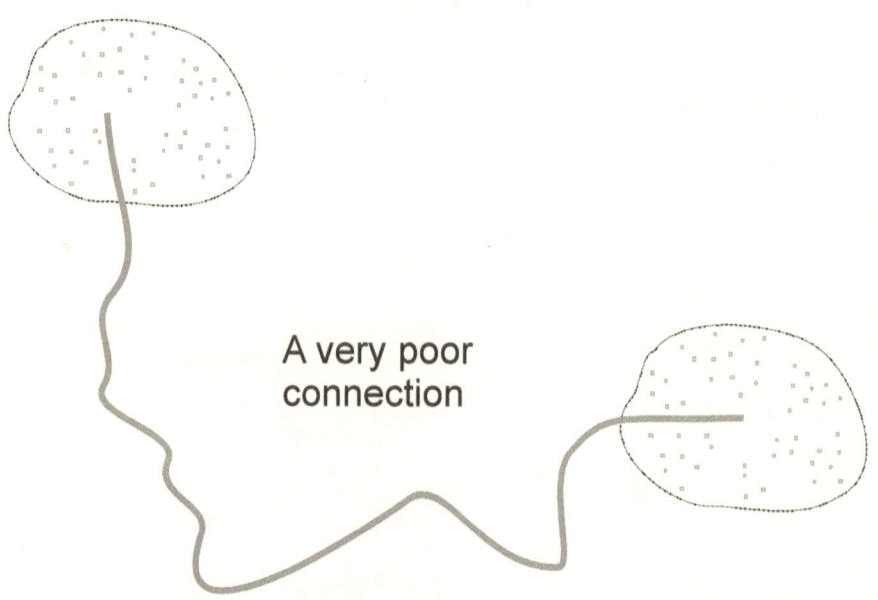

Remember that intercity traffic, and most rail travel, is very sensitive to the travel time, and a slow travel time will normally dramatically impact upon passenger numbers. A rail line like the one above is unlikely to be of much value, and may be cheaper to construct, but will be used by only a small number of people.

This problem also seems to be particularly acute with freight networks, which rarely seem to follow straight lines or the most direct path between where they start their journey or their final destination. Freight traffic is also very sensitive to grades, which means that a more direct route between two places is often impossible as the grades as too steep.

There are other network design problems that are also serious. Consider the network design below where there are three cities, and a need to connect the smallest of the cities to one of the other two. The smaller city will most likely have strong links and numbers of passenger movements to City B, as it is so close. City A has been connected to city C, and this may be because city C is slightly larger than city B.

Figure 5.23 Network Design with Multiple Cities

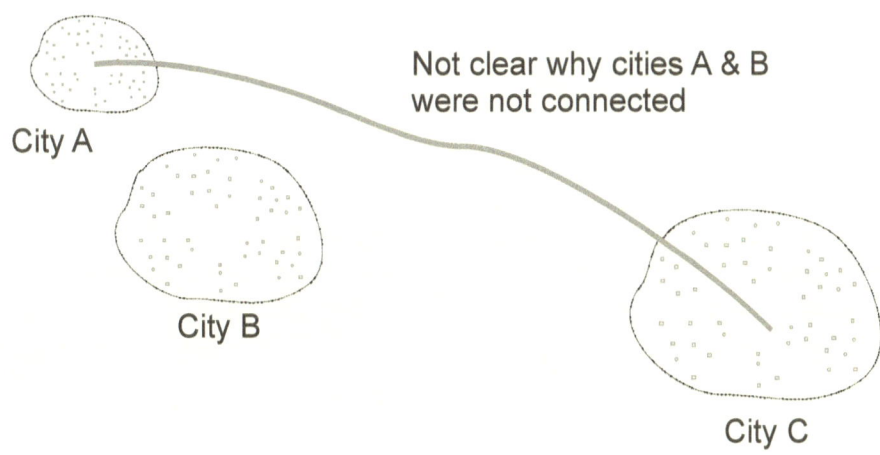

This type of rail transport connection creates many problems, other than the obvious one where the two closely located cities are not connected. It also encourages people to travel from A to C, when B is much closer. This may increase the number of long distance trips, which will sometimes be replaced with car journeys, which may cause road traffic to be higher than it needs to be. A much better network design is shown below, and of course A & B have been connected, so that this journey is now available.

Figure 5.24 Network Design with Multiple Cities

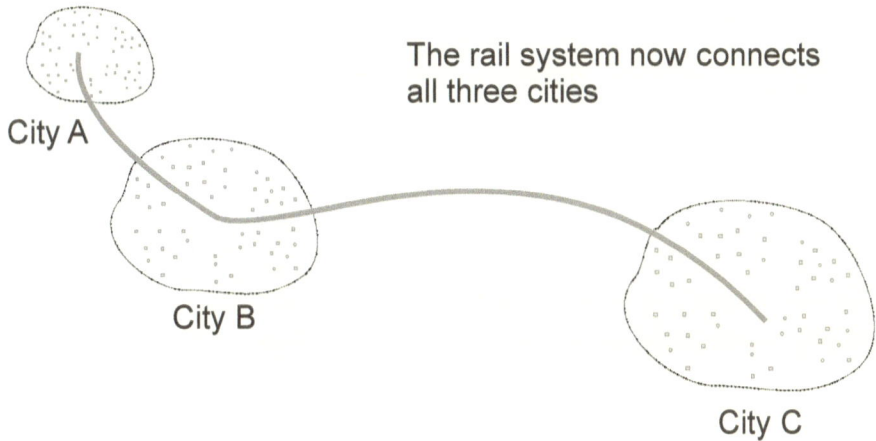

This design is far superior, and connects all the cities in a logical order. This network design will increase the number of passengers travelling between B & C, and so services will be more frequent between A & C (or probably will be, if services are not terminated at B).

Another mistake that is sometimes made is to have trains enter into a city, and then reverse out again having made a stop in the city or town. Below is the normal structure of a rail line passing through a town, and it enters from one side and then leaves from the other. Presumably there are other towns on both the entrance and exit side of the rail line leading into the city.

Figure 5.25 Network Passes through the City

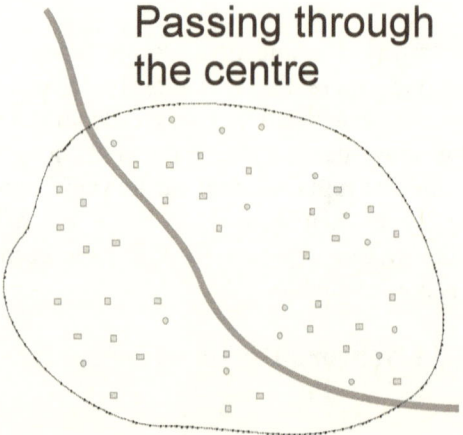

Below is another possibility, one that is not a good idea, but is done occasionally where there is no other choice. The rail line enters the city, and then the rail line terminates in the centre of the city. In the schematic below it is possible for a train to travel from city A to C through B, and to get out of city B a train would need to follow the same route that it used to get in. The train is essentially backtracking over the path it has taken to get into the city.

Figure 5.26 Trains Reverse out of City B

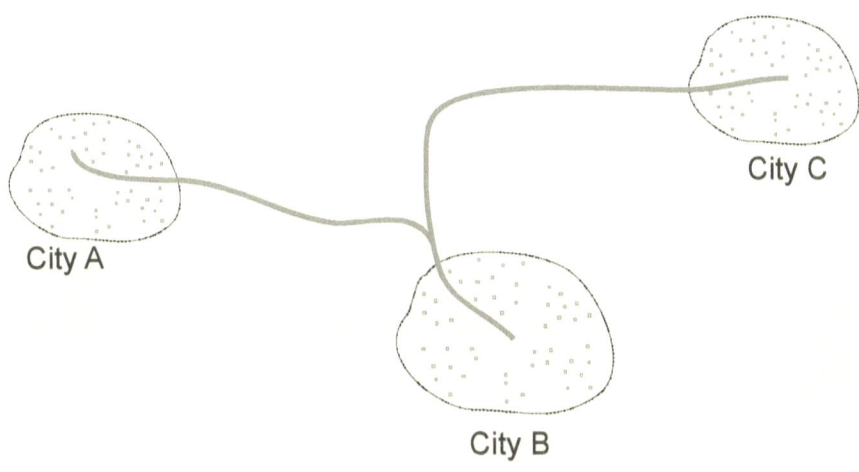

When the train arrives into city B the driver would need to change ends, and trains will leave the city in the reverse direction to the one it entered. Passengers will need to turn around, or flip seats around to face another direction (or sit facing backwards). Where the seats in the train are facing both forwards and reverse then maybe nothing is needed to be done.

The rail line from Venice to Rome has this structure when entering and leaving Florence. This rail structure, despite being sometimes unavoidable, is messy and inefficient, and should be not be utilised where at all possible.

Terminating trains early

Trains do not need to travel the entire length of all rail lines. A terminus or turnback can be installed at almost any station, and this can allow trains to be used more efficiently.

The schematic below shows a common scenario and potentially how trains can be managed. The main line runs from station A to station D, and the branch runs from B to E. A common rule is that trains can be terminated at any large station, but in metros and monorails systems trains normally only terminate at the major stations at the end of the rail line.

Figure 5.27 A Branch Line

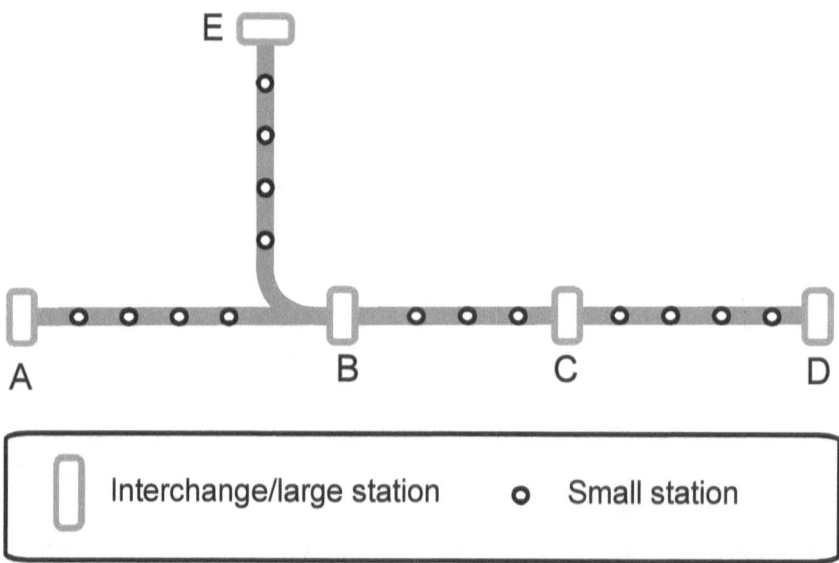

Trains can operate from A to D, but the number of passengers between A and B may be very low. If this is the case then trains may be terminated at station B, and sent back towards C and D. It is possible to terminate half or even most of the trains at station B, rather than send trains onwards. The branch line between stations B and E can also operate as a shuttle. Trains can be terminated at station B and then sent only along the branch line. The creation of shuttle lines has been discussed below.

Terminus's can be installed with significant cost, and can be expensive to maintain. A terminus can provide significant operational flexibility, and can be used to effectively manage a network. The main benefit of a terminus, such as in the schematic above, is to minimise the amount of rollingstock needed to provide a rail service along the line above. Rollingstock is expensive, and managing it efficiently can significantly reduce the cost of operating the network. Often if trains are terminated early, then the number of trains sets needed to provide a service drops.

A rail terminus or turnback should normally be provided at a large station. Whilst in theory it is possible to install a turnback at a small station, so doing means that trains are travelling to this station almost empty, as the train will terminate there and few passengers will use the station. The optimum solution is to install turnbacks at the largest stations, and when trains are being turned around, passengers can join the train.

Loops

A loop is sometimes put at the end of a rail line, so that trains can turn around without stopping. They are common on tram systems, and also for freight lines, especially ones that move bulk materials. They are less common on passenger lines, such as a commuter rail system or a metro, but are sometimes installed. Sydney has a loop in the centre of the city, which is heavily used by many train services each day.

The loop below is on the tram system in Hong Kong, and this one is located at Shau Kei Wan. Tram and light rail systems often have loops, and the benefits of installing a loop are quite significant. Whilst it is a little difficult to see on the photo below, the yellow tram has doors on the side facing the photographer, and the black tram does not. It is possible for trams and light rail vehicles to have a driver's cabin at only one end of the vehicle, and this can save space. Of course to achieve this there needs to be loops at each end of the tram or light rail system, so that the vehicle can turn around.

Tram Loop in Hong Kong

Loops have a number of benefits, and these include:

- Trains do not need to turn around, so the capacity of the rail line can be higher
- There is no need for a driver to change ends, which on many trains takes 5 – 10 minutes, and this time can be used for driving the train
- There is no need to divide or amalgamate trains, as the train does not break its journey

Of course it should be noted that for trams and light rail a loop can be quite small, maybe only 20 to 30 metres across. For metros and commuter rail, or any heavy rail really, a loop will need to be a number of kilometres across, so it will be very large, and quite expensive to build.

Freight systems seem to make the most use of loops. Loops for bulk materials are extremely common in Australia, and almost all collieries and loading ports are structured as a loop. A loop allows the freight train to slowly move around and either load or unload its cargo, and once complete the freight train makes its way back to its departure point to pick up some more material. It is expensive for freight trains to be shunted and trains marshalled and built up, so it needs to be avoided whenever possible. Freight loops are often operated in tandem with unit trains.

Loops seem to be less common for intermodal traffic, and this seems to be related to the land available to move containers. Intermodal terminals are often severely constrained for space, unlike coal ports in Australia which are built away from towns and have plenty of room. Intermodal terminals at ports are often located next to the port where containers are loaded and unloaded, and these are usually terribly cramped. A loop requires quite a lot of space, and most of the intermodal ports in Australia just don't have the space for a loop. The same can be said for intermodal terminals located away from port in cities, again, there is rarely room in an industrial suburb for a freight loop, and a siding is much more common.

The disadvantages of a loop are the cost, and the additional space required to install one. The land is often not available, and unless the rail line is being constructed away from residential areas, the land is very difficult to find.

Multiple Branch Lines

Rail lines can be split to cover more area than a single line. Radial designed systems often contain a large number of splits, and they can perform a very useful function. However, it is possible for a rail line to bifurcate too often, and the rail network below is a rail designer's nightmare. There are far too many splits on the right hand side of the network below.

Figure 5.28 Multiple Splits

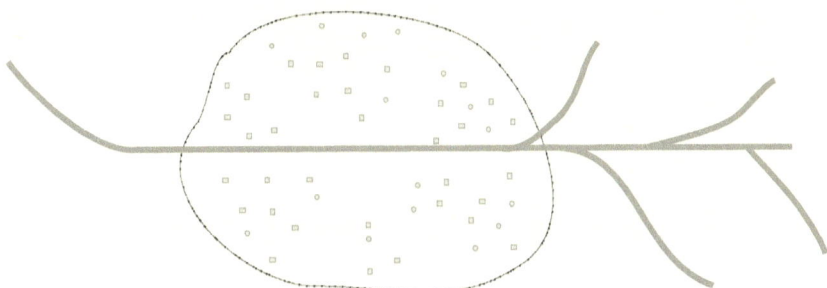

In this situation there would be many problems, but clearly the main problem would be that rail services from the right had side would not be able to get into the middle of the city, because too many lines feed into the centre. The left hand side of the network would be extremely congested, and there would be a very high number of services, regardless of whether these services were needed or not.

When confronted with this kind of rail nightmare, an operational railway has a small number of choices, and these include:
- Close one or more of the lines
- Convert one or more of the shorter lines to shuttles, so that services on this line don't operate all the way into the city centre
- Add additional tracks to the left hand side of the rail network so that there is somewhere for all these services to go
- Build another line into the centre of the city, and put some of the rail lines on the right hand side into this new line

For an operational rail network to balance this passenger loads on rail services in this network would be difficult or maybe even impossible. Another potential problem is of course that the rail line on the left hand side of the network does connect to any destination of any consequence, and so it is highly unlikely that all the services feeding into this line would be needed.

The schematic below shows what the rail system looks like when it has been repaired. The different colours represent different lines, and note that there are now two lines, whereas before there was only one. Also note that network has been extended on the left hand side, and now there are two termini for trains to terminate at and to be turned around. There is also a shuttle, in brown, on the bottom right hand side. This network design is a vast improvement to the one shown above.

Figure 5.29 The rail line re-balanced

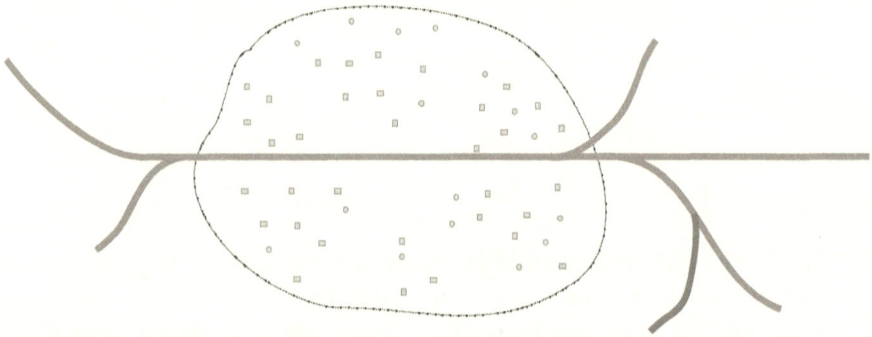

Rail Lines Passing Through the Centre of Cities

Rail lines often move passengers from suburbs into the centre of cities. This very common movement pattern occurs because city centres (CBDs) are congested, and parking, if it is available, is very expensive. This frequently means that in some cities the only rail lines that exist are ones directed at moving people from the suburbs into the city.

A pendulum line is one that passes through a large important destination, and then out again. Often considered to be the hallmark of high quality network design, a pendulum line can bring passengers into a city centre, and then take people out again. Pendulum lines are so described as trains move in and out of the city like a pendulum.

The scenario below shows how to get a pendulum wrong, and in this case the rail line doubles back on itself. The problem with this design is that passengers will alight from the train at the city centre, because then the train returns close to the direction it came from. Passengers will avoid this rail line because it will be quicker to travel from one arm of the rail line to another by another means, often private road vehicle. If the rail line continued through to the other side of the centre of the city, then passengers who needed this transport movement will remain on the train.

Figure 5.30 A poorly designed pendulum line

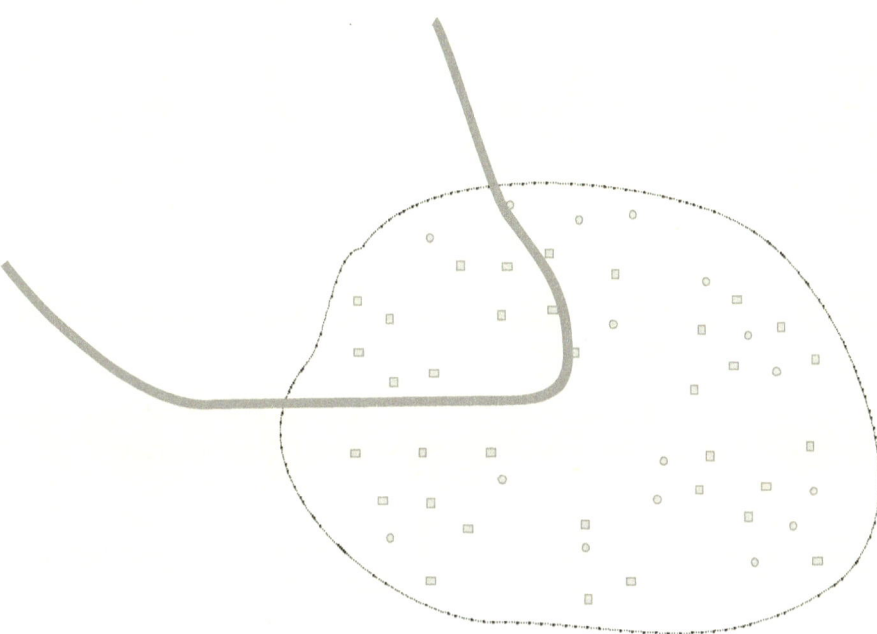

As always there are advantages and disadvantages for everything, including pendulum lines, and the advantages are:
- Trains passing through the city centre and pick up and drop off passengers at the same time
- Trains do not need to terminate, and change direction, so no time is lost at the terminus, which increases the efficiency of train use
- Passengers that wish to travel from one side of the city to the other can do so without interchanging

So it would seem that a pendulum line is a really good idea and should be the standard in rail transportation planning. However, in practise there are problems, and some of these are:

- In actuality it is almost impossible to balance the passenger load on one side of the city to the other, as there will almost always be more passengers travelling to stations on one side than another. This leads to some trains being overloaded on one side of the city, and relatively empty on the other which is undesirable
- There are often natural barriers preventing rail lines passing entirely from one side to another, such as river or a mountain
- Most passengers are probably travelling into the city centre, and would not be interested in continuing their journey into the suburbs to the other side of the city. As a rail path it may not needed
- In order to get the rail line through the city centre, the rail line needs to be positioned so that its path does not pass through some immovable object, and this location for the rail line is not ideal.
- Terminating trains in a city centre allows them to sit at the platform, and passengers can comfortably make their way to their seat without being rushed, and settle in for the trip home

So it really isn't clear if installing pendulum lines is a good decision of not, but some of the critical factors in making this decision are:
- Can a pendulum line even be built, is there a sensible place to put it?
- Will the number of passenger coming into the city be the same or similar on each side of the city?
- Which choice is cheaper; building the pendulum line or having two separate lines?

Some Examples of Network Design – Multiple Lines

Rail systems are often made up of multiple rail lines. A rail line is a part of a rail system in which trains traverse in one continuous trip from one end to the other. Rail lines are often separated from one another, but can also combine together and run alongside each other. Many network design decisions concern the design of multiple rail lines.

In the design of a passenger rail system, the system design is often described in terms of rail lines. Separate lines have services that are separate from one anther, and are timetabled independently. Multiple rail lines can share tracks with one another, and maybe some of the track will be separate. Alternatively they may be completely separate, and share nothing at all. This can be a little misleading. Perhaps the best way of considering a rail line is that services are separate from the rest of the network.

Things are simpler when designing a rail system with only one rail line. Where there are multiple rail lines, then the relationship between these lines needs to be decided. The relationship between the different rail lines can be very important for rail network design.

Junctions vs Interchanges

When rail lines pass over each other, there is a decision needed as to if the lines connect, or if there is no connection at all. Where rail lines converge, there is a junction that provides the ability for rail lines to merge together. Junctions are expensive to maintain, and create timetabling problems, and many rail systems installing junctions to connect two or more rail lines together.

This is an important decision, and in complex rail networks large number of rail lines might cross each other. Where rail lines are unconnected, but cross one another, they will be grade separated, so at different levels/heights. There is no real reason why rail lines should all be connected, and in the schematic below there is no connection other than the interchange for passengers. Trains themselves cannot move from one line to another. This network structure is commonly used for metros, and intermediate capacity metros.

Figure 5.31 Two rail lines, passenger interchange only

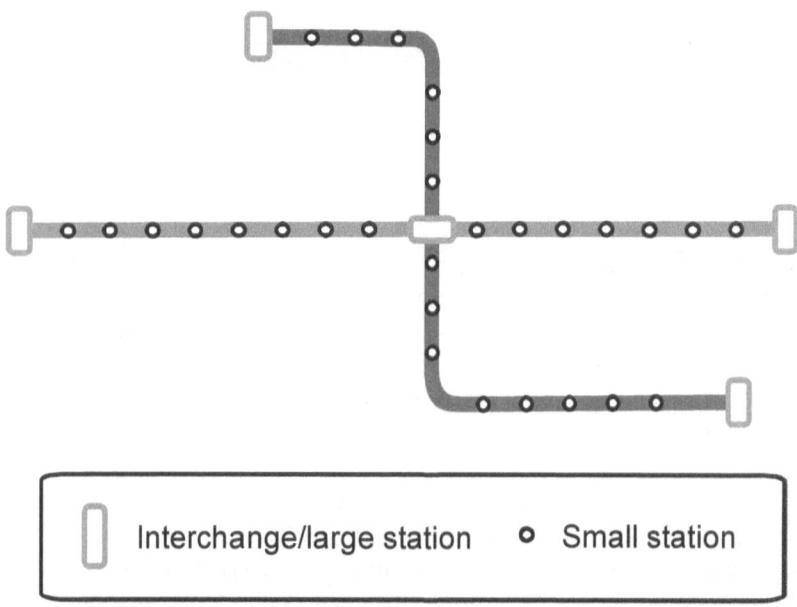

Alternatively, there are many systems where rail lines do connect, and it is possible for one rail line to connect to the other. The picture below shows how this works, and the green line is a path for trains to move from the blue line onto the orange, although it is not drawn this way. The green line is not an extra line, but rather a pathway that trains can take. Whilst it might seem that trains moving along the green line are separate from both the blue and orange lines, in practice there is probably no separation between the rail lines that are alongside each other.

Figure 5.32 Three rail lines, multiple paths possible

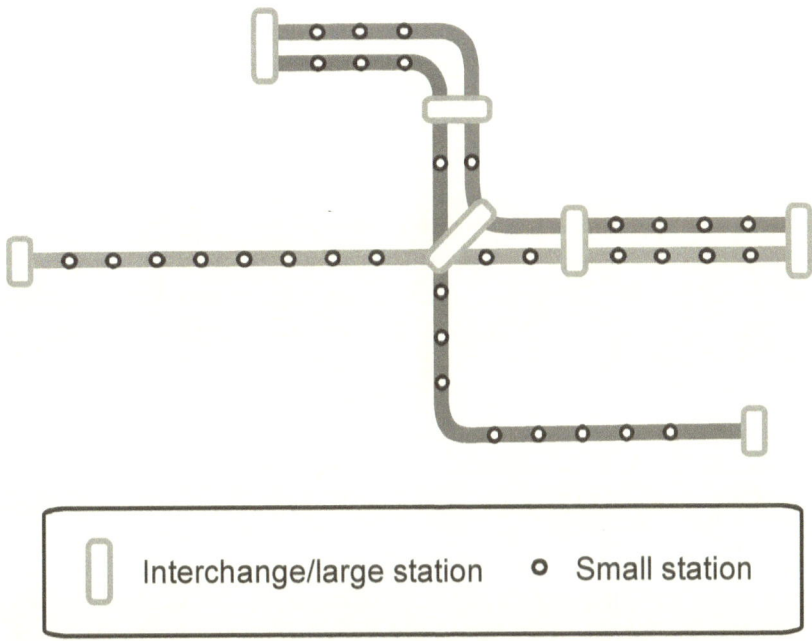

Where a railway can send trains to any direction, it is possible to tailor services to the needs of passengers. Multiple pathways are possible, and so in theory this must be better.

Of course there are also disadvantages, and these are:
- The rail network is more complex when providing this kind of connection, and the timetable will be more complicated and difficult to create, and for passengers to understand and use
- Incidents such as engineering failures will impact more of the network than where the network is separated
- Infrastructure is needed at the junctions to allow the different train movements
- Passenger information systems play more of a role, as passenger now have more options. This can be expensive in terms of maintenance and support
- Connections means turnouts, and this means a signal box somewhere with signallers managing the network. This is expensive

- The turnouts in the connections will need to have signallers managing them, and be thrown when trains need to go along a different path. This can increase the minimum headway.
- Trains when purchased will need to be able to be compatible with both rail lines, rather than just one. This can make rollingstock purchases more expensive.

Whilst one connection might seem fairly easy to manage, large numbers of connections in a complex network can make the system so complex that passengers have difficult knowing where to go. The number of possible combinations of routes will increase dramatically, and finding a pathway through is a little like navigating through a maze. The trend in Australia has been to attempt to minimise the number of different paths, as it confuses passengers.

Metros almost never have connections between lines, and this is one of the secrets to their overwhelming success. As connections are costly and messy to manage, passengers in most metro systems will interchange from one line to another. Even in a relatively short journey a passenger may interchange two or three times. No connections means that trains can operate more frequently, as trains do not need to wait for turnouts to move from one position to another.

Tram systems commonly have many connections, and a large tram network is full of them. Inter-connections between lines are very frequent in Melbourne, and the network map gets quite complicated with the number of different possible combinations. Connections (ie turnouts) are cheap in a tram system because the entire network is almost always at the same level, ie, one line normally does not pass over the top of another (of course there are exceptions).

Freight systems can also be quite complex, and full of interconnections between lines. Freight traffic can have a large variety of different destinations and departure points, and a large freight network will have an extremely large number of different possible paths for freight trains to use. In a combined passenger/freight system much of the complexity may be because of the freight system and it's need to send freight trains in many and varied directions. In some freight systems essentially everything is connected to everything. Where a passenger and freight line is mixed together, then the rail system can be extremely complex, and very difficult to manage. This challenging situation really needs its own chapter, and perhaps another book.

High speed rail lines do not normally cross each other, as they are so expensive to construct it is unlikely there would be 2 in the same place. Where there are 2, it is best for these rail lines to be grade separated, with a flyover to allow trains to pass over the other rail line without hindrance.

It is with regional and commuter trains that many of the decisions are needed with creating connections. Regional and commuter services may have many different paths and stopping patterns, and the number of different possible combinations can be very large. A decision should be made on an economic and public benefit basis on when to include a large junction, or not, but in practice these types of networks have large numbers of connections. This difficult area is not discussed any further in this book, but it is possible to analyse the cost of the junction and the number of passengers who get a benefit from the presence of the junction.

Shuttles

A shuttle is a train that moves back and forwards, captured within one part of the rail line. Shuttles terminate early, and often travel between only two stations. Shuttles require passengers to disembark at the connecting station, and then to transfer to the shuttle service. A shuttle service can be constructed on the branch line in the schematic above.

Shuttles usually only service a very small number of stations. Whilst 2 stations seems common, there is no reason why this number should be 2 and not 3 nor 4. Shuttles can connect lines that many people on the main rail line would not want to go down. Shuttles are a solution to the problem of how to balance the movement of trains down many separate lines.

Some examples of shuttles are:
- The Disney train in Hong Kong that connects the main metro line at Sunny Bay to the theme park
- The tourist shuttle from Beitou to Xin Beitou in Taipei, that connects the main metro line to the tourist area with the volcanic hot springs hotels
- The train in Sydney that connects Lidcombe station with Olympic Park, where the 2000 Summer Olympic games were held

- The Carlingford line is Sydney is operated as a shuttle, as the number of people wishing to catch the train from that line is very small

The network structure of a shuttle service is shown below. Trains start and finish on separated lines, and do not move along the entire length of the rail network, as shown below.

Figure 5.33 A shuttle and main line

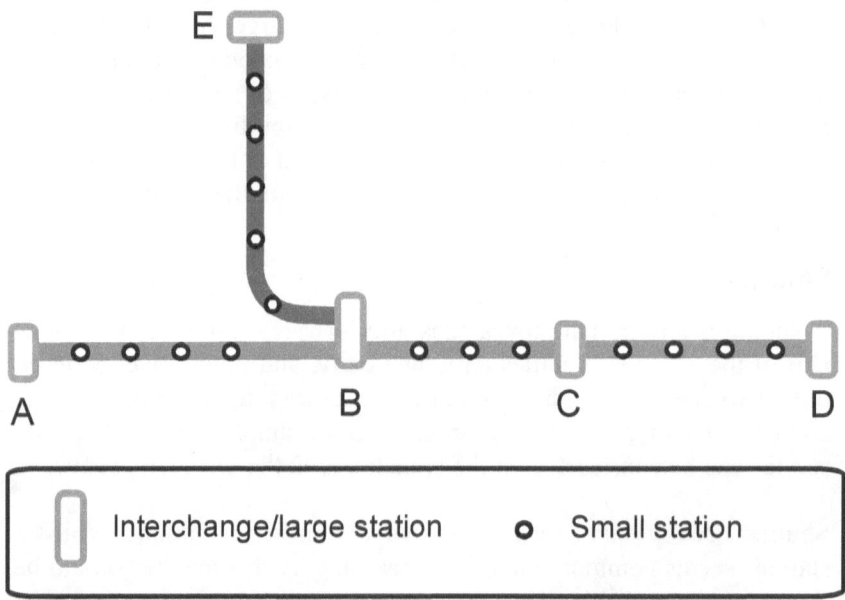

Shuttles are often unpopular with passengers, as they need to change trains and this can be time consuming. Passengers want to get settled on their train, read a book if they are sitting down, and then arrive at their destination. Interchanges, especially where they are poorly designed, which they often are, are extremely unpopular with passengers, and installing them will result in a far lower level of service. Shuttles also result in longer travel times, as the interchange time now is included in the total travel time.

In some cases shuttles are used because the other rail line is a different type to the main line, such as a monorail connecting with heavy rail system, or more commonly, a light rail system connecting with a heavy rail. In Taiwan very unusually a cable car system forms a shuttle service, because the steepness of the terrain, which is integrated into the transport system of the city of Taipei. It must be remembered that where a different type of rail system is used then a shuttle is almost always the result.

Shuttles are extremely popular with rail operators, as they divide the network up into sections and this makes the network far easier to manage. Problems with one line can be contained to one line, and the complexity of the network is far lower. Rail operators are often tempted to convert small lines into shuttles, but can be prevented from so doing by the government, passengers, the local community, and politicians (which is not necessarily a bad thing).

Some lines may operate as combined lines during part of the day, such as peak, and as shuttles during the rest of the day. Alternatively, on weekend the line may operate as a shuttle, and on a weekday as a combined line. Many variations are possible.

Perhaps the greatest importance of a shuttle is that it is often used when problems occur on a train system. Some rail systems are very prone to problems, and when these occur then trains can be formed into a shuttle service on either side of the problem.

When designing a rail system it is often tempting to create a shuttle. Where there are a small number of stations that need to be connected to the system, and there is limited capacity, then one solution is to use a shuttle. Overall it's best not to create shuttles, despite their cheapness and ease of construction, as they are generally not popular, but they can be a cost effective solution to a transport problem.

Two Rail Lines Sharing Stations

Rail lines can be combined together to provide a higher and more frequent level of services than with divided lines. The schematic below shows how rail lines might appear when not running alongside one another.

Figure 5.34 Two rail lines running side by side

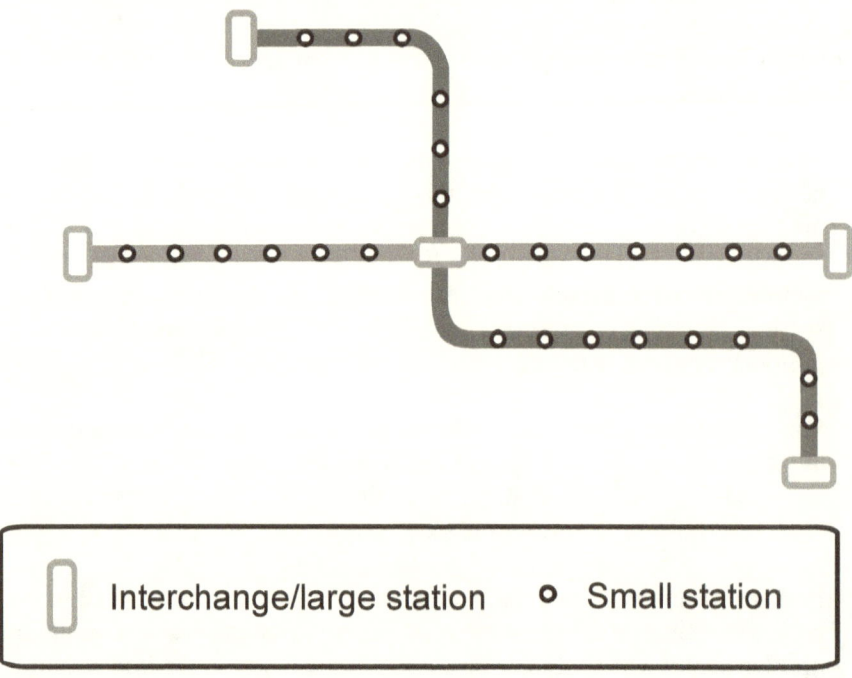

Note in the schematic above there is an interchange at one point, and the lines run parallel for a large part of their length. The alternative is shown below, and in this schematic the lines have been combined for their common length.

Figure 5.35 Shared Stations on Two Lines

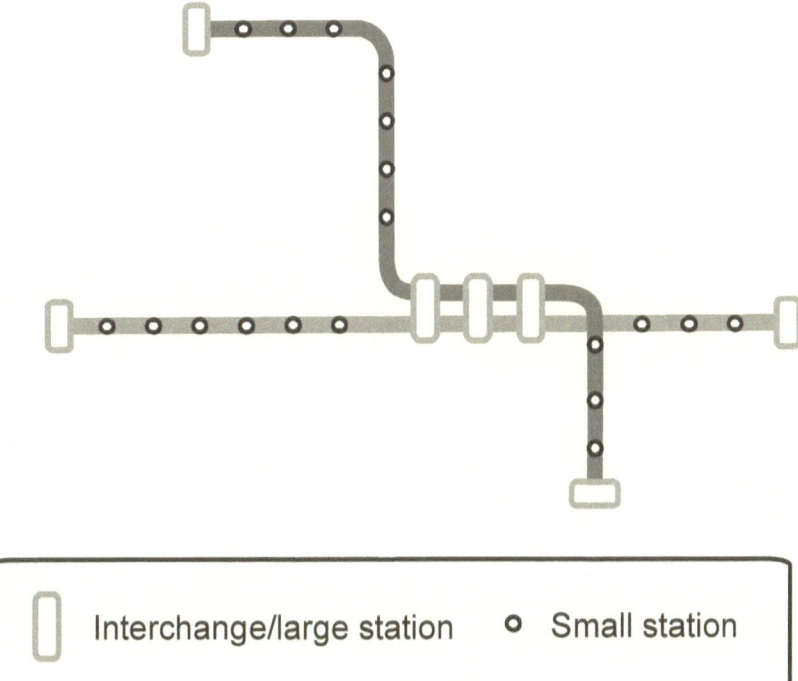

Interchange/large station   o Small station

The network lines are drawn as being side by side, by in reality these lines often would be running over the same track. In Hong Kong there are rail lines that run along side each other and are entirely separate This type of decision, whether to combine lines together, is a common one, and there are, like all the different decision needed in this section, advantages and disadvantages. There are a number of papers written on the design of transport networks, with a very heavy focus on buses, and the combined structure is almost always seen as being superior, but this is not necessarily the case.

So some of the advantages for sharing stations between different lines are:
- The number of services will be higher over the combined section, providing passengers with a higher frequency of services
- The construction cost of a combined system is lower, as either the stations are shared, or the track is shared.

- For high value locations such as the centre of cities, having lines operate together is better as people want to go to specific locations that both lines connect to

However, there are some disadvantages, and these are:
- If lines A & B are very busy, then combining them together will result in a lower number of services compared to separate lines, where tracks are shared.
- The coverage of the city or area will be better if the lines are separated, as there are more stations
- If there is a disruption on one line, then this disruption will impact the other line, as there is a common section in the middle. Separated lines are more reliable in general

So overall the recommendation is that rail lines should be separated if the traffic warrants it, and this is common in very large cities. This is especially the case for metro systems, where rail lines should almost never be combined. In smaller cities, with a small amount of rail traffic, combining rail lines together can make very good sense, especially for rail commuter traffic, or regional trains, where the train frequency would be too low to otherwise provide a good quality service.

Grid Layouts vs a Radial Design

Grid networks are very common, especially for large cities with multiple metro lines. The basic idea is that the entire city, or the centre of the city, has a very good level of service and is covered with a grid of rail lines. This type of network is unsuited for freight networks, but can be ideal for large cities.

Figure 5.36 Rail Grid Design

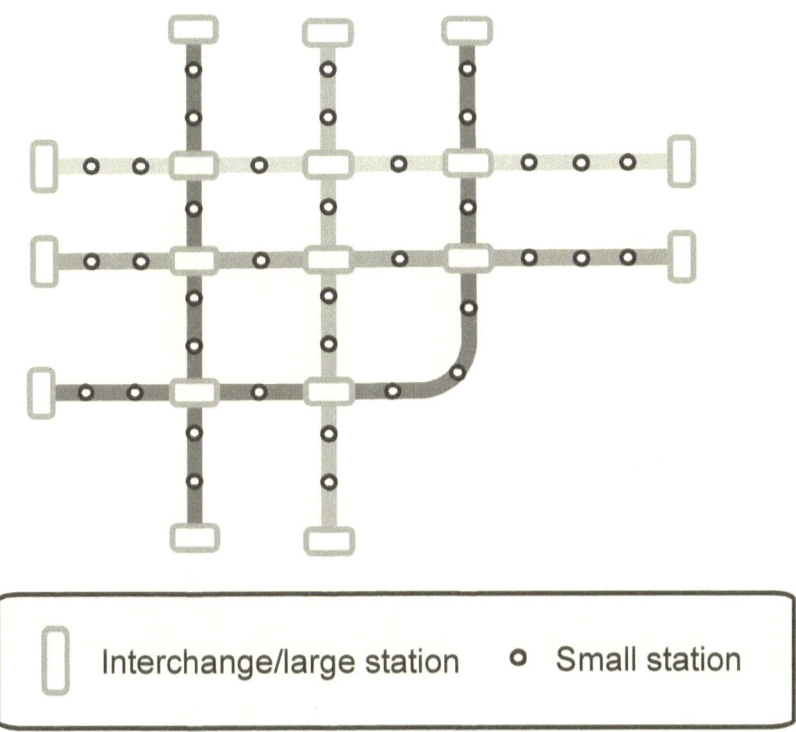

Interchange/large station   o Small station

Grid networks almost always require passengers to interchange between lines, but of course there are exceptions. The author's experience of Tokyo was that the rail system was dominated by rail services moving as in a traditional grid, but a small number of services were moved from one line to another, such as the express train to Narita airport.

Grid designs have a large number of interchange stations. In the relatively simple design above passengers can interchange at no less than 8 stations. A grid design will often require numerous interchanges for passengers, even for short trips.

The alternative to a grid design is a radial design, where trains radiate out from a central point. Radial designs are common in commuter and regional networks, where rail services move from the centre of the city to the suburbs and outlying towns. A radial design is shown below.

Figure 5.37 A Radial System Design

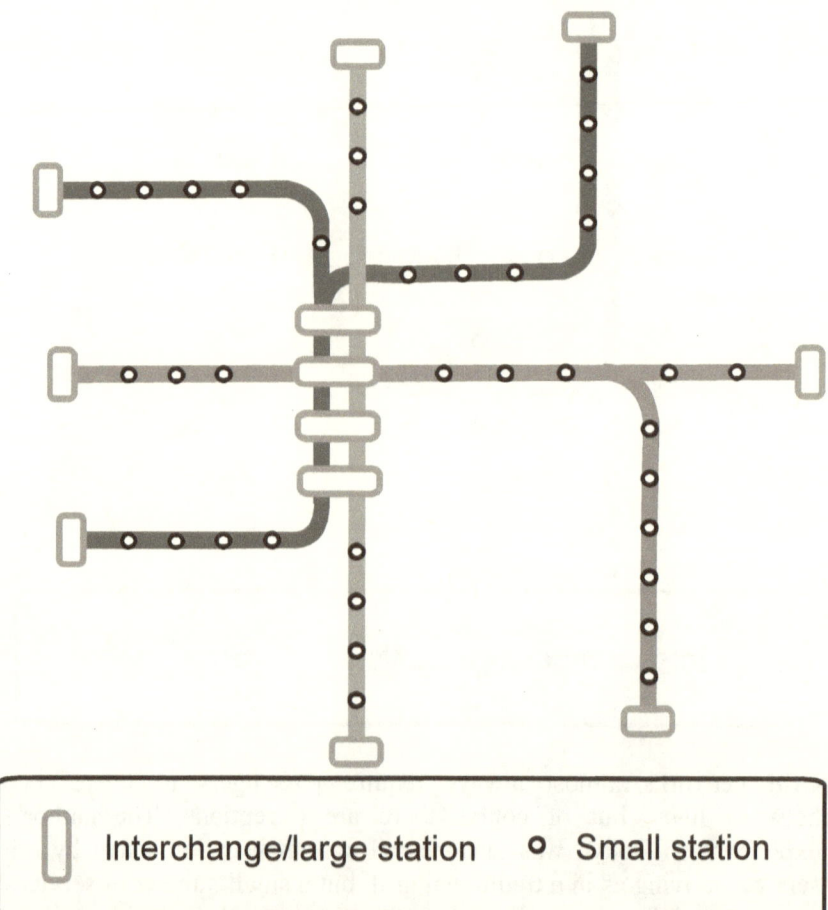

The schematic above shows trains moving from a central point through to the edges of a city or CBD, and further from the centre the green and the blue lines diverge.

Radial designs are also quite common, and seem to occur without any serious planning. Most medium size cities in countries with rail networks will have this kind of rail system, because there will be a major rail line into the city, and then a couple of others linking a few nearby towns, giving rise to the radial structure.

Ring Designs

A ring design is where the rail system has a ring around the centre of the city. A ring railroad may pass several other rail lines, and connect them all together. The ring line does not pass through the centre of the city, but around the periphery. Ring rail lines are uncommon, and seem to be difficult to build in practice.

The schematic below shows what a ring railroad might look like.

Figure 5.38 A Ring Rail Line

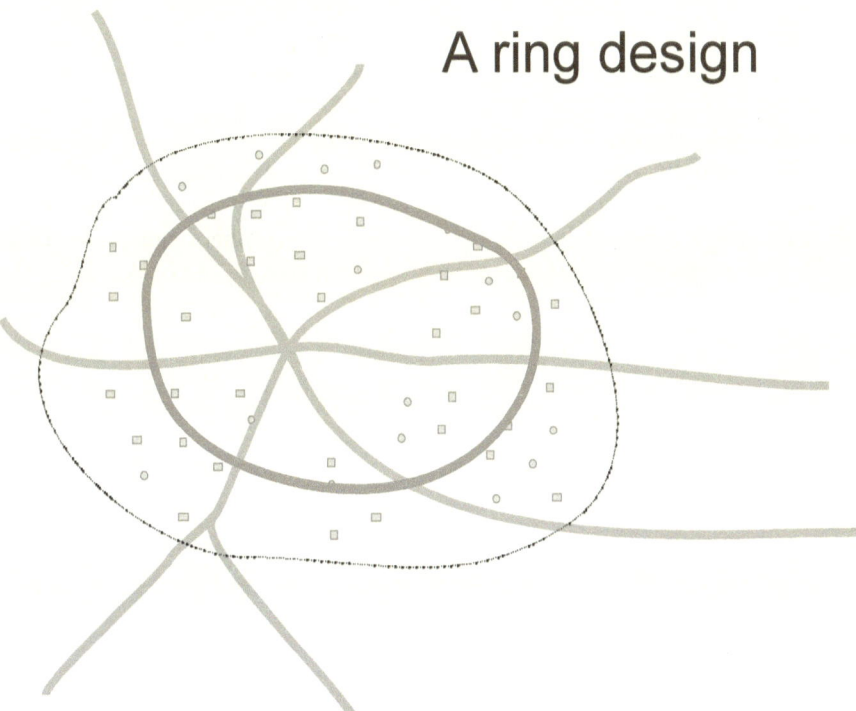

Ring rail lines seem to be often proposed as a new type of rail transport project, and in Australia there have been many suggestions to build these in one place or another. However, they are hard to economically justify, despite seeming to make very good sense to build. Buses seem to be able to maintain transport connections between different lines, and using buses is far more common than building a ring railroad.

The main problem is that ring railroads need large numbers of people using them to be justifiable, and as the ring does not pass through the centre of the city, getting these passenger numbers is difficult. Moscow metro has a ring railroad, but Moscow is the largest city in Europe, and has very large numbers of people using the system each day. Beijing also has a ring metro, and this was one of the first lines constructed. The general rule seems to be that only a very large city can justify having a ring railroad.

Rail Systems and Connections to HSR

HSR lines are very expensive to construct, and so there is a strong desire on the part of government to minimise the cost. One way of doing this is to construct the rail line so that it avoids the centre of the city, and another public transport connection is needed to provide passengers with a way to get into the centre of the city.

The schematic below shows the "normal" configuration of an HSR line, and where it terminates in the centre of a city. It terminates at an interchange between line A and B, and so passengers can make their way from the HSR system onto the local rail line.

Figure 5.39 Shared Stations on Two Lines

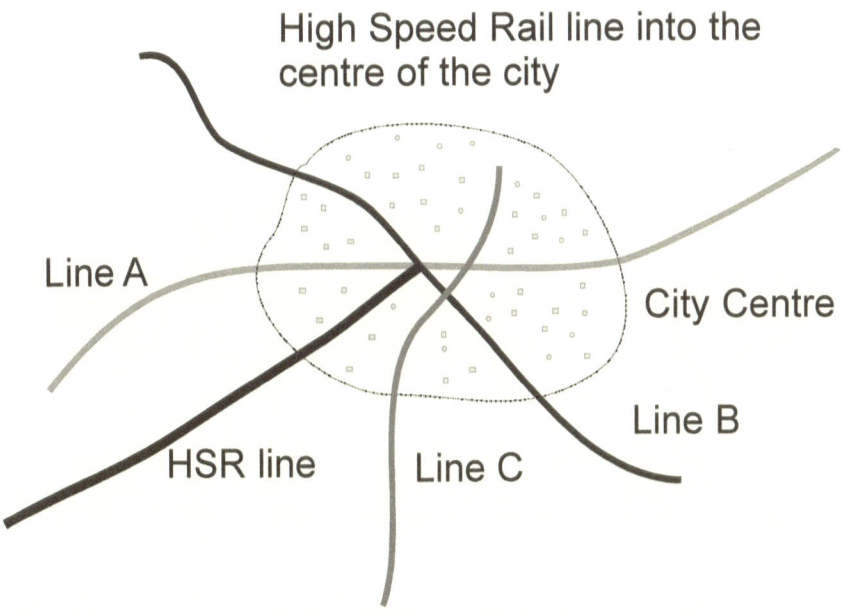

The alternative to this layout is a terminus or HSR station outside of the city. This type of network design is also common, and the HSR station Kaohsiung in Taiwan is built this way, and does not extend to the centre of the city. This design is shown below

Figure 5.40 Shared Stations on Two Lines

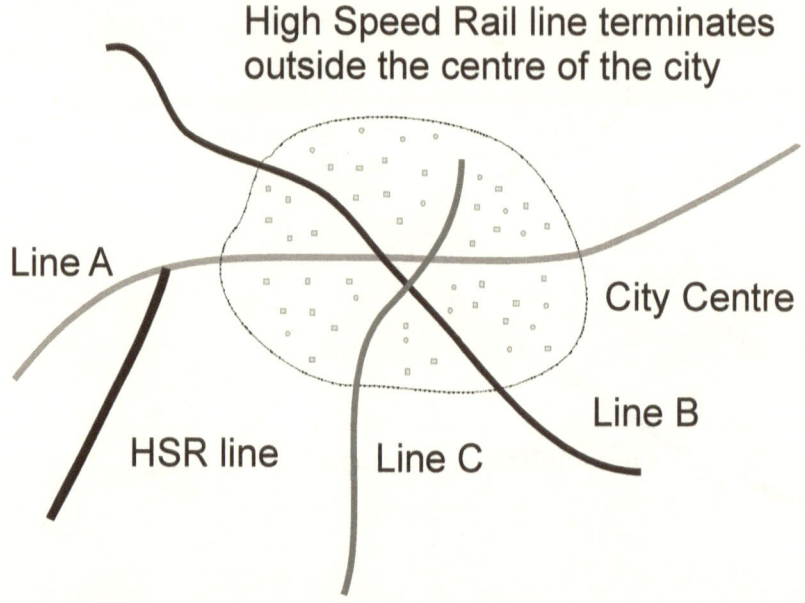

The HSR line does not enter the centre of the city, but terminates early, and then passengers make their way on the local rail line into the centre of the city. This type of design is substantially inferior to one where the HSR line reaches into the centre of the city, but can be dramatically cheaper. This network layout avoids the need to build a large terminal in the centre of cities where land can be very scarce, and difficult to obtain for a large rail terminal. The cost of the land in any major city can be very large, and again land does not need to be acquired to build this system.

REFERENCES

1. Cho-Lam Lau, J. *The Performance of public transport operations, land-use and urban transport planning in Hong Kong*, Cities, Vol 14, No 3, pp 145 – 153, 1997

Week 6

Structure/Loading Gauge and Platform Heights

This chapter is about the maximum size of trains, and grades. Many constraints are placed on what trains can move through rail networks, and in many cases these restrictions are quite strict. A train that can use one rail network may not be able to use another. In many cases these restrictions mean that only certain types of rollingstock can be purchased, potentially with a reduced capacity to what is needed.

Track and space around the track is very important for the choice of what rollingstock can use the track. Loading and structure gauge is a term that applies to the space through which a train moves. Structure gauge is the space that the infrastructure must stay out of for a train to make its way through a rail system. This includes platforms, where platform edges must not intrude into the structure gauge to the point where a train will strike the platform when entering a station. Platform strikes are uncommon, and when they occur can cause serious damage to a train. Usually the paint is stripped from the side of the train next to the platform.

Many different types of trains cannot accept large grades, and where the space around the track is small then the rollingstock will need to be small as well. In many ways, the track will affect many other rail systems, which is why it is so important. This chapter presented the basic of broadly describing some features and the space around the track.

Loading and Structure Gauge

Railways have specific terms for describing the space required for a train to pass through on a network. These terms are commonly used, and understood between countries. These terms are a rare example of some jargon that is used in Australia/UK and the US interchangeably. They are:
- Structure gauge
- Loading gauge
- Kinematic envelope

The structure gauge is a defined space around the track, into which no equipment or infrastructure is permitted. If any equipment strays into that space, then a train may strike it as is comes past. The structure gauge is the space allocated to trains to pass along the track and is larger than the train that passes through it, to allow for movement of the train and any possible slight deviations of the train from its design size. Trains are never as large as the structure gauge.

Structure gauge is what infrastructure maintainers use for maintaining clearances. They need clear cut guidance on what the structure gauge is, and any large railway and many smaller ones will have detailed standards on structure gauge and what sizes are required. It is not sufficient for an infrastructure maintainer to be told the loading gauge, as this is information is not useful and cannot be used for maintenance purposes.

The loading gauge is the area in which a train must fit in when stationary. Loading gauge is relevant to rollingstock and its design. It's important because the loading gauge determines which trains can be procured, what size they are, and hence their capacity. Loading gauges play an important role in determining the capacity of a system.

The kinematic envelope is the space through which a train might move, taking into account superelevation (cant), the suspension of the train, the end throw and centre throw. Calculating the kinematic envelope is a process called dynamic gauging. Calculating the kinematic envelope can be a paper exercise, and there are formulas that describe how to do this. The kinematic envelope increases where there are curves, as the curves result in the end of the train protruding away from the track.

Whilst changes to structure gauge are a common type of rail transport project, the cost can be high. Changes to structure gauge are very expensive, and can involve large scale changes to infrastructure. To complete a change from one structure gauge to a larger one, every point in a rail system or rail line at that structure gauge needs to be converted, it's not sufficient to convert some or even most of the track. There is no benefit for doing most of it, and so one problematic point in a rail system can stop the conversion to a larger structure gauge.

In many cases the maximum possible loading and structure and loading gauge is difficult to change. Train lines often pass next to structures and buildings that cannot be moved or demolished, and so it is not possible to change the width of the train, or the space through which the train passes. Some stations are heritage listed, and so major changes are not possible. In these cases rail operators need to manage their rollingstock as best they can, given the constraints on size. Problems with the maximum permitted size of trains can be very expensive to manage.

Loading gauges do not need to be square or rectangular. The diagram below shows a typical profile of a loading gauge. The shape down below is typical of what a loading gauge outline looks like. Whilst not always this shape, they often are, and so a train that is a perfect rectangle would not be permitted to operate on many rail networks if it were above a certain size.

Figure 6.1 Typical Loading Gauge

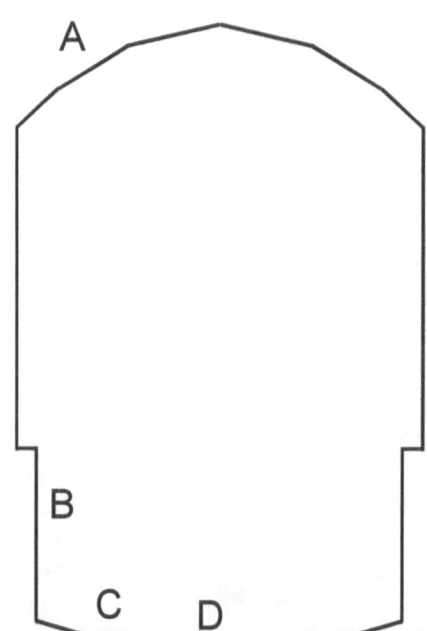

The letters in the diagram above refer to various parts of the outline. These are:

A/ This is the curved part of the roof of the train. Most passenger loading gauges are curved, and this allows the construction of arch shaped tunnels, which are cheaper to construct than tunnels with rectangular ceilings in many cases.

B/ There are often cut-outs for platforms for passenger trains. There is always a risk that passengers will fall between the train and the platform, and it's best if this gap is kept as small as possible. One way of managing this is to have the train overhang the platform, so that the gap is minimised.

C/ For the bottom of the train the loading gauge is flat and even all the way across, and is higher is some parts compared to others. In the schematic above the corner is cutout (same as D). This is to allow the many different types of rail side devices to operate and exist. Also the ballast is sometimes too high, and so contact with the ballast is minimised by having the train higher than the track.

D/ This is the lowest part of the train, and where the train runs along the track.

The kinematic envelope should be within the structure gauge, especially for curves. If the kinematic envelope extends to the structure gauge or beyond it, then trains may strike objects and structures next to the track (such as platforms). The kinematic envelope needs to fall within the structure gauge.

One way to determine the kinematic envelope is to run different trains along the track and see what happens. Whilst this is possible, it is far better to calculate the kinematic envelope, because if a train strikes an object it tends to make a bit of a mess, and the damage can be substantial. Also once a rail line is constructed it can be difficult for the structure gauge to be changed, so any errors can have a very long term impact. So for most rail projects, the kinematic envelope will be calculated first before construction begins.

So of the things that need to be considered in the calculation of a kinematic envelope are:
- The superelevation of the track
- Track movement
- The suspension of the train
- Loads on the train, for example, fully loaded passenger trains compared to empty ones
- Rail wear
- Tilting functions of trains, including both passive and active tilt
- Curves in the track

Structure, loading gauge and the kinematic envelope are most relevant to a railway in tunnels, but are also important at stations and particularly at platforms. Tunnels have very limited space available, and increasing the size of the tunnel once constructed is a messy and expensive business. If a train can't fit into a tunnel, there is little a rail organisation can do to get it to fit in, other than making major engineering changes. Some things can be done, and trains with hard suspensions and very little movement in the springs that support the train can move through slightly smaller tunnels. Also, trains that move at lower speeds can also fit into smaller tunnels, as they bounce around less when moving at lower speeds. Where a railway needs to move a large train through a small structure gauge, this can sometimes be achieved with dramatically reducing the speeds of the train to a point where the railway is confident that the train will not strike any object.

If a train strikes an object (again, such as a platform) the result can be very bad indeed. Whilst a glancing blow may not be very serious, a full impact with a fixed object is really a train crash, and passengers can be killed. That's bad, so railways will put a lot of effort into ensuring that trains cannot collide with anything fixed. One of the key responsibilities of maintenance staff is to ensure that a collision does not occur.

Vegetation often will grow into the space where the train runs. Trees often line rail corridors, and as trees grow they can come into contact with passing trains. This can be very common in some networks, and it's common in Australia. It's mostly harmless for trains to brush alongside trees, and most tree branches are quite soft. Trees can present problems to the overhead wiring system, or reduce the visibility of signals so that drivers cannot see them. In these situations trees can be a problem, or when they fall over in a big storm this can also block running lines.

In some cases trees may be planted on stations. The branches of trees may grow to the point where they intrude into the structure gauge, and even strike a train. Trees on stations, where they are healthy and continue to grow, will need to be routinely pruned to keep them outside of the structure gauge

It has become common to calculate the movement of trains, and the swept volume resulting from this, with software, and some packages have been written which work quite well. The software can visually display and calculate the movement of trains through tunnels, and so any problem areas that need to be addressed are identified. Whilst a hand calculation is possible, this method is increasingly rarely used. The calculation of the structure and loading gauges and a key part of the planning process, but given the technical detail necessary, and the cost, and the level of detail needed to carry out the analysis, this would typically be done very late in the process (but definitely before construction).

Loading gauges, as mentioned above, often have complicated shapes. To simplify things, they are often described in terms of height and width.

Figure 6.2 Simplified Description of Train Size

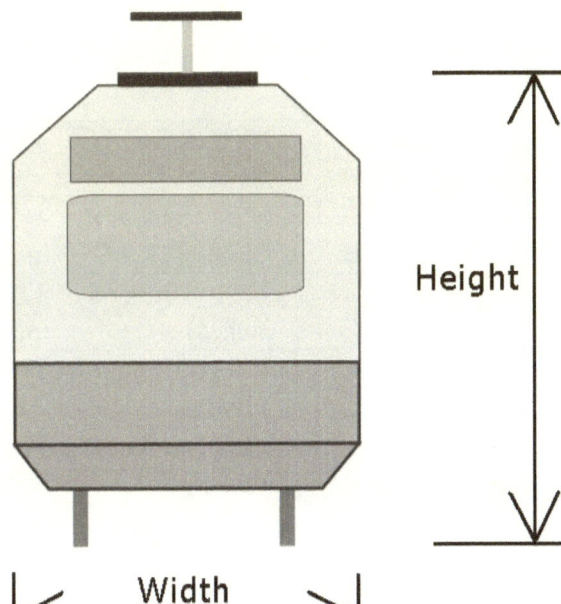

The pantograph above the train is not normally included in the loading gauge. In practice the pantograph is spring loaded so it can move up and down, and can usually be pushed down almost flat with the top of the train. Where the pantograph sits there is usually a hole/recess so that it can be strapped down, i.e. when transporting the train by sea.

The space in which the pantograph is sits into is called the pantograph well.

Below are some common loading gauges. It is only a small selection of the large number of loading gauges currently in use. Worldwide there would be hundreds of different loading gauges.

Table of Loading Gauges

Country	Name	Width (mm)	Height (mm)
UK	W6	2820 (9 feet 4 inches)	3965 (13 feet)
	W7	2778 (9 feet 1 inch)	3966 (13 feet)
	W9	2996 (9 feet 10 inches)	3967 (13 feet)
	C1	2744 (9 feet)	3772 (12 feet 4.5 inches)
(high speed)	UK1	2720 (8 feet 11 inches)	3965 (13 feet)
US, Canada, Mexico	AAR plate B	3250 (10 feet 8 inches)	4620 (15 feet 2 inches)
	AAR plate C	3251 (10 feet 8 inches)	4720 (15 feet 6 inches)
	AAR plate E	3252 (10 feet 8 inches)	4800 (15 feet 9 inches)
	AAR plate F	3253 (10 feet 8 inches)	5180 (17 feet)
European Union	UIC-A	3150 (10 feet 4 inches)	4320 (14 feet 2 inches)
	UIC-B	3151 (10 feet 4 inches)	4321 (14 feet 2 inches)
	UIC-C	3152 (10 feet 4 inches)	4650 (15 feet 3 inches)
Germany	G1	3153 (10 feet 4 inches)	4280 (14 feet 0.5 inches)
	G2	3154 (10 feet 4 inches)	4650 (15 feet 3 inches)

Table of Loading Gauges

Country	Name	Width (mm)	Height (mm)
Spain/Portugal	Iberian gauge	3300 (10 feet 10 inches)	4300 (14 feet 1 inch)

Platform Heights

Standardising platform heights in a rail network greatly aids efficiency and reduces cost. This is the ideal, and new modern networks are constructed such that all the platforms are the same height. However, in many older rail systems, there is more than one platform height, and potentially there could be several different standard heights.

Platforms are may not be at the same height as the train floor. It is preferable for modern train systems to have the platform as close as possible to the floor of the train, and at the same height, but this often does not happen. The photo below shows the regional tilt train in Taiwan, and note that the floor of the train is higher than the platform, and there is a step between the train and the platform.

Taiwanese Train with Door Flaps

Platform heights installed in rail systems have been decreasing over time. This is especially true for trams and light rail, where platform heights are dropping significantly. Trams often run at street level, and stepping into a high floor tram can be quite daunting, especially for people with disabilities. It's best for disabled people getting into trams to have the floor as low as possible. It is seen as desirable to reduce the height of platforms as much as possible, and rollingstock manufacturers are often keen to announce any reductions in floor heights of their products.

The step fills the space between the train and the platform. The step is often slightly higher than the platform, so that if the platform is curved or too close to the train then the step won't hit the platform.

It is engineering challenging to make the floor of the tram very low. Ultra-low floor trams have had some significant engineering problems, with cracks developing in the body of the trams, which were quite serious and needed substantial repairs. The lower floor puts higher forces on the body of the tram, and these stresses can cause higher maintenance costs and maintenance problems.

Ultra-low floor trams, notwithstanding their engineering problems provide a better service to customers. The step up into the tram is a small one, often only 180mm, which is low. This is enough for people to comfortably enter the tram from road level, and so this technology is still being developed (and perfected).

Low floor trams are higher than ultra-floor trams, and are about 300-350mm from the ground or platform, or about 1 foot in the English imperial system of measurement. Most people can negotiate this kind of step up from the road.

Higher speed trains will generally require higher platforms, at least as high as 550mm. The higher platform allows for structural changes in the rollingstock that make it stronger, and allow for higher speeds. Trams and light rail vehicles with ultra-low floors are limited in speed to about 100 kms/hr, or perhaps even lower.

There are many different platform heights in use around the world today. The variety is enormous, although attempts are being made to standardise to specific heights. It seems that 550mm is the minimum height for larger commuter trains, although 760 mm platforms are also used. In Australia and Hong Kong platform heights of 1100mm are used, which is high enough that if passengers fall off the platform onto the tracks then they will injured from the fall.

Where the platform is a different height to the floor of the train, the preference is to make the floor of the train higher. Passengers will step up into the train, and not down. It is considered by some that it's dangerous for passengers to step down into a train, and so this configuration is avoided if at all possible.

Rarely rollingstock is designed that can accommodate different platform heights. This can be achieved through steps that can vary in height to allow for the different platform heights. Rollingstock with this feature can be very expensive.

European Union decision 2002/735/EC specifies that high speed trains should be designed to a platform height of 550mm or 760mm. However, for trains that operate in the UK 915mm was specified, and for the Netherlands 840mm was specified. Even within a standard designed to force uniformity between member states, there is significant differences in the platform heights.

In designing a new rail line or more stations, and where platform height are different throughout a network and there is a need to extend the system, system designers face a number of choices:
1/ modify the existing platforms to a standard height
2/ have two different sets of platform heights, and different rollingstock that is designed for each
3/ continue with different platform heights, and order specialised rollingstock that can accommodate different platform heights.
4/ Design very long platforms that have two different heights, and so able to accept different trains with different floor heights

It's always best to have one standard height throughout a rail system, but there are many examples where this was not possible.

So overall we can observe the following with platform gaps:

- The higher the platform gap, the higher the structural stiffness of the corresponding train
- Lower platforms provide a better service to customers

- Platforms heights have steadily reduced over time in many countries

The Kinematics of Train Movement and other useful equations

It is important in the planning of any new rail line or extension to calculate the time taken to get from one end of the rail line to another. This information can be used to estimate how many people will use the rail line, or the utility of the rail line to people near the rail line. For freight it is beneficial to know the total trip time. The travel time of any rail service is an important metric that should be understood when assessing any change to a rail system.

Kinematics is the study of the motion of bodies, without any consideration of the forces involved in creating that motion. Whilst most readers may think of kinematics as something that is studied by high school students about small objects being thrown around, this topic is actually very relevant to the movement of trains, as they, strangely enough, are physical bodies, and many of the equations in kinematics can be applied successfully to train movement.

Travel time is a key parameter in the design of any rail system. Railways are very expensive to build, and rail systems are often implemented due to their superior speed. Rail needs to provide substantial benefits to justify its very high construction and maintenance cost, and speed can be one of those. To take one example of this, metro trains moving around a city need to exceed 30 kms/hr to really justify the expense of construction. Buses and other road vehicles may travel between 10 to 30 kms/hr, and trains need to be just a little faster than that. As we will see below, a common speed for metro services is 30 kms/hr.

So travel time is a key piece of information. So how can this be estimated? There are a number of equations that are used for calculating travel times, and these are the standard kinematics equations of motion that can be found in any high school textbook on physics. To write them down again, here they are:

$$Speed = \frac{distance}{time} \quad (1)$$

$$Time = \frac{velocity}{acceleration} \quad (2)$$

$$v^2 = u^2 + 2as \qquad (3)$$

$$s = ut + \frac{1}{2}at^2 \qquad (4)$$

$$v = u + at \qquad (5)$$

Another useful equation, derived from equation (3) above, is:

$$s = \frac{v^2}{2a} \qquad (6)$$

This equation is used for distances for stopping, and for distances to reach specific speeds when starting from 0 kms/hr.

The terms are:

v = final velocity
u = initial velocity
t = time
a = acceleration
s = distance

So how can we describe the motion of trains along a rail line? The graph below roughly shows how a train moves, and is applicable for trains moving through rail systems in a city, or in a metro line. The acceleration of a train as it leaves a station can be described in terms of speed and distance. As the train accelerates its speed increases, as what this looks like is shown below in graphical form.

Figure 6.3 An Accelerating Train

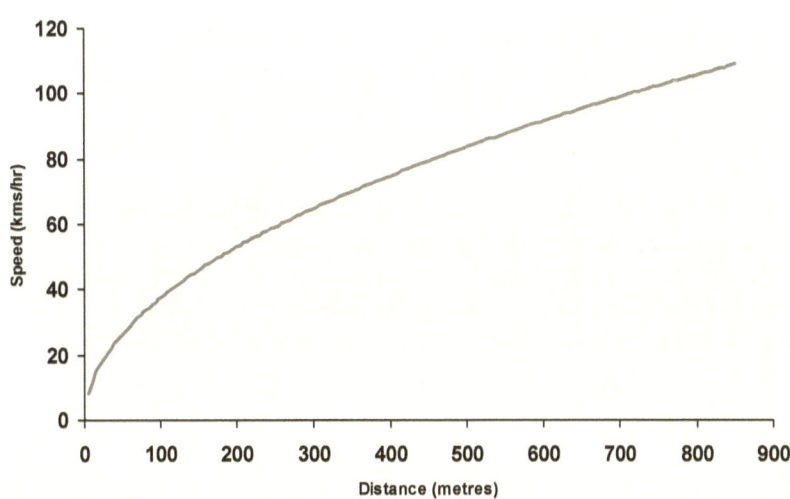

It takes hundreds of metres for a train to reach its top speed, or possibly even more. Cars can accelerate very quickly, and can get to maximum speed much faster. A train is not the same as a car, and accelerates more slowly. High speed trains make takes minutes to reach top speed, and sometimes people underestimate the time it takes for a train to reach top speed.

For closely spaced stations, such as in a metro system, careful consideration is needed of the spacing between stations. As a train takes so long to get up to high speeds, if stations are spaced too closely together then the train will never reach an acceptable speed. Furthermore, should the average speed drop too low, then the public will avoid the system. In practice a spacing of at least 1 km between stations is appropriate for metro stations, or even more, otherwise the average speed will be too low. The average speed is calculated below.

For a train system that needs to stop more frequently than once per kilometre, a light rail or a tram system might be more appropriate. These systems are more suited for frequent stopping. Light rail systems often run at street level, whereas metro systems are usually below ground. As light rail systems are faster and quicker to board, the slower travel speed is not such a problem. Light rail systems, especially where there are many frequent stops, should not be used for moving people long distances, typically more than 10 kms, and sometimes even less, as the travel speed is just too slow. Of course, with all of this, there are exceptions that could justify braking these simple rules. The author has travelled on the Hong Kong tram system on Hong Kong Island, which must be one of the slowest tram systems in the world. It has quite a long length, but to get from one end to the other takes several hours in peak time! It is nonetheless a very heavily used system.

The speed profile for trains operating in a metro style environment (or light rail in some cases) is shown below. Metros can maintain this profile all day, as they do not need to cross roads, or negotiate through complex junctions. Light rail vehicles, especially ones that cross roads, will have difficulty in matching the speed profile below.

Figure 6.4 Modelling Train Movement

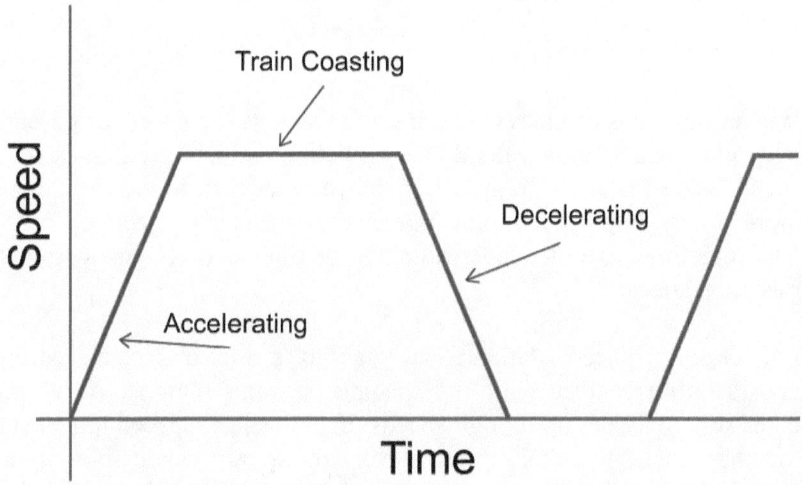

We can use this speed profile to estimate the time taken to move from one end of the rail system to the other. The time a train spends at a station is called the dwell time, and during this time passengers board and alight from the train.

Note that in this book it is assumed that trains accelerate and decelerate at the same rate. In practice this assumption is ok for simple calculations, but for any detailed work perhaps more accurate numbers should be used. The author has had long arguments as to the actual acceleration rate a driver must use, and it is generally agreed that it is easier for the train to decelerate faster than to accelerate. On the other hand, and this is true especially for rail systems without ATO, a driver is penalised if he misses the station, or "overshoots". This happens when he drives too far, and part of the front of the train is beyond the station, and some passengers may not be able to alight from the train. This is an undesirable situation, and one assumes that drivers will be liable to disciplinary action if it happens too often. So drivers will be careful in entering stations, and decelerate more slowly. Overall then, it's likely the acceleration and deceleration of trains will be somewhat similar, close enough for the simple and useful calculations contained in this book.

In actual practice train movements are similar to this speed structure, but not the same. A number of studies have examined the speed profile of trains moving through a rail system. In Sydney a very substantial study was performed on the speed profile of suburban trains, and again, it was found that trains move as per the diagram below. In actual practice trains moving between stations have the speed profile more similar to what is drawn below:

Figure 6.5 Practical and Theoretical Train Movement

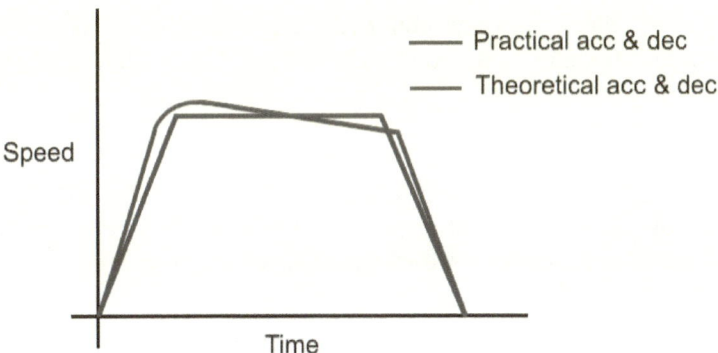

In practice drivers do not need to follow any particular curve or speed profile, they are usually free to choose any speed. However, it has been found that drivers mostly follow the curve drawn above. Some rail systems post signs that advise drivers of the "best speeds" to drive their train at. The best speeds are often chosen on the basis of energy efficiency, although operational considerations (i.e. the timetable) is also very important.

Where trains are moving between distant stations, and not closely spaced stations like the example above, and there are many different speed limits between the two stations, then the speed profile might look like something below:

Figure 6.6 Multiple Speed Limits from Station to Station

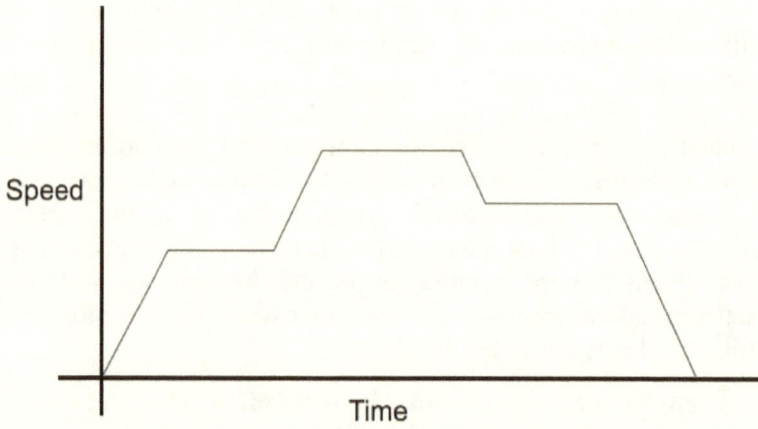

To calculate the travel time would require an analysis of the different parts of the trip, and then add them together. This is relatively straight forward, and easily done.

So let's analyse the movement of trains between stations. The train accelerates, then maintains a constant speed, and then slows down. We can assume that the train accelerates and decelerates at the same rate. The time taken to accelerate to maximum speed is given by:

$$Acceleration\ time = \frac{line\ speed}{acceleration}$$

Or we can put this as:

$$t = \frac{v}{a}$$

The distance covered when accelerating is given by:

$$s = \frac{v^2}{2a}$$

The travel time between one station and another is given by this equation:

$$\text{travel time} = t_{acc} + t_{coasting} + t_{dec}$$

Where:

t_{acc} = acceleration time

$t_{coasting}$ = time spent coasting

t_{dec} = deceleration time

The equation for travel time can then expressed as:

$$\text{travel time} = \frac{v_{max}}{a} + \frac{D_{station} - 2 \left(\frac{v_{max}^2}{2a} \right)}{v_{max}} + \frac{v_{max}}{a}$$

This can be simplified to:

$$\text{travel time} = \frac{2v_{max}}{a} + \frac{D_{station}}{v} - \frac{v_{max}}{a}$$

Which becomes:

$$\text{travel time} = \frac{v_{max}}{a} + \frac{D_{station}}{v_{max}}$$

Where:

$D_{station}$ = distance between stations, from the front of both stations

v_{max} = maximum velocity in ms^{-1}

Of course in calculating this formula we must be careful that the train has sufficient time to reach the maximum line speed, and we can test this using the equation below:

$$\frac{v^2}{a} < D_{station} \qquad (7)$$

If this condition is true then we know that the train can reach maximum speed before needing to begin slowing down to stop at the next station.

The speed profile of a train moving through a suburban network is shown below. The train accelerates and decelerates as it leaves and then arrives at stations.

Figure 6.7 Train Moving through Multiple Stations

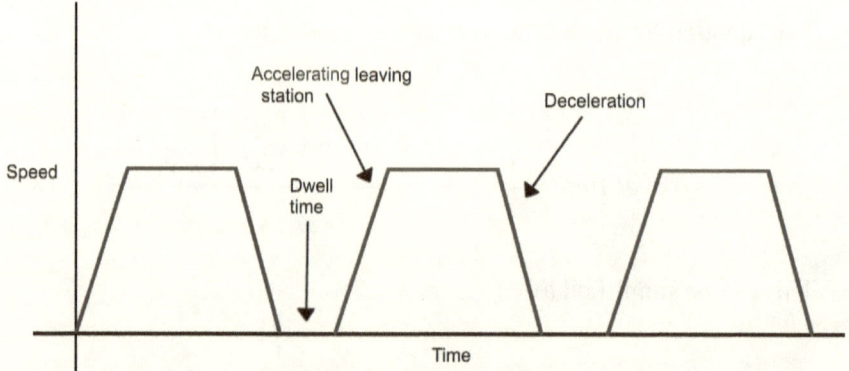

So what speeds can be achieved in practice? The limiting factor, especially for suburban networks or metros can often be the distance between stations, and the graph below shows the maximum speed based on the distance between stations. We assume that the train accelerates evenly and reaches the maximum speed, at which point it then begins to slow down to stop at the next station. To create the average speed between stations in the graph below, the assumption was made that train must spend at least 15 seconds at its top speed before starting to decelerate. Also an acceleration of 0.54 ms^{-2} was used. Dwell times were not factored into the calculation, so in practice average speeds will be a bit lower than what is shown below.

Figure 6.8 Top and Average Speed

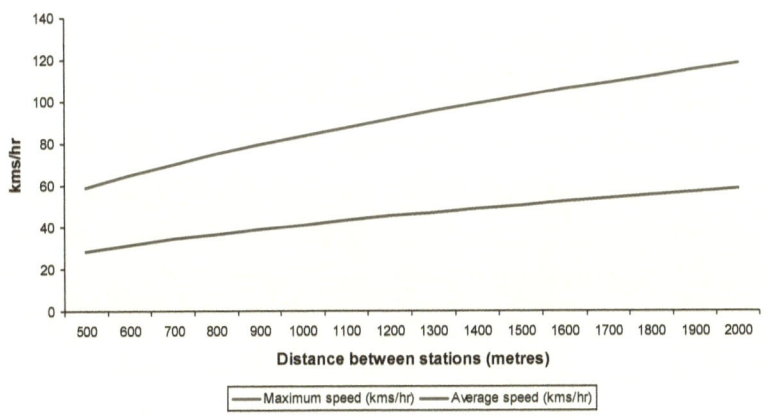

The table that accompanies this graph is:

Distance between stations (metres)	Maximum speed kms/hr	Realistic top speed kms/hr
500	59	29
600	65	32
700	70	34
800	75	37
900	79	39
1000	84	41
1100	88	43
1200	92	45
1300	95	47
1400	99	49
1500	102	51
1600	106	52
1700	109	54
1800	112	56
1900	115	57
2000	118	59

Notice how the average speed increases as the distance between stations increases. Something of a rarely stated rule is that stations for a metro style system should be at least 1000 metres apart.

A more complete explanation of average speeds is provided below. Once again the speed profile is shown below for the movement of trains throughout a suburban network with closely spaced stations.

Figure 6.9 Dwell Time and Maximum Speed

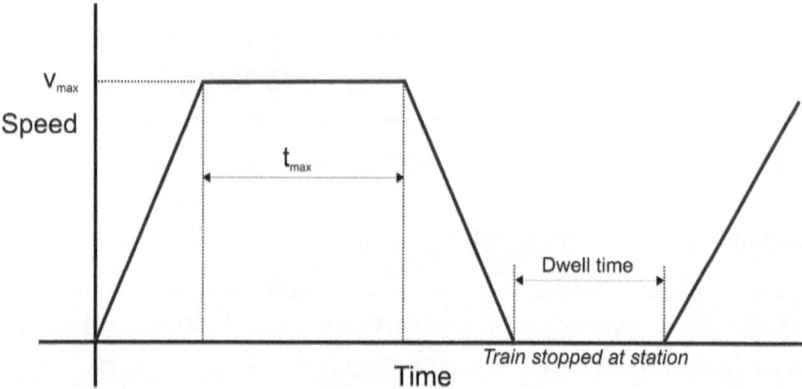

It is possible for a train to accelerate from a station, and then as soon as it has reached its maximum speed, start decelerating, but it is rarely done. Doing so is very wasteful of energy, and in practice very few rail organisations would do so. Drivers will accelerate until a target speed is reached, and then coast, and then start decelerating. The lower the maximum speed, the lower the power consumption. For this reason, and a number of others, trains usually will drive for at least a short period of time at the maximum speed.

We can calculate the maximum speed a train can reach, based on the acceleration and the distance between stations. Using equation (7):

$$v_{max} \leq \sqrt{aD_{station}}$$

This will give us the maximum possible speed between stations. With some simple manipulations we can derive the formula for the maximum speed between stations, including the time trains are coasting. The time t_{max} is essentially the time trains coast between stations.

$$v_{max} = a\left[\sqrt{\frac{D_{station}}{a}} - \frac{t_{max}}{2}\right]$$

The average speed along the rail line is a very important number. This number is often used in rail planning, as there are certain minimum speeds as for trains to travel at, as mentioned earlier.

The average speed of any train is:

$$Average\ speed = \frac{D_{station}}{travel\ time + Dwell}$$

It's important to have some reference on average speeds throughout cities and in transportation systems. Below are some typical values for average speeds, for reference, to compare with when calculating average speeds for new rail lines or other rail transport projects. As with any numbers in this book, the values are indicative only.

Typical Average Speeds

Location	Service Type	Average travel speed (kms/hr)
Cities	Trams	10
	Buses	10
	Light rail	20
	BRT	30 - 50
	Metros	30 – 45
	Commuter	50 – 80
Countries	Regional	60 – 100
	High speed	> 200

The table below shows some indicative values for acceleration.

Indicative Acceleration and Deceleration Rates

Acceleration	Comment
0.3 ms^{-2}	Typical acceleration for a freight train (and this changes depending of speed)
0.5 ms^{-2}	Acceleration used widely in metros and commuter services
0.8 ms^{-2}	Limit where passengers start to feel some discomfort in braking and acceleration
1.1 ms^{-2}	Limit of acceleration and deceleration of some metro trains
1.3 ms^{-2}	Commonly used acceleration rate in the US and Canada, also the limit of acceleration at which passengers can remain standing
1.4 ms^{-2}	Another common limit for the maximum acceleration and deceleration of metro trains
2.5 ms^{-2}	A common limit for the maximum emergency braking of light rail vehicles

In practice there are many other constraints on how quickly a train can move through a rail system. Congestion of the rail system is something that often slows trains down. Light rail vehicles moving along city streets will slow down for other road traffic, depending on how the rail line is constructed. The equations presented here work best for rail systems that are completely grade separated, and have regular patterns of acceleration and deceleration.

Top speeds are also limited by the geometry of the track. For top speeds around 70-80 kms/hr (50 miles per hour), the distance between stations will have a large effect on average speed. For metro systems especially, the calculations presented above are exceedingly useful. Also monorails, and intermediate capacity systems, and APM, also can make use of these equations. Other rail systems such as HSR, these equations are still relevant but not as important. HSR trains are limited by track geometry in most cases, and need to speed up and slow down at curves.

Freight was not mentioned above. Freight trains movements are a little more difficult to predict. For example, the loads the freight train is carrying will have a large impact upon the acceleration, and maximum speed. The weather conditions, and slipperiness of the top of the rail, is also important. Freight trains are affected by a large number of parameters, and tops speeds are difficult to calculate.

REFERENCES

1. Halpern, P *Non-collision injuries in public buses: a national survey of a neglected problem*, Emerg Medical Journal 2005 Feb: 22(2): 108-110

Getting People through Stations

Introduction

Some rail systems have very large numbers of passengers. Some metro stations move experience large passenger movements, for example, Mong Kok station in Hong Kong moves over 200,000 people per day. This level of passenger movements can create some real problems, and so the design of these stations is very important. The greater the passenger load through a busy station, the more important the design of the station becomes. Standard tools and process exist for designing stations, and these are discussed below.

Where stations are extremely busy, passengers may be unable to exit the station quickly, and when the subsequent train arrives then passengers may not be able to alight from the train quickly. This can slow down disembarkation, which results in the subsequent train have to wait while passengers attempt to alight. In severe cases, train movements may be severely disrupted, and the headway may grow significantly. Where a railway has invested heavily in improving the headway, this benefit can be lost where passenger overcrowding is so great that the better headway cannot be used.

In addition to the effect on train headways, passenger comfort is a very important factor in designing stations. Passengers do not like being cramped and crowded, and in a large station this can be a real problem. Some people dislike being touched by others, inadvertent or otherwise, and whilst people brushing against one another in a crowd is unavoidable, many people don't like it nonetheless. A slow exit from a station is in reality an increase in passenger travel times, and where travel times are too large then the public will not use the service. Severe overcrowding also provides the opportunity for all types of petty crime, such as pick pocketing and theft of bags, wallets and cameras. Also young girls and women may be touched in an inappropriate way, and so in general severe overcrowding should be avoided where possible.

Problems with passenger crowding typically arise in underground stations, but can also occur with above ground stations as well. Large metro stations are commonly seriously affected by overcrowding, as the numbers of people being moved can be very large and difficult to manage. More uncommonly, passenger crowding in tram systems can also be extremely severe, and the tiny platforms in the middle of streets provided for tram systems can be completely overwhelmed by large passenger movements. The tram systems in both Melbourne and Hong Kong suffer from extreme overcrowding, and in Hong Kong the tram service may be 2 or 3 times slower in peak times than on Sunday mornings. The small tram stops are insufficient in size for the number of people attempting to use them.

Light rail, HSR and regional rail systems seem less prone to overcrowding, as these systems may not have the same level of intensity of passenger movements. Also HSR and regional trains spend more time at platforms, and often have a large terminus where trains wait for the departure time, giving passenger plenty of opportunity to board the train. Commuter rail systems can suffer from severe overcrowding, but many of the services on these systems are relatively lightly loaded, and so severe overcrowding is uncommon.

In Japan and China rail services of almost any kind are overcrowded. In China regional services can suffer from severe overcrowding, and tickets are sold on long distance trains without seats, and passengers must stand for long journeys. Commuter trains in Japan are also very crowded, in addition to metro systems in big cities which are also often crowded.

In many cases managing overcrowding can be addressed with increasing the size of the station, at least within the station. Larger platforms, larger and more entrances and exits, and more barriers are clear and relatively straightforward solutions to overcrowding. The problem is that the space is not always available for platforms and walkways of very large size, or the cost of excavation of an underground station can be excessive. Trams systems may have very limited space because of the placement of stations in the middle of roads, and so cannot be increased in size without enormous difficulty. In many cases a compromise is needed to allow for stations that are not as large as needed, but can still cope with the passenger volumes predicted.

Smart station design can alleviate many overcrowding problems. Where space for a station is limited, use of the available space efficiently may present some interesting design challenges. One way to manage this situation is to create many different station designs, and then test them with modelling software to see which performs the best. The definition of best really means the rate at which passengers can exit the station, with the fastest being the best.

To get in and out of stations, walking is almost always required. Escalators assist with upwards and downwards movements, and moving walks are also used, but in almost every case at some point passengers need to walk to exit a station. Walking speeds vary enormously from person to person, and in lightly crowded spaces faster walkers will not be impeded. In heavily crowded spaces, the fast walkers will need to slow down, and in severely crowded spaces walking speeds are much slower. Modelling of the movement of passengers through stations involves estimating the speed of movement, with faster being better. Passenger speed will depend on their environment, crowding, the incline they are walking on, and a number of other factors. The rate of movement of people in different environments has been extensively studied, and fairly accurate and effective modelling of passenger exit speeds is possible.

Passenger Flow Modelling

Passenger movement speeds vary based on what they are walking on, in addition to a number of other factors. Some of the common structures that people must negotiate in a station includes:
- Stairs, both in and upward and downward direction
- Ramps
- Flat ground
- Escalators
- Moving walkways

People move substantially faster on flat ground than on stairs and ramps. This makes stairs and ramps the bottleneck for getting passengers on and off platforms, hence the focus they receive in the study of station design and managing dwell times.

Most basic calculations of estimating passenger exit speeds from a station are based on a flow rate. This is defined below.

f = *passenger flow per unit width of subway/walkway*
S = *passenger speed*
D = *passenger density*

So we can write:

$$f = S \times D$$

The flow rate of people per linear metre increases when their speed increased, or they are packed together more closely and so the density is higher. The passenger flow rate can then be used as follows:

Number of people moving through a corridor per minute = width of corridor x flow rate

The flow rate per unit width is often used for work with station design. Where crowding is heavy, and passenger movements slow, this can be accommodated by widening the available cross-sectional area to allow for more people. Widening corridors can be very effective, as this allows more people to flow through, and can increase the average speed as crowding is lower.

Notice that the flow rate is per unit width. Stations are a complex 2 dimensional design in many cases, but flow measurements are per unit width. This means that any modelling software will need to convert a station layout into a series of linear distances for which a flow calculation can be completed. In many cases this is relatively straight forward, but in others can be very difficult, especially where there are many different entrances and exits. Consider the example below:

Figure 6.10 Passenger Flow through a Bottleneck

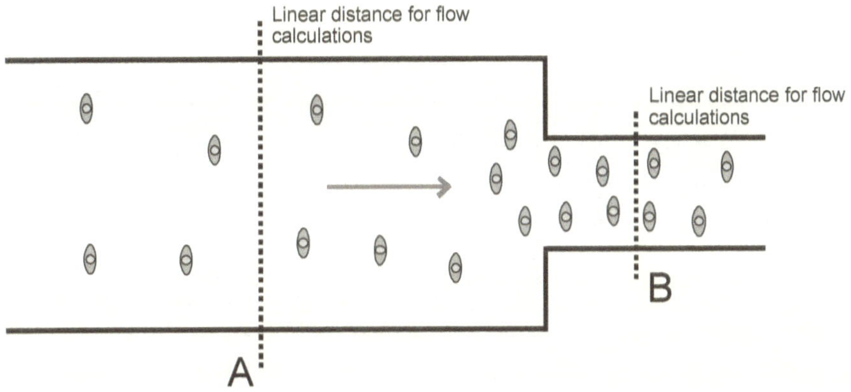

Passengers in the diagram above are moving from left to right. In the area with line A, passengers have plenty of room and can spread out, and so can move relatively quickly from left to right. Once they reach the area with line B, this more narrow area results in crowding, and so the average speed of passengers and their walking speed drops. The dashed lines represent the length used for the equations presented above. The length of the vertical line through A and B can be incorporated into the flow calculation, and passenger modelling packages commonly do this, quite effectively. Passenger flow modelling software packages can generate good results from this kind of analysis. The more passengers there are, the greater the effect of the bottleneck.

Station geometry is not always so clear and easy to calculate flow rates for. Where there are multiple corridors coming together into one area, with multiple entrances and exits, modelling of passenger movements is far more difficult.

Many studies have examined how quickly people walk, and this is needed to complete any flow calculations. As with anything involving people, there is a lot of variation, and some people move quickly and others are much slower. Numerous studies have looked at determining average speeds of movement, in a range of different scenarios. In practice two different sets of speeds are used for passengers in this situations; normal entry and exit from the station, and escape from the station under emergency conditions. Passengers will move much faster in an emergency situation.

Typical walking speeds for normal and emergency conditions are listed below. The speeds for emergency conditions are taken from the US standard NFPA130.

Walking Speeds Through Stations – A Rough Guide		
Structure	Typical Speed	Comment
Normal Conditions		
Flat ground	45 - 75 metres/min	Depends on crowding, see below
Stairs, down	17 -31 metres/min	Vertical direction
Stairs, up	12 - 21 metres/min	Vertical direction
Emergency conditions (from NFPA 130)		
Flat ground	61 metres per	Not linked to

Walking Speeds Through Stations – A Rough Guide

Structure	Typical Speed	Comment
	minute	crowding
Stairs	15 metres per minute	This speed is upwards/vertical, not along the pitch angle
Barriers – fare collection	50 per minute	This flow rate is only used when barriers are de-activated
Turnstiles	25 per minute	

There is a lot of potential variation in the walking speeds listed above, as many people do not walk at average speeds. Also notice the large difference between the speed on flat ground and speed on stairs, with the stairs speed being much lower than flat ground.

Crowding is an important factor in walking speeds, with crowding reducing average speeds. People dislike and avoid touching each other, and in a crowd will attempt to avoid this. Where there is substantial crowding, people will walk more slowly as they attempt to avoid each other, and in cases of severe crowding, the movement of people may stop completely. As people move through areas restricted in size, they slow down and crowding increases. Areas of restricted size can form into bottlenecks where the crowding is sufficient to almost stop the movement of passengers through the station.

When performing these calculations, normally 0.5 metres from each wall is not included. Most people will not walk so close to the wall, and so this space is largely useless. So a corridor that is 6 metres wide has a useful width of 5 metres, with 0.5 metres being deducted from each side.

In the US the Highway Capacity Manual, which is for road vehicles using roads, prescribes 6 "levels of service" for describing the volume of traffic on a road. These LOS have been applied to station design, and used to describe the rate of movement of passengers through stations. These levels can be used to give an idea of the movement speed of passengers/people in a station. For completeness, the LOS categories are described below.

Passenger Flows – US system

LOS	Space per pedestrian	Typical speed
A	>3.3 m² per person	79 metres/min
B	2.3 – 3.3 m² per person	76 metres/min
C	1.4 – 2.3 m² per person	73 metres/min
D	0.9 – 1.4 m² per person	69 metres/min
E	0.5 – 0.9 m² per person	46 metres/min
F	< 0.5 m² per person	<46 metres/min

This system is occasionally used outside of the US and Canada. London Underground uses this system as well.

The graph below shows the application of the above numbers to passenger flow rates per metre per minute. This is possible because there is both a speed and a density in the table above, which can be used to calculate the flow rate.

Figure 6.11 Passenger Flow (per metre per minute)

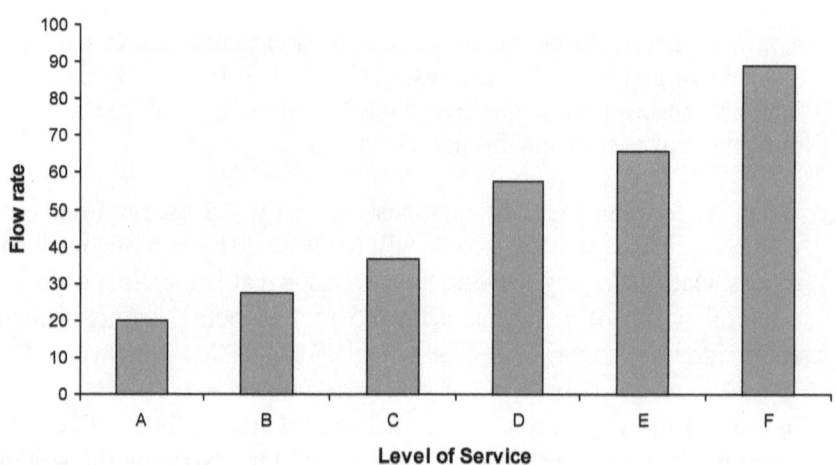

Notice that the flow rate increases as passengers become more crowded. At some point crowding becomes so great that the flow rate begins to decrease for any increase in crowding. It's not possible for the density of people to increase indefinitely, and an upper limit of about 100 people per metre per minute seems to be common, which can only be achieved at very high densities.

Some words about stairs; whilst on walkways people walk at constant speed and in no real pattern, on stairs people slow down as they climb, as they tire, and walk roughly one behind another. Stairs are often the major form of egress for underground and elevated stations, and so the rate at which passengers enter and leave is often strongly influenced by the size and number of stairs. Another consideration with stairs is that where passengers are moving in both directions on them, then the flow rate drops dramatically. Passengers ascend and descend at different rates, because climbing stairs is harder than descending.

Some simple definitions are needed for stairs. These are shown below.

Figure 6.12 Definitions for Stairs

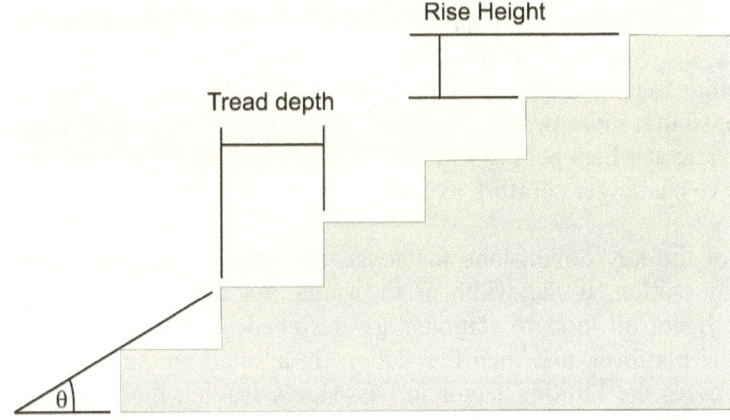

The simple diagram above shows some basic terms for stairs. Most countries have a building code or standard which prescribes the tread depth and the rise height. The pitch angle is commonly around 30°, but a range of pitch angles are common. It would be unusual for the rise height to be larger than the tread depth, which means most pitch angles are less than 45°. Steps in stations are no different from steps in any other facility.

For stairs three speed measurements are possible; in the vertical direction up and down, or along the stairs themselves. The third is the horizontal, and as most stairs are inclined less than 45° then this measurement will also be higher than the climbing speed, but lower then the speed along the stairs themselves. Where a number is provided for climbing or descending vertically, then this will be lower than any figures for the climbing speed measured at the same angle of the stairs.

Stairs for a station should be free of debris, clean, and even. Each step should be the same size, and even small changes in step height will result in a significant drop in speed for passengers either moving up or down the stairs. Stairs are also the same as walkways in the sense that overcrowding will result in a reduction in the speed of movement.

The size and shape of stairs will often be determined by any disability requirements in a country. Many countries have disability codes, legislation or regulations that describe how stairs should be designed. Station stairs will comply with national requirements on their design and geometry.

Station designers are confronted with a choice on the pitch angle of stairs; steeper stairs will require less space but will be more difficult to climb, and may not be suitable for the elderly and passengers with disabilities. In general stairs in a station should have a lower pitch angle, so that more people can climb them. There is however a penalty in the rate at which people will climb stairs. Shallower pitch angles also improve passenger comfort, as they are easier to climb.

One of the key dimensions for stairs, and then for any underground railway station, is the width of the stairs. As mentioned previously, most, if not all modern stations, are designed so that passengers can exit the platform, and then the station, in a small amount of time. In most cases the limiting factor in passengers leaving the station is the stairs, as they are limited in size and climbing stairs is in most cases slower then moving along flat ground. Another consideration is that most passengers, when confronted with a fire in an underground station, will attempt to exit the station through where they entered the station (assuming they entered the rail network through this station), as they know this path out of the station, and will attempt to use this route regardless of whether it is the most efficient and lowest distance to a safe place. This may mean that the number of people attempting to use a set of stairs in an emergency will be higher in one part of the station than another. This needs to be accommodated in any station design.

The wider a set of stairs, the more people that can use it. Flow rates for stairs are normally expressed in people per minute per metre. As an example of this calculation, consider the following example:

Flow rate = 50 people per minute per metre.

How many people would move through a staircase of 4 metres width in 90 seconds?

Total people = flow rate x time in minutes x width of staircase

So this is

Total people = 50 x 90/60 x 4 = 300 people.

Consider that the above example uses typical values, and this number of people being able to exit a station in this time may not be acceptable for a very busy metro station.

As the passenger density increases, the number of people moving up the stairs increases, until it reaches an optimum point. This density for stairs seems to be around 2.5 people per m^2, and after this point adding more people only slows down the rate at which they move through the staircase. Care must be exercised that in an emergency situation that this point is not reached when many people are fleeing to the stairs, as the movement of people will slow as more people want to exit and so a deadly situation may arise. At some point the movement of people through the staircase stops entirely, and the density is so high that no one moves at all. This point seems to be reached when the passenger density reaches around 5.8 people per m^2.

The graph below shows how the flow rate on stairs changes as the level of crowding changes. Notice that the flow rate seems to peak at about 2.5 people per square metre, or about 0.4 square metres per person. Recall that this was the highest passenger density used for flat open ground.

Figure 6.13 Passenger Flow Rates on Stairs

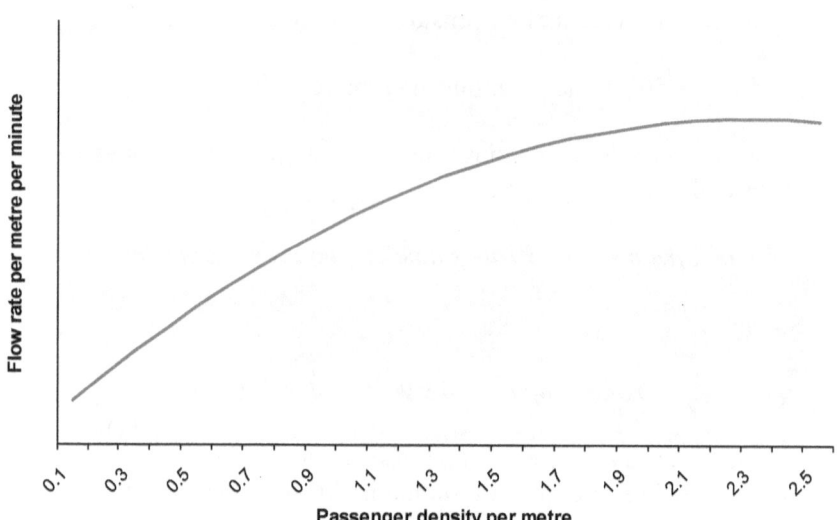

The pedestrian flow rate on stairs is almost always lower than on flat ground, which again, makes the stairs the bottleneck in any station.

Little has been said so far about escalators, and large stations will normally have many. Escalators are normally installed in groups of two, but are sometimes installed on their own, and less common in groups of three. In even more rare cases, for very large stations, four or more escalators may be installed together. The rate at which passengers move along the escalator is determined by the depth of the step, and the speed at which the escalator moves. Escalators typically move between 0.5 to 0.75 m/s although higher speeds are common in rail systems in Asia.

Many escalators are designed so that two people may use them at the same time. The width of the escalator is such that two people can stand side by side in relatively comfort. Typically people on one side of the escalator walk up the escalator, and on the other stand for their journey on the escalator. The author's experience on escalators is that usually less than half the passengers on a train will wish to walk upwards, and more people will prefer to walk down than walk up.

Assuming both sides of the escalator are fully used, the formula for the flow rate of an escalator is:

$$Passenger\ flow\ rate\ (per\ minute) = \frac{1}{step\ size\ (metres)} \times escalator\ velocity \times 60$$

Smaller steps for the escalator improve the flow rate, but are more uncomfortable for customers.

A run-off is the area at the top or bottom of an escalator where passengers can alight from the escalator. This area is important for station design, as the lack of this area will result in passengers "bunching up" at the exit of the escalator. This can cause slower movement of passengers throughout the station. The size of the run-off needed is dependent on the flow rate through the escalator.

Passengers can have accidents on escalators where clothing or even limbs can get caught. In rare cases passengers may fall down them, which can cause substantial injury. An important rule in allowing passengers to use escalators is that they must wear sensible shoes, and not be barefoot. Some types of shoes, such as crocs, can get caught in between the step and the side of the escalator, so injuries will occur from time to time. It is also important for escalators to be fitted with an emergency stop.

Lifts, or elevators in the US, are very common in many different types of stations. Lifts are commonly installed to move passengers from the platform to the paid area near the barriers on the mezzanine level, and then from outside the unpaid area to the road or outside area. For an elevated station, there will normally be lifts to the area with the barriers, and then down to ground level.

Lifts are not installed to move large numbers of passengers. Typically lifts can move 12 – 16 people, although in many stations lifts are significantly smaller than this. In some rare cases large lifts are installed that can move 30 people or more, but this is quite uncommon. The slow movement speed of lifts means that its contribution to moving people out of stations is actually quite small. For the purposes of modelling passenger movements, it is acceptable not to include lifts at all, especially for calculations involving fire and life safety.

Lifts are very good for moving people who have disabilities, or otherwise have difficulty climbing up stairs. This actually includes a lot of different people:
- Those in wheelchairs
- The elderly
- The blind and those with vision impairment
- Passengers with lots of luggage
- Women with small babies, especially when they have strollers or prams for the baby
- Passengers in poor health
- Passengers who are obese or otherwise overweight
- Those who have difficulty climbing stairs
- Passengers who have become ill or otherwise had a medical emergency on the rail system

The provision of lifts in a rail system is a valuable service for customers. It is however a little expensive, and some rail systems avoid installing them because of the cost. Lifts should normally be installed in pairs, so that if one is out the other can be used. A large station may need several lifts, or even more, as passengers may need to move from different parts of the station down to the platform. Also note that lifts rarely connect the platform to an unpaid area outside the station, as many rail systems segregate their stations into paid and unpaid areas, and allowing passengers direct access to the station in this way may be considered a security risk. Some commuter rail stations have lifts where they connect directly from the street to the platform level, but again it is relatively rare.

Designing better Platforms

The headway of a rail line is the time between trains when the trains are travelling as quickly as permitted by the signalling system. For a stopping station one of the key parameters in determining the headway was the dwell time. The dwell time at stations is a component of the dwell time, and so the longer the dwell time, the larger the headway. Headway in many rail systems needs to be reduced as much as possible.

Station design is very important to the headway in very busy stations. Passengers need to be able to disembark quickly and efficiently without any obstructions. Obstructions, especially where the crowding is heavy, can have a pronounced effect on passenger speed. For the best possible passenger movement speed, it is important for passengers to have a pathway which is unimpeded.

The station below shows a typical situation in many metro stations. The train has stopped at the station, and is shown in light blue. People are disembarking from the train, but there is only one exit to the right of the station. Also note the small squares in brown, these are columns supporting the roof of the station, and old stations were often built with these kinds of structures. Columns are structural items that cannot be removed once installed without undermining the structural strength of the station.

Figure 6.14 Passenger Flow in a Poorly Designed Station

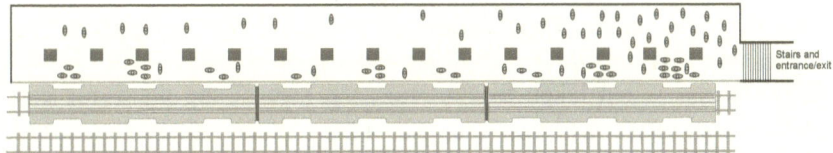

Also note in the above diagram that there is some congestion at the right end of the station, as passengers only have one exit. As passengers become more crowded they will slow down, and then they will slow down even more when climbing the only set of stairs into the station. This station is poorly designed.

In the station below many of the problems in the above diagram have been addressed. Notice that there are three exits rather than one, and these exits are located along the station. These exits can also be used as entrances. This station design will allow better loading and unloading of the train, and lower dwell times should passenger density get too high.

Figure 6.15 Passenger Flow in a Better Station

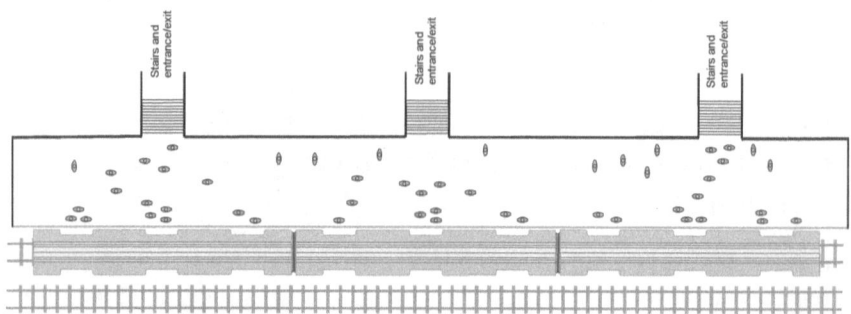

The station below shows as an example what can happen when construction costs are minimised to the point where the dwell time of trains arriving at the station is effected. One of the major costs of building an underground station is the cost of excavation, so minimising this cost through making the station smaller is one way to reduce costs. When taken to extremes, the size of the platforms can become very small, as in the diagram below. When side platforms are very small, passengers are crowded when alighting from the train onto the platform, and move very slowly when attempting to exit the station. The example below exists in some rail systems, and this kind of station can create major problems when passenger loads are high.

Figure 6.16 A Narrow Side Platform

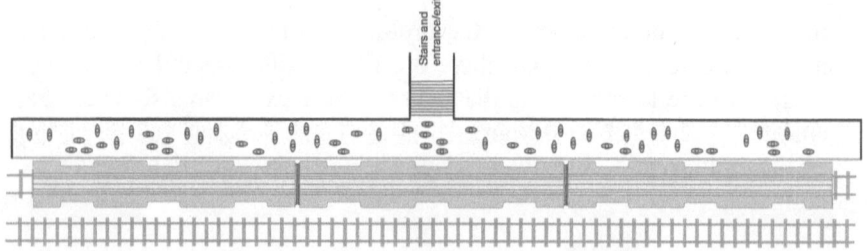

Platforms should be designed so that the highest anticipated passenger load will not result in excessive overcrowding. The ideal situation is that there should be at least 1 m^2 per waiting passenger at all times, although this may not always be possible. Where there is some special circumstance, or a special event nearby to a station, then in some cases it may be acceptable to allow for a more crowded station, and a space of 0.5 m^2 per waiting passenger may be acceptable.

Let's consider an example. Where a station is 160 metres long, and the peak passenger load is calculated to be 500 people per platform per minute. Assuming, a time between trains of three minutes, it would be necessary to allow for 1500 people standing along the platform. Without even allowing for passengers being closer to entrances and exits, and passengers alighting from the train, and surges in passengers entering the station, the platform would need to be almost 10 metres wide. With additional allowances, such as the space 0.5 metres next to walls which people rarely stand in, perhaps a platform width of 15 metres would be appropriate. This is quite large, and some platforms in metros are only 2 metres wide, far smaller than what is needed in many cases.

The example above demonstrates one of the advantages of an island platform. Island platforms almost always have two sides at which train can stop (although in rare cases three platforms are possible), with trains from each platform moving in opposite directions. Most stations have many more passengers travelling in one direction than another for many times in the day, so there will be large numbers of passengers moving in one direction, and a smaller number in another. Where this is the case, then island platforms will be able to accommodate more passengers as the other side of the platform can be used for waiting passengers. This idea is shown below.

Figure 6.17 A Narrow Side Platform

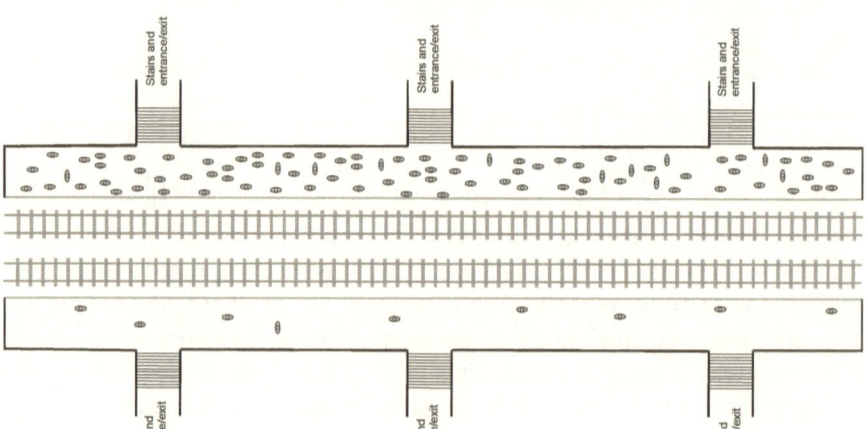

In the diagram above we can see that the top platform has a large number of passengers waiting for a train, and the bottom one only a small number. As a result the top platform is crowded, and the bottom one very comfortable. This scenario is very common in many metro stations.

Below is the same situation with island platforms, rather than side platforms. The same number of ovals representing people has been used in the diagram below as in other diagrams.

Figure 6.19 An Island Platform with the Same Number of People

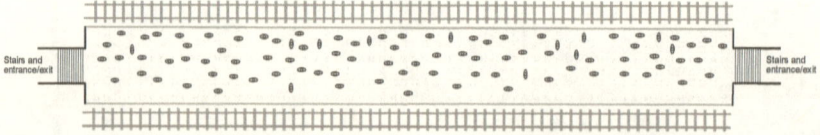

For an island platform the platforms are in the centre of the tracks, and the platform has far more space for passengers to spread out. This configuration is much more desirable, as the larger platform area will allow passengers to move around more freely, and so be able to board and alight much more quickly from trains. Passengers alighting from the train can also make their way along the other side of the platform to the exits, which in this case are drawn at either end of the platform.

Crowding on trains is often very severe. Crowding on trains can be as high as 4 people per square metre, or in some very crowded systems up to 6 people per square metre. In India some rail services operate with supercrush loads, where 8 or even more people are standing per metre. This high level of crowding is acceptable on some rail services, but is generally undesirable. For platforms and station design it is even more undesirable, and should be avoided if at all possible. The level of crowding that is permitted on a train should always be higher than what is permitted on a station.

In situations where passenger crowding on stations is extreme, then unusual problems start to occur. Passengers may not be able to get onto the train, and may need to wait for several trains before reaching the doors to board the train. Alternatively, for very busy services passengers may be overcarried, and not be able to alight at their desired station.

Stairs leading to and from platforms can also sometimes be a problem. Where passengers are crossings each others paths then problems can develop. The photo below shows one of the solutions to passenger flow in large stations, for stairs. One way to improve passenger flow is to keep the flow of passengers in different directions separate, so that passengers can move faster. This can often be achieved by drawing lines on the floor of stations to indicate which way passengers should walk. Below is a photo where this has been done. Notice that the blue arrows indicate a direction up the stairs, and the yellow down the stairs. This keeps passengers moving in different directions apart, so that flow speeds can be maximised.

Stairs in a Station in Osaka

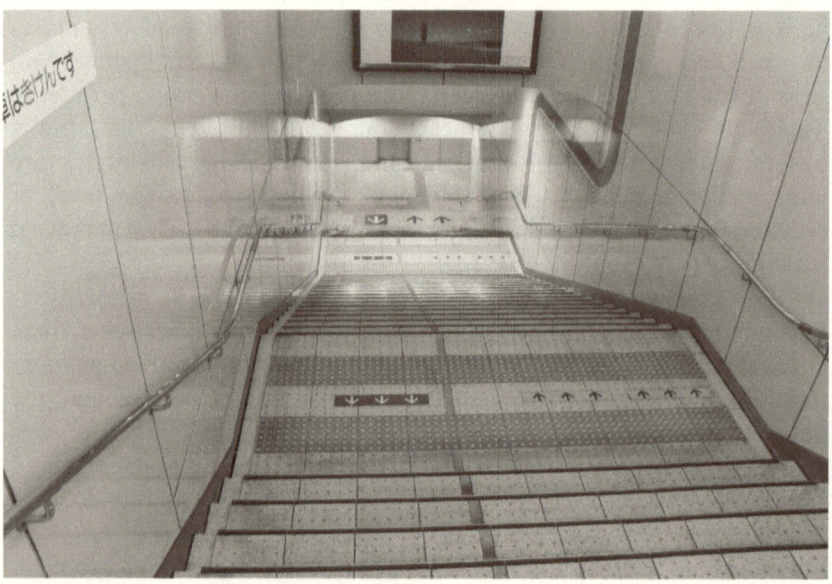

This photo was taken in Osaka in Japan. Notice that the space provided for passengers moving down the stairs is greater than moving up. This is because the platform is at the top of the stairs, and when passengers alight there is a large surge in passenger moving throughout the station, which is not the case for passengers entering the station, especially for stations that are not interchanges.

REFERENCES

1. European Commission, *Tracks for Tilting Trains*, Fast and Comfortable Trains (D8), July 2005

2. Mancini, G. et al *New developments with the Italian solution for tilting trains: optimisation of tilting system on new generation of Pendolino trains*,
www.uic.org/cdrom/2008/11_wcrr2008/pdf/R.2.4.3.5.pdf

3. Alessandro, E. New Developments for Tilting Trains, November 2001

4. Government of South Australia, Department of Planning Transport and Infrastructure, *PTSOM Code of Practice Volume 2, Track Geometry CP-TS-956*

5. Mochizuki, A. *JRTR Speed-up Story 2 Part 2: Speeding-up Conventional Lines and Shinkansen*, Japan Railway and Transport Review No 58 Oct 2011

6. Lindahl, M. *Track Geometry for high-speed railways*, Department of Vehicle Engineering Royal Institute of Technology, Stockholm 2001

7. Persson, R. *Tilting Trains Technology, benefits and motion sickness*, Thesis submitted to Royal Institute of Technology Stockholm, 2008

8. Forstberg, J. et al *Influence of different conditions for tilt compensation on symptoms of motion sickness in tilting trains*, Brain Research Bulletin, Vol 47, No 5, pp 525 – 535, 1998

Week 7

Emissions and Rail Systems

Introduction

Trains require energy to move, and it is important for any transport system that energy consumption is managed as efficiently as possible. The consumption of energy is expensive, and there are negative effects from its consumption. Emissions from energy consumption are directly and linearly linked to the amount of energy consumed. There is much to be said about energy consumption for trains, and how to best manage it.

Almost all trains are powered by either electricity or diesel fuel. Electricity required for propulsion is almost always provided through physical contact with a wire or other lump of metal, and flows all the way from a power station to the train. Diesel locomotives and DMUs store the diesel fuel on the train, and it is burnt to produce the energy required to move the train. The process of burning the fuel, called combustion, produces CO_2 gas, which is a gas that contributes towards global warning. Both of these methods of producing power have their advantages and disadvantages. More unusual methods of driving trains exist, such as rollingstock being pulled by cables, or steam power.

Power is also consumed in trains in managing and providing auxiliary services. This includes air conditioning, which can consume quite of lot of power. In hot environments, such as South East Asia, air conditioning is greatly desired on trains by the local population, and many of the rail systems in that area are fully air conditioned. Depending on the weather, weight and speed of the train, air conditioning can be quite a large part of the power consumption of any train. Other systems in a train that carries passengers can also consume power, such as doors, lights, CCTV cameras, and other systems.

Steam power is almost never used any more for power for trains, despite its popularity and sex appeal. Steam trains were very difficult and time consuming to maintain, and expensive to operate. Steam engines needed to be constantly supplied with water, and less frequently with sand, and of course coal. Steam as a power source is no longer used in any significant way worldwide.

Where trains are powered by electricity, then it needs to be generated somewhere and then moved to where trains are operating. Power is created at an electricity generator, and then moved using transmission lines, or cables, to where the trains are. The engineering of moving electricity from a generator to a place where it is used is quite complex, but this technology is mature and standard, and mostly operates efficiently without much fuss. The generator of power can be many different types, and which type it is determines the level of output of carbon dioxide. This is sometimes referred to as the mix of power generation.

One question that commonly arises is; which produces more CO_2 gas; diesel or electric power? At first blush it would seem obvious that diesel power produces more CO_2 than electric power, but this depends almost entirely on the method of electricity production. Countries that rely heavily on coal to produce electricity have a very high level of emissions per unit of energy generated, and those that rely on renewable sources or nuclear power have very low levels of emissions. The mix of power generation in a country is a powerful factor in determining the level of emissions for the rail mode of transport.

The main different types of power generation are:
- Coal fired
- Gas turbines
- Solar
- Nuclear
- Wind
- Hydroelectric
- Oil

Power consumption is often converted into a total emissions figure, and to do this requires an estimate of the amount of power that a rail system consumes, and then how much was the volume of greenhouse gas that was released. Electric trains produce no emissions on their own, they consume electrical energy, which when consumed produces no CO_2. The process of producing electricity for consumption by a rail system does produce emissions, and so to calculate the level of emissions a link is needed between the electricity consumed and the level of emissions. This is easy where a rail system possesses its own electricity generation, but this is now rare, and mostly rail systems buy their power from the local power grid. Almost all power grids are a combination of many different electricity producers and suppliers, and it is customary not to separate out any one industry as being better than another when they are all connected to the same power grid. For this reason the rail industry is almost always assessed as producing emissions at the same level as the local power grid.

It's useful to make an attempt to compare the energy used for diesel trains with that from electricity. In theory this is possible, because in both cases the energy is used to move the train along, so a direct comparison should be possible. Unfortunately things are not that easy, and these comparisons usually produce some very strange outcomes. The problem is that diesel fuel contains a lot of energy, and it is converted into useful work at a rate that changes depending on the efficiency of the diesel motor. Only a small percentage of the energy in diesel can be converted to useful work, but the release of CO_2 is correlated to the amount of energy released, regardless of the efficiency of any motor. This can make comparisons rather unfair.

Another problem is estimating power losses in the electricity network that feeds any rail system. This includes any power stations or generators. Generating electricity is not perfect, and as it is generated some of the power is wasted as heat and noise. These losses need to be included otherwise the comparison is unfair once again. There are also power losses in any transmission network, and again, these need to be included. Not including all of these factors generates the impression that electric power is always far more preferable to diesel, which is not the case.

An attempt is made in this chapter to compare the different modes of transportation, and the power they consume. Included in this attempt are some calculations on the emissions generated per seat kilometre, and per passenger. There are many challenges with this kind of approach, and the major ones are:
- Stations and other facilities also consume a lot of power, and depending on the study and the railway these may or may not be included. Up to half the power in any railway and potentially even more can be devoted to other rail related facilities, and their inclusion can dramatically change any calculation. As many studies in this area do not specify whether the power consumption for these facilities are included, direct comparisons are difficult. Rail systems often

include power hungry facilities such as maintenance centres, or washing sheds.
- Some studies only analyse peak passenger loads. Passenger loading has a powerful effect on the efficiency of a transport mode, and rail is no exception. Are all rail services included in any analysis, or only the ones on weekdays or during the peak? Again, this is not made clear in the many studies published in this area
- The on-selling of electricity is common for rail systems, as they consume power in large volumes, it is cheap for railways to buy power, and then just as convenient to on sell it. In some cases remote towns or villages might be entirely powered by "rail" power, where the railway buys the power and distributes it, and then bills consumers. Surprisingly this is the case in NSW, where a number of small towns receive almost all their power from a railway. This can distort the energy figures substantially

So direct comparisons are difficult, and perhaps comparisons within studies are the best way to examine the power consumption of different modes of transportation. An attempt is made below to create a "league table" of different transport modes, and the quantity of power they consume in comparison to one another. But first some definitions and equations are needed.

Formulas and Calculations for Energy Consumption

The basic unit of energy is called the Joule, and is given the letter J. One thousand Joules is one kilo Joule, and this is given the abbreviation kJ. An even larger unit for energy is the Mega Joule, or 1 million Joules, and this is given the unit MJ.

The first law of thermodynamics states that energy is conserved, and cannot be created or destroyed. When used energy is converted to other forms, and electrical energy is often converted into heat. When it is said that energy is lost or consumed, it is actually converted into a different form and no longer usable.

Power is defined as the rate at which energy is consumed, or the total energy divided by the time it takes to use the energy. The formula for power is:

$$Power = \frac{Energy\ consumed}{time}$$

The units of energy of course are Joules, and time is seconds. The units of power are Watts, named after the Scottish engineer who dramatically improved the steam engine.

The most commonly used units for power are the kilowatt, which is one thousand watts. The physical meaning of this unit is the use of 1000 watts per second.

Energy consumption is often expressed in Kilowatt hours. Kilowatt hours are calculated by finding the amount of energy that is used at a rate of 1 kilowatt for 1 hour. In Joules, one kilowatt is:

$$1\ kilowatt\ hour = 3.6 \times 10^6\ Joules$$

As the kilowatt hour is the standard unit for billing for power, this is what is commonly used for power comparisons. Notice that it is a very large unit in terms of Joules.

There are a number of measures for power consumption per distance travelled, and these are listed below.

For electric trains:

$$Energy\ consumed\ per\ kilometre = \frac{Energy\ consumed}{Distance\ travelled}$$

$$Energy\ per\ seat\ kilometre = \frac{Energy\ consumed\ per\ km}{Number\ of\ seats\ in\ the\ train}$$

$$Energy\ per\ unit\ capacity = \frac{Energy\ consumed\ per\ km}{No\ seats + No\ standing\ spaces}$$

$$Energy\ per\ passenger\ kilometre = loading\ factor \times \frac{Energy\ consumed\ per\ km}{Number\ of\ seats\ in\ the\ train}$$

Energy cost per seat km = Cost per kilowatt hour x energy per seat km

For diesel trains:

$$\text{Fuel consumed per seat kilometre} = \frac{\text{Fuel consumed per km}}{\text{Number of seats in the train}}$$

$$\text{Fuel consumed per unit capacity} = \frac{\text{Fuel consumed per km}}{\text{No seats + No standing spaces}}$$

$$\text{Fuel consumed per passenger kilometre} = \text{loading factor} \times \frac{\text{Fuel consumed per km}}{\text{Number of seats in the train}}$$

Fuel cost per seat km = fuel cost per litre x fuel consumed per seat kilometre

Note that sometimes attempts are made to calculate the energy consumed for a diesel train per kilometre. It is not recommended to perform this comparison, as the energy content of diesel fuel is very high, so the figures for diesel are always extremely high in comparison to electric powered trains. A much better way to compare is to use CO_2 emissions, and the formulas for this are presented below.

For emissions, for electric trains:

CO_2 emissions per pass kilometre = CO_2 per kilowatt x Energy per passenger kilometre

For emissions, for diesel trains:

CO_2 emissions per pass kilometre = CO_2 per litre of fuel x Fuel per passenger kilometre

It's best when calculating power consumption to use metric units, such as Joules, rather than such units as BTUs and others.

For freight, the standard unit is CO_2 emissions per tonne kilometre, which can be calculated from the formula below:

$$CO_2 \text{ emissions per tonne kilometre} = CO_2 \text{ per litre of fuel} \times \frac{\text{fuel consumed per km}}{\text{tonnes moved}}$$

As freight is mostly moved with diesel locomotives, this is normally how emissions are calculated for freight. There are of course some exceptions to this, and there is a coal line is Australia that is electrified and moves bulk freight to port, so it is possible for freight to be moved with electric power. Nonetheless in this chapter diesel will be assumed to be the standard fuel source for freight trains.

CO_2 Emissions per Kilowatt hour per Country

The emissions per kilowatt hr varies substantially from country to country. As mentioned above, this can impact upon rail planning decisions as it is desirable for a rail system to produce as low emissions as possible. There are tables published in reports on the emissions per kilowatt hr, and extracted below are some of those. These numbers were current around 2012. The differences between countries can be ascribed to a variety of reasons, such as the availability of fuel, the number of rivers that can be dammed to use for hydroelectricity, and a range of other factors.

Emissions Per Kilowatt Hour			
Country	Grams CO$_2$ per kilowatt hr	Country	Grams CO$_2$ per kilowatt hr
Canada	186	Germany	461
Mexico	455	Iceland	0
USA	522	Poland	781
Australia	841	Spain	238
Israel	689	UK	457
Japan	416	Russia	639
Korea	533	China	766
New Zealand	150	Taiwan	768
Austria	188	India	912
France	79	Hong Kong	723
Malaysia	727	Singapore	499

The data was extracted from "IEA Statistics", 2012 edition, International Energy Agency.

The country with the highest emissions per kilowatt hour is India, with its heavy dependence on coal. The emissions per kilowatt hour is really dependent on the fuel source used to generate the electricity, coal produces a lot of emissions, and hydroelectricity and nuclear power produce nothing. Many countries have a mix of these energy sources, which is why there is such a large range in the emissions per kilowatt hour.

Typical Emissions per Rail Mode

The table below is a list of the different types of rail systems and how they are powered. Electric systems will draw their power from the location power grid, and diesel systems use fuel. As diesel fuel is largely standard between different countries, emissions from diesel are vary little from system to system. Alternatively emissions from electric trains varies enormously, and the same train with the same number of passengers can different emissions, even on the same trip from one country to another.

Type of power used to Drive Transport Mode

Transport Mode	Power source
Metro train	Electric
Intermediate capacity metro	Electric
Commuter/regional	Electric or diesel
High Speed Rail	Mostly electric
Light rail	Mostly electric
Trams	Mostly electric
Buses	Mostly diesel or LPG, some electric
Minibus	Mostly diesel or LPG
Long haul air travel	Aviation fuel
Taxi	Petrol or LPG
Short haul air travel	Aviation fuel
Ferries	Almost all diesel

It is sometimes suggested in papers on power consumption for transport that countries that have high emissions per kilowatt should stick to diesel, and those with very low emissions per kilowatt convert to electric powered trains. Whilst this argument is very convincing, the emissions of any country can change, and with an investment programme will change, and so it may be a little premature to commit to one fuel source or another where the input power generation mix may change. This may not the case for countries with large coal reserves, such as Australia or India, where it is highly likely that this dependence on coal for power generation will continue for decades.

Typical values for a variety of different measures are shown below. Notice again the large ranges for each different transport mode. The table below lists typical values for CO_2 emissions for different transport modes.

Transport Modes CO_2 Emissions Typical Values

Mode	Typical Value
Metro	7 - 30 grams per pass km
Light rail	15 – 70 grams per pass km
Tram	17 – 75 grams per pass km

Transport Modes CO_2 Emissions Typical Values

Mode	Typical Value
Intermediate capacity metro	12 – 100 grams per pass km
HSR	15 – 30 grams per pass km
Bus	30 – 100 grams per pass km
Minibus	60 grams per pass km
Ferry	2250 grams per pass km
Regional train	25 – 200 grams per pass km
Commuter rail	25 – 105 grams per pass km
Road Vehicles	
Small road vehicle < 1.4 litre engine (petrol)	153 grams per km
Medium road vehicle 1.4 – 2.0 litre engine (petrol)	190 grams per km
Large road vehicle > 2.0 litre engine (petrol)	260 grams per km
Aircraft	
Long distance air travel	100 grams per pass km
Short distance air travel	150 grams per pass km

Some commentary is needed for emissions for intermediate capacity metros. The technology of intermediate capacity metros is well developed, and very efficient, and it is possible to have a very efficient metro system using these smaller trains and stations. Where intermediate capacity systems have large numbers of passengers, and the loading factor is high, then they can be just as efficient as a full metro system. In practice however, the emissions of these systems is often terrible, and the system in Porto in Portugal and the Vancouver Skytrain, as well as the Docklands Light Rail are all very energy intensive, and very poor energy performers. These systems are very well designed, and should be highly efficient, and yet seem to be very wasteful with energy.

The answer seems to be the loading factors of the trains. As intermediate capacity metros are mostly driverless, they can operate at very high frequency. As a result, the loading factor of these systems is extremely low, and 20% seems to be a common figure. This is particularly so for the light rail system in Porto, and the Vancouver Skytrain. The high frequency of trains means that the capacity of the system is quite high, and can be 8,000 to 10,000 per hour, and this can be maintained outside of peak times because there are no driver salaries to be paid. Whilst these numbers are small compared to metros, they are large compared to almost all other rail systems, for example, for intensively used commuter systems even 6,000 per hour is high. The result seems to be that most of these rail systems operate almost empty, and the author's experience on the intermediate capacity metro in Malaysia was the same. The grim truth for many of these systems is that they probably didn't have the passenger numbers in nearby areas to justify the service when constructed, and the aim of building the system was to create demand by providing the service. This can mean that when calculating the energy efficiency of intermediate capacity metros they can rate very poorly.

Intermediate capacity metros can also serve a purpose of encouraging rail demand in an area. As the trains and stations are small, and often driverless, providing the service can be cheap enough to run a high frequency system that encourages people to use the system more. A very high frequency rail system can be very attractive to people living in that area, and over time the system will attract more passengers. Nonetheless, in the interim, the energy consumption figures for intermediate capacity systems can be rather poor.

Regional trains have an enormous range for emissions and this is because again of the loading factor. Many regional trains are operated as a public service, and can be almost empty. Governments often want to support regional areas, and one way of doing this is providing uneconomic rail services to areas with little passenger traffic. This might sound harsh, and the benefit of this is that remote regional areas can have good quality transport services without large numbers of people. Because of the policy implications of providing services, energy consumption is not considered to be a priority and so energy efficiency can be a little low.

As an overall trend rail systems in Asia tend to be very efficient, and those in the English speaking world less so. Rail systems in Canada are quite efficient, and the country with the worst energy consumption per person seems to be the US. This difference between these countries is another of the reasons why the range for power consumption for even the same type of rail vehicle is so large.

Emissions for Freight

The following tables were extracted from an English report (listed in the references), and show the relativities quite well for the different transport modes for freight.

CO_2 emissions per Tonne Kilometre	
Transport Mode	**CO_2 emissions per Tonne Km**
Rigid van, 3.5 to 7.5 tonnes	591 grams CO_2 per tonne km
Rigid van, 7.5 to 17 tonnes	336 grams CO_2 per tonne km
Rigid van, > 17 tonnes	187 grams CO_2 per tonne km
Articulated van < 33 tonnes	163 grams CO_2 per tonne km
Articulated van > 33 tonnes	82 grams CO_2 per tonne km
Rail	21 grams CO_2 per tonne km
Small bulk carrier (marine)	11 grams CO_2 per tonne km
Large bulk carrier (marine)	7 grams CO_2 per tonne km
Small container vessel	15 grams CO_2 per tonne km
Large container vessel	13 grams CO_2 per tonne km

For air freight, the same report produced these figures:

CO_2 emissions per Tonne Kilometre	
Transport Mode	**CO_2 emissions per Tonne Km**
Domestic flights (UK)	1900 grams CO_2 per tonne km
Short haul flights	1320 grams CO_2 per tonne km
Long haul flights	1480 grams CO_2 per tonne km

Emissions for freight for flights is extremely high, and air freight is normally only used where the freight is very light or speed of delivery is required.

The numbers used here are drawn from *"2008 Guidelines to Defra's GHG Conversion factors: Methodology Paper for Transport Emissions Factors"*, written by the department of energy in the UK.

Diesel Vs Electric

Diesel powered trains have the advantage that they require less infrastructure. Overhead wiring, or alternatively a third rail, is not needed. To supply power to either the overhead or third rail systems, substantial infrastructure is needed, such as substations, transmission lines, and cabling running everywhere. This infrastructure requires a significant number of people to maintain, and the engineering skill set both difficult to trains for and retain, so the cost of wages for the maintainers is often quite high. The question is often asked; is this all worth it?

Electric power systems have a lot of problems associated with them, and these include:
- Anyone who touches the third rail or the overhead is usually killed instantly
- When performing maintenance, especially for track maintenance (i.e. fixing track geometry), the power needs to be switched off
- Accidental contact between equipment such as cranes and the overhead does happen, and this is a safety risk
- Substations, where the electricity is converted to the right voltage, sometimes catch fire and explode
- The presence of electricity in the rail corridor can cause electrolysis and other bizarre problems
- Electric overhead power line (the catenary and contact wire) are often considered ugly and unpleasant to look at

So if electric power is so problematic, then why is it installed? There are some advantages, and these include:
- In areas of large numbers of train movements, it's cheaper
- Tunnels and diesel trains are a bad combination, the smoke produced from diesel motors is unpleasant, and nasty to breathe in

- HSR diesel trains are limited to 200 kms/hr as a top speed
- Diesel motors are often considered to be dangerous to use in tunnels, and may require more infrastructure to accommodate their presence in the tunnel. In particular diesel trains introduce a fuel source into a tunnel, and it is possible for a poorly maintained diesel motor to explode
- In countries with low emissions per kilowatt hour, using electricity produces less emissions than diesel motors

One of the key questions for deciding to use electric powered trains, is the environment, and emissions. It's another important factor in the decision making. The commonly held view is that diesel trains are more polluting than electric trains, but this is not necessarily the case.

An attempt is made below to compare consumption of diesel and electric trains. Typical values are used to demonstrate which fuel source produces less emissions under certain circumstances. For the graph below it is assumed that 10 millilitres of diesel fuel is used for each seat kilometre, and 35 watts for each seat kilometre for electric trains. The CO_2 emitted for electric trains is calculated, and this is based on the amount of CO_2 emitted per kilowatt hr.

The quantity of CO_2 produced from a litre of diesel fuel is often assumed to be 2.65 kilograms of CO_2 per litre of diesel fuel. This number comes from an EU directive, 1999/100/EC, which is a directive concerning the level of emissions produced when testing cars. This number is specified in this directive, and it has become the defacto standard for the quality of CO_2 produced from diesel. In practice the actual figure can vary depending on the type of fuel and its source, but as a standard figure this one is useful.

Figure 7.1 Emissions Comparison Diesel vs Electric

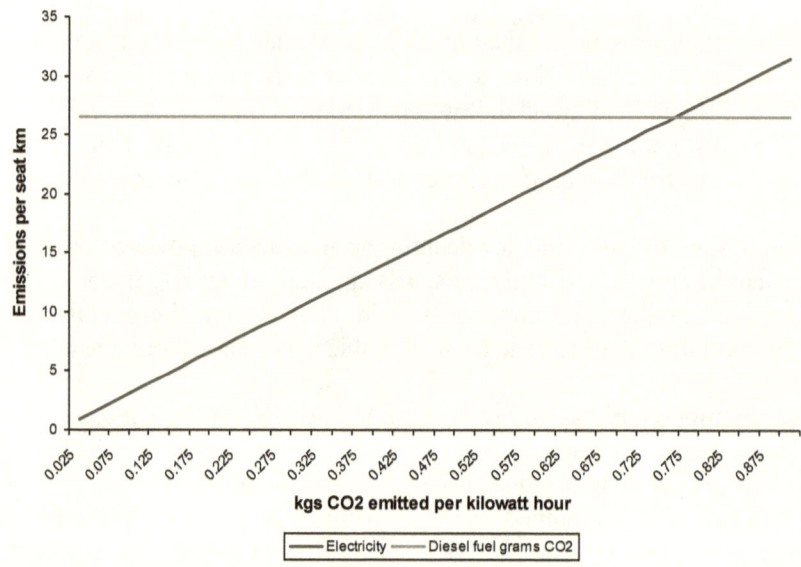

The blue line represents the emissions per seat kilometre with differing levels of emissions per kilowatt hr. Notice that for most of the graph that the blue line is lower than the green, and at very high values of emissions per kilowatt, it is possible for diesel trains to actually be more environmentally friendly than electric trains. This situation will be confined to countries where energy produced is dependent almost entirely on coal, such as Australia and India.

Overall most countries can reduce their emissions by changing their trains from diesel to electric.

REFERENCES

1. Bombardier, *EcoActive Technologies Mitrac Energy Saver*, www.bombardier.com

2. Kenworthy, J. *Transport Energy Use and Greenhouse Gases in Urban Passenger Transport Systems: A Study of 84 Global Cities, Institute for Sustainability and Technology Policy*, Murdoch University

3. Dearien, J. *Ultralight Rail and Energy Use*, Encyclopaedia of Energy, Elsevier Publishing, March 2004

4. Romo, L.& Turner, D. & NG, L.S. Brian *Cutting Traction Power Costs with Wayside Energy Storage Systems in Rail Transit Systems*, Proceedings of JRC2005, Joint Rail Conference, March 2005

5. Halcrow, *Energy Efficiency Opportunities Study Driving Style Modelling* ED-003-012, April 2011

6. World Nuclear Organisation, *Comparison of Lifecycle Greenhouse Gas Emissions of Various Electricity Generation Sources*, http://www.world-nuclear.org/uploadedFiles/org/WNA/Publications/Working_Group_Reports/comparison_of_lifecycle.pdf

7. Jernbaneverket, *Environmental Analysis Energy Consumption – Norwegian High Speed Railway Project Phase 3*, Dec 2011

8. Network Rail, *Comparing the environmental impact of conventional and high speed rail*, www.networkrail.co.uk/5878

9. Leung Michael KH *Carbon Emission Factors for Public Transportation in Metropolitan*, International Conference on Carbon Reduction, Sept 2010

10. Carruthers, J.J. et al *The application of a systematic approach to material selection for the lightweighting of metro vehicles*, Proc. IMechE Vol. 223 Part F: J. Rail and Rapid Transit, May 2009

11. Falvo, M.C. *Energy Saving in Metro-Transit Systems: Impact of Braking Energy Management*, SPEEDAM 2010, International Symposium on Power Electronics, Electrical Drives, Automation and Motion

12. RATP Group 2012 Sustainability Report, http://www.ratp.fr/en/ratp/c_5367/our-essential-documents/

13. Win van Beek The Effects of Speed Measures on Air Pollution and Traffic Safety, The Association for European Transport, 2008

14. Yangzhen, Z et al *A Simulation Model of Energy Efficient Automatic Train Control* (ATC 1999), http://citeseerx.ist.psu.edu/viewdoc/summary?doi=10.1.1.508.9800

15. Kemp, R. *T618 – Traction Energy Metrics*, No 2, Rail Safety and Standards Board, Engineering, Dec 2007

16. International Energy Agency, *Transport Energy and CO_2*, 2009, https://www.iea.org/publications/freepublications/publication/transport2009.pdf

17. Defra, *2012 Guidelines to Defra/DECC's GHG Conversion Factors for Company Reporting*, https://www.gov.uk/government/uploads/system/uploads/attachment_data/file/69554/pb13773-ghg-conversion-factors-2012.pdf

18. Lang, P. *Emission Cuts Realities – Electricity Generation*, Jan 2010, http://bravenewclimate.com/2010/01/09/emission-cuts-realities/

19. Commissioner for Environmental Sustainability Victoria, *Public transport's role in reducing greenhouse gas emissions*, July 2008

20. Dearien, J. *Ultralight Rail and Energy Use*, Encyclopedia of Energy, Elsevier Publishing, Cutler J. Cleveland, Editor-in-Chief, March 2004

21. Romo, L. et al *Cutting Traction Power Costs with Wayside Energy Storage Systems in Rail Transit Systems*, Proceedings of the JRC 2005 Conference March 2005 Colorado

22. Williams, M. & Schmid, L. *The Effect of Rail Running Surface Irregularities on Energy Consumption*, Railway Engineering Conference Newcastle Australia Oct 1993

23. Bae, C.H. et al *Simulation Study of Regenerative Inverter for DC Traction Substation*, Electrical Machines and Systems, 2005, ICEMs

24. Griffiths, M. *Energy management of traction power substations on the Dallas Area Rapid Transit System*, Proceedings of the 1999 ASME/IEEE Joint Railroad Conference, 1999

25. Henning, U. et al *Ultra low emission traction drive system for hybrid light rail*, SPEEDHAM 2006, International Symposium on Power Electronics, Electric Drives, Automation and Motion

26. Jong, J.C. & Chang, E.F. *Models for Estimating Energy Consumption of Electric Trains*, Journal of the Eastern Asia Society for Transportation Studies, Vol 6, pp 278 – 291, 2005

27. Tourism and Transport Forum Public Transport and Climate Change, Nov 2009, http://www.ttf.org.au/Content/ptclimatechange.aspx

28. Thong, M. & Cheong, A. *Energy Efficiency in Singapore's Rapid Transit System*, Journeys May 2012

29. Hong, W. & Kim, S. *A study on the energy consumption unit of subway stations in Korea*, Building and Environment 39 (2004) 1497 – 1503

30. Kennedy, C. *A comparison of the sustainability of public and private transportation systems: Study of the Greater Toronto Area*, Transportation 29: 459 – 493, 2002

31. Viswanathan, C.N et al *Energy Conservation in Subway Systems by Controlled Acceleration and Deceleration*, Energy Research, Vol 2, 133 – 151 (1978)

32. Oak Ridge National Laboratory, *Transportation Energy Data Book, Edition 29*, July 2010, cta.ornl.gov/data

Power Consumption

Introduction

Rail systems are very energy efficient, and a rail system will normally consume far less power than any other comparable transport system for the same purpose. Rail systems require far less energy to perform the same function.

The lower power consumption is one of the great advantages of rail. In performing an economic assessment of the benefits of rail, special consideration should be made of the lower energy consumption. Depending on the government policy at the time, this may or may not be important to the decision maker for a new rail project. Regardless of the views of the decision maker, it is a real benefit, and should have significant value placed upon it.

Typical Values for Power Consumption

Below are summarised the results of many reports that have examined the energy consumption of different types of transport modes. An attempt has been made to summarise many different reports into a ranking of power consumption per passenger, or per seat kilometre. Problems abound with this approach, but for rail planning it's a necessary step. Many of the papers available are of varying quality, and separating out fact from fiction was not an easy process.

Technology has been improving, and the power consumption per passenger kilometre, and the fuel consumed per kilometre, has been dropping. This improvement has been steady for at least the past 20 years, so the power consumption and fuel figures listed below will change over time, and improve. References and reports produced more than 15 years ago often quote higher consumption figures, and the drop in power consumption per vehicle, and per passenger, has been quite substantial. No doubt in the future improvements will continue to be made, so it seems likely that the rankings in the tables below may change into the future.

Transport Modes Typical Values		
Mode	Metric	Typical Value
Electricity		
Metro	Energy per pass km	14 - 60 watt hrs per pass km
Light rail	Energy per pass km	33 – 115 watt hrs per pass km
Tram	Energy per pass km	33 - 150 watt hrs per pass km
Intermediate capacity metro	Energy per pass km	20 – 200 watt hrs per pass km
HSR	Energy per pass km	30 – 55 watts hrs per pass km
Commuter rail	Energy per pass km	30 – 100 watt hrs per pass km
Diesel		
Bus	Fuel per pass km	12 – 60 ml per pass km
Minibus	Fuel per pass km	22.77 ml per pass km
Ferry	Fuel per pass km	850 ml per pass km
Regional train	Fuel per pass km	10 – 70 ml per pass km
Commuter rail	Fuel per pass km	10 – 40 ml per pass km

The numbers above should be treated with a great deal of caution. The power consumed by any railway per person can very by an enormous amount, and the rankings above are really only a rough guide. Nonetheless some important points should be made:
- A heavily loaded metro will always be the most power efficient per person, as people stand and many metros operate fully loaded
- Air and sea transport is wasteful of energy in comparison to rail, and is always less efficient

- High Speed rail is surprisingly efficient, and very similar to commuter and regional rail systems

There are an enormous number of factors that could potentially change the energy consumption per person. Perhaps the most important is the loading factor, which can substantially change the energy efficiency per person, because most of the weight of trains is in the body of the train, and the weight of passengers is small in comparison, so increasing the number of people always improves the energy efficiency. So it is always energy efficient to pack as many people as possible into each vehicle.

High Speed Rail and Energy Consumption

The energy consumed by high speed rail (HSR) is very important. As HSR trains travel large distances, and large numbers of people are moved, then it is critical to know how much power an HSR train will consume. The energy cost of moving large numbers of people with HSR is quite significant. Whilst this question is easy to propose, getting the answer is quite difficult.

The conventional wisdom is that HSR trains should consume large amounts of energy. Pushing against the air, at high speeds, should require large amounts of energy, and the faster trains go then the greater the energy consumption. It would be easy to assume that a trains travelling at 250 kms/hr would consume more power than one travelling at 100 kms/hr. Often, experiments have been performed that calculate the forces on trains, and they are almost expressed as a function of speed, and they always look like:

$$Force = a + bv + cv^2$$

Each of the terms in the above equation represent some part of the resistance to movement for each train, for example, the cv^2 part of the equation is often though to be related to aerodynamic drag, which is important at high speeds. The other terms are related to friction in the train, bogies, and wheels, which does not change with the speed of the train (or shouldn't anyway).

We also know that *Work = Force x distance*, and work is measured in Joules, so as the force increases then the energy consumed should also increase. So it is easy to expect that the energy consumed by HSR trains is very high, even at relatively moderate speeds.

In practice this is not the case. As surprising as it may seem, HSR trains travelling at 250 kms/hr consume the same energy per person as a regional or commuter train travelling at 100 kms/hr. The author, after first calculating this result refused to believe it, but there is no question that it is true. This value of energy consumption is one of the key reasons why HSR systems and technology are so desirable, and why many countries are considering installing them. But why, how can this be?

The author suggests the following reasons for the energy efficiency of HSR systems, and it is difficult to know which factor is more important than any other:
- HSR trains are aggressively streamlined, and so the aerodynamic drag is much lower than a conventional train
- HSR systems mostly are built on open ground, so energy is not wasted pushing air along a long tube
- HSR systems have very few stops, often 6 to 10 on one line, so stopping and starting occurs infrequently
- HSR trains are often able to maintain constant speeds from one end of the line to the other, so acceleration and deceleration is limited
- There are no large vertical curves in HSR systems, so trains rarely climb and descend hills, which can waste power, especially if the station is at the bottom of a hill
- HSR trains are very long, so the drag from the train per unit length will be lower for a longer train, as drag is mostly calculated relative the frontal cross-sectional area. IN practice a longer trains will have a higher aerodynamic drag, but a longer trains is always more energy efficient than two trains that add to the same length. One HSR trains may be the same length as three regional trains.

So for these reasons, energy consumption of HSR trains is similar to commuter and regional trains, and maybe a little more efficient. From an energy consumption perspective, this makes HSR trains very attractive.

The Shinkansen is the most energy efficient HSR train at the time of writing of this book (2012), and it seems that a number of innovations were employed to get the drag as low as possible, and these include:

- Further streamlining the front of the train
- Putting aerodynamic covers on everything underneath the train
- Making the outside of the train as smooth as possible, including the area where carriages are coupled together
- Reducing the number of pantographs from 8 to 2
- Designing a low drag pantograph, with a specially designed cover
- Even redesigning the windscreen wiper for the front of the train

The Japanese were partially motivated by the desire to reduce emissions, but also were motivated by the desire to reduce noise from the train, as much of the Japanese HSR system is built on slab concrete track, and that's noisy, so there was great political pressure to reduce the noise. As it turns out, reducing the noise is almost the same thing as reducing power consumption, so the Shinkansen trains became very energy efficient.

The graph below shows a comparison of the running resistance for two types of Shinkansen, the 300 series and the 700 series. This information was extracted from a paper published in 2000 called "*Improvement to the Aerodynamic Characteristics of Rollingstock*". It shows the benefits of improved technology to the drag of HSR trains, and how reducing the drag effectively increases the maximum speed of the train. Since this paper was published the Japanese have built the E5 series Shinkansen train, and this train is even more streamlined than the 700 series.

Figure 7.2 Shinkansen and Drag

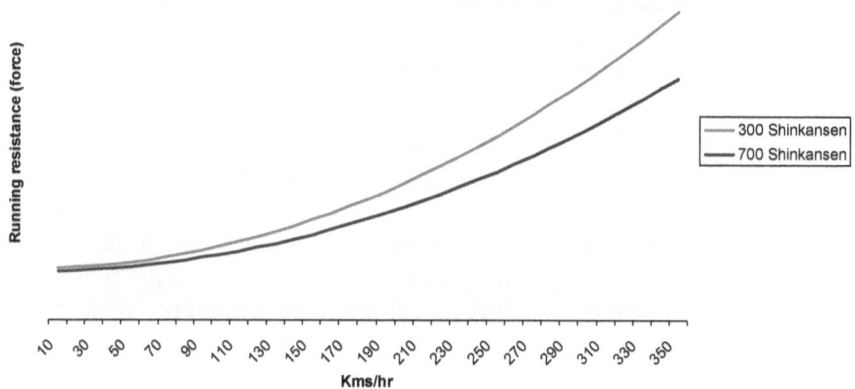

Notice that the running resistance increases at the power of 2 compared to the velocity.

It seems that the Japanese have settled on a energy consumption value of around 30 watts per seat kilometre. As their technology improves, they are able to increase the speed of their trains, but are currently limited to about 320 kms/hr. Their trains could probably go much faster than this, and modern European trains can do 350 -360 kms/hr, but as mentioned above, the noise restrictions on HSR trains within Japan means that they are not permitted to travel above these speeds. European trains seem to average about 50 watts per seat kilometre, which is a little high but not excessively so.

So what about the length of the HSR train, does this help with reducing the drag? Is this a more energy efficient option? It seems that increasing the length of the train does actually help, and the equation below shows the relationship between the different variables.

We start with the formula for the aerodynamic drag for a train:

$$D = \frac{1}{2}\rho A v^2 \left(C + \frac{\lambda}{d_h} l \right)$$

Where:

D = aerodynamic drag
ρ = density of air
v = velocity of the train
C = constant based on the drag caused by the front and back of the train
λ = constant for the drag from the surface of the side of the train
d_h = the hydraulic diameter of the train

The hydraulic diameter is a standard term used in flow calculations, for produced a diameter that is roughly the same, in terms of fluid flow, as the equivalent diameter for a round object. It is normally defined as follows:

$$d_h = \frac{4A}{P}$$

Where A = area, and P = the perimeter.

The only terms for this equation that could be found were for the Shinkansen 100 series train, which at the time of writing is an obsolete model and has been removed from service in Japan. Nonetheless, for the purposes of the analysis, we can assume that the relative weights of the drag coefficients are similar comparable to more modern trains. The numbers for this equation were:

$$D = \frac{1}{2}\rho A v^2 (0.15 + 0.004521)$$

From this equation we can see that drag increases linearly with length, but is quite large to begin with. The longer the train, the drag increases, but there is a large constant term, so per passenger, it's always better to make the train as long as possible. A length of 200 metres, from this equation, seems to be a reasonable compromise, and anything lower than this would be energy inefficient. A 300 metre train is better than a 200 metre one, and the energy consumed per person will be lower. Of course it would be helpful to have these coefficients for more modern trains.

So does HSR travel compare well with air travel? Above we saw that the figure to use for comparison with HSR for air travel was an emissions level of about 158 grams of CO_2 per passenger km. For the purposes of comparison, the table below shows all the different scenarios under which an HSR system might operate, and what the comparable emissions might be.

Scenario Analysis – HSR – High and Low loading factors			
HSR type	**Emissions**	**Load factor**	**Grams CO_2 per km per passenger km**
European	High	30%	133
European	Low	30%	67
European	High	50%	80
European	Low	50%	40
Japanese	High	30%	80
Japanese	Low	30%	40
Japanese	High	50%	48
Japanese	Low	50%	24

The assumption was made that the Europeans have not improved their HSR technology so that it's similar with the Japanese, but it is likely that this gap in efficiency will soon close. A value of 800 grams per kilowatt hour was used for high emissions, and 400 grams per kilowatt hour for low. A value of 50 watts per seat kilometre was used for European HSR trains.

There is a lot to be said about this table. We can see that even the worst emitting HSR system produces less CO_2 than a domestic flight in the UK.

Also note that increasing the load factor is very helpful in reducing emissions. The graph below shows the effect of increasing the load factor on emissions per passenger km, and it's very helpful. We note that even the worst emitting train performs extremely well when it's full of passengers.

Figure 7.3 Emissions per Passenger Kilometre 700 Shinkansen

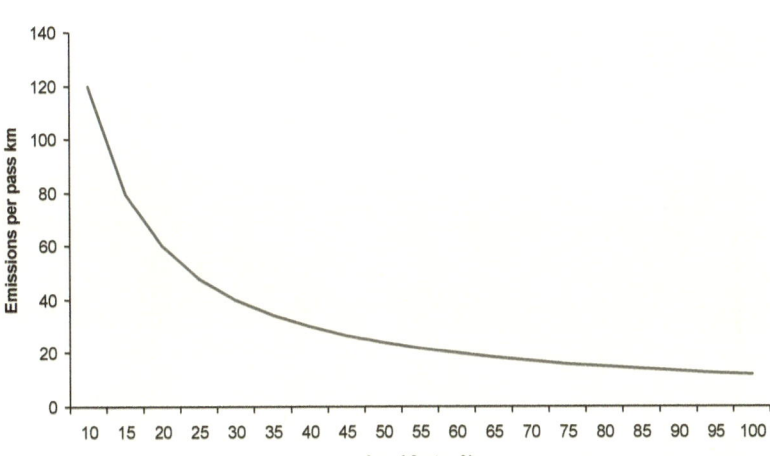

From this graph we see that a rail system really needs at least 30 – 40 % loads to be energy efficient, and for a well-designed rail system this should be no problem.

Driving Trains Efficiency

It is possible for railways to minimise their power consumption through driving trains differently or more efficiently. For a railway that has already been built and commissioned this represents one of the few ways that power consumption can be reduced. Obviously changing driver behaviour is relatively cheap, so railways will always be interested in reducing power consumption this way.

There are two main ways to reduce power consumption, through driver behaviour. These are:
- Driving more slowly
- Driving the train in an efficient way

Driving the train in an efficient way refers to the way that a driver applies the power to the motor in the train. As with any motor, there are a number of settings for the amount of power applied to a motor, and the output of the motor increases as the power applies is increased. A number of studies have been performed to examine how to drive the train the best, and an optimal speed profile has been developed. Essentially, the best way to drive a train is to accelerate as hard as possible, and then coast until time to decelerate, and then decelerate as quickly as permitted for passenger comfort. This optimal speed profile is shown in the figure below.

Figure 7.4 The Optimal Speed Profile

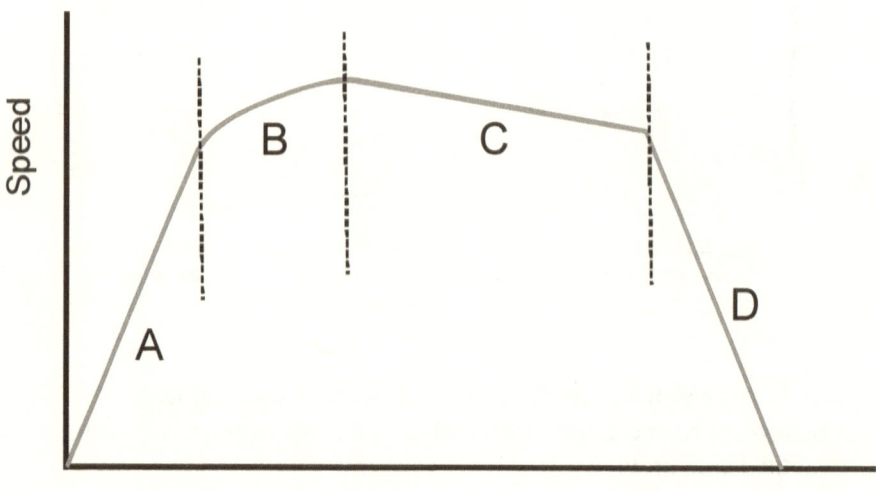

This graph has speed on the vertical axis, and time on the horizontal. As a train leaves a station it speeds up, and then slows its acceleration, coasts, and then decelerates. The time to get from one station to another as shown above may be only 1 or 2 minutes, or could be substantially longer.

Each of the stages in the speed profile are:
- A: acceleration away from the station
- B: tapering off of acceleration
- C: coasting, where no power is applied
- D: deceleration and stop

The height of the profile, ie, the final speed reached when leaving the station, as well as the acceleration, will determine how long the train takes to reach the next station.

It is particularly important that the train does not apply power throughout the entire distance, or until the end of section C.

The optimal speed profile can be calculated ahead of time, and then speed boards placed at the correct places alongside the track to indicate to drivers when to accelerate, stop accelerating and coast, and then decelerate. Without some guidance it may be a little difficult for all drivers to know when to apply power or to coast. One of the benefits of an ATP system is that it can, when designed to allow this, provide a target speed to the driver so that the motor and brakes can be applied at the correct time. Significant power savings are available for implementing this type of system, but it is unlikely to be a saving more than 10% of total power consumption.

Top speed is also very relevant, and has a profound effect on the energy consumed to drive trains. The energy and hence power consumed for a train, for short distances, can be very roughly approximated using the formula for kinetic energy, which is:

$$Kinetic\ energy = \frac{1}{2}mv^2$$

Where m = mass, and v = velocity in ms^{-1}. As the velocity increases, then the energy stored in the movement of the vehicle increases with the square of the velocity, so the energy consumed increases very quickly. This equation is rarely used for energy and power calculations for rolling stock, but does neatly illustrate the point, that increased speed increases power and energy consumption substantially. In practice there are losses associated with almost all aspects of transferring power from a power station to a train, and these would need to be considered as well to improve the accuracy of this equation.

So driving trains more slowly almost always reduces the power consumption, but from a customer perspective, is often unacceptable. It is sometimes possible to increase the acceleration of a train to compensate for a lower top speed, as acceleration is not a term in the above equation. For any given railway this may or may not be possible, as many different types of trains are limited in their maximum acceleration, or for passenger comfort purposes there are limits on the maximum acceleration. Nonetheless increasing the acceleration and reducing the velocity of a passenger train should reduce power consumption.

Power Consumed in Stations and other Facilities

The power consumed in stations, workshops, shops and cleaning equipment, can be a significant percentage of the power consumption for a railway. Certainly in Sydney the power consumed at stations is relatively low, as the pleasant and comfortable weather means that air conditioning at stations is rarely needed, something that consumes a lot of power. In Singapore on the other hand and on some lines the power consumed in stations is greater than the power used for moving trains, and this is probably because of the need to air condition stations in that country. It is possible to achieve reductions in power consumption in stations, and below are some fairly standard measures that can be implemented in stations to reduce the power consumption:

- Platform screen doors retain the air conditioned air within the station. The are particularly effective in cities where the temperature is either very hold or cold
- Special lighting systems can reduce the power needed for lighting by about 30%. There are a number of different technologies, including voltage regulation and special types of fluorescent tubes
- Reducing the number of entrances and exits into the station
- Installing escalators that slow down when no one is using them. These escalators can detect when passengers step onto them
- Special types of lifts consume less power moving people up and down
- Overall the energy consumption of a station is usually proportional to its floor area, so smaller stations consume less energy
- Smaller numbers of escalators and lifts
- Installing solar panels on the rooves of outdoor stations
- Technology in stations, especially the air conditioning system, that can air condition the station more efficiently

These initiatives can reduce the power consumption in stations by up to 50%, and should be implemented where economically feasible to do so.

Much larger railways may have other facilities to which they need to provide power. Maintenance depots, or large facilities such as washing sheds, can be run from railways power. In some cases workshops, and machine tools such as lathes, can also be run from railways power. This is especially true where the workshop is located in a rail corridor, and away from any other power source or the local power provider.

Providing power to shops on stations is common in Australia, and is a good way to supplement income derived from leasing out parts of the station. It is not possible to find any publicly available information on what railways do in other parts of the world as regards on-selling power, but we can probably make some educated guesses on the conditions that increase the probability that railways on-sell power:
- Railways that consume large amounts of electricity are better equipped to on-sell electricity, those with only diesel trains may not be in a position to do so
- railways would on sell power to shops located on platforms, or wholly within the paid area
- where stations are located in places where there are no other buildings, then the railway is likely to provide the power
- where it is technically challenging to provide power to shops, ie, in a very strange place, the railway may provide the power as the local power company does not have the skills to do it

There are occasionally special situations where a railway may be required to supply power to facilities where there are no other providers. Examples include army facilities, hospitals, hotels and mines located in places where there is no other supply of power. In these cases the railway may need to supply power, and bill for its provision.

It is very difficult to reduce or even manage the power consumed by external parties, towns, workshops, or maintenance facilities. Where the power is supplied, it is not the railway's concern as to the size of the power consumption, unless the power consumed overloads the rail system power grid, in which case the something needs to be done. For reporting purposes any power on-sold should be excluded from any analysis of power consumption. Railways often set targets for energy consumption reduction, and including these makes things very difficult indeed.

Power consumption is something that should be considered in the design of any station. Whilst it might seem to the reader that design choices are limited, the reality is that there is much that can be done to reduce power consumption in a station. This is especially so for underground stations, or those that are covered and require artificial lighting.

Stations consume a lot of power. Stations may consume over 50% of all the power consumed by a rail system. Many of the systems installed in stations can consume a lot of power. Some of the typical systems and facilities that consume all this power include:
- Shops, especially those that cook or provide food
- Advertising displays
- Lighting
- Wireless internet
- Lifts and escalators
- Facilities for stations staff
- Air conditioning
- Platform screen doors

Larger stations consume more power than smaller ones. Reducing the size of a station is one way to reduce power consumption, and the power consumption per square metre of public area can be constant across many different station types, so smaller stations consume less power than large ones. A modern trend has been to increase the size and space of stations, as this give a feeling of space and luxury, and many large terminus stations have been designed this way. One should remember however that larger stations, with a greater floor area and volume, will need more power to be air conditioned and lit.

Deeper underground stations will consume more power. As mentioned above, it is generally recommended for any station built underground to be as close to the surface as possible, as this makes evacuation easier in the event of a fire or any other emergency. Deep stations require more power to move people from the platform to the surface, and the deeper this is the more power that is consumed. Where the station is particularly deep, multiple escalators may be needed, as one escalator will be either too short to reach from the platform to the surface, or the capacity may not be enough, or that there is no room to fit the escalator in. Multiple escalators will consume more power than one on its own.

Lifts and escalators have been substantially redesigned in recent years to reduce their level of power consumption. Escalators have been designed that operate only when passengers are detected moving onto it (or standing on it), so escalators operate only very slowly when no one is using it. This can save a lot of power.

Being more efficient with Power Consumption

It is important for a railway to attempt to minimise the consumption of power, and to be as energy efficient as possible. There are lots of things that can be done to reduce power consumption, and some are easy to implement, and some of them are politically difficult, or difficult to implement. These include:
- Reducing the mass of rollingstock, by using lighter materials such as aluminium
- As mentioned above, driving slower. A very unpopular option
- Operating trains with a high loading factor, which either means fewer services, or shorter trains.
- Limiting the maximum speed of the train, and procuring trains designed for lower speeds
- Using special lubricants on top of the rail to reduce friction, and save power
- Using better electrical infrastructure with fewer energy losses
- Closing stations, or designed rail lines with fewer stations, so that trains do not need to accelerate or decelerate as often
- Operating a metro style system, where people stand, so only a small number of seats are needed
- Installing regenerative braking on rollingstock, or buying trains with this feature included
- Removing any grade crossings, ie, so that trains can accelerate and decelerate smoothly
- Streamlining rollingstock so that drag is minimised
- Increasing the length of carriages, so that the average weight per metre is reduced
- Single bore rather than twin bore tunnels

The best time to plan and implement any energy initiatives is when the railway is being constructed. Once a railway is built, it is very difficult to change the energy consumed. Most passengers will not accept slower travel times in exchange for lower power consumption, passengers are very sensitive to travel times, and so not want them increased. In some countries perhaps with very strong environmental sentiments, it may be possible politically to do this, but the author recommends not doing so. Rail as a system is a solution to reduce emissions and power consumption, and slowing trains down to save a small amount of power undermines one of the main benefits of the system by discouraging people from using the system.

It's really important for any rail system to reduce the weight of its rollingstock. Heavier trains require more power to move, so lighter trains are more energy efficient. Modern trains are a little lighter than trains 30 years ago, and much of this has been achieved by using more aluminium. It is possible to design the trains with lower weight by redesigning many of the fittings inside the train. Beware however that in many cases the weight of trains is increasing in some countries, as heavier trains are more crash resistant, and in the US and Australia some trains are heavier than a comparable train on the same rail line with the same stopping pattern than 20 years ago.

Streamlining is common on all modern rollingstock. Trains more recently manufactured have become progressively more and more streamlined, and this has reduced the drag they experience as they move. The appearance of many modern trains has changed as the streamlining has become more pronounced. Streamlining may even include the underneath of the train, and may include the bogies and the underside of the train. Significant energy efficiencies can be gained by streamlining the front of the train, especially low in front of the bogies. This is especially true of high speed trains, where streamlining underneath the train is common.

One thing that is commonly done is to the track at stations slightly raised in comparison to the track between stations, so that when the train comes to stop at the station, gravity assists. When the train departs from the station, it is assisted again by gravity, which pushes the train down. London Underground has this design on some of its lines. This is shown below.

Surprisingly only a few metres of depth between stations is needed to reduce the power consumption dramatically. To use the correct physics terms, when the train climbs to get to the station, energy is transferred from kinetic energy to potential energy, and when the train leaves the station, it is converted from potential to kinetic.

Raising the track at stations was a common practice even 50 years ago. Some water stations for steam trains were designed in this way, and placed at the top of hills.

Regenerative braking has become very popular with new rail systems. This type of braking involves storing kinetic energy from the moving train when the train brakes and comes to a stop. Until very recently when trains braked the energy was converted almost entirely into heat, and wasted. Modern trains are often equipped with regenerative braking, where the energy is "regenerated" and essentially can be used again. There are a number of different regenerative braking systems, and the most common is to use capacitors to store energy as a train comes to a stop. Once the train resumes motion, this stored energy may be used to accelerate the train.

Regenerative braking needs to be distinguished from dynamic braking, and occasionally these two things are confused. Dynamic braking is a type of braking where the kinetic energy is dissipated by using the motor to generate electricity when braking, and then sending this energy into a bank of resistors. It is a particularly efficient form of braking, but as with friction braking, the energy is wasted.

There are a number of different types of systems of energy storage used in regenerative braking, and it is also possible to put the energy back into this electricity grid, which is discussed below. Capacitors are commonly used for energy storage, and they need to be very high performance to be able store the power needed, and sometimes these capacitors used are called super capacitors. Capacitors electrically wear, and come with all sorts of problems, but many of these engineering problems seem to have been overcome.

Another way of storing the power generated in braking is to use flywheels. This is a mechanical system with spinning wheels, and they are heavy, and as the train decelerates the wheels spin faster and faster, storing the energy as rotational energy. If the train sits at a station for a long period of time, the flywheel will slow down and energy will be wasted, so it's a system that is more efficient where the train accelerates away from the station fairly quickly after coming to a stop.

As with any type of regenerative braking, energy is lost in the conversion from one type of energy to another. Energy is also lost if the train does not resume its motion as quickly as possible, and the stored energy is slowly dissipated as time progresses. There are also some potential risks with energy stored in batteries or similar, as very rarely batteries may explode, particularly when they are not handled correctly or properly maintained.

Another form of regenerative braking is to put the energy back into the power grid. Electrically powered trains can put energy back into the overhead wiring or third rail, so that it can be used by either other trains or in stations. Whilst in theory this idea is very good, in practice the energy put back into the overhead or third rail needs to be used by a train in the nearby area, i.e., at most a few kilometres away. A train on its own with no other trains or stations nearby, if it puts power back into the railway power system, will not achieve anything and the power will be wasted.

It is often not possible to put power back into the city or country power grid. One obvious way to deal with the power generated from regenerative braking is to put the power into the grid that supplies local houses and businesses. Whilst on paper this seems like a good idea, in practice it is often not possible. Railway power is often very dirty, and the quality of the power is low. In technical terms, the power is full of harmonics, which can damage or destroy electrical equipment. Railway power is often so dirty that only the railway itself will accept using for any purpose, and even then special equipment is needed to manage the power. This is unfortunate, as the often occurs that a lone train is passing through the country or regional area, and putting its braking energy back into the power grid would solve a lot of problems. This is especially true of trains powered with DC power.

It should be noted that regenerative braking can only save around 10-20% of the power consumed. It might seem that much more than this can be saved, but no. Losses in conversion of the energy are significant, but more importantly, regenerative braking only works at moderate to high speeds, and at low speeds traditional friction brakes are needed. Regenerative braking is often used in combination with friction brakes, and almost never used on their own.

Twin bore tunnels are less energy efficient than single bore. In the paper *"Twin-tube, Single track high speed rail tunnels and consequences for aerodynamics, climate, equipment and ventilation"* a graph is provided that would suggest that energy consumption in a single bore tunnel is about 20% lower than that of a twin bore tunnel. The key to reducing the power consumed in a tunnel would be to decrease the blockage ratio, which is the ratio of the train area to the area of the tunnel. A smaller area will mean less energy is wasted accelerating air in the tunnel when a train passes through, and hence is more energy efficient.

It is also possible to reduce the power consumption by applying lubricants to the top of the rail. This very interesting area offers opportunities to reduce the power consumption with just applying oils and grease to the top and side of the rail. A device exists called a rail lubricator, and it stores and pumps out lubricant as trains pass over the rail. It's a standard and common technology. This is typically done for freight traffic rather than passenger, and in freight systems so doing is common. Whilst there is a lot of argument in several papers on this topic as to the exact benefit, and the existence of any kind of benefit seems controversial, an energy saving of 10% seems typical. The benefit for a passenger rail system seems to be less than that of a freight system.

Power Consumption, the Environment and the Population Density of Cities

Global warming is a serious issue, and the emission of global warming gases is something that, as much as possible, countries should attempt to avoid. Railways are a key part of this situation, and are a very effective way for entire cities and countries to reduce their emissions.

Encouraging citizens, residents and visitors to use public transport can be a very effective way of reducing emissions. Emissions from cars and private vehicles is far higher than for public transport, and moving people into public transport will reduce emissions. There is however much more to this story, and the population density of any city is also very important. If a city builds apartments, and high rise buildings, then the population density of the city is higher, and the overall size of the city is lower. This makes public transportation much more attractive, and much easier to use. A higher population density makes public transport much easier to economically justify, and a smaller number of lines will be more effective in moving people around the city.

The population density of a city is for some, in countries like Canada and Australia, a passionate issue. Whilst in Asia and Europe cities typically have very high population densities, this is uncommon in Australia, Canada and the US. The internet has many discussion pages where arguments are made for low population densities, and this is not seen as a problem for providing cost effective public transportation. These public discussions sometimes get very heated.

The reality is of course that more dense cities require less energy for transportation, and public transportation works much better with people concentrated into small areas. The graph below was extracted from a paper called *"Transport Energy Use and Greenhouses in Urban Passenger Transport Systems: A Study of 84 Global Cities"*, and demonstrates the concept quite well. This graph shows the energy consumed for transportation based on a large number of cities, and there was a clear relationship between the population density and the energy consumed.

Figure 7.5 Energy Consumer per Person (MJoules)

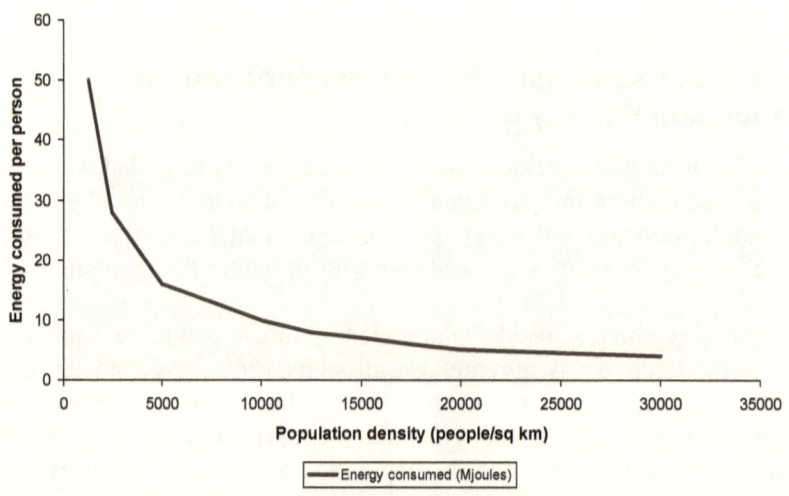

This data was calculated for 84 cities, and represents real data, not a theoretical calculation. We can see that the energy consumed per person falls dramatically as the population density increases. Most of this benefit is realised for cities where the population density is over 10,000 people per square kilometre.

There are two reasons why the energy consumed per person drops so rapidly, and these are:

- The city is smaller in size, as a higher population density means that trips throughout the city are much shorter in distance
- Public transport becomes more efficient, and the smaller size of the city means that the rail or bus system reaches more people

Many cities in Canada, Australia, and the US have population densities of less than 2000 per square kilometre. This is very low, and it is difficult to provide effective public transport in cities of this size. Brisbane in Queensland has a population density of only 350 people per square kilometre, and this ludicrously low number makes rail transport difficult to provide economically.

We note that cities with population densities of less than 2000 people per square kilometre can be very large. Australian cities are enormous, and a trip from one end to another takes hours. Even very large numbers of stations and rail lines are not enough to remove many of the cars from city streets, and the traffic every where is terrible. Rail transport planning in this environment can be a nightmare, because there are never enough people to justify the large expenditure required to build a rail line or system, and HSR systems are impossible because the urban area is large and too expensive to build through. And of course the emissions per person are very high, and the entire situation is really very unpleasant.

Note that this type of city is not only confined to Australia, the US, and Canada. The Chinese city of Ningbo has a low population density, about 770 people per square kilometre, and is similarly spread out over a very large area. Ningbo has 7 million people in it, so a city with a population density this low has a very large urban area.

REFERENCES

1. Bombardier, *EcoActive Technologies Mitrac Energy Saver*, www.bombardier.com

2. Kenworthy, J. *Transport Energy Use and Greenhouse Gases in Urban Passenger Transport Systems: A Study of 84 Global Cities, Institute for Sustainability and Technology Policy*, Murdoch University

3. Dearien, J. *Ultralight Rail and Energy Use*, Encyclopaedia of Energy, Elsevier Publishing, March 2004

4. Romo, L.& Turner, D. & NG, L.S. Brian *Cutting Traction Power Costs with Wayside Energy Storage Systems in Rail Transit Systems*, Proceedings of JRC2005, Joint Rail Conference, March 2005

5. Halcrow, *Energy Efficiency Opportunities Study Driving Style Modelling* ED-003-012, April 2011

6. World Nuclear Organisation, *Comparison of Lifecycle Greenhouse Gas Emissions of Various Electricity Generation Sources*, http://www.world-nuclear.org/uploadedFiles/org/WNA/Publications/Working_Group_Reports/comparison_of_lifecycle.pdf

7. Jernbaneverket, *Environmental Analysis Energy Consumption – Norwegian High Speed Railway Project Phase 3*, Dec 2011

8. Network Rail, *Comparing the environmental impact of conventional and high speed rail*, www.networkrail.co.uk/5878

9. Leung Michael KH *Carbon Emission Factors for Public Transportation in Metropolitan*, International Conference on Carbon Reduction, Sept 2010

10. Carruthers, J.J. et al *The application of a systematic approach to material selection for the lightweighting of metro vehicles*, Proc. IMechE Vol. 223 Part F: J. Rail and Rapid Transit, May 2009

11. Falvo, M.C. *Energy Saving in Metro-Transit Systems: Impact of Braking Energy Management*, SPEEDAM 2010, International Symposium on Power Electronics, Electrical Drives, Automation and Motion

12. RATP Group 2012 Sustainability Report, http://www.ratp.fr/en/ratp/c_5367/our-essential-documents/

13. Win van Beek The Effects of Speed Measures on Air Pollution and Traffic Safety, The Association for European Transport, 2008

14. Yangzhen, Z et al *A Simulation Model of Energy Efficient Automatic Train Control* (ATC 1999), http://citeseerx.ist.psu.edu/viewdoc/summary?doi=10.1.1.508.9800

15. Kemp, R. *T618 – Traction Energy Metrics*, No 2, Rail Safety and Standards Board, Engineering, Dec 2007

16. International Energy Agency, *Transport Energy and CO_2*, 2009, https://www.iea.org/publications/freepublications/publication/transport2009.pdf

17. Defra, *2012 Guidelines to Defra/DECC's GHG Conversion Factors for Company Reporting*, https://www.gov.uk/government/uploads/system/uploads/attachment_data/file/69554/pb13773-ghg-conversion-factors-2012.pdf

18. Lang, P. *Emission Cuts Realities – Electricity Generation*, Jan 2010, http://bravenewclimate.com/2010/01/09/emission-cuts-realities/

19. Commissioner for Environmental Sustainability Victoria, *Public transport's role in reducing greenhouse gas emissions*, July 2008

20. Dearien, J. *Ultralight Rail and Energy Use*, Encyclopedia of Energy, Elsevier Publishing, Cutler J. Cleveland, Editor-in-Chief, March 2004

21. Romo, L. et al *Cutting Traction Power Costs with Wayside Energy Storage Systems in Rail Transit Systems*, Proceedings of the JRC 2005 Conference March 2005 Colorado

22. Williams, M. & Schmid, L. *The Effect of Rail Running Surface Irregularities on Energy Consumption*, Railway Engineering Conference Newcastle Australia Oct 1993

23. Bae, C.H. et al *Simulation Study of Regenerative Inverter for DC Traction Substation*, Electrical Machines and Systems, 2005, ICEMs

24. Griffiths, M. *Energy management of traction power substations on the Dallas Area Rapid Transit System*, Proceedings of the 1999 ASME/IEEE Joint Railroad Conference , 1999

25. Henning, U. et al *Ultra low emission traction drive system for hybrid light rail*, SPEEDHAM 2006, International Symposium on Power Electronics, Electric Drives, Automation and Motion

26. Jong, J.C. & Chang, E.F. *Models for Estimating Energy Consumption of Electric Trains*, Journal of the Eastern Asia Society for Transportation Studies, Vol 6, pp 278 – 291, 2005

27. Tourism and Transport Forum Public Transport and Climate Change, Nov 2009, http://www.ttf.org.au/Content/ptclimatechange.aspx

28. Thong, M. & Cheong, A. *Energy Efficiency in Singapore's Rapid Transit System*, Journeys May 2012

29. Hong, W. & Kim, S. *A study on the energy consumption unit of subway stations in Korea*, Building and Environment 39 (2004) 1497 – 1503

30. Kennedy, C. *A comparison of the sustainability of public and private transportation systems: Study of the Greater Toronto Area*, Transportation 29: 459 – 493, 2002

31. Viswanathan, C.N et al *Energy Conservation in Subway Systems by Controlled Acceleration and Deceleration*, Energy Research, Vol 2, 133 – 151 (1978)

32. Oak Ridge National Laboratory, *Transportation Energy Data Book, Edition 29*, July 2010, cta.ornl.gov/data

Week 8

Supply and Demand

Introduction

In many cases rail systems and transport is provided for the public good. Governments collect taxes, and use these taxes and other resources to provide services for their taxpayers. This includes providing infrastructure and other services, which for whatever reason, cannot be paid for from a user pays basis. There are many such goods and services, and rail is one of these. Rail systems rarely recover their costs from their users, but the economic benefits from possessing a rail system far outweigh the cost of providing them. For this reason, many rail systems are build and provided that do require subsidies from government for their continued operation.

Given this, it is important for government to fully assess the economic benefits of rail systems before subsidizing them. Economics possesses the methods and tools to perform this assessment, and through economic analysis that a rail system can be assessed and its worth determined. These tools are common, and are based mostly on the supply and demand model that is taught throughout any economics course. Economic appraisal of almost any rail project is made through attempting to assess the demand and supply curves of a rail system, and then determine the overall economic benefit, which is made of consumer and producer surpluses. This basic principle is used extensively throughout transport economics, and indeed, economics for rail systems.

Projects are the way in which improvements are made to rail systems, and it is through the project approval phase that the economic benefits of projects are really examined in detail. Many countries have formalised systems and manuals on how to perform these appraisals, and they vary in quality from place to place. The appraisal of large projects is a well researched area, and there are numerous good quality references available to the reader to further explore this process. The process itself can generate a lot of meaningful insight rail projects, and a good appraisal is both logical and easy to read.

Large and small transport projects are approved based on the economic and financial case that is prepared to substantiate them. Large transport projects can cost billions of dollars, and it is important for governments and large corporations that the economic return that is often promised with large projects is genuine. Governments and corporations assess benefits differently, governments use an econometric evaluation, and corporations use a financial one. Financial appraisals are normally made on a purely financial basis, which does not include an assessment of economic benefits. Government cost benefit analysis includes (or should include) all economic costs and benefits.

Economic appraisals are often performed by economists in the private sector, or more commonly working in universities. These departments normally have databases of economic information relevant to the local area in which they operate, and have detailed reports on externalities, costs of congestions, pollution, etc. They also have information on the Willingness to Pay (WTP) of the local population for different transport services, and can predict what level of demand will be generated by different transport services. They can do quite a lot, and often in large rail projects their services can be quite helpful.

The underlying principle for assessing whether projects should proceed is cost benefit. Cost benefit is the ratio of the benefits to the cost, and the ratio for these two numbers should normally be greater than one for the project to be considered. There are a number of variants on this system, where the benefits are quoted as an absolute number in dollars, as a ratio of benefits to costs, or as a rate or return over the life of the project.

This book will not consider in depth how to evaluate the financials of large private sector projects. Costs for the buying of locomotives, wagons, and the construction of terminals change with time, and so any discussion of these costs would be out of date even as this book was being printed. Also the mechanics of evaluating this type of project is quite well known, costs are estimated and tallied, and then compared to the money saved through the project, or the additional capacity that can be created. Capacity calculations for freight are based on the number of trains that can be moved per day, and how much freight they can carry.

Economics plays a role in many different aspects of rail transport planning and this includes:
- The assessment of large capital projects

- Setting the prices for tickets throughout a rail system
- Setting the price for access to a rail network
- Estimating the demand for rail services when new rail lines are built
- Estimating the change in demand for rail services when critical parameters such as train frequency or punctuality are changed
- Estimating the change in land values when rail lines a built nearby
- Changes to industries such as tourism when new rail lines are built
- And for freight, increases or changes in the amount of freight moved on each different transport mode

The Supply Demand Curve/Model

A standard concept in economics is the demand supply curve. Supply and demand, often thought of as a graph and a curve, is actually a model that is used to estimate how price and quantity of any good is determined. This curve/model is extensively used to explain how free markets are able to determine the price of goods sold, and the quantity of goods sold. The supply demand model is applied to only one good at a time. The supply demand model is taught in economics at a very early stage, and is one of the key basic concepts upon which microeconomics is based.

The amount of a good demanded will change depending on the price, and the lower the price the more of the good that will be demanded. Alternatively the supply curve shows the prices at which suppliers of goods will be prepared to sell the good, and the higher the price the more of a specific good that suppliers are prepared to provide. Market equilibrium is the point where the number of goods sold is equal to the number of goods made, and the price and quantity at equilibrium is very important for economics.

There is almost no limit to the number of goods that the supply demand model can be applied to. Transport is one good to which this model can be applied, and commonly is applied. Not all goods have a market, for example the sale of air is in most countries not a good that is manufactured and sold, and so there is no supply and demand curve. This might potentially change in a country where the air quality is very poor, and clean air can be bought.

The graph below shows the standard supply demand curve used in economics. This curve demonstrates the way markets find an equilibrium point which determines both the price paid and the quantity of a good supplied. The supply curve slopes up, as more and more of the good can be supplied where the price paid is higher. The demand curve slopes downwards, as when the price drops the quantity demanded increases. The two lines meet at the equilibrium point, which is where the market stabilises at. Note that the two lines do not need to be straight, curves of almost any shape are acceptable (with some conditions).

Figure 8.1 Consumer and Producer Surplus

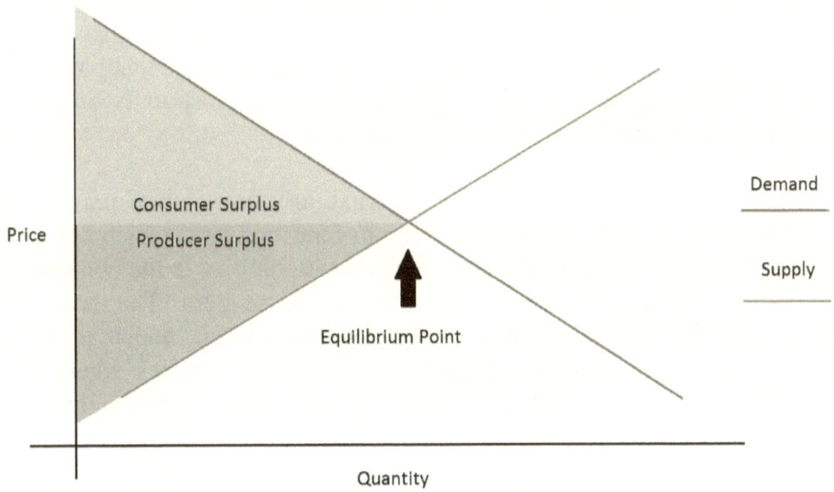

The supply and demand curve drawn above also shows the consumer and producer surplus. The consumer surplus represents the benefit to consumers from buying and consuming any good. As some consumers would be prepared to pay more for the good than the equilibrium price, their economic benefit for buying the good is the difference of the price they were prepared to pay, and the final equilibrium price. The consumer surplus can be calculated by estimating the area as shown on the graph, which can be calculated through an integral.

The same can be said for producer surplus, where the equilibrium price is far higher than the price some producers were prepared to provide goods at. The difference between the equilibrium price and the sale price the producer was prepared to accept is known as the producer surplus. In economics the producer and consumer and producer surplus are considered to be real money, and included in any estimate of the economic benefit of creating or changing a market. Combined the producer and consumer surplus are known as social surplus.

All this works well when the supply and demand curve includes all the costs and benefits to society. In many markets, the supply and demand curve as presented above is more than adequate to represent the social benefit of creating a market, and for rail systems such as a tourist railway this curve is perfectly adequate. Unfortunately, often, the full benefits of providing rail services are intangible, or there may be benefits to third parties other than the buyer and seller, and so may be a little difficult to include, as they cannot be directly measured. For rail, most of these other factors are benefits, and regardless of good or bad, these other factors are called "externalities". Externalities impact upon other parties, or members of society, other than the ones that partake in the transaction between the buyer and seller. Transport is one good where the externalities are very significant.

The existence of large positive externalities for rail transport is the reason why governments are so keen to fund railways, which are often loss making. In many cases the value of externalities to the community are greater than the benefit provided to passengers. The economic benefits from a rail system can be very substantial, and it is in the interests of governmental bodies to provide rail services where they need to be subsidised. Externalities, by definition, are not included in the graph above, and need to be considered by other means in making an economic appraisal of a project. Care needs to be exercised that the benefits to society are real, and the rail system is not just another cost placed upon tax payers.

The demand supply curve is used as the basic model for predicting changes to quantity demanded when changes are made to a good, which is how things are calculated for transport. Investment in infrastructure will often (or should) change the supply curve, or in some cases the demand curve. Infrastructure projects will allow more for less, which means that more can be done with the infrastructure for a lower cost. For example, redesigning a freight line so that it allows double stacking may increase the capacity of freight trains by 30%, reducing the cost of the freight movement because more of it is moved at one time. The reduction in cost allows the supply curve to move, and in economics it is said to "move to the right". A constriction in supply moves the supply curve to the left.

The graph below shows a common result of an infrastructure project. The supply curve has moved to the right, which normally means a successful infrastructure project. The equilibrium point has been moved, so that it is now lower in price and higher in quantity than the original equilibrium point. There has been a change in consumer surplus, which is clearly larger than before, and producer surplus may or may not be higher, but if the supply curve is straight as shown below then it will be higher. This situation, desirable, is the economic benefit of many infrastructure projects.

Figure 8.2 Change in Supply for Rail Transport

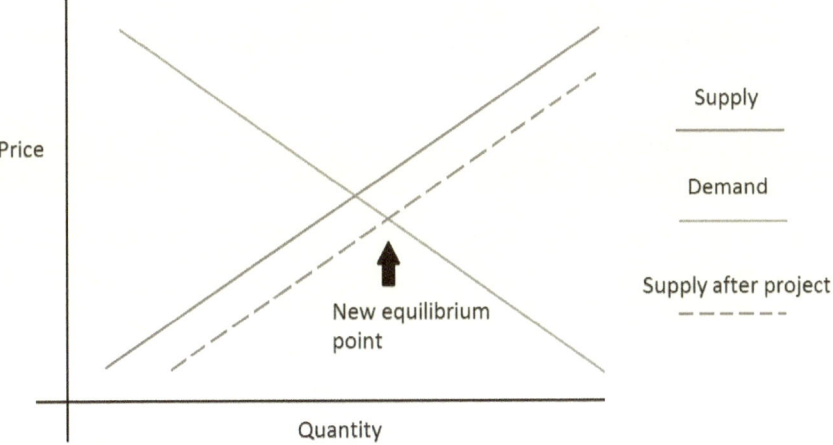

The rail industry is a very capital intensive industry, and requires substantial investments of money to make changes to it. In a modern economy, it is possible for the suppliers of goods to make changes to the supply curve, by upgrading their production equipment when they are too old and need to be replaced, or buying better equipment, so that their productive capacity is greater. In these cases the slow replacement of old equipment can increase the performance of any business, and this happens in the rail industry as well. Rail infrastructure can be upgraded to provide a better service, but the costs can be high. Changes to the supply curve ordinarily take time and effort.

In economics the situation is often discussed or considered where the demand curve is moved about, and this is a result of population changes, or change in income levels, or a change in consumer preferences. Demand shifts in economics are considered to be common, and with transport they are also common, but usually not as the result of the actions of government planning. Demand in transport may change, and this may be the result of changes to population centres, or freight and the type of freight moved on freight trains. It is often considered, especially in Australia, that demand for rail services is fixed, but this is not necessarily so. In unusual cases the government may be able to shift the demand for transport, and to increase it for great advantage. Some of these more unusual situations for increasing the demand for passenger services include:

- Feeder rail lines are built, such as a light rail that connects into a heavy rail system
- Building a network of overpasses, so that people can walk comfortably into train stations, increasing demand for rail services
- Transport orientated development (TOD), where apartments, shops and other facilities are installed around a station to increase demand.
- A very major facility such as a theme park, or a casino, is also built at the same time as the rail line

Changes to demand are also possible for freight. Some of these include:

- Changes to the regulatory environment, making transport modes that compete with rail less attractive (particularly license fees or increases in fuel taxes)
- Increases in terminal capacity, which allows more goods to be shipped at a cheaper price. Many terminals are not part of rail lines, and so there is a change in demand
- Approval given to a variety of mining leases, which increases demand in the area for rail transport
- Free trade agreements, or other diplomatic efforts to allow greater access to foreign markets

The supply demand curves drawn below show what happens where this is an increase in both supply and demand, at the same time. This highly desirable situation shows that there is a new equilibrium point, where the price may be maintained, and the quantity demanded increases. This has a wide variety of economic benefits, GDP increases, the size of the market increases, the taxation and revenues base increases, as potentially productivity increases as well. Managing demand for rail transport is a key way to successfully managing a rail system, and the Hong Kong rail system has used this strategy successfully for decades.

Figure 8.3 Movement of both Supply and Demand Curves

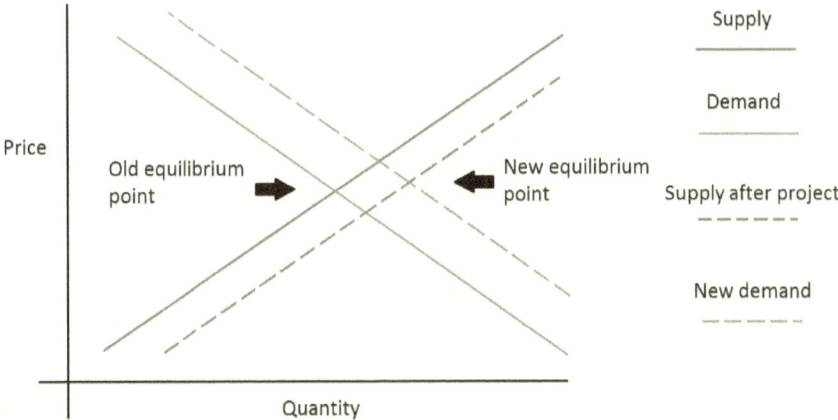

Supply side projects are far more common, and represent the majority of rail projects. Supply side rail transport projects, such as building a rail line, will provide a service where previously there was none. Other projects will improve the quality or cost of a service, and this will shift the supply curve to the right. When the supply curve shifts a new equilibrium will form, and there will normally be an increase in quantity demanded, with a drop in price. This is beneficial for the economy as a whole.

Changes in price do not represent changes in demand, but the level of use of the service will of course increase or decrease as the price is changed. In economics terms changes to the amount of a produce or service demanded is called the "quantity demanded", but changes in demand refer to movements in the demand curve. Railways and governments can set the price of their services, and for lower prices the quantity demanded will increase, and vice versa for price increases.

The reader may notice that moving around the supply curve will result in the equilibrium point moving from one place to another on the demand curve. As the demand curve infrequently shifts, at least as a result of rail projects, it is possible to use this knowledge to determine some forecasts for the change in demand based on changes to services. Particularly important is the slope of the demand curve, and a gently downward sloping demand curve will result in a large change to demand when the supply curve shifts, and a steeply sloping demand curve will result in very small changes to demand. This situation forms the basis for demand elasticity.

Figure 8.4 Demand Elasticity

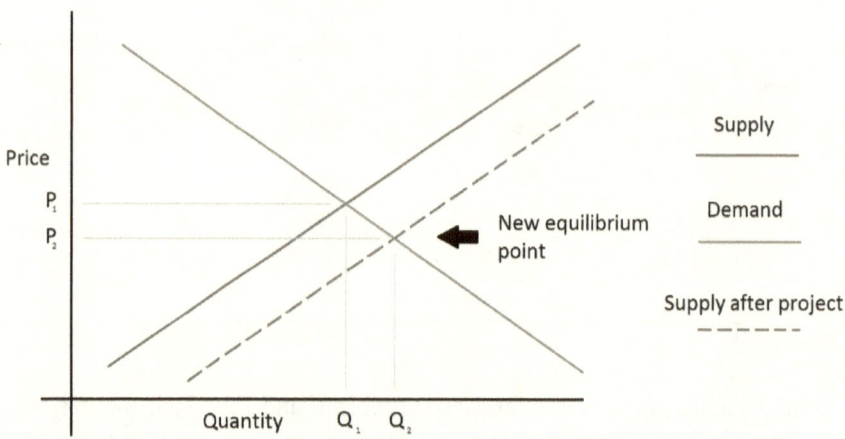

The graph above describes changes to demand as a result of changes to the supply of a good, which can include rail transport. Notice that the price has fallen, but the quantity demanded has increased. This is common with infrastructure projects.

In economic assessments of rail projects, it is desirable to know the shape of both the supply and demand curve. In practice obtaining the precise shape of these curves is a time consuming and difficult process, and any econometric department that has succeeded in obtaining them should be commended. Detailed surveys of both providers and customers of a rail service would need to be surveyed, and analysis made of any potential new entrants into the market should a rail service be improved. Acquiring a complete picture of the supply and demand curves is not easy, and is an expensive exercise. In practice only two points are needed, the starting point and the final point where the market stabilises when any infrastructure changes are made. It is much easier to calculate two points rather than an entire curve.

Elasticity of Demand

An extremely useful concept is the elasticity of demand. This represents a change in the quantity demanded, and is the ratio of the change in quantity demanded to the change in price. The equation below is for "arc elasticity", and is a commonly used and useful formula.

The P's represent price, and the Q's represent quantity. P_1 is the price before the movement along the demand curve, and P_2 the price after the movement.

$$E = \frac{(Q_2 - Q)_1 / Q_1}{(P_2 - P)_1 / P_1}$$

This equation can be re-arranged as:

$$\frac{\Delta Q}{Q} = E \times \frac{\Delta P}{P}$$

Where $\frac{\Delta Q}{Q}$ is the change in quantity demanded. Note the format of this equation, a value of 0.1 is a 10% increase in demand for a doubling in price, a value of -0.1 is a drop of 10%. A value of 1 is a 100% increase in the quantity demanded for an increase in price, and -1 a drop of 100%.

Demand elasticity is a very commonly used concept in attempting to predict what changes will result from an infrastructure project. Demand elasticity is also used to attempt to estimate the change in demand for rail transport for a wide variety of government policies, such as ticket prices, changes in the frequency of services, or the cost of alternatives or their components, such as the fuel price. Demand elasticity is commonly used as below:

Change in demand = E x Δ cost or parameter

The cost or parameter can be almost anything. Note that where the cost increases, then the demand will almost always decrease, so there should be a negative sign in front of the E (but is excluded because it seems a common practice to exclude it). Demand elasticises are mostly negative, so when cost increases demand will fall, but most reports into transport demand elasticises leave off the negative sign, which can be very confusing. The reader should remember that in most cases demand elasticises have a negative sign.

In practice the above equation seems to be applied to changes to a market for a good that can be either a supply side change or a demand one. For example, a change to the price of tickets for rail passengers is a supply side change, but an increase in the price for parking for road vehicles in city areas may increase the demand for rail, which is a competing market for road transport. Nonetheless, both of these changes can and are assessed through the same mechanism.

For an example, let's use a change in frequency of rail services to determine the change in demand. So for this example, we will use an increase in frequency of trains of 15 trains per hour to 20, and a demand elasticity of 0.1. What is the change in the demand for rail services?

This would be:

$$\frac{\Delta Q}{Q} = -0.1 \times \frac{(15-20)}{15} = +0.033$$

We interpret this as a 3.3% increase in the quantity of passengers using the rail service. Also note the addition of the negative sign, often left out of the equation, but very important.

Where the demand elasticity is equal to one, then this is referred to as unit elasticity. If the demand elasticity is less than 1, demand is inelastic, and greater than 1, elastic. A higher value (in absolute value terms), means a greater change to quantity demanded when prices and parameters change.

A large body of research exists that attempts to determine the demand elasticises for a variety of different parameters. The published research has produced many of these and the range over which the demand elasticity is possible for any one parameter is very large. In general demand elasticises are challenging to use successfully, as published elasticises vary so much it is difficult for economists to know which one to use. There is a very large difference between an elasticity of 0.1 and 1, and yet it is common for published elasticises to vary between these two numbers, or even more.

An important distinction needs to be made between short and long run. In economics many studies look at what happens when changes are made to a market, and many of these changes will result in the short run price and quantity changing only slightly, but in the long term the change is more pronounced. For example, where the government increases the prices of tickets, in the short term there will be a reduction in the number of passengers, but in the long term the effect of the price change will be much more pronounced. The long term effect is almost always far more pronounced than the short term effect, and it is common to use the long term impact in assessing projects and infrastructure changes. Studies attempting to estimate the demand elasticity of changes to government policy may calculate two elasticises for the same change, one long term and one short. Care must be taken in choosing which one to use.

For freight, as price is the most important variable in determining the quantity demanded, most of the published research concerns this. Even given the vast body of literature on freight elasticises, things are still rather difficult. Freight elasticises, even for the same product within the same country, can vary enormously, with some studies reporting low values, and others high.

Fixed/Variable Cost, and Marginal Costs

An important distinction needs to be made between fixed and variable cost as this can play an important role. In accounting it is very common to divide the costs of running a business into two separate categories, fixed and variable. Fixed costs, also sometimes called sunk costs, are those large costs that are incurred in setting up the business, and do not change if the business produces either a large or small amount of product, within a practical range. Variable costs are those that change with the number of products produced, or units sold, and are directly related to the volume of business that a business might have, in a short time period such as a week or a fortnight. The distinction between the two is an important concept in accounting, and also for rail transportation.

Rail transportation is an industry with extremely high fixed costs. Many large rail lines may take 10 years to build, and cost billions of dollars, so the fixed costs of almost any rail business is extremely high. Some rail operators, such as passenger service companies, may have much lower fixed costs, as they do not own much fixed infrastructure, and are not required to invest in rail lines that take 10 years to build. Nonetheless rail is often correctly considered to be an industry with extremely high sunk costs.

For any industry with high fixed costs it is important to maximise the utilisation of assets. Once constructed, infrastructure should be fully exploited, and not left unused. Whilst this might seem obvious, one potential trap for any railway, when allowing access to its network, is to charge the full cost of infrastructure and the network to any rail operator, as the full cost is, for most railways, dramatically different to the variable costs. The full cost is in many cases far too high for any operator to pay, such as a private passenger company, or a freight company, but the variable cost is much lower and these companies mostly can afford that.

The variable cost for a freight company might be the cost of fuel, access charges for the network, wages for train crew, and any other fees that might be incurred in performing a freight movement. For a private passenger rail company, variable costs will be similar. For an infrastructure company, variable costs might be the cost of preparing the train plan, creating a path in a timetable, or maintenance costs for equipment and facilities that are only needed for that rail operator. The costs of installation of the fixed infrastructure, such as the track, signals and electrical power system is often not included in any access charges for the network. This makes the distinction between fixed and variable costs very important.

Fixed costs may include depreciation. Fixed costs can also include interest charges for any money borrowed for construction of the rail line. Many of the costs associated with operating a railway are fixed, and very few are variable. Railways have such a large volume of equipment, and need so many people to oversee their safe operation, that the fixed costs of most railways are very large.

The marginal cost is the cost for a business of providing any additional service or product. It also is the slope of the cost curve, and it is really the derivative of the cost curve. Marginal costs often drop as more and more trains are added to a rail system. The graph below shows the common situation where the total cost of operating the rail system increases as the number of rail services is added. Fixed costs must be paid, even where there are no rail services operating. Also note that the cost of adding more rail services is lower each time a service is added.

Figure 8.5 Fixed and Variable Costs

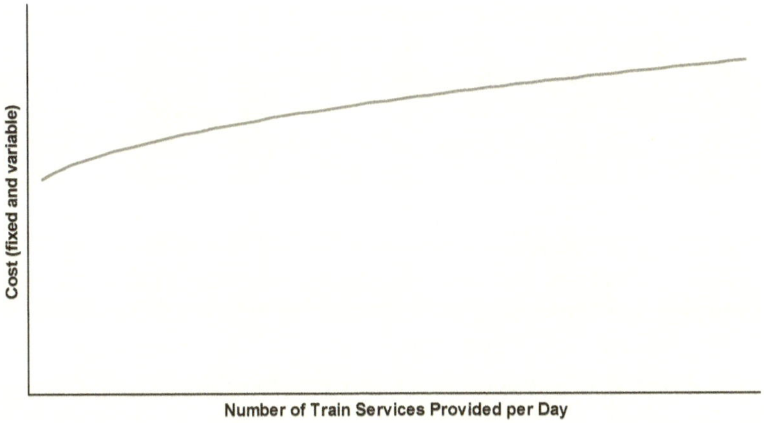

Cost (fixed and variable)

Number of Train Services Provided per Day

The graph above is typical for what a rail company would experience. The fixed costs are high, and with each additional trains added to the system the costs increase, but that increase reduces for each additional train.

Financial Comparison of Train Travel to Automobiles

One of the key benefits of installing rail lines, especially for passengers, is the reduction in cost to society for providing transportation. Rail systems are often much cheaper than road travel, and so the "derived demand" of transportation can be met with lower resources. Consider that the alterative to rail travel is often road vehicles, which are expensive to buy and maintain.

Some of the advantages of rail transportation over road is:
- A train carriage can take hundreds of people, whereas a private road vehicle can take only up to six or eight
- The fuel consumption of a train is mostly much lower than a car or a bus

- The separated right-of-way means that most rail systems are not delayed by heavy road traffic, and so are able to move into city centres without much difficulty
- Rail carriages typically last over 20 years, whereas road vehicles often last only 10

The costs of road vehicles varies substantially from country to country, and even city to city. Many highly densely populated cities have taxes, and levies that discourage people from buying cars, and these costs make the ownership of cars the exclusive domain of the wealthy. Alternatively, some countries have cheaper running costs for cars, especially where fuel is cheap.

In Australia a number of attempts have been made to estimate the cost of running and owning a road vehicle. It's a complicated calculation, as insurance, servicing, and taxes need to be paid regardless of the use of the vehicle. There are also some direct costs associated with operating the vehicle, that increase as the number of kilometres the vehicle is driven increases. Also bigger cars tend to be a lot more expensive to operate, and consume more fuel than smaller vehicles.

Perhaps the best way to estimate the cost of operating a road vehicle is to use the taxation deductions allowed for owning a road vehicle. In Australia, when used for work related purposes, the cost of operating a vehicle is deductible from the income of a business, and the Australian tax office provides a table which is to be used. The cost per kilometre ranges from 63c to 75c per kilometre (Australian currency in 2012), based on the size of the engine. These figures seem appropriate for comparing with rail.

Consider that in Hong Kong, where the metro system is not subsidised, that the cost for adults is about $9 to $12 Hong Kong dollars for a trip of about 15 kilometres, which is about $1.40 US (again for 2012). This translates to a cost of about US 10¢ per kilometre. This is far less than the cost of operating a road vehicle, and remember that this is the cost for an adult, and in Hong Kong , as in many rail systems, there are discounts for the elderly, children and those with disabilities, so they pay even less.

Australian rail systems tend to be expensive to operate, as they have smaller numbers of passengers, and operate on long sections of track through wilderness where rail infrastructure is difficult to maintain.

Even in this very difficult environment, the cost per kilometre for a rail passenger is no more than about 35¢ US per kilometre (2012), which is substantially less than the cost of road vehicles. Rail, as a system for moving people, is usually more cost competitive than private road transport, unless the rail system has low loading factors, or has some specific problems that make it very expensive. This is one of the key advantages of operating a rail system.

The reduction in cost to society in providing transport is one of the key benefits of the installation of any rail line entirely within one city. A reasonable heavily used metro line may move 100,000 people per day, and a typical trip distance is about 12 kilometres. On that basis, if passengers switch from private vehicle use to rail, then the cost saving is staggering, and can be over $100 million US per year, which is normally more than enough to justify the construction of a metro line, even without all the other benefits such as better air quality and safety included.

For HSR (High Speed Rail), the situation is a little different. Passenger numbers are lower, and the travel distances are much higher. HSR competes with road transport for shorter distances such as 200 – 300 kilometres, and with aircraft for large distances such as 700 – 1000 kilometres. Rail is seen as a premium service, and superior to air travel, and is priced accordingly. HSR systems are NOT installed to reduce the cost of travel, but for convenience, environmental reasons, and most importantly financial ones (i.e., profit), and so HSR systems are not judged the same way as short distance metros and light rail.

Commuter travel, from a suburb to the centre of a city, and then out again at the end of a working day, is an expensive service to provide, for a number of reasons. These include the need to provide seating to passengers which results in a lower capacity compared to a similar sized metro, the large central terminus that needs to be maintained for these trains to terminate at, and the difficulty with rostering rail staff to work on these trains. The cost per kilometre of a commuter system can be high, and normally a commuter system is not justified on the basis of cost reduction. Commuter systems are used where people in the regional area, or the distant suburb, want to travel by train as they don't want to drive long distances. Even in Australia, where driving 1.5 hours to and from work each day (so that's 3 hours per day) is seen as reasonable, people are reluctant to drive further than this, and prefer to take a train. The fatigue that arises from long distance driving can be very draining, and long distance commuter trains are far easier to travel on. Passengers commonly sleep on these trains, or eat, something that is either difficult or impossible to do whilst driving a car.

Externalities

Introduction

The correct assessment of the economics of any rail system involves the calculation of the full economic benefits, including those for which there is no market. In many cases there are benefits other than the consumption of rail travel or rail freight associated with a rail system. These need to be included in the calculation of any economic benefits.

A rail system provides a whole host of different benefits. In many cases the benefits of a rail system are much larger than the benefits from the passenger travel. Road congestion is reduced, emissions reduced, less energy consumed, and near passenger stations property values increase. Passenger rail systems are very safe, and provide a much safer system than road travel. All of these benefits are real, and need to be included in any economic appraisal.

An externality is a cost or benefit that is generated by some activity, usually trade related, that is not included in the cost of production of a good or service. For example, a typical externality is pollution, which is generated by many different manufacturing processes, and if it is not controlled may cause negative health effects to those nearby, but may not be counted as a cost during the manufacturing process. In a rail environment, a common externality for rail operations is noise, as the generation of noise by a freight train creates no cost for the freight company, but a cost to the community as a whole, depending on where the noise is generated. Externalities may be counted in the finances of freight companies, depending on the country.

Externalities need to be accounted for separately when performing cost benefit analyses of transport projects. A large part of the economics of transport is the assessment of the value of externalities, and putting a value to society of them. Externalities are difficult to assess correctly, but externalities are very important for assessing any rail project, and not considering them reduces any economic appraisal to farce. The method of assessment of externalities can strongly influence the result of any economic appraisal.

Externalities may also need to be considered in markets that are related to rail transport. For example, the market for road freight is a related market, as it is a substitute for rail freight in many circumstances. A negative externality of road freight is congestion on roads, and where more road freight will take up space on roads, and where congestion already exists, add to this congestion. A rail project to take road freight off the road will impact on traffic congestion, in a positive way, so this benefit needs to be considered in any economic appraisal, even though the benefit is not actually in the rail freight market, but in a related market.

The problem with externalities is that there is no market for them, so assessing their impact to society gets quite difficult. There is no market for noise produced by a freight train, or for the benefits to road transport of getting more trucks off the road and onto trains, but a value needs to be assigned to them. As projects are assessed on a cost benefit basis, and costs are in money, then externalities need to be converted into money to be included as part of that analysis. In economics there is a method to complete this transformation, and it is briefly outlined below.

Some of the more common externalities and associated with rail and related markets include:
- Noise increase or reduction
- Reduced congestion on roads
- Reduction in carbon dioxide and toxic gas emissions
- Improvements in safety for motorists
- Wear and destruction of roads by trucks

Many of these benefits are not included in the price of the rail ticket, price to access a rail system, nor in the cost of supply. This makes them externalities, as they are outside of the pricing of rail tickets. No money from rail tickets, nor provision of the supply of the good, goes towards these benefits (usually). This makes the normal supply demand curve analysis so typical of many economic appraisals incomplete, and needing more information to make it representative.

Quantification of the benefits can be challenging. Many studies have been performed to attempt to understand the various intangible benefits. The transport economics field has researched this problem extensively, and many high quality references exist which can provide guidance on how to quantify the many externalities associated with rail transport.

Changes in Asset Values from Building Rail Lines

Passenger rail projects provide improved transport services for those who live near it. As stations are fixed and don't move, the presence of a rail station typically causes an increase in property values which should increase as rail services are introduced or improve. Any improvement should produce an increase in property values, such as faster services, more frequent services, or an increased number of possible destinations.

Asset value changes are externalities because there is a change in the economic position of members of society that is not included in the market for the good. The price of a rail ticket for passenger travel does not include any provision for changes in property values. Changes in property values can be significant for new rail lines, or even for changes in the frequency of rail services.

An increase in property values can be an argument for property levies to pay for new rail lines. A typical levy is a property tax on nearby properties, which should be levied in proportion to the increase in value of the property. Thorough studies into any increase in property values can be very helpful in convincing local residents to pay more taxes, especially if their overall wealth position improves.

In practice the situation is a bit more complicated that what it would seem. There are a number of reasons why property values may decline because of new rail services, and not increase, and these include:
- Areas of high wealth are often very exclusive, and are not easy to access, especially for the general public. Putting a station in the middle of an exclusive area may rob it of the exclusivity that makes it attractive. This situation arises often in Sydney, but arises in many cities with high wealth.
- A new rail system brings noise, especially where the system is used for both passenger and freight trains. Depending on the level of the noise, property values may decline significantly
- Many freight trains carry materials that are dangerous, such as chlorine, or highly flammable, such as LPG or fuel. A new rail line may increase safety risks to local residents
- Many rail services are priced very cheaply, and crime may be much higher near a station compared to locations away from the station. In some parts of Asia such as Singapore, there is very little crime so this issue is not a problem, but in the US

- with their very high crime rates rail systems and stations may bring a lot of crime, which will reduce the value of property in the area
- The rail system is not needed, so there is no increase in property prices as local residents are indifferent to the introduction of the new rail line
- The rail system is poorly designed, so the travel times are too high for the rail line to be used by large numbers of people, and so the rail line is poorly patronised
- With each rail line includes some stabling, maintenance centres, freight yards, and intermodal terminals that are needed somewhere, and these facilities are ugly and visually intrusive. Any property next to these facilities may drop in value substantially.

On the other hand, there are many situations where the introduction of rail services provides a large increase in property values. If the increase in property values can be maximised, this is ideal for any rail project, and something that should be encouraged. Some of the situations where property values might rise quickly include where:
- The new rail service is very high quality, fast, frequent, or cheap. If the rail service provides a very efficient connection to highly desirable locations, then this is attractive and will increase property values
- If as part of the rail project other facilities are included in the project, such as shopping centres or parks. Areas with good quality facilities are more attractive to live in
- Remote locations with poor transport connections can be completely revitalised where vastly improved transport is provided. This sometimes occurs where old dockland or port land is revitalised, and a rail line included as part of the process. Access becomes very good, and property prices changes accordingly
- Regional centres that are connected with High Speed Rail often experience a renaissance, and grow. The availability of high quality transport allows people to line in that location and work in others, which is very desirable.
- Large cities with very high congestion can be difficult to move around in, especially by any transport that uses roads, such as buses, taxis or cars. Building a rail line allows people to get in

and out of the area much more efficiently, avoiding traffic, and getting to work and other activities more quickly.

So it would seem that the increase in property values will depend on the situation and the needs of local residents. Certainly it is a very difficult relationship between land and property values, and calculating any future increases is not easy at all.

A number of reports completed in Hong Kong have assessed the increase in property values, and found a relationship between several variables and increase in property values. Some of these reports are very detailed, and assessed the benefit of improved train frequency, for example. The highest increase in property values in these reports for Hong Kong was about 10%, and this was for good quality properties very close to the rail line, with a highly frequent service. Certainly the increase in property value was not 100%, but really quite modest.

It must be kept in mind of course that even in Hong Kong, a city with a very well run metro system, has the highest property values in a place called "the Peak", which is on top of Hong Kong Island, and has no rail line at all (other than the cable car, a tourist rail system). The property there is some of the most expensive in the world, so it is possible for high value property to exist even in places with virtually no public transport.

The Pricing of Road Congestion

Road congestion is relevant to a rail system because building a rail line is one of the solutions to relieve congestion. Road congestion in a large or even a moderately sized city is a major issue, and has substantial economic, environmental and social impacts. Road congestion is seen as a great negative, and something that should be avoided if at all possible. As the construction of a rail system can substantially reduce congestion, the benefits of reduced road congestion is often included as part of the assessment of any rail project. Reducing road congestion can provide substantial economic benefits for any city or country, and this can be used to justify large rail projects.

Typically congestion is not a word commonly used for rail systems, but as a concept is very applicable. Rail systems can behave in a similar way to road ones when there are too many trains. Rail and road systems both slow down when the number of vehicles increases beyond a certain critical point, but the solutions for each can be quite different. Congestion in a rail system would normally be the result of the capacity of the network being inadequate for the number of trains, which can be often remedied with structural changes to the network . Whilst conceptually this is the same for roads, the engineering solutions can be quite different.

Road congestion in any large city or region can have a powerful and very negative effect on business. Costs increase as businesses need more drivers and vehicles to get product around to their customers. Operating costs of trucks and light vehicles increases with the frequent starting and stopping that is typical in highly congested road systems, and fuel consumption is higher per kilometre travelled. Furthermore, in areas with high traffic congestion, the variability of the time of any travel increases, so that additional drivers and vehicles are needed to guarantee delivery times.

Perhaps the largest impact to business is the loss of scale, and this needs to be explained further. Businesses in areas of heavy road congestion will have a reduced area for customers, as there will be limits on the distances that can be effectively reached in a reasonable time throughout any busy city with deliveries. In a city with an excellent and effective road system, one business may be able to provide services to the entire city, and so have a large volume of business over which to spread their fixed costs. Where congestion is very bad, a large number of business supplying the same goods will be needed to cover each small part of the city, which will be less efficient, and need to charge higher prices. Competition will be reduced, as congestion will convert a free market into a series of tiny monopolies, in which suppliers of goods can charge higher prices.

Property prices will also be negatively impacted by road congestion. Roads with large amounts of traffic are very unpleasant to live near, they are noisy and smelly, and the noise from trucks can continue well into the night. Crossing major roads is also dangerous, and takes time. Property prices may be 10 – 20% lower in areas with heavy road congestion compared to similar areas without any congestion, and the loss of wealth is a serious factor that needs to be considered. Alternatively, when congestion is reduced there should be an increase in property values. Amenity is increased when road traffic declines, because the area is now more pleasant to live in.

For the travelling public, the use of taxis in a heavily congested road system is problematic. As taxi fares are calculated either on the distance travelled, or in congestion, by time, the cost of any taxi fares can be very large. Even short distances in heavy traffic can be very costly for any passengers, and this is unfortunate as taxis are another form of public transportation that should be encouraged.

In the context of economic appraisals of rail projects, it is often necessary to assess the benefits of providing more rail transportation, and hence the theory is that there will be fewer cars on the roads. The benefit of removing cars from roads needs to be assessed, and included in any assessment of the merits of rail projects. The benefits of removing cars from roads, as mentioned above, falls into four major categories:
- The time saving resulting from less cars on the roads to other road users
- The financial cost saving of operating less cars and more trains
- The improvement in air quality from operating less cars and more trains. The benefit is especially pronounced with freight trucks and replacing them with trains
- The gain in wealth from the improved rail service, and the reduction in unpleasant road congestion near places where people live

In economics, the overuse of public roads, and the resulting traffic jams, is sometimes referred to as the "tragedy of the commons". Roads are mostly free to use, and once a person enters the road system then typically there are no further charges. This situation leads to overuse, as the public good is free, and the price rationing mechanism of capitalist economics cannot be used because roads are free to use. There are of course strategies to avoid this problem, such as tolls, congestion charges, and setting licenses costs at a level to eliminate congestion. These strategies, all quite nasty and unpleasant, which involve in taxing people for just wanting to drive down the street, can be avoided by building a rail line that reduces the congestion on roads, without the need to damage people financially.

As with all economic analysis, benefits accruing from rail projects should be quantified in terms of dollars, so that comparisons can be made. Once again this means that the benefits of rail projects need to be quantified in dollars, and for travel times this is relatively straight forward. If the average trip is, say 40 minutes, and there is a reduction in the travel time, then this can be translated into dollars. A common way to make this conversion is to use the average wage in an area, and to multiply this by the time saving. So the formula for the reduction in travel time for a rail project is:

$$Economic\ benefit = avg\ wages \times trips\ per\ day \times \left(\frac{Dis}{Sp_1} - \frac{Dis}{Sp_2} \right)$$

Where:

Dis = average trip distance
Sp_1 = average traffic speed before the rail project
Sp_2 = average traffic speed after the rail project

This formula represents a rough but useful approximation.

Emissions from vehicles is a topic which is very contentious. Cars, in burning fuel, produce a number of quite nasty compounds and particles, and these include:
- CO_2, carbon dioxide, which is a greenhouse gas and causes global warming
- NO_x, which includes NO and NO_2, and these two gases are nitrous oxides. These gases can cause breathing problems, such as emphysema, and also potentially heart attacks
- CO, which is carbon monoxide. This odourless and colourless gas can cause brain damage and in severe cases death.
- Ozone, which has the chemical symbol O_3. Ozone is helpful for the upper atmosphere where is blocks ultraviolet light and protects animals and plants living on the surface, but at ground level can cause lung inflammation and induce asthma attacks.
- Particulate matter, given the abbreviation PM, which refers to tiny grains of organic material. The smaller the material, the more likely it is to get into the lungs, or the bloodstream and cause damage. Particulate matter is referred to either as PM_{10} or $PM_{2.5}$, which means the particle is this size or less in microns. Particulate matter is considered to be particularly nasty to people's health.
- Lead, which is was an additive commonly used in fuel, now banned in many countries. Lead in the atmosphere causes reductions in IQ in children

- Sulphur oxides, given the chemical symbol SO_x, which can cause acid rain.
- Highly toxic organic compounds, such as benzene, which is carcinogenic.

We note that there are a large number of different unpleasant gases and other products from gasoline burnt to power motor vehicles. Combined these emissions seem to be quite dangerous, and there is research to suggest that, even in the developed world, the number of deaths from car emissions is in the tens of thousands. Particulate matter is considered to be particularly dangerous, and something that countries should avoid producing.

There are two ways that a rail project can reduce the level of toxic emissions; by reducing the number of kilometres driven by road vehicles, and by increasing the average speed at which road vehicles move. The graph below shows the basic idea, and many different versions of this graph have been published. The basic premise is that the emissions per unit time change based on the speed of the vehicle. As the vehicle slows down, not only is the travel time longer, but the efficiency of the engine drops, and more toxic gases are produced. Vehicle speeds need to be above 30 kms/hr (or 20 mph), so that the engine of the vehicle avoids producing large quantities of toxic gases.

The same applies for high speeds, once a vehicle travels at over 100 kms/hr, emissions tend to increase. A key question is: do all of the nasties in the emissions increase evenly as the overall emissions increase, and the answer seems to be yes. A small number of studies, quoted at the end of this chapter, have investigated this question, and it seems that as a rough approximation that each component tends to increase fairly uniformly.

Figure 8.6 Gas Emissions and Speed

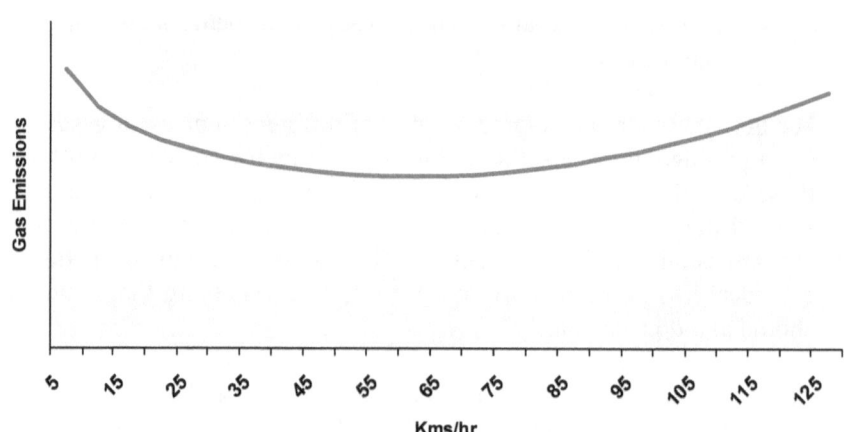

So getting back to the economic appraisal, and the inclusion of road traffic congestion, it is traditional to assign a cost per kilometre to the negative externality of traffic pollution. A cost of about US 5¢ per kilometre per vehicle seems to be about the right number (in 2012), which, the astute reader will notice, is quite a large amount. The cost per kilometre of providing metro services is often around 10¢ per kilometre, so the economic benefit of eliminating road trips is comparatively quite large. This is particularly so where the average traffic speed is below 30 kms/hr, and the movement of these trips from road to rail will mean that the remaining road vehicles are more efficient, so the economic benefit will be even larger. This figure includes all the different gases, but it is also possible to separate out all the different gases and apply a figure to each one, and then tally them. This approach is acceptable, but more complex, and it is left to the reader to choose which approach is the best.

In most large countries there will be a government department that determines the cost per kilometre that should be used in any economic appraisal that reduces the number of road trips.

The Economics of Safety Benefits

Rail is much safety as a transport mode than road transport. Often overlooked, rail transport is vastly safer, and per distance travelled the number of deaths is much lower. This safety benefit is quiet significant, and should be included in any economic appraisal of the benefits of building rail lines.

Statistics on the death rates of different types of transport modes are commonly available. There are a number of very good websites that provide this information, and the reader can use these very effectively. In the US there are a number of government bodies that publish statistics on transport modes, and their comparative safety, and these are also very helpful. It should be noted that there has been consistent action on safety in most developed countries for many years, and that the death rate per distance travelled is constantly falling. The numbers presented below should be taken only as a guide, and current figures should always be used when writing economic appraisals for new rail projects.

The unit of measurement adopted here is deaths per 100 million kilometres. This measure was chosen because it can be used to compare across different transport modes, which is the purpose of this section. Other measures include deaths per 100,000 people per year, and deaths per number of road vehicles owned. These measures are commonly quoted in different papers and documents, but are difficult to use for comparative purposes.

Of course the numbers presented here do not include suicides. Sadly in some countries suicide on the rail system is quiet common, and Australia is one of those countries. Whilst it is often difficult to implement a solution to prevent suicides, platform screen doors can be very effective in eliminating attempted suicides from platforms. The experience in Australia has been that the riskiest place for suicides is express trains passing platforms at high speed, where the train is not stopping, and the platform can be accessed when no trains are stopping there.

The numbers listed in the table below are useful for comparison purposes. It should be noted that these death rates per kilometre are appropriate for countries in the OECD, or countries in Western Europe. These numbers are not appropriate for use in countries like India, where the death rate is extremely high. The same can be said for China, where the number of road deaths per kilometre is much higher than in Australia/UK and Canada.

Comparison Table Road and Rail Related Transport Deaths – English Speaking World only

Transport Mode	Death Rate	Place and year
Trucks, road freight	1.69 per 100 million kilometres	US, 2002
Buses/coaches	0.7 per 100 million kilometres	Australia 1999
Rail (all types)	0.15 per 100 million kilometres	NSW 2012
Motorcycles	25.3 per 100 million kilometres	Australia 1993
General aviation	8.5 per 100 million kilometres	1985 Australia
Large passenger jets (domestic in the US)	0.004 per 100 million kilometres	US, 2010
Cycling	7 per 100 million kilometres	NSW Australia, 1985
Walking	36.2 per 100 million kilometres	US, 1995
Road (all vehicles)	0.7 per 100 millions kilometres travelled	Australia 2009
Road (all vehicles)	0.6 per 100 millions kilometres travelled	UK 2009
Road (all vehicles)	0.8 per 100 millions kilometres travelled	USA 2009

General aviation refers to the many different types of small aircraft that might be used to transport people, or perform some sort of commercial function. Crop dusting falls under the heading of general aviation, and can be quite dangerous. Helicopters are more dangerous then general aviation. The death rate in Australia for large domestic passenger is 0, and has been since Qantas was founded in 1921. The death rate used for large jets for passenger traffic was the US domestic figure.

Trucks have a surprisingly high number of fatal crashes. A majority of the deaths from truck accidents are the occupants of the other vehicle that is hit when the truck impacts another vehicle. Trucks thus represent a major hazard to other road users. In Australia in 1996 almost two thirds of the people killed in accidents involving trucks were in the other vehicle. The death rate associated with articulated trucks is even higher, and the larger the vehicle the greater the death rate. Rigid trucks are far safer than articulated ones, on a per kilometre basis.

The Relationship between Property Values and Freight Systems

Rail freight systems are dirty and messy, and often noisy. They are beneficially environmentally compared to moving freight with trucks, but that is small comfort to anyone living alongside one. Houses alongside a freight line may also be exposed to the risk that there will be a derailment and a train crash into a house, or a derailed train release a poisonous chemical that injures or even kills anyone near it. Freight trains often operate late into the night, and so anyone that is a light sleeper will have difficulty sleeping when living next to a busy freight yard or line.

The drop in property prices around a freight line seems to be about 5-7%. This range is taken from a study done in Ohio, but seems consistent with studies in Hong Kong showing an equivalent rise in property values of this amount when a metro station is placed next to housing. The more freight trains that pass through an area, the greater the reduction in property prices.

Particularly irritating to those living nearby is the use of horns on trains. Trains, like cars, have horns to sound if they approach a level crossing or other area where there is likely to be a safety risk. The horn is a warning to other users of nearby roads that trains are near. The use of horns for trains is sometimes banned, as it is so noisy, but this increases the safety risk for rail freight movements.

In countries where property values are very high, any government action which results in reductions to property values is met with very determined and vigorous resistance. Whilst a rail freight line will reduce traffic congestion overall, the local residents alongside the new rail freight line will lose out as their property prices fall. Any government that plans to implement a transport plan that reduces property values, and the rail project is not desperately needed is likely to experience a lot of trouble. Even a 10% reduction in property values can translate to enormous amounts of money where average property values are over US $1 million per property (like it is in Sydney, Singapore or Hong Kong). Thousands of properties may be affected.

So how can this situation be managed? What controls or measures can the transport planner make to allow for this reduction in property values? So what possible solutions exist? Some of them include:
- Putting rail freight into industrial areas where noise from container terminals won't be noticed, or next to other industrial sites such as oil refineries
- Developing an area with the freight terminal on it before houses are built
- Putting freight terminals onto islands away from people. This solution is surprising common
- Banning, or limiting the use of horns on freight trains
- Putting sound barriers up around rail lines with freight
- Moving freight yards from high value areas to low value ones.
- Perhaps even shutting down freight operations, and moving all freight onto road vehicles, as was done in Hong Kong
- Relocating freight into freight corridors where the impact of the noise and unsightliness of trains is reduced
- Where possible, moving freight terminals away from areas where people live
- Electrifying rail freight lines, as electric locomotives are quieter

Freight lines are rarely put into tunnels, as diesel locomotives emit a lot of fumes. Freight lines in tunnels may seem a sensible option, as the noise from the train will not penetrate through the ground to the houses above, but in practice this solution is rarely implemented. In many situations is may be difficult or even impossible to reduce the negative impact of freight trains on property values, and a freight tunnel underground built. At present freight tunnels are limited to water crossings and tunnels under mountain ranges, but there is no technical reason why more freight tunnels cannot be constructed.

Week 9

Demand Estimation

Introduction

Demand estimation refers to any attempt to predict the patronage of a rail system either before it is built, or before changes are made to the system. Demand estimation for an existing line is often done via elasticises, which are very commonly used, researched and reported, and are discussed at length above in this chapter. Demand estimation for entirely new rail lines is much harder, as an estimate needs to be made for a service where presently none exists.

It should be noted that it is not always necessary to have a comprehensive model of the demand for a rail service. Some rail projects are built because of reasons in addition to moving lots of passengers, and some projects have a highly political nature and may not need large passenger numbers to be approved. Some of the projects in Hong Kong that connect the city to mainland China are being completed for integration purposes, and the number of passengers is not the primary consideration. However for most projects passenger numbers or freight movements are a key consideration.

It is not always possible to have access to detailed and complex demand forecasting models, and at early stages of project development these will not be available. As projects progress however, the expectations as regards passenger forecasts grow, and more detailed analysis is needed. Demand estimation will start very basic, and become more sophisticated as any project progresses. Many governments, before providing the substantial funding required for any rail project, will expect some pretty thorough research into passenger numbers to be completed. Demand modelling techniques that are quick and easy to perform are sometimes described as "sketch planning". This term refers to the need to create very simple demand estimates in the early stages of any demand estimation.

One of the key considerations for any the demand estimate for passengers is the time frame over which any analysis is performed. Demand for rail services changes over time, and mostly increases. In some cases the increase in demand can be quite dramatic, and increasing the size of the analysis window will often produce much better results. A typical time period for analysis may be 10 years, or 20, or 25. When comparing different project alternatives, it is important to use the same time window for comparison.

Demand estimation for a new freight line is quite different to that of a passenger line. Freight companies, and companies that produce items that need to be shipped, are often in a position to provide the transport planner with substantial information about what freight movements a new line will have. Freight companies often have industry bodies where the demand on new rail lines can be estimated with a good degree of certainty, and freight companies will have a good understanding of their demand patterns, it is easier to determine the freight movements on any new freight line.

Different Techniques

There are a range of different techniques that can be employed to estimate the demand for new passenger lines. Some are very simple, others are very complex. What type of technique is used will depend on a number of factors, including the budget that is available, the technique that was used in past studies, and the information on hand at the time of the forecast. It should be remembered that all attempts to predict the future are fraught with difficulty, and no one technique can guarantee success.

So, from the most basic to the most complex, the types of forecasting of demand, for new rail lines, is:
- Statements about the potential for high demand for rail services, such as the number of people in an area, the demographics of those people, the number of trips, and other factors such as the income level or the number of cars owned. From a relatively simple analysis of these factors, much can be learned, and a competent planner can get a sense of the viability of a project or rail line
- Rules-of-thumb to generate a simple estimate of demand, such as comparing the location and type of service with a comparable service and location elsewhere that already has the service. There are many cities and regions worldwide with varying rail characteristics, and an observant rail planner can normally find one that is quite similar to the one being studied.

The demand levels in the comparable place may very well be similar to the place where the rail line is being proposed
- Analysis of the rail travel patterns in a region that has a lot of rail, but where there are gaps in the rail service, and the proposal is to close those gaps. This situation may occur where a large city is seeking to build another metro line, and wants to estimate passenger numbers, and has a large number of other stations to study to determine what travel patterns are. A regression analysis may be performed on the number of passengers at existing stations, using variables such as the number of people in the surrounding area, location of schools, parks and shopping centres, available employment, incomes, etc. This type of analysis is recommended in this book because of it's accuracy, cost, and is relatively easy to complete
- Catchment analysis, where the number of people living nearby to the station is determined, and then multiplied by a factor that represents how many trips will be generated by each household per day by rail. The choice of factor is based on any previous study that estimated how many people used a rail service per day, who lived nearby to the station.
- Formulas for the percentage of travel expected based on travel time. This type of analysis is sometimes used for high speed rail, where travel times of over 4 hours will attract a low percentage of the total number of trips, and a travel time of 2 hours resulting in rail capturing almost 100% of all trips.
- Surveys of the people in the area surrounding where stations are proposed to be built. There is nothing wrong with launching a survey to determine what local people think of a new proposed project, but the results need to be interpreted with caution. In small towns people will rarely say no to a new rail line, but that does not mean that there will be adequate patronage of the rail line once it is built. Nonetheless, surveys are one way of obtaining a clear picture of the travel habits of the people near the rail line.
- Activity based modelling, where a model is built that contains estimates of the movements of every passenger in the relevant area. A model of the utility of the transport trip is created, and then applied to each different trip pattern. This modelling technique is particularly useful where new rail lines are to run along existing highways. This type of model is sometimes considered to be the best way to produce a forecast, but it is very resource hungry, and expensive and time consuming to

produce. Where a strong modelling group in an area has built one of these models, then it is possible to make use of their system, and for the privilege fees must be paid.

The type of demand modelling used can vary greatly, even for the same country, and for the same project. In the feasibility stage of any project to build a new rail service, it is likely that money is quite limited, and there will be relatively little information on the proposed new service. Not every project starts with a clear set of requirements, and for some projects the objectives and goals can be quite vague. In that situation demand planning using "sketch planning" is entirely appropriate.

Regardless of the type of model used to estimate demand, there are a number of key variables that need to be defined in order to determine what the demand will be. These include:
- Service frequency
- Cost of tickets
- Type of service
- Punctuality
- Number of rail interchanges to reach important destinations
- Crowding
- Travel speed and time

It's best if these variables are known, and as a project progresses more information will be known about a project. It is the author's experience that often projects may be publicized with high frequencies, high average speeds, and low costs, but as the project nears completion then some of these key assumptions may change, and the cost of tickets increase, the frequency of service might drop, and overall the project may not seem as rosy as when it was announced. Furthermore, punctuality figures almost never match those promised, and train delays, especially in a newly constructed rail system, will be higher than what was promised.

Activity based modelling, as mentioned above, is a way modelling the movements of people in a city or region. The results of a model using this technique can produce a lot of information, and this information centres on the trips that will occur when the transport project is completed. Some of the information that is produced about the trips includes:
- The purpose of trips in the area

- The time trips occur
- The origin and destination of all trips
- The travel mode, be it car, train, bus or any other mode
- The route that the trips take
- And the frequency of the trips

That's a lot of information. It is for this reason that activity based modelling is seen as the preferred way to model new transport projects, and produces far more information than how many people will use a particular station or transport service each day.

The underlying premise of any activity based modelling is that demand for transport is a "derived demand", which means that the service is not demanded for it's own sake, but is demanded as part of another activity. People rarely take trains without having any other purpose, but in some cases, especially on railways or on other speciality railways, then the trip itself is all that the consumer wants. Notwithstanding this, the vast majority of trips are related to work, buying groceries, social activities, or children going to school, and occur because of work, social activities, or educational requirements. As transport is related to other activities, it is possible to work out from the location of offices, places or work, school and shopping centres how many trips will be generated. It is this way that is the key to modelling transport in an activity based model.

Utility is a concept in economics that concerns the satisfaction of consuming a good. Utility is a different concept from cost, as the cost of a service or good may not be the same as the satisfaction of its use. For example, the cost of purchasing a good may be $10, but someone buying it may be prepared to pay much more, because their utility from the consumption of that good is far higher than the $10 that the good cost. Utility, as the satisfaction from consuming a good, is what economists use to model transport demand. Unfortunately, as utility is not the same as price, an activity based model that maximises consumer utility will need a lot of information about how consumers perceive utility, and then this should be entered into the model. Once again, as mentioned before, this requires a lot of groundwork, and this is one of the major barriers to creating an activity based model.

Sensitivity analysis is a term that is used to describe the analysis of options and input variables to any process. Transport planning is a process, and in planning for a new rail line, or modifications to one, input parameters such as the type of new line, frequency of trains, type of trains, and capacity of new rollingstock, are the input parameters to the process. The transport planner attempts to produce some outputs from the process, which is the number of passengers, the economic benefit to society from the transport project, the cost, etc. A sensitivity analysis attempts to determine how much the outputs change based on the inputs. A normal process, to perform a sensitivity analysis, is to modify the inputs a small amount, and then calculate the new outputs. How much the outputs change relative to the inputs, is what a sensitivity analysis is all about.

With a sensitivity analysis, it is possible for the transport planner to answer questions that are normally posed during the planning process; what happens if this is changed, how can costs be reduced, or how can the inputs be changed to increase the number of passengers. These sorts of questions are normal, and when asked indicate that the planning process is worked normally. These questions are not a sign that the planning process is under attack (usually!).

Demand Elasticises

A demand elasticity is the change in demand for a transport service given a change in the way the service is supplied, or in the nature of the service. Demand elasticises can be applied to changes in service frequency. If a rail service is very slow, then fewer passengers will want to use the service. A very quick and efficient service will result in higher number of passengers. From a rail transport planning perspective, it is necessary for an estimate to be made of the number of passengers who will use a service when transport times are either increased or decreased. This can happen when service frequency is increased or decreased, or when passengers need to interchange where previously services were direct. Changes to travel times are common in any rail system.

Elasticises are used in economics, and they describe the effect on demand of changing a variable on the quantity demanded of a good, and commonly the price is the variable that is changed. An elasticity is how much the demand changes, and an elasticity of more than 1 means the good is elastic, and small changes result in large changes in demand. An elasticity of less than one means that the good is inelastic, and that changes to price and other variables means that the quantity demanded will change only a little. Goods such as food and fuel are inelastic, as they are basic necessities and are needed regardless of the price. Goods that are discretionary are often strongly elastic.

This concept of elasticises is commonly applied to rail transport, and it is possible to develop a formula relating travel time to number of passengers. Much research has been done on establishing the relationship between travel time and passenger numbers, and this is presented below. This research often focuses on the value of the elasticity, rather than any other statistical parameter such as the correlation, or the shape of the curve that relates travel time to passenger.

So the basic variables are:

TT = travel time

P = number of passengers

η = elasticity of demand

The formula for the elasticity of demand assumes a base level of passengers is known, and the formula applies to changes from this base level. The classic formula for demand elasticity is:

$$\frac{\Delta Q}{Q} = E \times \frac{\Delta P}{P}$$

We modify this to account for changes in travel time, rather than price, and we obtain:

$$\frac{\Delta P}{P} = E \times \frac{\Delta TT}{TT}$$

We can express this differently as:

$$\frac{P_2 - P_1}{P_1} = E \times \frac{TT_2 - TT_1}{TT_1}$$

Where

P_2 = *number of passengers after the change*

TT_1 = *travel time before the change*

TT_2 = *travel time after the change*

Also note that the travel time is calculated from:

TT = transit time in train(s) + interchange time + maximum waiting time/2

The maximum waiting time is divided by 2 because it is assumed that passengers arrive randomly, and there will wait on average half the maximum waiting time.

One challenge applying this equation is that for any rail line passengers will be alighting and boarding at all the stations along the line. Passengers will have many different destination choices, so a change in frequency of service will impact upon passengers differently. In particular, where passengers are travelling a short distance a change in frequency of service will have a very large impact, because a change of a few minutes can be very significant for a travel time of 10 minutes. A long distance trip is much less sensitive to small changes in service frequency, as a percentage it is much smaller. This is one of the reasons why metro services operate at such small headways, as trip distances are quite short, and the waiting time has more of an impact to the number of passengers.

Transport planners should use the elasticises of demand for travel time that are mandated for use in that country, if there are any. A large number of studies have been produced in the past 40 years that have analysed elasticises of demand for transport, mostly in reference to the price charged, but also concerned with the travel time. Whichever country is planning a new rail system should take account of the most relevant study with the most relevant elasticity figures. Elasticity values can vary through an enormous range, and most likely the best way to obtain any elasticity figures is to use the study conducted in the most similar transport environment.

An excellent resource is the website of the Australian Government Department of Infrastructure and Regional Development, who maintain a database of different studies conducted into transport elasticises.

Their database is impressive, but seems to contain information that is a little dated, much of it being from the 1970's and 80's. It contains hundred of entries on different transport modes. The link, at the time of printing of this book, is:

http://www.bitre.gov.au/tedb/index.aspx

Some typical values for η are shown below, for both trains and buses:

Different Travel Mode – Time Passenger Demand Elasticities (η)	
Mode	**Elasticity**
Bus, urban	-0.60
Rail, urban	-0.60
Bus, intercity	-2.11
Rail, intercity	-1.58
Air, intercity	-0.43

The elasticises are negative because an increase in travel time will result in a reduction in the number of passengers. Only rail cruises and tourist railways have a positive elasticity.

Interestingly elasticises for rail and bus is very negative for intercity trips, presumably because the travelling public dislikes this mode of travel for intercity trips, and will only choose it when the trip is very efficient and quick.

The graph below shows how passenger demand changes with travel time. This scenario has used the base case where the number of passengers per day is 10,000, and the travel time is 30 minutes. As the travel time gets shorter the number of passengers gets larger, and the increase in number of passengers using the system gets large. As can be seen clearly from this graph, there are significant increases in passenger demand for reductions in travel time.

Figure 9.1 Passenger Demand P = 10,000, travel time = 30 min, η = -0.6

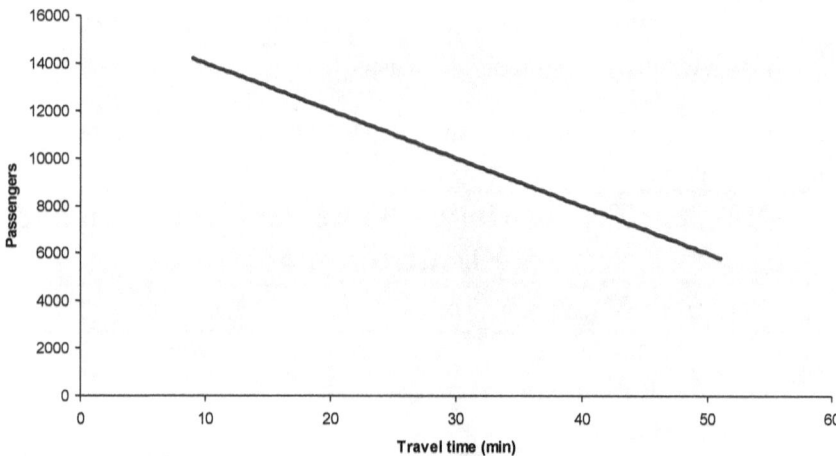

This equation for passenger demand can be used in transport models, where new rail lines or changes to a rail system are modelled.

Financing Large Projects

Introduction

Large rail projects require large sums of money. Most governments are severely constrained by the amount of money that can be provided to invest in any project, including rail, and finding a source of funding is always difficult. Most governments would prefer that large scale funding is sourced from other places than the government, and in many cases this is possible. How should this be done? What strategies can governments employ to encourage any other party to pay for the costs of any large rail infrastructure?

Seeking alternative sources of funds for a rail project is difficult. They are often provide very poor returns, and so very few private sector organisations would want to pay for a rail line or project. In some limited circumstances there may be situations where a very specific project met their need they may be willing to pay, but in general things are quite difficult. Nonetheless governments have been searching for a way to find someone to help them pay for the enormous cost of building rail lines.

Broadly, there seem to be a small number of ways that governments can obtain funds:
- Pay for the project themselves out of consolidated revenue
- Seek contributions from local government and other organisations, such as shopping centre owners for any rail project
- Raise taxes and direct the money to the rail project
- A private sector corporation may wish to pay for the entire project if it is very lucrative, or if the project is structured to be so
- Provide incentives to a private sector corporation to build the project, such as the right to build property around the railway line

Small projects may be funded through the actions of local government, or local business people. Local government may be able to provide funds for some projects, but the larger project they will be unable to contribute any significant amount of money. The larger the project, the more difficult things become.

Many governments consider that the involvement of the private sector in a construction project will bring major benefits, and so is something that should be encouraged if at all possible. This includes obtaining funding, and there are a number of mechanisms that can be deployed to involve the private sector more.

Apart from the cost saving from involving the private sector in a large infrastructure project, involving them is seen to produce other monetary or economic benefits as well. There include:
- The private sector is seen as more efficient and goal orientated that large government bureaucracies, and able to deliver projects with lower costs
- The private sector will take the risk associated with any large rail project, and any project overruns and cost blowouts will be absorbed by the private sector rather than the government
- The financing costs of the project, as well as the loans for the project, not the responsibility of government, and so the government accounts for the country will not show the debt, and the budget position of the government will be better

It is a commonly held view that the private sector is more efficient than government in operating businesses. It is definitely true that private sector companies are more profit driven, and do not have the nebulous goals that make operating a government department difficult. Government departments often have many competing goals based on the politics of the government in power, and these can be very diverse, from procurement, equal opportunity, supporting regional areas, environmental, etc, whereas private companies are often not bound by the same government policies.

The differences between government and private companies and they way they operate is beyond the scope of this book, but nonetheless a very interesting topic. The way these two types of business operate is vastly different, and both systems have strengths and weaknesses. In many countries it is the strong preference of government that as many businesses as possible are operated by the private sector. Alternatively, in many countries, rail systems and operators are still very much operated by the government.

As a final comment on the different approaches between public and private sector organisations, there always seems to be more risk with private sector organisations. Many of the companies that compete for work from the rail industry seem to be small, or temporary ventures, or something with very little stability. In Australia many of the companies that have bid for and won work often have flashy sounding names, but only have the revenue from one contract, and when that contract expires is often wound up. It always seems risky trusting the lives of the travelling public to companies that existed only for a few weeks before the start of performance of the contract.

As regards getting more involvement from the private sector, there are surprisingly many different strategies that can be employed. A short summary of those would be:

- Selling off the rail system or the operation of the rail system, so that any future investment is carried out by the private sector.
- Encouraging private sector investment by providing "sweeteners", such as paying for part of the investment, or providing generous tax incentives to allow the investment to occur. Sometimes governments will provide generous cash grants to any organisation that will take on any transport project.
- Allowing development of the land around a large rail infrastructure project, which will generate large profits, which can be used to offset the cost of the large rail project. This strategy is commonly used in Hong Kong to provide the funds for investment
- A major rail project may be split into two parts, the unprofitable part that is paid for by government, and a profitable part that can be financed by the private sector, and revenues from that part being used to generate the financing needed.
- Offering a monopoly on the use of certain lines, in exchange for funding for infrastructure projects. This kind of funding arrangement can cause a lot of friction with the users of the service that becomes a monopoly, as the cost of the service can rise substantially. Users of the monopoly service will have no alternative but to accept the higher charges, causing resentment. Nonetheless, converting a service that was competitive to a monopoly has substantial value to the company that acquires the monopoly, and the buyer may be prepared to invest substantially to acquire the monopoly

A rail line may connect a facility of enormous value or size, such as a Disney theme park or a shopping centre of large size. This facility may be so profitable and wealthy that they may pay for the new infrastructure outright, or make a very substantial contribution to the cost of any rail project. Casinos often have the funds to pay for rail projects, and deals can be struck between government and private companies that provide for the financing of this type of project. Hong Kong Disney land is an excellent example of this type of financing.

Levies and Surcharges

Governments have the authority to raise taxes of many different types. This power can be applied for the purpose of raising revenue to pay for any new rail project. Whilst it is possible to raise broad taxes such as income tax to pay for projects, more targeted measures are generally preferred, and there is a general perception that a user pays approach to additional surcharges is the best approach. As such there are a number of approaches that can be used to raise revenue, and these include:

- Applying levies to the owners of properties around the new rail lines or projects, which is then used to pay for the new rail project. Care must be taken in applying this kind of levy that the local property owners see the rail project as something they would want, and provides a benefit to them or the residents of their property. A rail line that has no station or is an express line, or moves freight, will not be a suitable candidate for this type of system for raising funds. This system is used for the Vancouver Skytrain.
- A country or government may apply a levy to a service or business that is unrelated to rail, that is imposed only for paying for the project or infrastructure. This is sometimes done with gambling, a cash business that generates large revenues. Gambling is often seen as something of a shady industry, morally questionable, and the operators of gambling establishments may be required to contribute to some sort of public investment scheme in order to dignify/redeem their business operations. Lotteries are also sometimes used as a source of funds for infrastructure and transport investment.
- Applying surcharges to particular parts of the rail network, especially where the patrons of the service have the resources to pay for it. Surcharges on rail tickets are very common for rail lines to airports, as the cost of the rail ticket is normally only a small part of the cost of any trip. Care must be taken to

ensure that there is some sort of system to allow for employees of the airport or the facility with the surcharge applied to avoid the charge, otherwise those that need to use the station routinely may be penalised.
- Seeking contributions from freight companies where the efficiency of a rail line increases from a project. In some cases the contribution of a freight company may be substantial, especially if the improvement is large.

Government Support of Different Forms

Government can provide incentives to private sector corporations to encourage them to participate in any project. Also the government has control over many different aspects of legislation, and can motivate many different parties through the use of various different and varied strategies. This is separate from providing benefits such as the right to build and develop around the rail system. Some possible strategies include:
- Governments can guarantee the debts of the private sector organisation that is making the investment, which reduces the funding costs. Debt guarantees can be a very effective way of reducing the cost of borrowing, which can substantially help with reducing the costs of building infrastructure. This was done with the High Speed Rail system in Taiwan.
- Infrastructure bonds are a specific type of borrowing where governments go the debt markets and raise cash for specific projects. This type of funding is used where the governments approach the public for funds, and bonds are sold to raise cash for the infrastructure project. These bonds may be paid for using government revenue, or revenue from the infrastructure project.
- Superannuation funds, or other wealth fund such as a sovereign wealth fund, may be compelled through government legislation or other means into providing the funding for transport infrastructure projects. Care must be taken with this approach, as these funds are really public money, and large losses may create political problems for any government that compelled the fund to support the project.
- Offering a long term contract that generates an income stream, and then guaranteeing this income stream, so that the private sector can borrow against the income stream. This type of financing is commonly used in public private partnerships,

where the income stream is used as collateral for any financing. The income stream may be in the form of a lease, and the private sector leases the infrastructure back to the government, or as a guaranteed stream of income for the provision of services.

Public Private Partnerships

PPP stands for public private partnership, and is a common way of attempting to reduce the cost of major infrastructure projects. The key to a PPP is for the private sector to assume the risk in any major project. Governments often are prepared to accept large costs in transport projects, as long as the benefits are there and there is substantial public support for the project. Risk, on the other hand, is something that governments genuinely dislike, and will generally pay substantially more on a project to reduce any risk as much as possible. Government dislike of risk is one of the reasons why the private sector is able to compete more effectively than government businesses, as the appetite for risk is higher, and governments sometimes avoid risky projects that could potentially return very large benefits to the public.

PPPs have become a very common way for governments to get private sector involvement in the funding of rail infrastructure projects. In Australia PPP's are popular, and a commonly used investment vehicle to attract private sector investment. PPPs can be used for a variety of different purposes, including hospitals, prisons, rail project, and road tollways. PPPs are very versatile, and can be an attractive option.

PPP projects have a very specific structure, which is:
- Governments make partial payments early in the life of a project
- The construction consortium continues to operate and maintain the constructed assets after construction is complete
- The operation period if defined ahead of time
- As the construction consortium continues to operate the assets, the remaining capital is paid from the government to the consortium
- Detailed performance requirements are provided for how the assets should be managed
- The construction consortium also receives a fee for managing the assets

PPP structures allow governments to convert a high up front capital cost into a series of payments over many years. The construction consortium borrows against the stream of payments, and so the construction cost is spread over many years, even decades. This structure is very attractive to government.

We should note that governments can almost always borrow more cheaply than private sector companies. The quality of the infrastructure, and the nature of the project, will also contribute to the final cost of raising capital. High quality projects will be able to raise money cheaply, not so good, more expensive. Even the best projects will struggle to raise money as cheaply as a government. This problem does cause some involved with the creation of PPP's to sometimes question the overall benefits of a PPP structure.

As governments are so reluctant to accept any risk, one of the key advantages of a PPP structure is that a private party can innovate regarding the design and implementation of any transport project. As technology advances, solutions to problems can be found where none existed previously, and private companies may want to adopt these designs or techniques, where government may be reluctant. As private companies are generally more flexible, the employment of foreign consultants is easier, and headhunting of talent from overseas employment markets easier, allowing for more rapid technology transfer.

Gifts and Aid

Rail projects are very expensive to implement in any country. In countries with low labour rates the cost of rail projects will be significantly lower, however there are many engineering systems that are produced in a handful of countries that need to be imported. This equipment is not provided at reduced prices as a charitable act, and so full price needs to be paid. For many third world countries complex rail systems are too expensive to implement.

Organisations exist across the world to provide funding for a variety of different infrastructure projects. Almost all wealthy first world countries have aid programs that direct funds towards poorer countries that are unable to provide for themselves. There are also many departments of the UN that also work to provide the same service.

These organisations can be a very useful way for many countries to obtain funding for rail projects.

Major countries such as Japan and China has established investment banks who purpose is to fund major construction projects of all kinds. China has established the Asia Investment Bank to fund all sorts of different projects. Japan also has the Japan bank for International Cooperation. These banks provide funds for a variety of different projects.

The provision of these monies often have strict conditions attached, many of which concern corruption and the theft of the funds provided. Many companies are vary of providing funding to countries with notorious corruption problems, and any money provided may be stolen and used for other purposes.

Investments in third world counties are assessed on an economic basis as they should be. A variety of different measures are used to make the assessment, including most importantly the benefits to the local population. Money will be provided where the economic benefits are very large, and local government cannot raise the funds on their own.

Wealthy countries clearly will not be the recipient of this kind of funding, and even relatively strong third world countries would not often receive funding for these kinds of projects, even where there is a very large economic benefit.

This kind of investment is suited only for a small number of rail transport modes. Flashy sexy rail systems such as high speed rail will not be funded this way. Tourist railways may be, as there could be old rail systems left over from the colonial era that could be converted into a tourist railway. Rail systems funded in this way are low tech, and cheap so that they can be used by the local population. Driverless trains would also not be deployed as this restricts employment opportunities.

The best of these types of rail projects are ones that are cheap, connect impoverished areas to areas of employment, result in large economic benefits, and permanent employment. This often means investing in town and cities, with whatever type of rail system is suitable for that area. Freight lines are also common, which allow access for major countries to raw materials that they require.

Success and Failure

Obtaining funding from different sources comes with a degree of risk. Organisations that provide funding have expectations that the money will be used in an appropriate way, and that the promises made about the project are actually delivered. Projects need to be delivered on time, and on budget.

All manner of problems can occur in a project, and these can affect any future funding that might become available. Where projects in a specific location obtain a bad reputation, seeking more funding in the future may be difficult. Where projects are successful things will be a lot easier.

There have been instances in Australia where large private sector companies have been almost destroyed by entering into a large contract that provided limited benefits, or did not provide the expected revenues. One of the consequences when this happens is that the private company suffers considerable financial damage, and the CEO of the company is fired. After this any company that thinks about dealing with the government prices in so much risk that the financial benefit is really not there to let the contract, and the contracts for any services have so many escape clauses as to be virtually worthless. Even worse, as companies get more cautious about accepting government contracts more money is needed to entice them into the contract, which defeats the entire purpose of getting the private sector involved in the first place.

The experience in Australia has been mixed. Care must be exercised in getting the private sector involved in any rail project, because getting it to work well is really hard, and things go wrong really easily. Things do seem to be getting better, and some hard lessons have been learned. Some of the problems include:
- Contracts are poorly written, so that the scope of the contract is wrong, or key terms are missing. Often the requirements are incorrect, so key needs are not addressed
- The project price is either too high or too low, and the company either goes bankrupt or they make an enormous amount of money which embarrasses everyone.
- In rail especially, the government attempts to remedy a shortfall of qualified experienced technical staff by creating a PPP contract and company to complete the work, only to find

- that the PPP company cannot recruit skilled people either, as there are none to be found
- The PPP company puts clauses into the contract so that the government will bailout the company if it makes a loss, so the risk to the government is not reduced at all
- Estimates of revenues from the project are wildly optimistic, and the private company that builds the infrastructure goes bankrupt
- Projects have technical requirements that are difficult to measure and even more difficult to monitor. Rail projects often have requirements in the contract concerning reliability and other rather abstract performance measures, and depending on the project these can be almost impossible to manage effectively. Without clear goals management of the project can be very difficult
- Private companies install equipment for the new infrastructure that is very poor quality, cheap, and that public government companies would never install. This equipment is often so poor that maintenance staff are displeased to even see it in service, and when any infrastructure is handed back to the government, will immediately need to launch a project to remove all the low quality infrastructure and replace it with something more suitable.

For any rail project it is best if projects for revenue and economic benefit are realistic and achievable. High quality analysis up front, especially for demand estimation of the use of the railway can help reduce the impact of any problems.

Tourism and Rail Systems

Introduction

Most rail systems have regular users that patronise the system very frequently. Price, frequency of service, and reliability are very important for these passengers. Tourist railways are very different, where passengers may use the service only once in their lives, price is not as important, and experience and look and feel are very important. Tourist railways are the "quiet achiever" of rail systems, and there are many of them that operate at a profit.

Tourists have different travel patterns from business travellers, and other travellers that are visiting family, working, studying or attending a conference. Tourists travel for leisure, and during their travel want to experience new and different things, and to see things that are interesting or have historical value. Tourists are prepared to take trips that are more expensive than normal transport if the experience offered is seen to justify the expense.

Rail systems are very suited for tourists. Any large city or region that has large numbers of tourists should have a good quality rail system. Tourists like rail systems, and their presence and quality can significantly affect the number of tourists that come to a region. Tourism brings valuable money into an economy, generates jobs, and earns foreign exchange. Tourism, when done sustain ably, is a good thing that should be encouraged.

Tourist railways are railways that are specifically designed and marketed to tourists. They are not typically used by passengers to move around an area, but are designed to provide an experience that is far beyond what is normally obtained from a "normal" railway. Tourist railways can be quite effective in bringing tourists to a region, and there are many famous examples. The street cars of San Francisco are a very known example, and there are many others. Tourist railways fall into a number of small categories:
- Train journeys that are very scenic, and may take between 1 to 2 hours. The train often travels over and through mountains, and this type of rail service is designed for day trips, rather than trips that take days. Examples of this type of tourist

railway is the Kuranda railway in northern Queensland in Australia.

- Rail cruises, where the trip is meant to resemble that of an ocean cruiser liner in splendour and quality of travel, where the trip can take several days or even longer. The tickets for this type of travel are very expensive, and the quality of service very high. Sleeper compartments are common on this type of rail system, and the trip length can be over 30 days. Perhaps the best known of this style of rail system is Orient Express, which used to travel from Paris to Istanbul. Another example would be a long distance train trip through the Canadian Rockies.
- Short train trips that allow tourists to access difficult to reach places. One very good example of this is the Peak Tram in Hong Kong, which allows tourists to reach the top of Hong Kong Island. Another example is the monorail that connects Harbourside in Singapore with the resort island of Sentosa, where one of the casinos is located in Singapore.
- Historical tramways, which meander through the centre of cities on old tram routes. In addition to San Francisco, there are some of these in Melbourne and Adelaide in Australia. This type of tram is often free, and offers a quite poor service for getting people from one destination to another, but provides a nice scenic ride through the city.
- Rail systems so exotic that people will travel on them for the experience, such as the Maglev in Shanghai. This train is a very interesting experience as it is, at the time of writing, the fastest commercial train in operation. Another example is the very short rail line in the Blue Mountains near Sydney that operates at an incline of $55°$ to the horizontal. To a lesser extent HSR systems are also an experience, and tourists will use them just for the experience.

Tourist railways can attract significant numbers of tourists, in the order of tens of thousands each year for very good quality systems. The economic benefit of this should not be discounted.

Other than the special case of tourist railways, in general tourists also greatly like using efficient and cost effective rail systems in areas where they want to visit. Tourists often do not bring their cars with them when travelling, especially when travelling large distances, or to countries over seas. The further tourists want to travel, the less likely it is they will want to bring their car. This leaves tourists at the mercy of the local transport systems, which can include car rental, taxis, buses, rail, and other forms of public transportation. Some tourists will rent cars, but this is not always possible, and many tourists will be travelling on a budget.

Tourists often want to use rail systems to get around at their destination, but only where a good quality service if offered. The amenity of a good quality rail system is hard to understate, and there are many examples of cities with well developed rail systems that allow tourist to move around with ease. Rail systems suit tourists, for a variety of reasons listed below, and these include:

- Rail systems are normally immovable, unlike bus lines which change frequently. Rail systems require very heavy investments, and so are normally permanent. For tourists who have only been to a city or region a small number of times, this can be very helpful, as the stability of the system allows tourists to use it more effectively.
- Rail systems are more spacious than buses, and cheaper than taxis. They are often very cheap to use, especially metro systems in large cities.
- It's not necessary to be able to speak the local language when using a metro system, as there are signs in the Latin alphabet which can be easily read (in most rail networks), and the need to explain to a taxi driver where the passenger wants to go can be avoided
- In some countries taxi drivers participate in scams to extract money out of passengers, and can be violent. One unfortunate example of this is the island of Phuket in Thailand.
- Information for rail systems can be obtained from the internet easily, as rail systems are permanent, a map can be downloaded before going to the new city or country.
- Bus stops can be very poorly signposted, and tourists can be overcarried very easily. Bus stops in some countries are clearly signposted, which makes things easier for tourists, but this is often not the case. In Australia it is common to rely on the driver to tell passengers what stop the bus is approaching.
- Ferry services on large rivers or harbours can have an extremely large number of stopping patterns. With a large number or piers/jetties, a very large number of different routes can be generated, which can be extremely confusing. Rail

systems have very consistent stopping patterns which are almost always advertised well in advance of the trip.
- Rail services are often faster than buses and ferries
- Bus services stop on edge of the road, on opposite sides of the road, so any passenger that is overcarried may have terrible trouble crossing a highway to get to the bus service in the other direction
- Rail systems can move large numbers of people for large events, such as the Olympics, or a football match, that would be impossible in any reasonable numbers on any other form of public transportation.
- Rail systems such as HSR systems offer ticket sales through internet sites, which means tourists can buy tickets well in advance. Bus or ferry tickets are commonly only available in the city once the tourist arrives there. This is of course not the case where the bus or ferry system is integrated into the region's ticketing system.

So rail systems generate more tourist income for a city or region, which is due to the larger numbers of tourists that are attracted to a city or region. Some of the disadvantages of rail systems, and there are not many, but some drawbacks for tourists are:
- Rail metro services are slower than taxis, unless the traffic is very bad
- Rail systems can be dangerous, with thefts and petty crime common. This of course depends on the country where the rail system is located
- Very large rail systems can be very confusing to use. Some of the stations in Tokyo are enormous and interchanging can be very difficult
- Rail systems are not suited to get people to remote areas, or mountains or swamps. Areas of great natural beauty frequently do not have any rail system at all, and the cost of constructing it would be far greater than the economic benefit
- Most rail systems do no operate past midnight, and so tourists "hitting the town" may not be able to use a rail system when returning back to their hotel room
- Some rail systems are too crowded for luggage, and may even ban passengers bringing luggage onto the rail system.

So what makes a good tourist rail system? What makes the rail system attractive to use for a tourist? Is it any different to what a commuter passenger would want? Below is a list of some of the things that attracts tourists to a rail system:

- It has a simple ticketing that provides tickets that cover where tourists want to go
- There are direct connections to and from the airport, or major transport interchange
- The rail system is simple and easy to use
- The rail system connects to tourists attractions
- The crime rate is low
- Plenty of space for luggage
- Lifts and escalators for passengers with baggage
- Reasonable pricing
- Good quality signage, in languages that many of the tourists would read, often English, or at least Latin characters. This is particularly important for metro stations with large numbers of exits.
- Interchanges are small or convenient, and do not involve walking kilometres to another station to change trains. This is often difficult to avoid, and even a well planned system such as Hong Kong has large interchanges that involve a lot of walking.

Tourism can represent a large part of the GDP of modern economies. In Australia tourism represents about 4% of GDP, which is a large amount for one industry. It also provides about 5% of the total employment in Australia (in 2013). Likewise tourism accounts for 4.5% of the GDP of Hong Kong, and employs about 6.5% (in 2013). Tourism is also a good way for countries to earn foreign currency, and in many ways tourism is like an export.

Much of the focus of tourism and the related economic studies is related to the construction of places to visit, and theme parks and gardens seem to be a common thing to build. Also countries can build exhibition halls, which can be used to cater for large exhibitions, such as car shows or gift expositions. This too can bring in a large amount of income to a country. One consideration is of course the construction of the infrastructure to support tourism, which normally means airports and hotels, but includes rail systems.

So a good quality rail system can have a profound effect on the tourism in an area. That's a nice statement to make in any cost benefit study for the construction of a new rail line, or a large new project, but how is this assessed?

Economic Benefits of Tourist Railways

Assessing tourist railways is conducted on a different basis to almost all other types of rail system. The purpose of a tourist railway is to provide an experience to tourists, and the economic benefit of a tourist railway is assessed similar to any other government project, such as cost to build, economic benefits, money brought into the economy, jobs provided, etc. For a more general rail project, such as building a metro line in a city, the rail system supports the tourist industry in general, and is often not linked to one specific project. In a small number of cases, the construction of a rail line is directly linked and part of the construction of a larger tourist attraction, and so the cost of the rail line is included in the cost benefit study of the larger project. This was the case for Hong Kong Disneyland, where the rail line was constructed specifically for the theme part.

Many rail projects will clearly have no impact to tourism in the city or region. This is particularly so for:
- Commuter rail lines, where trains operate between city centres and the suburbs. Tourists will rarely be interested in the suburbs of large cities, unless there is some sort of tourist attraction there or are visiting friends or family
- Rail lines that operate between cities and small regional centres that do not attract tourists
- Freight lines of all types
- Rail lines that are designed to take workers to specific worksites, such as large industrial area, where tourists are unlikely to want to go. This can include light rail as well as heavy
- Feeder light rail lines that connect the suburbs to heavy rail lines.

These rail lines will have almost no impact to tourism, and changes in tourist numbers should not be included in any cost benefit economic appraisal.

Some rail lines clearly will have a benefit to tourism, although an indirect one. Changes to rail lines with these characteristics, or the construction of new ones, will increase tourism when:
- The rail line connects to the airport or other major transport interchange such as a cruise liner terminal
- The rail line connects to an exhibition centre
- The rail line passes through the centre of any major city
- The rail line is an HSR line. This is particularly the case the faster the system operates.
- The rail line connects areas with many hotels to other locations where tourists may want to go
- The rail line offers a good view of an important tourist attraction, or natural area
- The rail line connects to major tourist attractions such as theme parks or museums
- A tram line that passes through the centre of a city and offers a convenient way to see different parts of the city

For these projects it is much more likely that the tourism benefits will be high, or at least worth considering.

So, where appropriate, the benefits to tourism of any infrastructure may be assessed through an economic tourism impact study. This type of study is very common, and falls within an area of economics called tourism economics. The benefits of tourism can be broadly characterised as:
- Direct benefits, which is the money spent by tourist when in the region or city. This is normally calculated as a total dollar figure per day per person.
- Indirect benefits, which refers to the money spent by businesses that sell products to tourists. These businesses need to buy supplies to provide their services, which is an indirect benefit.
- Induced benefits, which means the spending and income effect of the employees and owners of businesses supplying goods to the tourist industry. For example, airport employees spend money on renting properties near the airport, and this raises rentals in the area, which is an induced benefit.

It is important for any economic appraisal of tourism to include all the benefits, not just the direct ones. A lot of economic activity is generated by tourism, and this extends to the infrastructure needed to provide the services that tourists want. A restaurant will need to buy chairs, tables, cooking equipment, uniforms, and the business that supply these goods will also benefit. A large tourist industry can support the employment of a lot of people.

A description of the benefits of tourism for a rail project would be described in the following terms:
- The number of additional people that will visit an area or region as a result of a rail project.
- The amount of money they will spend, and inject into the local economy.
- The economic activity that will be generated as a result of the increase in tourism.

In tourism economic benefit studies a common concept is an economic multiplier. The multiplier effect refers to the economic activity that is generated by tourism that is beyond the direct spending by tourists. The multiplier effect is:

$$Multiplier = \frac{(direct\ benefit + indirect\ benefit + induced\ benefit)}{direct\ benefit}$$

Major industrialised counties will normally have a government statistics department that collects this type of information, and should publish the economic multiplier of the benefits of tourism. They will also publish information on the number of arrivals, time spent in the country, and where they went. This information is extremely useful in compiling a tourism economics benefits study.

The Australian Bureau of Statistics has published a number of studies examining the economic benefit of tourism and reported in July 2013 that the multiplier for tourism in Australia is 1.9. The economic multiplier for tourism seems to be commonly somewhere around 1.5 to 2, but this varies significantly based on the country and many other factors.

A related concept is what is called the "leakage effect", where money generated from tourism leaves the country where the money is spent. Leakage of money from an economy for tourism is common, especially in developed countries, where services provided are by foreigners that take the profits offshore. Many of the products provided in countries that have undeveloped infrastructure and industry are imported, which means that the people where the tourism is do not benefit.

Modelling for a tourism impact study seems to be quite complex, but similar to that of modelling changes to demand for rail services. Demand elasticises are commonly used, as well as more complex models using utilities. Recall that utility is the benefit that consumers derive from buying a good, and is not necessarily the same as price.

Complex models for tourist behaviour have been developed. Once created, it is possible to introduce changes to this model, and from this an estimate of the changes to tourism from large scale rail projects. Tourism is driven by major factors such as the sights and places to visit, cost of accommodation and food, as well as the convenience of the travel required to get to the destination, and often this is air travel. Rail services play more of a role in getting people around in their tourist destination, rather than bringing people into the region for tourism.

Of course HSR is the exception to this, and an HSR service may bring in large numbers of tourists. Domestic tourists are much more likely to travel to a location when HSR services are cheap, comfortable and frequent, and the increase in tourism from an HSR system can be significant. This is especially so for places where access before the introduction of the HSR system was difficult or time consuming.

Unfortunately demand elasticises, so useful for estimating the increase in passengers or freight for new rail projects is not really useful for tourism. Rail transport mostly plays only a small role in the cost of any travel, especially where all the long distance travel is by air.

REFERENCES

1. Tourism Research Australia, *Tourism's Contribution to the Australian Economy, 1997-98 to 2011 – 12*, July 2013

2. Ang-Olson, J. & Mahendra, A. *Cost Benefit Analysis of Converting a Lane for Bus Rapid Transit – Phase II Evaluation and Methodology*, National Cooperative Highway Research Program, Research Results Digest 352.

3. Kenworthy, J. *Transport Energy Use and Greenhouse Gases in Urban Passenger Transport Systems: A Study of 84 Global Cities, Institute for Sustainability and Technology Policy*, Murdoch University

4. Kemp, R. *T618 – Traction Energy Metrics*, Rail Safety and Standards Board, Interfleet Technology, Dec 2007

5. Brons, M & Givoni, M., Rietveld, P. *Access to Railway Stations and its potential in increasing rail use*, Transport Research Part A 43(2009) 136 – 149, The Department of Spatial Economics, The Free University

6. CFL, *Rapport Annuel*, 2011 (In French)

7. Koppenjan, J. & Leijten, M. *How to Sell Railways: Lessons on the privatisation of Three Dutch Railway Projects*, European Journal of Transport and Infrastructure Research, Sept 2007

8. Andersonn, M. *Marginal cost of railway infrastructure wear and tear for freight and passenger trains in Sweden*, Swedish National Road and Transport Research Institute (VTI), Department of Transport Economics, 2011

9. Bradbury, N, *Face the Facts on Transport Safety*, Railwatch Nov 2002

10. Bureau of Transport and Regional Economics [BTRE], 2007, *Estimating urban traffic and congestion cost trends for Australian cities*, Working paper 71, BTRE, Canberra ACT.

11. Damart, S. & Roy, B. *The uses of cost-benefit analysis in public transportation decision-making in France*, Transport Policy 16 (2009) 200-212

12. Centre for International Economics, *Business Costs of Traffic Congestion*, August 2006

13. Department of Infrastructure, Transport, Regional Development and Local Government, *Road Deaths Australia 2008 Statistical Summary*, May 2009

14. Paulley, N. et al The Demand for Public Transport: The Effects of Fares, Quality of Service, Income, and Car Ownership, White Rose Research Online, http://eprints.whiterose.ac.uk/2034/

15. Litman, T. *Understanding Transport Demands and Elasticities*, Victoria Transport Policy Institute, www.vti.org, March 2013

16. IBI Group, E&N Railway Corridor Study: Analysis of Tourist Train Potential, (Date Unknown)

17. Daniel J Stynes, Economic Impact of Tourism, Michigan State University

18. Kockelman, K. et al *The Economics of Transportation Systems: A Reference for Practitioners*, Center for Transportation Research, University of Austin, January 2013

19. Baldry, C. Off the rails: factors affecting track worker safety in the rail industry, Employee Relations; 2006;

20. Joint Transport Research Centre of the OECD *Survey on price and demand elasticity in terms of reliability in freight railway services*, International Transport Forum, May 2008

21. West, R. et al *Identification and Evaluation of Freight Demand Factors*, National Cooperative Freight Research Program, Sept 2011

22. Beuthe, M. *Freight transportation demand elasticities: a geographical multimodal transportation network analysis*, Transportation Research Part E 37 (2001) 253 - 266

23. De Rus, Gines *The Economic Effects of High Speed Rail Investment*, OECD International Transport Forum, Discussion Paper No 2008-16, May 2012

24. Cervero, R. & Murakami, J. *Rail and Property Development in Hong Kong: Experiences and Extensions*, Urban Studies, 2009 46:2019 Aug 2009

25. Chun-Hwan, K. *Transportation Revolution: The Korean High-speed Railway*, Japan Railway & Transport Review 40, March 2005

26. Agostini, C & Palmucci *The Anticipated Capitalisation Effect of a New Metro Line on Housing Prices*, Fiscal Studies, vol 29, no 2, pp 233 – 256 (2008) 0143-5671

27. Scarsi, G.C. & Smith, G. *Different Approaches and Responsibilities for Investment Sustainability in EU Railway Infrastructure: Four Case Studies*, EUI Working Papers, RSCAS 2010/88

28. Bureau of Infrastructure, Transport and Regional Economics (BITRE), 2010, *International road safety comparisons 2009*, Canberra ACT.

29. Shughart, L. *Trends and Issues in Container Transport*, TRF Annual Meeting, March 2012

30. Arnott, R. & Small, K. *The Economics of Traffic Congestion*, American Scientist, Volume 82, Sept 1994

31. Victoria Transport Policy Institute Transportation Cost and Benefit Analysis II – Air Pollution Costs, www.vtpi.org/tca/tca0510.pdf, **March 2011**

32. Australian Government Department of Climate Change and Energy Efficiency *National Greenhouse Accounts (NGA) Factors*, July 2010

33. Fouquet, R. *Trends in Income and Price Elasticities of Transport Demand (1850 – 2000)*, Basque Centre for Climate Change, BC3 Working Paper Series, Feb 2012

34. Hess, D.B. & Almeida, T.M. *Impact of Proximity to Light Rail Rapid Transit on Station-area Property Values in Buffalo*, New York, Urban Studies, Vol 44, Nos 5/6, 1041 – 1068, May 2007

35. Burge, P. et al Modelling Demand for Long-Distance Travel in Great Britain, www.rand.org, 2011

36. Australian Transport Safety Bureau Cross Modal Safety Comparisons, https://www.atsb.gov.au/media/36229/cross_modal_safety_comparisons.pdf

37. Li, K & Tiong, R. *Financing and Operating of Singapore's Urban Rail Transit Infrastructure*, 4th International Conference on Wireless Communications, Networking and Mobile Computing, 2008

38. Torija, A.J. *Relationship between road and railway noise annoyance and overall sound exposure*, Transportation Research Part D 16 (2011) 15-22

39. Nijkamp, P. & Pepping, G. *Meta-Analysis for Explaining the Variance in Public Transport Demand Elasticities in Europe*, Journal of Transportation and Statistics Jan 1998

40. Haworth, N. & Vulcan, P. & Sweatman, P. *Truck Safety Benchmarking Study*, National Road Transport Commission, March 2002

41. Flyvbjerg, B et al *Comparison of Capital Costs per Route-Kilometre in Urban Rail*, European Journal of Transport and Infrastructure Research, Feb 2008

42. Queensland Co-ordinator General Northern Link Road Tunnel, April 2010, http://www.statedevelopment.qld.gov.au/resources/project/legacy-way-project/northern-link-road-tunnel-cg-report.pdf

43. BSL Management Consultants GmbH & Co. KG *Survey on price and demand elasticity in terms of reliability in freight railway services*, Hamburg May 2008

44. Nilsson, J-E. *Restructuring Sweden's railways: The unintentional deregulation*, Swedish Economic Policy Review 9 (2002) 229 – 254

Week 10

Freight

Introduction

Freight is an important part of any economy of any country, and the efficient fast and cost effective movement of goods is critical to productivity and maintaining low prices for goods, and hence international competitiveness. Rail freight went through something of a decline in the 60's and 70's, and despite reports of the death of the rail freight industry, it is still alive and well, albeit a bit smaller in percentage terms compared to road transport.

In Australia, as in many developed countries, there was a boom in constructing railways from around 1850 to 1920. Rail technology was invented before automobiles, or before automobiles could move freight in any kind of significant economic way, and so was the standard for the movement of freight for decades. The development of many industrialised economies depended on the creation of large very comprehensive freight systems, and countries like Canada and the US were criss-crossed by rail lines. The growth of large rail companies was one of the drivers that led to the creation of common stock companies, ways of raising money for investment into large enterprises. The rail industry in many countries, such as Germany, the UK, France and Australia expanded very quickly, becoming very large.

As trucks improved, and road freight became cheaper and more efficient, rail started losing its competitive advantage, and through the 60's and 70's rail freight in most developed countries dramatically contracted. Rail lines were closed, and much of the freight moved to road transport. As road transport was cheaper, and more flexible, the maintenance of expensive rail infrastructure could not be justified, and many freight lines were closed. In Australia the closure of rail lines was particularly dramatic, and freight corridors were converted into walking paths, housing, light rail, roads, etc. Large freight yards next to old disused wharves were also common, and these freight yards became quiet as rail lost its ability to compete. As part of this process, and the development of new technology that made rail services more productive and require less staff, there were dramatic contractions in the number of employees working in rail companies. This contraction was also very pronounced in British Rail.

In many cases rail freight stopped operating entirely, such as in Hong Kong. In others rail freight become something of a niche player, and catered only for small markets with very specific needs. The cost advantage of rail systems for bulk materials such as coal and grain guaranteed their survival, but many goods that were previously moved by rail were rarely moved this way. In Australia wool was very commonly moved by rail, but now, or even since the eighties, is almost never moved with the rail freight mode. Also the development of the "road train", a truck/traction unit with a large number of trailers, allowed the movement of large amount of goods by road. Road trains can be extremely large, and large ones are not permitted to enter urban areas. The record for the largest number of trailers pulled by one large truck is apparently 112.

This great contraction in rail freight has left many rail lines either underutilised, and many freight yards are almost empty. Large numbers of freight lines were closed, and many rail systems shrank. In the US things seems to be a little better, and through very prompt action rail freight has survived in a much more substantial way there than in many other countries. This contraction has had a profound effect on the rail freight industry, with many deserted yards, little used freight wagons, and old rail freight lines covered with grass.

One advantage rail freight has is its fuel efficiency. Road vehicles such as trucks and articulated vehicles require more fuel than rail, so for intensely used freight corridors, rail freight can still be viable. For mines with large amount of material to be moved, rail freight works quite well, and so large rail lines often service mines. For non-bulk materials, the picture is more bleak, and even in areas where it has survived, there is relatively little moved by rail. In Australia, rail freight has about 20% of the market for non-bulk freight, in the UK it is about 10% and in the US about 40%. Rail has genuinely struggled to compete, but has survived nonetheless (as of 2012).

One of the main challenges with rail freight is the need to provide specialised infrastructure. Rail freight requires rail corridors, and rail tracks, which need to be built and maintained. The cost of rail freight infrastructure needs to be at least partly recovered, and so there are charges for the use of rail infrastructure. In many parts of the world, and Australia is no different, use of roads by trucks and road freight is taxed in a preferential way, or the full cost of the damage to roads is not covered in the cost of licenses, so rail freight needs to compete with road when it is paying for the infrastructure, and road freight is not. This is a very difficult situation, and one that is problem for the rail industry.

Rail freight is almost always heavy rail. Heavy rail is a rail system where the loads are very large and the trains very long. High speed rail for example is a heavy rail system, because of the large locomotives and the weight of the train. Some freight systems are however light rail, and sugarcane railways are a light rail freight system.

Despite the contraction of rail freight 50 years ago, and the difficulty of competing with road freight, rail freight is now perceived as being superior to road in many countries. Rail freight has many advantages, included the low level of emissions, its better safety, the benefits to urban spaces in terms of amenity and quality of life from removing road freight from roads, and the reduction in damage to roads. Many countries are encouraging rail freight through subsidies to the rail industry, taxes to road freight, and projects to improve the efficiency of rail freight. This level of support has been very beneficial to improving the amount of freight moved.

Much of the research and reports on rail freight focus on getting as much freight as possible onto the rail system and off roads. All sorts of different strategies have been investigated, and these are discussed below. Rail freight is seen as not being able to compete with road freight, but a commonly held view is that rail freight is something that should be encouraged. This view, coupled with constant study of rail freight systems, has provided a wealth of information on freight and how it is managed, and what is needed to improve it. The chapter below explores many of these options.

Overview of Freight Systems

Almost anything can be moved by rail freight, and almost any item that is sold or manufactured can be moved by rail. For example, washing machines could be moved by rail, or milk, or books, almost anything. What can be moved by road or air can be moved by rail. The choice of transport mode is an important one for any freight system, and this decision can have a large impact upon costs, delivery times, and punctuality.

To provide the reader with an idea of the broad range of goods that can be moved, consider the list of different goods below. It is not at all an exclusive list, but provides some indication of the broad range of goods that can be moved by rail:
- Whitegoods and furniture
- Food products
- Livestock
- Animal products, such as wool
- Bulk food products such as wheat or milk powder
- Petroleum products
- Gases of all types such as chlorine
- Liquids used in production process such as ethanol or methanol
- Bitumen or other organic compounds
- Lumber
- Minerals and bulk materials such as coal, iron ore or sand
- Parcels
- Weapons, such as tanks or missiles
- Road vehicles, cars and trucks
- Mail
- Industrial machinery
- Sugarcane

Many different products can be moved by rail. In competition with rail, the main transport modes are:
- Road freight, which means mostly trucks. Road freight is more flexible than rail, and often suited to short distances or small numbers of shipments
- Air freight, which is used for long distance freight, and where the item is needed to be transported quickly. Air freight is very expensive and struggles to compete with other transport modes
- By ship, which are mostly ocean going. This transport mode is frequently the only serious way to transport goods from one country to another that is not linked by land.
- By barge, a type of boat that is suitable for large navigable rivers. Barge transport depends on the location of suitable rivers, and whilst not common in Australia is still common in the US.
- Other more unusual means of transporting products, including dedicated pipelines, or conveyors.

Freight trains are quite different to passenger trains, although some of the design concepts are the same. Some of the key differences are:
- Freight trains accelerate and brake much more slowly than passenger trains
- Freight trains are almost always much longer than passenger trains, and are often over 1 km long
- Freight trains can be diesel or electric, in Australia freight is mostly diesel
- Freight trains have difficulty climbing grades, and even small grades can be a problem
- Passenger trains often have powered passenger cars (EMUs), freight trains are almost always powered by separate locomotives
- Passenger trains are rarely divided and amalgamated, freight trains are often split and amalgamated
- Freight trains are mostly much noisier than passenger trains
- Freight trains are almost always much heavier than passenger trains, and frequently do much more damage to the infrastructure than passenger trains
- Freight trains are limited to an economic speed of about 100 kms/hr, although there are exceptions to this rule. Passenger trains often are much quicker than freight trains.

Australia has a number of very successful freight rail systems, which are able to survive and thrive because of the high price of coal (which at the time of publishing this book has changed substantially), and the energy efficiency of moving bulk materials by rail. Successful rail freight companies, which in Australia can even generate enough revenue to pay for the infrastructure and signalling, move very large quantities of coal for export to overseas markets, mainly China and Japan (in that order). The volumes of material moved are truly extraordinary, and by weight rail is by far the most commonly used mode of transport for freight in Australia.

The photo below shows a typical freight locomotive. Large and extremely powerful, these locomotives can be combined together to be able to generate the motive force to move large number of wagons. The fuel consumption of diesel locomotives can be very large, although it should be noted that freight trains can be very fuel efficient compared to the loads they are moving.

A Freight Locomotive

Freight trains are often barred from entering a rail passenger network during peak times, when there are large numbers of passengers moving around the system. As freight trains are slow moving, and accelerate and decelerate slowly, putting them into a passenger system in peak times causes problems. The most common effect of mixing these two rail modes is that the total capacity of the system is reduced, and top speeds are lower. To mitigate these problems, a rail system may impose a curfew, which is a blackout period where freight trains are not permitted to enter a rail system. Curfews have a profoundly negative impact of freight movements, and should only be implemented where absolutely necessary.

Maintainers of rail infrastructure tend to dislike rail freight, and this is because of the changes in infrastructure needed to accommodate freight trains. Broadly, more infrastructure is required, and some of the infrastructure required is different to what is normally required for passenger services. Some of the changes/additions to rail infrastructure include:
- The spacing between signals is increased, so the headway increases, even for passenger trains. This can be extremely inconvenient when a small headway is needed
- The track structure needs to be stronger to accept freight loads that are normally much heavier than passenger loads
- Freight trains have paths through the rail system that are different from passenger trains, and normally more junctions will be needed to accommodate those paths. For example, passenger trains, especially commuter train, operate from the city to the outskirts of large cities, but freight services may move from one remote part of the city, to another remote part, in a direction completely different from the passenger traffic.

These different direction may require substantial amounts of additional infrastructure (turnouts commonly)
- Some sort of billing system is needed for the freight trains, as access to the network is often based on the number of wagons and the weight of the train. Whilst in theory it might seem ok to trust the freight company when they provide data on what trains went where, experience in Australia has shown that freight companies will understate the loads on their trains. Weighbridges are needed to weight trains are they enter the rail network to accurately bill freight companies for the trip through the rail system
- Freight companies will need marshalling yards, where wagons are combined into trains, and where locomotives are stored awaiting use. Marshalling yards can be very large, and are not pretty to look at, and so any rail network with large amounts of freight will need to have at least, and maybe several of different sizes
- Freight trains are often not as reliable as passenger trains. This is frequently because passenger trains use electric power, and operate as EMUs, and so have natural advantage compared to freight trains. This means that they break down more frequently, and there needs to be a system of "recovery" or "rescue" of broken down trains. A normal high powered locomotive is often enough to rescue a broken down freight train, but there are also speciality rail vehicles that perform a similar function. Rescue is often provided at a fee, and a failed freight locomotive will block the rail line in at least one direction, depending on where it has broken down. This needs to be considered in the design of any freight system
- Freight trains pull wagons that can have a bearing failure, which can derail the freight train. Special infra-red cameras are available to look for heat in a rail wagon, and this system is often called a "hot box" detector. These will be needed in strategic places around the network to prevent large derailments
- Facilities will be needed to store freight trains when faster moving passenger trains need to pass. Alternatively, the freight train may need to wait to get access to a freight terminal, because it is full, or there is a curfew that prevents the freight train from entering a certain area of the network at a certain time. Freight trains seem to spend a lot of time waiting, and

sidings, or sometimes called a refuge. Will be needed at strategic places in the network. Passing loops can also be used.
- Special precautions may be needed before hills to ensure that freight trains do not stop before a hill. Whilst freight trains will be able to start moving on level ground, and climb moderately steep grades, if they stop on a high grade they may not be able to pull the load up the grade. Special signals may be needed to ensure that once a freight train enters a section of track before a steep grade, that there is nothing to stop the train on the grade, until the track is in a place where the grade is lower. A freight train may need 10 kilometres of clear track to ascend a particularly steep grade, and stopping halfway through the climb can mean that the freight trains gets "stuck". In Australia this special type of signal is called a "tonnage signal", which will tell the driver of a freight train that the road (ie the rail track) is clear and that it is ok to proceed at normal speed for several kilometres.
- Freight trains are often diesel hauled locomotives, and these produce diesel fumes. Whilst this is fine in the open air, in a tunnel the fumes can rapidly build up and create a toxic environment. In a narrow tunnel the diesel fumes will need to be removed, and this means additional ventilation. A rail tunnel with mixed freight and passenger traffic will need very good ventilation systems to ensure that the air is acceptable to the passengers, and not smell or be full of soot. Ventilation systems in tunnels are expensive
- Modern intermodal container freight trains are often "double stacked", where a second set of containers is placed on top of the first. Where this is done the height of any overhead wiring will above the containers will need to be extremely high, maybe as high as 7.5 metres, and this can impose a substantial cost to have either the overhead wiring moved higher, or built high when first installed.

The damage caused to a rail system from freight can be quite significant, especially where the rail freight is very heavy. The main damage to the rail system is the rail and supporting infrastructure, which will be "pounded" by the heavier loads. Damage to the infrastructure consists of :
- The top of the rail will develop metal defects, such as flat spots and cracks

- Trains carrying bulk loads will often drop some of their load onto the rail track, fouling the ballast and filling points/turnouts with coal or grain or whatever material is being carried. This can cause many problems, especially with the points filling with this unwanted material, and this if often a problem at the entrance to the final terminal where the bulk material is unloaded.
- The track infrastructure will degrade with the constant passage of heavy trains, and need more frequent maintenance

Many types of passenger rail systems cannot accept freight onto their system. If anything, freight on a rail system is becoming less common for a variety of reasons discussed below. Some of the rail systems that cannot accept freight, or rarely do, are:
- Metro systems, where the high frequency of service makes it almost impossible to fit freight trains in between passenger services
- Light rail, where the track structure is rarely strong enough to take large freight trains, and freight trains are rarely suited for running down the middle of streets (although freight trams still exist and were common in Australia for decades)
- Monorails, which are utterly unsuited for freight trains, unless the monorail has been specifically designed to accept freight
- High speed rail, where the slow speed of freight trains will not permit HSR trains to operate at their normal commercial speed. HSR freight is something that does exist, and is discussed extensively in Chapter 16, but is quite rare.
- Some specialised rail systems, especially medium capacity metros that operate with rubber tyres, are not suited for freight

Some of the passenger rail systems that are better suited to accepting freight are:
- Commuter systems, where the heavy commuter trains run on infrastructure that is often the same as what is required for freight
- Long distance and overnight trains, which are often not high speed, and so can intermingle with freight trains quite effectively.

Overall it is extremely important during the planning of any rail system to consider if freight will be allowed onto it. If so there a number of changes and modifications will be needed to the infrastructure, which usually adds substantially to the cost of the construction of the rail system. An economic assessment will be needed of the benefits of allowing freight trains onto rail systems, and for large amount of freight this assessment will normally be quite positive. Where road traffic is extremely congested, then there will be large positive benefits from rail freight, or where bulk materials are being moved. Otherwise it may be very difficult to justify allowing freight onto the network.

Large cities may need freight movements from one part of the city to another. A very large city may be 40 kilometres across, and so large that freight trains are needed to move freight from one side to another. Sydney has this type of freight traffic, and normally the rail freight originates from somewhere on the outskirts of the city, and then moves to the port. This situation arises in part because of severe road congestion, and trucks moving containers may take long periods to get to the port and back again. In theory containers can be moved around at night when roads are empty, but in practice is seems that most intermodal traffic that is short distance needs to take place during business hours. This requirement gives intermodal traffic a chance to be competitive in a rail system even over short distances in very large cities.

Some of the different types of freight are:
- Bulk materials, such as coal, iron ore, grain, milk, fuel, sand, flour, gypsum, etc
- Intermodal freight which consists of large metal containers. Intermodal freight is very important, because this is how most items are shipped around the world today
- Other more unusual freight types, such as steel coils, or road vehicles. In theory many different types of large materials may be moved, should a freight wagon be designed to move it.

The photo below shows some of the different types of freight wagons that can be used. At the front are flat cars, in the middle hoppers for powder of different types, and then after that tank wagons for transporting liquids.

A Freight Yard

There are a number of useful numerical terms that can applied to a freight system. These can be used to describe many aspects of a rail freight system, and some of the key parameters are:
- Axle load. This measure normally has the units of tonnes, and there are mostly 4 axles per freight wagon, so the axle load is the weight of the wagon divided by 4. Freight companies often want to operate with the highest possible axle load, as this increases their efficiency, and reduces the number of trains needed. A typical limit for the axle load would be about 20 tonnes, depending on the freight network of course. In Australia some railways have been able to achieve up to 40 tonnes per axle.
- MGT, which stands for Million Gross Tonnes, which is one measure of the number of tonnes that have been moved through the network in any given year. The measure is made at one point, and the same network will normally have different MGT figures throughout the network. A network with a low number of freight trains may only have an MGT of about 5, and with a moderate amount may have 10 to 15 MGT, Some freight systems in Australia have only 100 MGT, or even over 200, which is a very large amount
- GTK, which stands for Gross Tonne Kilometres. The GTK represents the weight and the distance that freight has been moved, and it is the multiplication of the number of kilometres travelled, by the distance the train has travelled. GTK numbers are often very large, and so are commonly quoted in millions

of GTK. A rail network with only a small number of trains may still be able to have a large GTK figure if their trains travel large distances.

A freight corridor is a dedicated rail freight line that does not have any passenger traffic. Freight corridors can move large quantities of freight, and are very popular with freight operators. The safety risk of freight is much lower than for passenger trains, a freight train can have a derailment where many of the wagons are derailed and destroyed, and there is no loss of life because the freight locomotives are the only places where there are any people. Freight corridors are a very effective infrastructure strategy, and can be spectacularly successful in increasing rail freight movements. Many of the problems associated with moving freight are eliminated, the higher priority given to passenger trains, the lack of network capacity, and curfews that are often placed on freight movements are all eliminated as types of problems.

One problem that commonly arises in freight networks is balancing loads between destinations. It is common for intermodal trains to operate between only 2 destinations, and pick and deliver at both ends. What is desirable is for the loads and freight traffic to be balanced, and so the same number of intermodal containers, or really any other freight traffic, to be the same in both directions. This will reduce cost as the cost of the train is spread over a larger number of containers. In practice things are rarely so nice, and often there is a much higher flow of freight in one direction than in another, and so in one direction trains operate at capacity an in the other are only partly full.

Bulk materials freight almost always has fully loaded wagons and trains moving in one direction, and empty ones in the other. In Australia trains make their way from mines to ports, so that raw materials can be exported, and there is nothing to bring back from the port to the mine. As a result bulk material trains almost always operate half the time full, and the other half empty. This is very difficult to avoid.

A derailment is when train wheels no longer sit on top of the rails, and in severe cases can lose contact with the rail entirely. Derailments are one of the major safety risks for any railway, and for passenger trains this risk should be kept to an absolute minimum. For freight systems derailments have a much lower risk, as the locomotive will rarely derail, but wagons can and often do, especially towards the back of the train. Derailments are much more common for freight trains than for passenger trains. Many freight systems have dozens of derailments per year, and this is because the risk associated with the derailment is so much lower, so mitigations to prevent derailments are not as commonly applied as for passenger trains. Given the relative frequency of derailments, any significant freight system needs to have a method or re-railing any derailed freight train. There are a number of methods for doing this, and a common and easy one is to use jacks to lift freight trains up and back onto tracks.

Freight trains are almost always driven by a human driver. Many freight drivers consider the driving of a freight train to be an art, and requires a special skill. Recall that freight drivers mainly control the speed and braking of a train, and mostly cannot control direction. Managing the acceleration of a freight train is apparently quite difficult, and mistakes can result in separated trains, damage to rail, slow movements of freight, and safety risks. In Australia there have been attempts to automate the driving of freight trains, especially in large mines in the desert where salaries are very high, and up until the writing of this book these attempts have been almost entirely unsuccessful. This may change in the future, as research is continuing into this topic.

Rail Freight Lines

Rail freight lines have some differences from rail passenger lines. The structure and loading gauges need to be larger than a minimum size, and the track infrastructure needs to be quite strong. Many rail lines do not permit the movement of any freight over them, as they are not designed to allow the movement of freight trains. A rail line that allows the passage of freight will need to be designed to allow freight to pass over it, and including freight is a conscious decision that a rail planner will need to make.

Once a decision is made to allow freight through a rail line, then there are some design considerations that need to be taken into account. The grades that a rail system passes over is very important to a freight operation/train. Freight trains are very heavy, and climbing a hill requires a lot of power. The more steep the grade, the more power that is required. A large grade, such as 3% can be climbed by a freight train, but this requires more locomotives, which are expensive, and freight companies prefer to use as few locomotives as possible. Where there is only one high grade along a rail corridor, the freight company will need to put more locomotives onto a freight train to get over this one hill, something that is inefficient to do.

It should be remembered that passenger trains can climb high grades. Some light rail vehicles can climb grades of almost 10%, which is extremely high. A rack and pinion railway can allow for grades even higher than this, and 12 or 14% is possible. The grades for a rail freight system are far lower than this, and a freight train would need to be specially designed to allow for a grade of even 3 to 4%.

The largest grade on any freight path is called the "ruling grade". It has this name because the highest grade will determine how many locomotives are needed, and this is an important parameter for any freight movement. Freight train movements will be more profitable when the ruling grade is low, and so only a small number of locomotives are needed. In Australia the ruling grade is often high, because there is a mountain chain running from the top of Australia to the bottom, along the eastern seaboard, and there are many rail lines that have comparatively steep grades because of this.

Where the ruling gradient is very high, or comparatively high for a freight system, there is greater load on the wagons closer to the locomotive than at the end of the train. Rail wagons are all connected together in a long string, and the force to pull the end wagon is passed through the wagon second from the end, and so on. In some cases the weight of the wagons is such that the stress and load on the wagons near the locomotives is so great that there is a risk that these wagons will be damaged. Care may need to be taken in position the right wagons close to the locomotives, which can accept the higher loads. Other strategies for managing the forces on freight wagons is to put multiple locomotives in different positions in the freight trains, so that the load on any one wagon is not excessive.

Passenger rail lines are mostly duplicated, which means that there are two tracks so that trains moving in different directions are free to pass one another. Rail freight lines are often only single track, especially in Australia, where track maintenance costs are high and the number of freight movements is low. Single line tracks allow the movement of trains in both directions, and a track that has this feature is said to be bi-directional. Freight lines that are single track need a place for trains moving in different directions to pass one another.

A passing loop is a section of track, along a single line section, where the track is duplicated. Where tracks are uni-directional a passing loop may be on one line, to allow trains to pass. Many freight lines have very low volumes of traffic, and need only one track. Freight trains moving along this rail line, in opposite directions, will need to pass each other, and the purpose of a passing loop is to allow this to happen. One train will be held in the passing loop, waiting for the other, and then when the other reaches the passing loop then the first train is free to proceed.

A Passing Loop

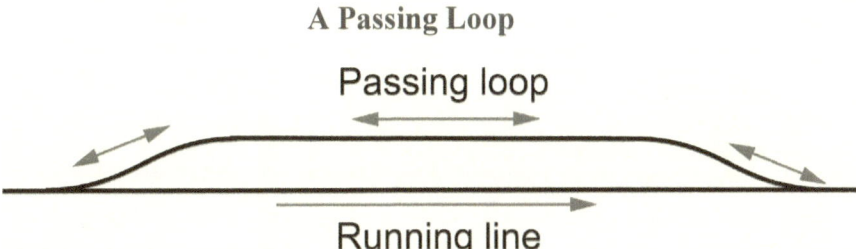

Passing loops are common, especially in areas of single track. Single tracks are much cheaper to maintain, and are very common in Australia. To get more capacity out of a single track line, passing loops are necessary. For a freight system with low amounts of traffic, many rail transport projects may include the construction of passing loops.

Passing loops are also needed where passenger trains and freight trains share the same track for long distances. As freight trains are limited to about 110 kms/hr, passenger trains that move faster than this will be unable to pass the slower freight train. One solution to this problem is to build a passing loop, allowing freight trains to sit in them whilst the passenger train passes. To achieve this the passing loop needs to be long enough to allow the freight train to sit in it without intruding onto the mainline. The lengthening of a passing loop is a good way to cheaply improve the capacity of a rail freight system.

Structure and loading gauge are very important for freight trains. Narrow and low structure gauges will result in small freight wagons that are not economical, and cannot carry the goods or the containers that are needed. Small loading gauges will result in the use of small freight wagons to fit into the space allowed, and so to transport the same amount of material more wagons are required, which will be more expensive, and sometimes not possible because of restrictions on the maximum length of freight trains. Structure and loading gauge also arise as issues when double stacking for intermodal containers is needed. Double stacking requires a much higher loading gauge, which if often not available.

Rail Freight and Government Policy

Government policy is very important for any rail freight network. Rail freight as a industry is heavily dependent on government support to survive, and a hostile government will quickly reduce the amount of rail freight moved to almost nothing. Government policy is normally favourable to rail freight, as it is seen as a positive and beneficial thing, but where this is not the case rail freight will struggle to survive. There are many ways that a government can influence the amount of rail freight moved, and this support is critical to the continued survival of any rail freight industry.

The target of much government action is to increase the modal share of rail. Governments will often have policy launches where rail freight is discussed, and options for increasing it are laid out. In the European Union the European Commission produces policies and reports into rail freight and how to encourage it. Governments often have strategy documents that address how to increase the rail modal share, and which seem to have mixed success, but nonetheless have a lot of useful information in them on the rail industry. Where sensible and useful policies are chosen and implemented, the amount of rail freight moved can increase dramatically.

Rail operators are commonly split from maintainers of infrastructure. The cost of maintaining infrastructure is very high, and often borne by the government, whereas the rail operators may be privately owned. An alternative to this structure is to have a large government organisation that owns and operates everything, so it operates the trains and freight as well. Rail infrastructure is extremely expensive to maintain, and is often the largest group of costs for any rail company. To encourage some private ownership and participation in any rail industry, it is possible, and commonly done, for government to pay for the infrastructure only, and not the cost of operating trains.

Rail freight companies are often privately operated. In Australia, even till recently, there were some freight companies that were government owned, but now all freight companies in Australia have been privatised, and owned by the private sector. The private sector seems able to manage their freight trains and rosters more efficiently, and seem to be able to move freight more cheaply than the public sector. Employee conditions in the public sector are often quite good, and inflexible, which does not help things. It is not clear at to the author why rail freight seems to operate so much better when privatised, and the experience in Australia for privatising freight rail operators has been almost uniformly positive.

So this leaves many governments in the difficult position of needing to provide constant support to an industry that is often completely privatised. In some countries the support of private organisations by government is commonly accepted, but in many others, and Australia included, government support to a private organisation is seen as a negative. This perception is particularly strong where the freight operator is owned by a foreign company, and providing support for this company may be perceived very negatively. Nonetheless government support for rail freight is still critical to its survival.

"Modal share" is a term that refers to the percentage of freight that is moved on different forms of transportation. Road transportation of freight is a "mode", and the mode share refers to how much of the freight travels on this form of transportation compared to any other mode. Other modes are rail, water, and air transportation. Rail and road transportation are often the most direct competitors; water transportation requires rivers or seas, and ports, which are not easy to move or change. Regardless of the mode of transportation for freight, it will need to be moved somehow, and what is not moved by rail will need to be moved through another transport mode. A lack of government support will mostly result in rail freight being moved on roads, and in an area with lots of people there will be a large number of trucks moving around the road system.

Governments control access to most infrastructure, including roads. Even where rail freight operators are privatised, governments can exercise substantial control over freight of all types through taxation, and regulation. Governments may want to encourage any type of freight transport mode, and there are a large number of mechanisms to achieve this. Government support is quite critical to any rail freight operation, and without support it will shrink to almost nothing.

So why is government support for rail freight so important? What can governments do to help rail freight along? The list is quite long, and below are some of the areas and facets of a rail freight business that governments can influence or control:
- Curfews on access to rail systems used by passenger systems
- Investment in infrastructure
- Setting access charges for freight trains to pass over rail infrastructure
- Allowing rail freight lines to operate through suburban areas
- Regulations on what products can be moved
- Standardising the safety and regulation regime for rail freight
- Setting aside land, and resuming land when needed
- Supporting the construction of efficient port infrastructure, that has good quality rail sidings next to it.
- Installing technology that is "freight friendly"
- Financial support when appropriate
- Participating in international efforts to allow freight to operate through many countries more efficiently
- Building rail systems where freight is not excluded

Curfews are sometimes placed on rail networks to stop rail freight from using the network during certain hours. Rail freight, because of its low speed and long length, can seriously interfere and impede faster moving passenger trains, and one solution to this problem can be to prohibit the entry of freight trains into the rail network, or parts of the network during certain times. This is called a curfew. Curfews are a real problem for freight operators, as they limit the number of usable hours per day for freight movements, and generally increase the expense of moving freight. Curfews will often also reduce the punctuality of rail freight, as a freight train that reaches an area with a curfew as the curfew is imposed will need to wait until it is lifted. Freight trains often sit outside curfew areas waiting to enter, which is expensive and makes predicting the arrival time of the freight train difficult.

As the government will often control the infrastructure company, which is heavily subsidised, and freight trains do so much damage to the rail infrastructure because of their weight, the pricing of access charges is a key question. A low access charge will encourage large numbers of freight movements, and there will be little recovery of the cost of the damage to the infrastructure. Alternatively, a high access cost will result in very few freight movements, and types of rail freight that generates only a small profit, often intermodal traffic, will shift onto roads.

Many modern rail signalling systems are an additional cost burden for rail freight. Automatic Train Protection (ATP) is a safety system that checks that trains are braking correctly then they need to, and is becoming more common. This system can only be applied with difficulty to freight trains, and only with the support of the rail freight industry. ATP is being implemented in Europe as a way of allowing freight and passenger trains to operate in many different countries, for which it is quite suited, but in one jurisdiction ATP is a barrier to rail freight, because it is an additional cost to implement.

Trans-national rail freight operations are now common in Europe, a continent with many small countries. Government policy in one country may be to encourage one freight operator over another, and having a preference such as this can strongly influence the ability of freight companies to enter the market. Governments may support companies domiciled in their own country, especially where these companies are government owned. Support for these companies may include subsidies, or cheap finance, or outright gifts of money. This is yet another way that governments can influence the rail freight market.

Perhaps the area where governments play the greatest role is in investment. Wealthy freight operators will be able to pay for some or all of investment in freight systems, but there are also many others that generate meagre returns, or no returns at all, and are operated as a benefit to the community. Where this is the case, the rail freight industry will be completely dependent on government to provide funds for investment in infrastructure, and if this is not done rail freight will struggle to compete. Any government that wants to encourage rail freight will need to take a lead role in improving productivity, as the rail freight companies will want to do this, but will often be unable. Rail freight operators may form industry groups to lobby government for support, but will be unable to provide anything more than moral support when the time comes to provide funds.

Many rail infrastructure companies in Europe publish a document called a "network statement". A network statement provides comprehensive information about the conditions and infrastructure in a rail system, and what a rail operator needs to do to run trains in that network. Network statements are very comprehensive, and detail the infrastructure that is present in a rail system. Some of the information contained in a network statement include:
- Typical tops speeds
- Structure and loading gauges
- Gauges, ie, standard/narrow
- Location of freight/intermodal terminals
- The location of refuelling facilities
- The process for applying for a path through the network
- Location of water supplies
- How access charges are calculated
- The maximum length of freight trains
- Other services provided (for a fee)

Network statements are fascinating documents that contain a great deal of information about how a railway operates. Network statements are often produced by government departments, as many infrastructure companies are government controlled, and government policy will play a role in determining the content of the network statement, and many of the access charges.

Where freight companies are privately owned, and the government owns the infrastructure, and the company that maintains it, then the question arises as to how access is given to freight operators to run trains on the network. A rail freight operator does not just arrive at the boundary to the network, contact the signal box and proceed into the rail system. The rail freight operator will need to be licensed or certified to operate on the network, and this license can be quiet difficult to get. The approval process is mostly overseen by a government department, and the rail freight operator will need to submit an application to operate trains on the network. In addition to this license a rail operator may need to obtain separate certification for safety, sometimes called a rail safety certificate. Some of the approvals that are needed to get a freight train onto a network include:
- Certification of rollingstock
- Certification of drivers
- Certification of companies, and with that procedures of work

- Permission to move goods of certain types
- Application for a path through the network

That's a lot of approvals, and these are usually obtained from each infrastructure company, or from the central government. This can be quite a burden where a freight train must move between many infrastructure boundaries. Managing this situation is discussed in depth below.

Studies have shown that freight transport is very sensitive to price. Encouraging freight onto the rail system is best done through price mechanisms, although other factors are also important. One study detailed a market survey where the different factors relevant to freight were assessed for their importance. The study found that order of importance to rail freight was as follows:
- Price
- Punctuality
- Transport speed
- Other factors such as safety, flexibility, and frequency of service.

The other factors are important, but price is really central to how much freight is moved on any rail system. Governments are in a position to substantially effect the prices that are charged.

Some of the goods moved by freight operators can be classified as dangerous. For example, some poisonous chemicals, if released by harm or kill people nearby to the railway. Alternatively, where goods moved on a rail systems are highly flammable, then there is a risk of fire or even explosion. LPG containers can explode under the right conditions. It is even possible to transport weapons by rail, such as tanks or firearms, and their associated ammunition. The carriage of dangerous goods on a railway in most countries is subject to strict rules, and often a separate licensing regime. Some governments may not permit some types of dangerous goods to be moved on their rail network.

Last but not least in our list of parameters over which governments have control is taxation. In many countries the level of taxation is very high, and there are taxes on almost everything. Governments are in a position to strongly influence which mode of transport is chosen for freight through transportation. Taxes can be imposed on road use, or on road vehicle licensing, or on the carriage of freight. A government can always make rail freight more competitive with the right taxation, but as a lever through which to control people's actions care must be exercised other serious damage can be done to an economy.

Different Types of Freight

Bulk Material Freight

Bulk materials includes bauxite, coal, iron ore, sand, wheat, etc. In Australia the three largest bulk materials moved by rail freight are coal, iron ore, and grain. Bulk materials are particularly easy to load and unload into wagons as they can be poured, rather than lifted with a crane or individually handled into the train or onto a wagon.

Below is a photo of a coal train passing through suburban Sydney. This particular train is empty, and notice that it is quite long and the end of the train cannot be seen. Also note that it is passing a suburban rail station, and there are occasionally injuries to passengers who attempt to "touch" the passing freight train.

Coal Freight Wagons

The coal, or similar bulk material, can be poured, using gravity as the motive force. Not all bulk freight moved is solid, some is liquid. The freight wagon in the photo below was used for moving milk, although based on its condition has not been moved or used for a while.

Sometimes the freight wagon below is called a tank wagon. This one is quite old, at least 30 years, and has seen a lot of use.

Liquid Wagon for Freight

Bulk material freight is often more economic and profitable than intermodal freight. The relative wealth of companies who move bulk materials means that they operate their rail operations differently; their trains are often in much better condition than intermodal locomotives, they can brake more quickly and have a superior braking curve, and can pay higher prices for paths through complex networks.

Below is the final destination for the coal, the loader terminal where the coal is put into a boat, and then sent to it's final destination, which in many cases, is China.

Intermodal Freight

After World War II increasing trade volumes placed great pressure on ports and transport systems, and there was a need to develop a better way of moving goods from one place to another. In the 1950 a trucking company owner called Malcolm McLean developed the modern shipping container, which was a standard size and can be used to move a large variety of different goods. The key advantage of the shipping container was its standard size, which meant that trucks, rail wagons, and ships could be specially adapted to move the containers.

Shipping containers, also called intermodal containers, can be moved on almost any transport mode. The containers are strong, durable, and can survive bad weather and rain. They are easy to move and transport, and can be placed on top of one another. Each corner of the intermodal container has a locking mechanism called a "twistlock", that allows containers to be secured to each other when they sit on top of each other. The twistlock mechanism also allows the container to be placed onto transport, such as ships, trains, and trucks, and then locked into place so that it does not fall off when the vehicle bounces around of passes through heavy seas. The introduction of the intermodal container has been one of the great successes of the 20th century, and has revolutionised the movement of freight worldwide.

Intermodal containers come in many different types. Whilst the early versions were little more than steel boxes, modern intermodal containers can be quite different to one another. Intermodal containers can be refrigerated, for the shipment of ice cream, and other foods that need to be frozen. Containers can also have air conditioning, or ventilation. Bulk containers are also available, suitable for moving bulk materials much like the specialised wagons in the section above. Also available are container to move dangerous goods, which have special flooring to contain spills, may be have special insulation, and of course have different signage.

Intermodal freight is a very important part of any modern economy. Whilst in Australia intermodal freight is often seen as the poor cousin of bulk material freight, in many countries and especially the US, intermodal freight is a very central part of the transport system. The US has a high rail intermodal freight share, with rail moving 35-40% of all intermodal containers countrywide.

Intermodal containers come in many different sizes, but are classified according to their volume. The standard intermodal container is 20 feet long, and 8 feet wide and 8 feet high. In metric units this corresponds to a length of about 6 metres, and a width and height of about 2.44 metres. Intermodal containers are wider than rail gauges, and so will overhang the rail gauge. Recall that trams are typically 2.45 metres wide, and light rail 2.65, and metros about 3 metres (9.8 feet), so intermodal containers are about the same width as a tram. High shipping containers are also available, and these are about 2.9 metres in height.

Intermodal containers seem to be limited to carrying about 28-30 metric tonnes of goods, regardless of their length or height. Containers often weigh about 3 to 4 tonnes, so the gross weight of a container should not exceed 32 tonnes. For most rail systems that is not a lot of weight, and most railways should be easily able to accommodate this amount of weight on one wagon. Where double staking is employed, even 64 metric tonnes is easily carried by the right rail wagon, and with 4 axles on the rail wagon this corresponds to a per axle load of about 16 tonnes, not a large amount for most heavy rail systems.

It is a commonly held view that moving intermodal containers by rail is only economically viable when the transport distances are very large. By large this can mean over 500 (around 310 miles) kilometres, or even further, over 800 kms. This is quite a large distance, and many countries and not this wide or long, especially in Europe where many countries are very small. In the US, Australia and Canada this is not a particularly large distance, and freight movements of this distance are common. In Europe a 1000km (620 miles) freight movement would almost definitely require transport through 2 or more countries, or in some cases more than 5.

Below is a photo of an intermodal container loaded onto a train. This particular one is quite unremarkable, and seems to be relatively old. Notice that the container is a nice square shape, and it's quite long, so probably 40 feet in length.

An Intermodal Wagon

One each corner of the container is a device called a "twistlock". It is on the corner that containers are secured to each other, and onto other objects. To secure a container effectively requires a matching unit underneath the container, and if needed, on top.

Intermodal containers are rated according to units of Twenty foot Equivalent Units (TEUs). The standard intermodal container is 20 feet long, so a 40 foot long intermodal container would represent 2 TEU's. Most containers now moved worldwide seem to be the 40 foot or longer container, rather than the shorter containers.

The table below shows the TEU rating of different sizes of containers.

Container size and TEU rating	
8 feet high x 8 feet side by 20 feet long	1 TEU
8 feet high x 8 feet side by 40 feet long	2 TEU or 2.25
8 feet high x 9 foot 6 inches side by 20 feet long	1 TEU
8 feet high x 8 feet side by 48 feet long	2.4 TEU
8 feet high x 8 feet side by 54 feet long	2.65 TEU

The TEU is a very important unit of measure for intermodal shipping. Trains and terminals are rated in terms of the number of TEUs moved. A typical intermodal terminal might move 100,000 containers per year. This does not mean that 100,000 containers were moved, only that the total TEU ratings of all the containers add up to that figure

Intermodal containers are often stacked on top of a rail wagon called a flat car. Flat cars, as the name would suggest, are entirely flat, and can be an excellent way of transporting many types of goods, in addition to intermodal containers. The photo below shows a modified flat car that is used for moving intermodal containers.

A Flat Car

The photo below shows a well car, where the container sits lower to the track, and is contained within the sides of the wagon. This type of wagon is useful because the container is held more securely, but also because the height of the top of the container can be a little lower, which can be useful where the structure gauge of the freight line is restrictive. Well cars are particularly useful where the track gauge is wider than standard gauge, ie, broad gauge.

A Well Car

In Australia rail is more competitive than road for moving bulk materials even over short distances, and the economic distance where road transport is more competitive than rail is very short indeed, perhaps 20 kilometres or even less.

For bulk materials where the amount moved is relatively small, the freight task may be performed with a road transport to a rail hub/terminal, and then moved by rail to its final destination.

Double stacking

Double stacking is a method of transporting more intermodal containers for a given train length. A second layer of containers is stacked on top of the first layer, and so more containers can be moved than a single stack. Double stacking is very common in the US, where it is widely considered to have dramatically improved productivity. In the US it is common for governments and private companies to have considered investing in their local rail systems to allow double stacking, and many of these reports have been published to the internet.

Double stacking is not as straightforward as it might seem. There are many different configurations of stacking that just simply don't work, and can't be used. In practice special software, deployed in the terminal where the trains are loaded, is often used to allow the efficient and safe double stacking of containers, and avoid many of the unacceptable configurations that cannot be used. The effort involving double stacking means that it is sometimes more economical to not double stack, especially where trip distances are short.

One of the main advantages of double stacking is the reduction in cost. As more containers can be moved, and the weight of containers is normally not that high, for a given locomotive it is often possible to move more containers. This increase in volume moved per locomotive results in a cost decrease, which for the highly competitive freight market is very important.

Overall the effect of double stacking is to either reduce train lengths or to increase the capacity of trains. It is not the case that introducing double stacking can reduce the length of trains by 50%, in practice there is a reduction of maybe 25-30% in train length, as not all intermodal containers can fit together or sit on top of one another. Some of the more heavy containers cannot sit on top of lightweight or weak containers, as it cannot be guaranteed that the lower container won't be damaged. The table below shows which configurations are acceptable and which are not.

Often the sidings where freight trains are loaded with containers is not the ideal length, and too short. Double stacking allows an increase in capacity for a train of a given length, and this can be very important where sidings are too short. In remote areas land will often be very abundant, and so rail sidings can be almost any length, but around ports the length of sidings may be very restricted. Allowing double stacking is one way of making more efficient use of scarce land around ports, as a train of a given length can move more containers when double stacked.

The table below shows what configurations of double stacking are acceptable and which are not.

Double Stacking – Acceptable Configurations

Configuration	Comment
	The top container is not the same length as the two bottom containers combined. Fastening the top container will be difficult, and this configuration is not acceptable.
	The bottom two containers are not the same height, and so the top container cannot be placed evenly across both. Whilst it is possible to fill the void between the two containers, in practice it would not be economic to do this on a large scale. This configuration is unacceptable.
	The top two containers cannot be fastened to the larger container below them. This configuration for double stacking is not acceptable.
	The top container sits evenly on the lower two containers, and can be fastened effectively. This configuration is

Double Stacking – Acceptable Configurations

Configuration	Comment
	acceptable
	The four containers sit evenly on each other, and all the corners line up. This configuration is acceptable
	The flat car is much larger than the intermodal containers, but if secured properly, this is an acceptable way of double stacking.

The photo below shows some intermodal containers being transported through Sydney. Notice that the cyan/light blue container behind the red one is a different height to the red one, and the top of the container is not flat. The red containers can be used for double stacking, but the cyan ones cannot (unless they are sitting on top).

Different Intermodal Containers

Double stacking requires higher structure and loading gauges than single stacked trains, and this is the major reason why double stacking is so difficult to achieve in practice. Typically the height/structure gauge required is about 6.5 metres (21 feet), although a loading gauge of 5.9 metres(19.3 feet) will also allow two standard height containers to be placed one on top of the other. Even a loading gauge of 5.9 metres is quite a lot, and the loading gauges of many rail networks is about 4 to 4.5 metres. Increasing the loading gauge is not cheap, and an increase of 2 metres (6.5 feet) is a large amount.

Some of the changes that are needed to achieve double stacking include:
- Increasing the height of tunnels. This can be done either by boring out the top of the tunnel, or reducing the height of the floor of the tunnel, or both.
- Increasing the height of any overhead wiring that is used to supply trains with traction power, or removing the overhead entirely
- Raising bridges, and many bridges on a track designed only for single stacking will be very low to the track and the train, and raising bridges is a standard infrastructure investment. Raising bridges is not cheap, and depending on the local roads, can be extremely difficult to achieve in practice

Of course intermodal terminals will need to redesigned and changed to accommodate double stacking.

Sugarcane Railways

This type of freight operation is common in some parts of the world, especially where sugar cane is grown in large quantities. Sugar cane railways are a form of light rail, and move much lower tonnages and quantities than say a freight train moving iron ore or sand. They are normally built on 2 foot gauge (61 cm) and radiate out from the sugar mill and the system length can be very large.

The sugarcane railways in Australia are very large and run for over 4000 kilometres (2500 miles). Sugarcane is more economically transported by rail when volumes are large, and the ground is very flat. There are also some large sugarcane railways in Egypt, as well as a number of other countries.

The photo below shows two locomotives coupled together to pull sugar cane wagons back to the mill. These locomotives are always diesel, and need to be built to the 2 foot gauge. Notice the unharvested sugar cane on the left of the photo.

Sugar Railways Locomotives

Below is a photo of some sugar cane wagons waiting to unload their sugarcane to the mill. The mill can be seen in the background with the smoke stacks. Notice the very small size of the wagons, which are completely unpowered and unbraked.

Sugar Cane Wagons

The total weight of sugarcane moved in Australia was 36 MGT in 2007, or about the same as weight of all intermodal traffic moved in Japan for that year. Despite being a light rail freight system, the volume of material moved can still be quite large

In some cases where sugarcane is no longer grown in some countries or areas, the railways has been converted to run as a tourist railway, and even as a passenger railway. There are tourist railways in Taiwan and Fiji that use the old converted 2 foot gauge tracks.

Other types of Freight

It is possible to move many other types of freight, other than bulk materials and intermodal containers. Rail wagons can be customised to move almost any type of freight, and in Australia the main type of freight that is moved is steel products and coils. The steel coil is manufactured in a large steel mill and then shipped for final processing or for export. The photo below shows steel soils waiting to be shipped in Australia, in a custom designed rail wagon.

Steel Coils Moved by Rail Freight

Piggyback operation is a type of freight system where semi-trailers (lorries) which are carrying freight are themselves put onto the train, and then transported. The driver of the truck or semi-trailer will get out of the vehicle and then sit in a special rail car where many drivers can sit. This type of system is rail in the Chunnel, the rail tunnel that runs from the UK to France.

Terminal Design

The design of terminals is very important to any rail freight operation. Passengers get off trains by themselves, however rail freight does not unload by itself, and needs to be removed. Bulk freight is often easier to unload, and intermodal freight is lifted off the train using a crane, or a forklift truck specialised designed to lift containers. Terminal design can be influential in determining what freight transport mode is common in a country or area. Well designed terminals can greatly assist with reducing the cost and time required for successful freight operations.

Any terminal needs to be designed for the type of freight that moves through it. An intermodal freight terminal is not suitable for use as a bulk material terminal, and vice versa, so there might need to be several terminals catering for different types of freight in one area or region.

Modern intermodal terminals can perform some of the functions of international border clearance, such as customs and quarantine. It is more efficient, and better for the senders of the containers, for these government checks to be performed at the same place as where the container is dropped off and delivered to. Intermodal terminals might also offer ancillary services, such as cleaning of containers, or repairing them if they are damaged. Some containers may need to be disinfected, and this service can also be offered for a fee. Perhaps the most important service is to store intermodal containers, as they are not expensive to buy, and companies often buy too many, or have procured some for freight movements that only occur occasionally. The storage of shipping containers does not generate much revenue, but it is an important function in support of intermodal freight.

Freight terminal are often linked to ports, where goods can be exported and imported. In rare cases goods may be taken to a port to ship to another port in the same country, although for reasons that are not clear this is unusual in Australia. Small countries will normally have only a small number of ports, and would not ship containers from one port located close to one another.

Bulk material freight terminals are often located outside large cities, in a regional area. Material shipment such as coal or grain, destined for export, does not need to pass through a major city, and doing so only adds cost and time. On the other hand intermodal traffic is often destined for major cities, much of the contents of intermodal containers are consumer goods, and these end their journey in a shop or retailer.

Freight terminals that move intermodal containers can be classified on the basis of the number of containers moved through the terminal per year. Some references discussing intermodal freight traffic distinguish between terminals that move more than 10,000 TEU's per year, and those lower than that being a small terminal. Some major intermodal terminals handle millions of TEU's per year, and a terminal that handles less than 10 thousand is really quite small.

The photo below is of the intermodal terminal in Yennora in Sydney. The train sits in between the two long gantries, and the gantry crane moves along the length of the train to remove or place intermodal containers onto the train. This type of lifting arrangement is more efficient than a diesel powered container forklift, but more expensive to construct.

A Intermodal Freight Terminal and Gantry Crane

Below is a photo of the coal bulk terminal no 1 in Newcastle. This terminal is structured as a giant loop, and freight trains arrive, move around the loop, and unload their coal onto a conveyor, which moves the coal to where it is stored. Many of the coal freight terminals in Australia have some limited storage capacity, called a stockpile, where coal can be stored for a short time until loaded unto a ship for transport to the final consumers. This particular coal terminal loads ships with coal, and they are not in this photograph. The large orange machines are coal loaders.

A Coal Freight Terminal

Many terminals have restrictions placed upon them by government as to their hours of operation. Many terminals in Australia are required to close at certain hours. The placement of a terminal, especially if it is placed in an industrial area that has no housing, will give the terminal a better chance of being permitted to operate longer hours.

Freight terminals are often built on a slight grade, allowing wagons that are de-coupled to move slowly in one direction. In the past it was common for freight wagons to be uncoupled, and then be allowed to move slowly downhill under their own weight, but more recently this practice is banned in many places and all freight movements and marshalling of wagons to be performed with locomotives. In Australia all movements of wagons in yards are now done by locomotives. Not withstanding that, it is convenient for a freight yard to be on a slope, as this makes runaways much more unlikely, and if they do occur, in a consistent direction.

In the past and still today there was a position in many freight yards called a shunter (as opposed to the light engine of the same name), who was responsible for coupling and uncoupling wagons. In some cases they would run alongside the wagon or wagons are they moved from one side of the freight yard to another. Accidents and deaths in this environment were common, and shunters were occasionally crushed between two freight wagons. In some cases freight wagons needed to be physically coupled together with the shunter between the two wagons to complete the connection; this extremely dangerous situation was allowed to persist for a long time. Fortunately this practise is now banned in Australia.

To move wagons around in a yard often a specialist locomotive was used, rather than the locomotive that propels the train through the network. In the US this locomotive is called a switcher, and has performance characteristics suited for moving wagons around. High torque, low maximum top speed, and relatively small, these locomotives were and are still relatively common.

REFERENCES

1. Wardrop, A and Suess, P, *Strategies to Increase Line Capacity and Reduce Travel Time in a Mixed Passenger and Freight Corridor*, The Institution of Railway Signal Engineers Inc Australasian Section Incorporated, Nov 2009

2. Gifford, J. & Moore, T. *Axle Counters – For Heavy Rail Applications*, The Institution of Railway Signal Engineers Inc Australasian Section Incorporated, March 2007

3. Andersonn, M. *Marginal cost of railway infrastructure wear and tear for freight and passenger trains in Sweden*, Swedish National Road and Transport Research Institute (VTI), Department of Transport Economics, 2011

4. Hassan A *The Role of Light Railway in Sugarcane Transport in Egypt*, Infrastructure Design, Signalling and Security in Railway, Chapter 1

5. Wardrop, A. & Suess, P. *Strategies to Increase Line Capacity and Reduce Travel Time in a Mixed Passenger and Freight Corridor*, IRSE Australasia Technical Meeting – Sydney, Nov 2009

6. Joint Transport Research Centre of the OECD *Survey on price and demand elasticity in terms of reliability in freight railway services*, International Transport Forum, May 2008

7. West, R. et al *Identification and Evaluation of Freight Demand Factors*, National Cooperative Freight Research Program, Sept 2011

8. Beuthe, M. *Freight transportation demand elasticities: a geographical multimodal transportation network analysis*, Transportation Research Part E 37 (2001) 253 - 266

9. Troche, G. *High-speed rail freight*, KT Railway Group, Stockholm 2005

10. Shughart, L. *Trends and Issues in Container Transport*, TRF Annual Meeting, March 2012

11. Lin, CY. *Causal Analysis of Passenger Train Accidents on Freight Rail Corridors*, 2013 World Congress on Railway Research, November 2013, Sydney Australia

12. ABC Containers *ABC Container Guide*, http://www.abccontainers.com.au/downloads/abc-refrigerated-container-guide

13. Department of Infrastructure, *Transport, Regional Development & Local Government Adelaide Rail Freight Movements Study*, Oct 2009

14. Bureau of Infrastructure, Transport and Regional Economies, *Information Sheet 34 Road and Rail Freight, Competitors or Complements*, April 2009

14. Bureau of Infrastructure, Transport and Regional Economies, *Information Sheet 65 Australian Container Ports in an International Context*, Sept 2009

15. Woodburn, A. *The role of rail in port-based container freight flows*, Maritime Policy Management, Aug 2007, Vol 34, No 4, 311-330

16. Piyaatrapoomi, N et al Freight Intermodal Terminal Systems for Port of Brisbane, Melbourne, and Sydney, 2006, http://eprints.qut.edu.au

17. van Geldermalsen, T. & Leviny, D. Viability of Providing Double Stack Access on Railway Lines in SouthEast Australia, 28th Australasian Transport Research Forum, http://www.atrf.info/papers/2005/2005_vangeldermalsen_leviny.pdf

18. Rahall, N. Central Corridor Double-Stack Initiative Final Report, Appalachian Transportation Institute, Feb 2003

19. Yang, Q. *How to Improve the Efficiency of Railway Freight Transport in the Urban Area?*, Service Operations and Logistics, and Infomatics, 2008

20. Freight Infrastructure Advisory Board *Railing Port Botany's Containers*, July 2005

21. Shipping Australia Ltd *Metropolitan Intermodal Terminal Study 2011*, http://www.transport.nsw.gov.au/sites/default/files/b2b/freight/rail-access-review-shipping-aust-mits-attachment.pdf

22. Iawasa, K. Rail *Freight in Japan – The Situation Today and Challenges for Tomorrow*, Japan Railway and Transport Review 26, Feb 2001

23. Sydney Ports Corporation *Intermodal Terminal Guide Metropolitan & Regional New South Wales*, October 2009

24. Colliers International *The National Intermodal Terminal Challenge*, 2010, www.colliers.com.au/research

25. BSL Management Consultants GmbH & Co. KG *Survey on price and demand elasticity in terms of reliability in freight railway services*, Hamburg May 2008

26. Bureau of Infrastructure, Transport and Regional Economies, *Report 114 Optimising harmonisation in the Australian railway industry*, 2006

27. Park, H. *Rail Freight Transport in NSW Briefing Paper No 8/09*, November 2009

28. Radosavljevic, A. *Measurement of train traction characteristics*, Proceedings of the Institution of Mechanical Engineers; Sept 2006; 220, F3; Proquest Central

29. Lukaszewicz, A. *Running resistance – results and analysis of full-scale tests with passenger and freight trains in Sweden*, Proceedings of the Institute of Mechanical Engineers; Jun 2007; 221, F2; Proquest Central

30. Andersson, M. *Marginal cost of railway infrastructure wear and tear for freight and passenger trains in Sweden*, European Transport no 48, (2011): 3 – 23

Week 11

Timetabling

Introduction

Timetabling is a key activity within managing rail operations. Timetables can have profound effect on the quality of service provided, as a high frequency of service is considered to be highly desirable, and a low level may result in rail systems being dramatically underutilised. For more complex rail systems timetables also include decisions on what trains go to which line, and which stations to stop at. A good timetable can help a rail system operate efficiently, and a poor one can similarly damage rail patronage numbers. Property prices can be impacted by the number of services, so the choice of the level of services can change the financial position of people who do not even use the rail system.

Companies operating large rail systems will have substantial departments many people working with timetables. Timetabling is often a labour intensive process, and even small changes to timetables can generate a lot of work. Those involved in timetabling will need a very good understanding of the network to be able to create effective and efficient timetables.

Timetables are often needed to keep passengers informed about trains and when to expect them. Where the service frequency of a rail line is high, then this need will be lower than that of a rail system with very few services. Perhaps the only information passengers will need for a high frequency system is the service frequency, and when the rail line opens and closes. For rail lines with very low frequency, passenger timetables are essential.

This chapter does not discuss how to create a roster for rail staff for stations and trains. This falls outside, for the purposes of this book, the definition of transport planning. The aspects of timetabling that are relevant for transport planning for this book are:
- Setting service frequencies
- Determining stopping patterns
- Deciding where trains will go, what their final destination is
- How quickly trains will get from origin to destination

- The relationship between the timetable and train trip punctuality
- How much rollingstock is required

All of these topics will be discussed in this chapter. Excluded from this book is a discussion of the following:
- Rostering of all staff
- Calculations involving power and fuel requirements
- Scheduling of maintenance for tracks, rollingstock, and stations

Large rail systems may have multiple timetables. A large system may need several timetables, and these can be almost completely independent of one another. A rail system with several large timetables may be able to make changes to one or more of these without changing any of the others. Partial changes to the timetable are possible, and commonly done. For a very large timetable, there may be a schedule of changes to timetables, and each timetable may have large changes implemented every 5 years. For a rail system with 10 or more independent area or rail systems, this can mean a new timetable every 6 months for one part of the rail system or another. This approach has many advantages, as the scale of the change to timetables is smaller when performed, but the timetable change will be less noticeable to the general public. Alternatively, the constant change in the rail system may make managers in the company a little weary!

The timetabling of trains has a profound effect on the people in and around the rail system, including employees. Even those railways that do not have a publicly available timetable will have a private timetable which is used for rail employees, sometimes called a working timetable. The timetable is used as a basis for the creation of a roster for drivers, operators, guards if there are any, and station staff. The timetable is a very important document which has far reaching implications throughout the rail organisation.

A working timetable has much more information than the passenger timetable. Train movements that do not move passengers are also shown. The movement of trains from one stabling yard to another, often at night, are shown on a working timetable. In some cases trains do not start revenue service from the stabling yard, but start from another station. The movement of the train from the stabling yard to the start of its run is shown in the working timetable. Another use of the working timetable is to move trains from stabling yards and revenue service to maintenance centres, where maintenance is performed. This also needs to be scheduled.

The table below shows what type of rail system is likely to need a rail timetable, and which do not. If a timetable is needed, then the level of complexity is also shown:

Rail Systems and the use of Timetables

System Type	Passenger Timetable Needed	Comments
Monorail	No	Frequency based timetable
Tram	Maybe	Depending on size of the system
APM	No	Frequency based timetable
Intermediate capacity metro	No	Frequency based timetable
Metro	No	Frequency based timetable
Commuter rail	Yes	Highly complex timetable
High Speed Rail	Yes	Simple timetable
Regional	Yes	Simple or complex depending on the size of the rail system
Tourist	Yes, for infrequent services	For passenger convenience only
Rail cruises	Yes	Simple timetable
Intercity and overnight	Yes	Can be very complex

Even if a railway does not strictly speaking need a timetable, there are still benefits in creating one. Simple railways like monorails can create a timetable of services moving back and forth along the rail line, but as a timetable it will be very simple. The timetable will tell passengers the start and finish times of revenue service, the stopping pattern, and the frequency of rail services. The timetable also informs passengers of the travel times between stations.

Most tourist railways have only a small amount of rollingstock. The trains in use on a tourist railway often are very old and have a special look and feel that makes them attractive. This type of train is unlikely to be very common, so most tourist railways the number of trains available is very limited which makes timetabling very easy. Tourist railways will need a timetable for passengers, as the number of services per day is often small. Alternatively, a rail line running through a theme park may have a very simple timetable, and a very small number of stops.

Commuter railways have very complex timetables. A timetable created for a large commuter railway, such as Sydney, can be very complex, and even for a single day can run to hundreds of pages. Some of the reasons why commuter railways are so complex include:
- Trains can move through large numbers of different paths, which makes describing the train movement very difficult and complex
- Most commuter railways contain large complex junctions. A very complex junction, or where there are multiple junctions next to one another, creates a powerful requirement for a timetable.
- Commuter railways move passengers from the suburbs to a city centre, and then out again at the end of the day. Services funnel in to a central point, and to allow this to occur a timetable is needed to permit the movement of trains in an orderly fashion through the city centre
- Large commuter networks can have many places to stable trains, so it is easy, if not managed properly, for too many trains to be at one stabling yard, and then not enough at another stabling yard. Balancing the number of trains in different locations can be very important for commuter rail systems

Alternatively, where rail systems are composed of single lines with few or no junctions, then passenger timetables may not be needed. This type of rail system has become increasingly common, and the simplicity and low cost of the system is partially because of the lack of a need for a complex timetable. Again, it should be mentioned that even without a passenger timetable a railway should have a timetable of its own.

One important step in the creation of a timetable is the addition of a unique identifier to each trip. A trip is a one rail movement, usually from one terminus to another, where the train does not change direction. Trips can be identified with a unique code, which may be a short alphanumeric which identifies the train. Trip numbers are not normally provided to the public, but on rare occasions they are made available. Some regional trains, and high speed trains, may have the trip number printed onto tickets, or can be seen when ordering tickets online.

The station display below is from Taiwan for their high speed rail system. Notice in olive there is a train number, and there are two of these. The first is 0656, and the second is 0660. This is the trip number, which in Taiwan is visible to the public.

High Speed Rail Pass Info

Whilst it is up to the individual railway whether to provide trip numbers to the public, in general only long distance trips, with ticketed seating may bother. Where seats are ticketed, trip numbers can be useful in identifying which trains passengers should board. Tickets for long distance trains often have unique identifiers, although this is not always strictly speaking necessary.

One important consideration is the difference between a weekend and a weekday timetable. For rail systems where only frequency needs to be considered, service frequencies in most cases, but not all, are reduced on weekends. Train frequencies are particularly reduced where services are provided for city workers making their way from the suburbs to the centre of a city for work, and then back again in the evening. In this type of rail system the timetable for a weekday and weekend are substantially different.

In busy metro rail systems, the weekend and weekday timetable may be quite similar. The timetable for Hong Kong MTR is substantially different for a Sunday compared to a weekday, and service frequency is reduced. This is particularly so for early on Sunday morning.

In some cases the rail infrastructure used may have an effect on the creation of a timetable. Rails are made of steel, and this rusts, so over a period of time the top of the rail rusts. This can interfere with the signalling system, which then cannot detect trains. Trains need to move over rails with track circuits with enough frequency to keep them free of rust. For example, perhaps a train will need to operate over a all rails with track circuits at least every three days.

The need to run trains over every section of track periodically can have a significant effect on the timetable. Many turnouts are only used periodically, and are used only in an emergency, or when maintenance work is being performed. These will need to have trains operate over them, and services that do this are sometimes referred to as "rail cleaners". Having a large amount of track only used occasionally will cause the working timetable to become very complicated, and there will be movements everywhere that are needed to keep the rails clean. Other types of train detection, such as treadles, or axle counters, or manual systems of train working such as train order working, so not require trains to clean the tops of rails. This can be a significant factor in the decision on which type of signalling system to use.

The photo below shows the contact band on the top of the rail. The rest of the rail is rusted, and not surprisingly a rust colour. The contact band is kept clean through the passage of trains, and without them the top of the rail would be the same colour as the rest of the rail. Without this clean band of metal at the top of the rail, track circuits, if there are any, would not operate. The need to keep the rail clean means that trains need to run regularly over the rail to keep it clean. This can significantly complicate the working timetable.

Rail Wear Band

An important use of a timetable is to estimate staffing needs for thinly used rail lines. Many stations in rarely used rail lines are only staffed when a train is scheduled to stop. Whilst this might seem strange for large busy stations inside large cities, many smaller regional stations are unstaffed, or staffed only when trains arrive. The roster for stations and their staffing will depend heavily on the timetable when created.

Something that needs to be considered in creating a timetable is the management of rollingstock. A railway will rarely create a timetable where all of the rollingstock is in use at any one time. Rollingstock need to be maintained, and sometimes fails, and other problems occur on trains. Where people are sick on trains, or the train hits an animal, then the train will need to be cleaned. Sometimes vandals paint offensive graffiti on trains, such as inappropriate political slogans, so these need to be cleaned immediately. Where crimes are committed on trains, they may be unavailable for use as they may become crime scenes, and forensic investigators need to examine the train for clues to determine who committed a crime. So for many reasons, it is reasonable to assume that not all rollingstock will be available at any one time, and allowances need to be made for that.

The maximum utilisation of a fleet is something that can be calculated. The fleet utilisation is the ratio of the number of sets in service compared to the total number. The highest number of sets in use in any one day is used for the calculation. Very efficient railways may make use of almost 90% of the total number of trains available, but percentages lower than this are also common. As part of the creation of a timetable calculations are needed to determine how much of the fleet is in use at any one time.

$$Rollingstock\ utilisation = \frac{number\ of\ sets\ in\ use\ in\ timetable}{total\ number\ of\ sets}$$

The utilisation of a rollingstock fleet becomes an issue where additional services are needed for special events. A special event is a large football match, a grand final for a major sport, or a concert given by a leading music singer. There are many different types of special events, which can require a number of additional trains to cater for the need. Racecourses in Australia often have stations which are opened only on race days, and some of these attract very large crowds. Flemington station in Melbourne is one such station, although there are several in Australia of this type.

As a rough guide, a figure of about 85% is about right for the peak use of the number of sets for a passenger service. A figure significantly lower than this indicates that there might be spare rollingstock not being used, and more services could be potentially timetabled.

Where a special event is scheduled, rollingstock will need to be found to provide passenger services. In many cases special events are held on weekends, which makes things a little easy, but some events are held on weekdays. The Melbourne Cup (a horse race) for example is held on a Tuesday. Provision needs to be made to allow special events to be catered for.

There are two different types of signalling; speed signalling, and route signalling. Speed signalling is a system which tells the driver what speed the train is permitted to operate at. Route signalling tells a driver what path the train will take, without necessarily informing him of the speed. Speed signalling is more complex than route signalling, but drivers know their maximum permitted speeds from speed boards posted along the rail line. In a route signalling system, drivers know the speed permitted based on experience, which means that they need to constantly use a rail line to maintain their knowledge. Whilst the maximum speed is posted, speeds under more restrictive signals are not, so driver knowledge is very important.

At first blush the significance of this may not appear obvious. Drivers only know the speed of a rail line through knowledge, so how do they obtain this knowledge? They get this by being driven around the system with someone who knows the speeds, who gives them training on what the speeds need to be. In a large rail system, there may be numerous lines, and drivers will need to be rostered to different parts of the rail system to maintain their knowledge.

A driver that has not driven on a section of track for a while may have forgotten what the speeds are on that section. A system is needed to track where drivers have driven trains, and how long ago. Rules and policies are needed for how long a driver can go before he or she needs to be retrained on the speeds of a section of track. The complexity of this situation is difficult to understate, and problems abound with this situation. Where a driver is compelled to drive on a section of a network that he may have limited experience with, then there is a real risk of a derailment, or even fatalities.

Express, Limited Services and All Stoppers

It is not necessary for trains to stop at all stations along a rail line. It is common on many rail systems for trains to pass through smaller less used stations without stopping, which speeds up the travel time for all the other passengers. For many types of rail system, trains stop at all stations, such as tourist trains, light rail and metros. HSR systems often have only a small number of stations, and often trains stop at every station. Commuter, regional, intercity and for some HSR systems, some trains do not stop at every station, and stop at only larger stations. This allows passengers to get to their station faster, as smaller stations are bypassed, reducing the travel time.

In the context of timetabling, a large station may refer to a station that is physically large, but more commonly refers to a station where there are large numbers of passengers. Usually stations with large numbers of passengers are also large in area or volume, but not always so. For the discussion here, a large station is one with large numbers of passengers. This means that passengers board and alight at this station, rather than just passing through.

An express service is one that does not stop at many stations along a rail line. Some express services stop at a very small percentage of stations, possibly as low as 10%. Limited services are express services that stop at many more stations, but also skip a large number of stops. A local service is an all stops service, which stops at all or almost all stations. Transport planners are confronted with the choice of what stations to include for an express service, and which for a limited service. Clearly residents living or working near the station will want the station to be classified as a large station, and so the service is better because more trains stop there. Classifying a station as a small station can have large consequences, and the number of passengers using the station may drop significantly.

So for many rail systems a decision is needed on what is called the "stopping pattern", and this may be the responsibility of the operating railway, or a rail transport planning department. A stopping pattern is the stations that the train will stop at, and many different stopping patterns are possible on any normal sized commuter line. The number of possibilities for a rail line or 15 to 20 stations is very large, and some rail lines may have several different stopping patterns, or even more. A major factor that influences what stations to stop at is the size and number of people using the station. A station with a very high number of passengers will have almost all trains stop there, stations with small numbers of passengers can be skipped, and very small stations may have only a small number of trains stop there. In some cases a station may have so few stops there that it begins to become a "ghost station", which no one uses. In the Melbourne rail system, there is a station called East Richmond where very few trains stop, but many trains pass through, and it is almost never used.

So, for the purposes of characterising how stopping patterns are commonly constructed, there is rough hierarchy for stations used in this book, from largest to smallest. This ranking is not used widely in the rail industry, as far as the author can tell, but seems to be very helpful. This hierarchy is:
- Extremely large stations, or stations with very large numbers of passengers both getting on and off. These stations are often interchanges, or termini, where trains cannot proceed any further
- Large stations, often co-located with shopping centres, large developments, tourist attractions, and/or interchanges
- Medium size stations, with significant numbers of passengers, and many people living in the local area to the station
- Small stations, which often have a smaller number of services, and few people living in the area around the stations, very few

shops, and almost no transport orientated development around the station
- Tiny stations, where the number of people getting on or off is very small. These stations may be unmanned for a large part of the day, even on work days. Often the only traffic these stations get is for peak services, outside of these times trains do not stop.
- Halts, or stations where the train stops by request only. Halts are common in Australia, where they are often little more than a mound of earth and some wooden flooring. Halts are often shorter than the length of the train, and passengers may need to disembark from one or more doors at the back of the train to get onto the platform.

We can roughly characterise each of these stations and the number of services that stop there in the table below.

Stopping Patterns and the Size of Stations

Station type	Stopping Pattern, and how frequently or pass the station
Extremely large, or a terminus	ALL
Large	Almost all trains will stop at these stations, other than a small number of very unusual express trains
Medium	Express services may or may not stop, depending on timetabling. A mix of express services may stop at these stations
Small	Express services do not stop at these stations, but special local services do
Tiny	A small number of services per day, most trains do not stop. This station may close after a small number of trains have stopped.
Halts	Trains stop by request only

The decision of a rail planner to characterise a station as a small one, which receives fewer services, is a controversial one. Things can get quite heated, and the public can get very passionate about designating a station as small, as this can be interpreted as a statement about their town and community.

Timetables will show which train stops at which station. Below is a example of what a timetable can look like, and what stations they stop at. A theoretical example has been used, not to offend any railway that might not want its timetable reproduced.

Timetable Examples – Stops						
Station	Service Type					
	Express	Local	Limited	Express	Local	Limited
	7:00 am	7:05am	7:20am	7:30am	7:35am	7:50am
A	YES	YES	YES	YES	YES	YES
B		YES			YES	
C		YES	YES		YES	YES
D					YES	
E	YES	YES	YES	YES	YES	YES
F		YES			YES	
G		YES	YES		YES	YES
H	YES	YES	YES	YES	YES	YES
I		YES			YES	
J	YES	YES	YES	YES	YES	YES
K	YES	YES	YES	YES	YES	YES
L	YES	YES	YES	YES	YES	YES

This rail line runs from station A to station L. The times represent departures from station A. Express services stop at a mixture of stations, and the 7:00 am stops at E, H, J, K and L. The following local service stops at all stops except D. The express at 7:20 after that stops C and G in addition to the stops that the 7:00am train has, so it is still an express service, but not as fast as the express at 7:00 am. This is sometimes called a limited service.

Notice that for station D, even some of the local services do not stop there. Station D is a very small station, and so only one of the trains listed above stops there.

In Asia the different levels of stopping pattern are sometimes given names, and in Japan these names are used on parts of the High Speed Rail system:
- Nozomi – the fastest trains with very limited stops
- Hikari – express service with a few additional stops, but similar in travel time to the Nozomi
- Kodama - the all stops service

Remember that slower local services will often delay faster moving expresses, and it is common in Australia that express services are only slightly faster than the local services. The express service frequently catches up to the local, and then travels a comfortable distance behind the local as it stops at all stations. This is unfortunate, and doing something like this is a real and genuine timetabling mistake. It would be far better to have the express service stop at all stops, take passengers, then pretend that it is an express service, but just happened to be a bit slow most of the time.

So how to decide on which trains stop at which stations? Whilst there is no easy process here, there are a number of key factors that should be considered, and these are:
- Generally speaking, stations that have roughly the same number of passengers move through each day should have the same number of trains stop there. As choosing the number of trains that stop at certain stations is a highly political process, equality in stations with the same number of passengers is important
- Express services within cities should reach an average speed of at least 50 kms/hr, and 80 kms/hr is even better. Any slower than this is probably too slow, and more suitable for a local service.
- Rail lines with only two tracks and very high numbers of trains probably can't support an express service, as it will run behind a local service throughout its entire trip. Express services work best where there are substantial time gaps between trains, such as 15 to 20 minutes at least
- Express services often run between two large population centres, and often for marketing, it is nice for this service to achieve a certain minimum time. For example, if a service between two very major cities takes 2 hours and 3 minutes,

then perhaps cutting out a couple of stops to achieve a time of 2 hours would be appealing.
- Timetabling is very important, as expresses need to be timetabled so that they are not delayed by slower moving local services. Often a local service will lose 1 to 2 minutes per station when it stops (compared to not stopping), so if trains are 10 minutes apart then the local service could stop at 5 or 6 stations before the express is delayed.

Also note that where there are too many small stations, and it's just not possible to get the express and local services up to a reasonable average speed, then it might be necessary to close some stations. Rail services are time sensitive, and slow services will struggle to attract passengers.

It is possible to model the number of passengers who will use a rail line given the frequency of rail services. The classification of stations can be tested to determine what impact there will be on the number of travelling passengers. Another possibility is to assess the amount of revenue earned, and an attempt can be made to maximise it. These calculation methods can use elasticities of demand, a topic discussed extensively in previous chapters.

One final point about stopping patterns; it is generally best to not have too many variations and different patterns. Whilst it is possible for large numbers of stopping patterns to be created, that doesn't mean that this is a good idea, and in practice it is better to limit one rail line to 5 or 6 different stopping patterns. Over 10 stopping patterns becomes difficult to remember, and stations staff will have difficulty explaining the different stopping patterns to customers. Worse still, a rare and uncommon stopping pattern may be confused with other similar stopping patterns, and customers may be overcarried when their stop is skipped because the rare and unusual stopping pattern does not include that station.

Increasing Trip Speed as Much as Possible (Using Timetables)

In many rail systems a premium is often placed on getting trains as fast as possible to their destinations. In some cases a different price is charged for faster rail services. For example, Nozomi services on the HSR system in Japan on the HSR system are charged at a different rate to Hikari and Kodama services. These names are given to different stopping patterns, and tickets on each service type are different. Alternatively, tilt trains may be deployed on a rail line, and those trains that tilt may be charged at a higher rate than trains that do not.

A government or railway may want to offer higher priced rail tickets for faster trains. There may be sound commercial reasons for so doing, or for political reasons these services need to be offered. It is often desirable to advertise that trains can get from one important destination to another in a very low time, to attract customers. The reality may be that most services do not get to their destination in this time, but that may not necessarily matter. Either way, it may be desirable to attempt to get trains from origin as quickly as possible.

Whilst track condition and geometry are often the most important factors in determining track speed, timetables can to a certain extent be used to manipulate the travel times from one end of the rail system to another. Some of the tricks used to do this include:
- Reducing the number of stops
- Reducing the number of services that would delay express trains
- Moving slower all stopping trains out of the way of express trains
- Providing a large time window for the express train to run unimpeded

Timetabling can be used to compensate for the lack of additional tracks or places for trains to pass. In many cases rail lines between cities have only two tracks, and it is not really possible for a local service to be passed by an express. Depending on the configuration of the rail line, it may be possible to speed up the express by scheduling the local service after the express, so the express is not "catching up" on the previous local service. This concept is demonstrated below.

Consider trains with two stopping patterns, A, and B. A trains are express, and B are all stops. Assume that A trains cannot pass B at any point. One possible timetable, with a departure frequency of 20 minutes, is as follows:

Week 11   Page 460

Example Timetable 1 Union Station	
Departure Time	**Service Type**
14:20	A - express
14:40	B – all stops
15:00	A - express
15:20	B – all stops
15:40	A - express
16:00	B – all stops
16:20	A - express
16:40	B – all stops
17:00	A - express

This timetable has a number of advantages, including that the services depart station Union Station evenly, so passengers will have only a modest wait time at the station. Express services leave the station only 20 minutes after A, so if the all stops service is very slow, the express may catch up behind the all stops, and then move at the same speed.

Another possible timetable is below, and this one is also common:

Example Timetable 2 Station α	
Time	**Service Type**
14:20	B – all stops
14:55	A - express
15:00	B – all stops
15:35	A - express
15:40	B – all stops
16:15	A - express
16:20	B – all stops
16:55	A - express
17:00	B – all stops

Notice that the B all stops services leave shortly after the A express trains. In this timetable A express trains have 35 minutes to catch the slower B all stops trains, which means A trains can have a faster timetable, or fewer stops. The effect of structuring a timetable this way can be profound, and the A express services may be very popular with passengers. In Australia where this is done services have proven to be very popular.

There are limits to the use of this tactic to create express services on lines with limited capacity. Where trains are scheduled 5 minutes after one another, it is very hard to create a large time window for an express to be much faster than an all stops service, and so all services really move at the same speed. A classic mistake of timetabling is to create an express service that is constantly trapped behind a local service, and does not stop at stations, but is not faster than an all stops service.

Structuring a Timetable

For passenger convenience it is often better for a timetable to have a nice clear structure. This means for trains arrive and leave from stations at regular and consistent times. Even better is for the entire day's timetable to be very clearly structured, so that passengers can remember what trains arrive and depart at what time.

The photo below is the timetable of the Keihan railway in Osaka in Japan. In this photo, the rail line is drawn at the bottom of the board, and each of the different stopping patterns is given a colour. There are about 6 different stopping patterns here, and what stations are included in the stopping pattern is also shown on the rail map.

A Commuter Timetable in Osaka

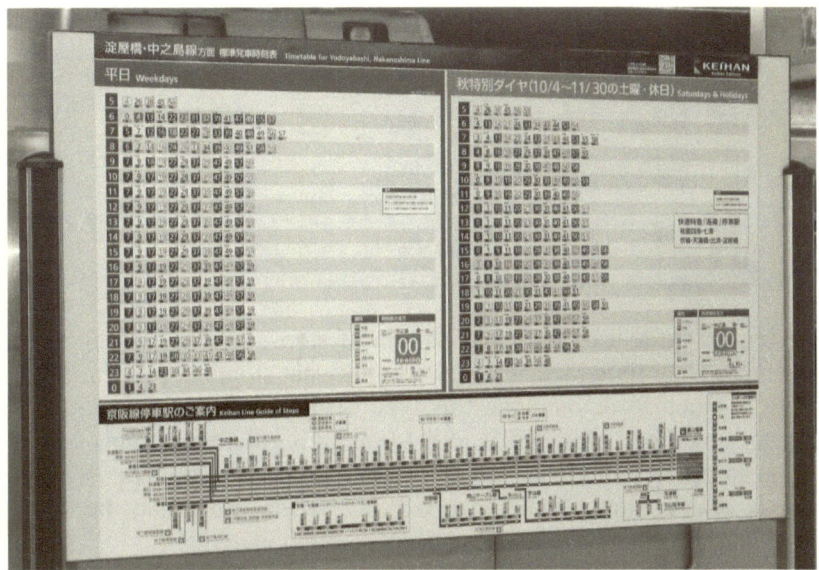

The timetable for weekdays and weekends are different, with workdays on the left, and weekends on the right. Notice that there are some stopping patterns that are only used in peak times.

The author considers the above timetable to be a masterpiece of rail transport planning. An excerpt of the timetable is shown below. The number in black along the left hand side is the hour and the smaller number is the time in minutes. So, for example, at 10:09, a train with the black stopping pattern will be leaving the station, and then at 10:17, a train with the burgundy pattern will be leaving the station. The burgundy trains are an express, and the black stopping pattern is an all stops.

Timetable detail

The regular structure, and clear pattern of stops, allows passengers to remember what time their train leaves and what stopping pattern it has. There is much to recommend this type of timetable structure, as it is easy to remember. Notice that at 8:14 and 8:33 there are trains with a purple stopping pattern, which is not included in the trains past 9am. This is also common with peak periods, where there may be some additional trips that have more unusual stopping patterns.

In Japan these stopping patterns have been extended to the trains themselves, with display windows on the side of the train identifying the stopping pattern. The same colour is used for the stopping patterns on the train as on the timetable. That level of coordination is very impressive, and adds to the level of service provided by the railway.

Managing Dwell Times

Dwell times are the time that a train spends at station allowing passengers to board and alight. More specifically they are the time that a train spends at a station stationary, regardless of whether the doors are open or not. Dwell times depend on the number of passengers boarding and alighting, as well as the number and size of doors. Dwell times increase the headway for a rail line, and need to be accounted for in a timetable.

The challenge with dwell times is that they can vary. People are not machines, and on busy stations the times that people take to board and alight will vary. This variation can mean that the same train on one day, with the same number of people, will be on time, and then on another day will be late. The variability in dwell times presents some major challenges to those creating a timetable.

There are a number of solutions to this problem, and these include:
- Allowing for longer times for dwell at stations (which makes the rail trips slower)
- Inserting a timing point
- Using rollingstock that has more doors, or wider doors
- Putting staff on stations to get passengers onto trains faster
- Other more exotic strategies, such as skipping stops when a train runs behind, or closing doors before all passengers have boarded or alighted from the train

Rail companies and governments dislike increasing the travel time of a rail service unless there is a very good reason. Also allowing for large dwell time of a train at a station should be done only where this is a very good reason to do so, and is generally avoided in many cases. Where insufficient time is permitted to passengers to board and alight, then trains will frequently arrive late at their destination. Where the allowed dwell times are too short then they should be extended so that trains have a better chance of arriving on time. The key here seems to be to get a good balance, not to long, and not too quick.

A timing point is something that is more commonly used on bus networks. A timing point is a place where a bus, or train, may wait if needed to get back onto its scheduled time. Timing points are places where, if early, a train will wait for the correct time before leaving. A timing point is very useful to correct minor problems with a timetable.

Timing points are not standard terminology in the rail industry, at least not in Australia. Nonetheless, the principle is commonly used throughout different transport modes, and timing points can be very useful. Small problems, such as delays from disabled passengers, can be compensated for. A driver of a train, or where the train is computer controlled, will need to wait to the exact time when the train is scheduled to depart. In some cases trains may wait 5 minutes or even more, before the correct time to leave. This addition time, allowed for the in the timetable, will slow the average travel time of trains. It is a difficult decision for any railway to do this, but is some cases it may be acceptable to exchange speed for punctuality.

From a rail transport planning perspective, the decision on what to do with dwell times takes on strategic implications. Whilst a short dwell time on one station probably won't have much effect, typically railways and governments will have unofficial policies on how much to allow. Where the government is trying to increase the number of trains moving through a rail system, or reduce the travel times, then allowances for dwell in a timetable will be reduced. Where the government is under pressure to improve on-time-running, and punctuality, then dwell times will be increased. In practice modifying the timetabled dwell times can be a very effective tool in changing the performance of a railway.

Adding more trains into a Timetable

Rail systems are always limited in the amount of capacity. There is no rail system that has an infinite amount of capacity, and commonly rail systems are limited to about 16 to 20 trains per hour on one track in one direction. It is however possible to put more trains into the system, above the practical capacity of the system, and when this occurs there can be a deterioration of the performance of the system.

Mostly timetables include a trade-off between punctuality and on time running. The less trains that are included in a timetable, the better the on time performance. This is in addition to the dwell times, discussed in the previous section, which can be modified in a timetable to increase or decrease the punctuality. The addition of more trains can be problematic, and regardless of the number timing points, can introduce serious on-time-running problems for a rail system.

Not only are trains more frequently late when more trains are added, but the average speed of trains through a system also decreases. Trains will start operating under more restrictive aspects, and not full proceed/clear. The reduction in average speeds, often at peak times, can significantly contribute to the requirement for more rollingstock. Care must be taken when adding more trains into a timetable.

The addition of too many trains to a timetable can have perverse effects that are not immediately obvious. One of the functions of a timetable is to allow trains to pass through complex junctions. These exist in some rail systems, typically commuter systems, or regional or intercity rail systems. They are uncommon in metros. A timetable allows trains to pass through a junction in an orderly fashion, and each train that arrives at a junction is allocated a path through. Without this the capacity of a junction is significantly reduced, and trains will be allocated paths as they arrive. This situation, common in some rail systems, is not a good way of running a railway, and results in substantially lower capacity. Figures such as 70% of the original capacity have been quoted in conference papers, but in reality the reduction in capacity will depend on the complexity of the junction. The more complex, the more important it is to schedule trains through it.

Adding too many trains will adversely affect the performance of any rail system. Once train movements become too random, or a rail system controllers struggle to move trains through junctions, performance will deteriorate rapidly, until large numbers or trains are late. It is very important that trains keep to timetable, and not be allowed to deviate from this if at all possible.

Something that needs to be considered for any timetabling changes is the consumption of energy, especially where the number of trains operating in the system increases. Train consume either diesel fuel, or electrical energy. For either, changes to consumption may require modelling to determine if the energy consumption in one area is beyond what the system can provide. Electrical traction systems provide power for trains to move, and all rail systems are limited in the amount of power that can be provided. Timetable changes can have a profound effect on the amount of energy consumed, and where the power is insufficient, problems can occur.

Where the limit on the power supply for a railway is reached, there can be substantial operational consequences. These include:
- Trains cannot accelerate at the full rate
- Trains may need to operate in a state where less current is drawn, ie, lighting reduced, air conditioning switched off, or some auxiliary services are not available
- Trains may need to wait for other trains to depart stations (the time of maximum current draw) when on completely separated tracks
- The overhead wiring cannot take any more electricity, and so breakers at one or both of the substations open, removing power entirely from the train. Trains in tunnels may be in complete darkness
- Station power supplies may need to be curtailed, and power hungry systems such as escalators or lifts may need to be switched off to allow trains to operate at peak times

Care may be exercised in creating any new timetable that the capacity of the power system is not exceeded.

Where diesel trains are used, there needs to be enough fuel in the depot to keep trains running. Depots have limited capacity, and large timetable changes may result in the depot running out of fuel. It may be necessary to restock the fuel into the depot as more often as the number of trains operating increases. This all needs to be considered in the construction of a new timetable.

A classic mistake of rail transport planning is to build a new rail line or extension, and then not have enough power to operate it. When this occurs, the government can become extremely frustrated, as they have spent money building the rail line or extension, and then cannot use it. It is best to avoid this situation and consider power consumption well before the construction of any new rail infrastructure, and timetable, is complete.

Making Changes to a Complex Timetable

Minor changes to timetables are commonly made. Timetables may be changed to accommodate additional maintenance work, or working on trains, or allowing for additional trains for freight or privately operated rail cruises. Maintenance vehicles may need access to track, and so small short term changes are made to timetables to allow access. Small changes to large timetables are very common.

Where large changes are needed to a timetable, then the time period required to implement the changes can be quite long. Six months to a year would be common, as large scale changes to a timetable need to be propagated through the rail business. Many rail companies are very large, and have thousands, if not tens of thousands of staff, and so changes, and information about changes, will be implemented slowly. Propagating this through a rail organisation takes time. Crewing rosters need to be changed, staffing levels adjusted, and new infrastructure tested to ensure it is ready for different or increased rail traffic.

The need for large notice periods for making changes to timetables can cause problems. Rail freight operators may need paths through complex networks for new freight movements, as the rail freight business may have won more work. The freight company may not be happy if approval for the freight path requires a waiting time of six months, which commercially is a very long time and normally not acceptable.

The addition of new trains and paths to an existing timetable, without modification to the existing trains scheduled to operate, should be pretty easy. For example, scheduling an ad-hoc rail freight service in the middle of the night, in a rail system that typically does not have many rail movements in the middle of the night, should quite straight forward. Larger changes, and especially where additional staff is needed to operate trains, might be more difficult, depending on how many drivers or operators are available. In some cases it may be very difficult to find additional staff.

The Process of Creating a Timetable

A timetable can be created using roughly the following process:
- Changes, needs, opportunities and requirements to a timetable are identified
- Proposed changes are implemented into the timetable, and then a new timetable generated
- Power/fuel consumption modelling is performed
- Timetables are simulated to ensure there are no conflicts or trains moving through the same place at the same time
- The results of the simulation are used to make changes to the timetable
- Changes to infrastructure required for the new identified, and then implemented where possible
- Rollingstock requirements are identified and changes made to rollingstock where possible
- Rosters for staff are created for stations and train crew
- Rosters once created are resourced and staff organised
- A date for the introduction of the new timetable is issued to the public
- The timetable is implemented

So let's discuss each of these steps in turn:

The identification of changes to timetables comes about through a variety of different mechanisms. There is always pressure from the public and others that receive the benefits of rail services to increase the frequency. These requests may or may not be reasonable, and this will depend on passenger numbers in that area. The government may decide to provide additional funding to provide these services, and so it becomes possible to provide them. Another reason for changing a timetable is that infrastructure has been built that allows more services, or services along a different path, and so changes are needed to the timetable to take advantage of the new infrastructure. It should be remembered that for a rail system that uses timetables extensively, the benefits of new infrastructure often cannot be realised until the timetable is modified to accept the new infrastructure. An example would be a large project to reduce the headway of a rail line, which cannot be used until the timetable is modified to put additional trains down that line.

For freight operators, it may be possible that a freight company has expanded its operations and needs additional paths through the network. Whilst it is generally preferable to allow some flexibility in a rail system to allow changes to freight train numbers, in some cases freight trains will need to be timetabled. This is particularly so where passenger and freight trains share the same tracks, so freight paths need to be explicitly created.

Alternatively, many railways take the view that timetables need to be constantly modified and updated to keep them fresh and consistent. Small changes are helpful to get a timetable really running well, and the process of improvement to a timetable will produce lots of small changes. When a timetable is updated then the opportunity arises to make these changes.

Once the changes are identified then they are implemented into the timetable. This can mean more trains, or less, or a different stopping pattern. Where new extensions to a rail line are built, then a new timetable is needed to accommodate them.

Power consumption needs to be modelled as part of the creation of a new timetable. Where this is done, and a shortfall in the amount of power that can be generated is identified, then an infrastructure project can be identified to redress the lack of power. This often may involve the construction of new substations or for diesel, new or larger fuel depots. Where trains are diesel power then checks are needed that diesel storage is sufficient for the new timetable and services. Also note that some diesel trains have a lot of storage capacity for fuel, and in some cases the time needed to refuel the train may need to be taken into consideration.

A timetable needs to be simulated to ensure that it performs as expected. A timetable simulation is a bit different to a normal simulation. Simulations are often performed of factories and production, or customers entering a bank, or planes arriving and landing at an airport. In these cases the arrival of orders, customers or planes, is assumed to be random, and when these inputs to the simulation are generated, the performance of the system is monitored. A rail timetable is a little different, as the timetable is fixed, so the simulation performs a different function. A simulation is there to ensure that the logic of the timetable is correct. For example, only one train can use a turnout at any one time. Once a turnout is in use, then the track near the turnout cannot be used either, as the train is passing over the turnout. A mistake with timetables is to have two trains using the same turnout at the same time, which is impossible, and so this conflict in train movements needs to be resolved. A simulation of a rail timetable will ensure that no two trains move through each other, or collide, or move through the same turnout at the same time. Whilst the signalling system will prevent this from happening anyway, there is nothing to stop an impossible movement being timetabled, and then on the first day of the new timetable, the operating railway finding that the movement is impossible, and then needing to change the timetable. If this happens this would be considered a large failure of the transport planning process.

Some railways implement large scale timetable changes without simulation. Simulation is expensive, and takes time. It is possible, and in Australia some large railways do this, to implement a timetable without simulation. When this happens, there will invariably some problems with the timetable, and months may be needed to smooth out some of the more serious problems. It is not recommended for any railway to do this, but seemingly it is common practice.

Some timetable changes result in the change in use of some types of infrastructure. For example, some turnouts may be used more or less after a timetable change, and as a result may perform differently. Intensely used turnouts may need to be rebuilt, so that the equipment can withstand the additional pounding from many additional trains. This will need to be planned to be completed before the timetable is implemented.

Rosters will be needed for staff when a timetable is changed. Rostering is a very complex and difficult process, and rosters will need to be created in advance before any timetable change. Where rosters are substantially different, time is needed for staff to be briefed on any roster changes, and potentially time is needed for staff to make adjustments to any new timetable. This will depend on the industrial situation for the rail workforce. Whilst it is easy for some to be critical of inflexible workplaces, note that rail employees may have commitments such as picking up children from school, and need notice to change these plans. Large scale changes to rosters, with little notice, may result in children waiting at school for parents for are working.

The use of rollingstock needs to be calculated for any rail system. It is important to ensure that more trains are not allocated to be used than are available.

An important part of the generation of a new timetable is community consultation. When a timetable is created there can be large impacts to a local community, and these need to be explained to locals. This is particularly the case where the number of services to a station are being reduced when a new timetable is introduced. Another consideration is the first and last train, and changes to this can have a large impact to some passengers. Consider that some shift workers may be reliant on one particular train to get to work by a certain time, and where this train is cancelled, may have to leave their job, or move to a place closer to work. This kind of change can be very adverse to some people.

Large timetable changes should be announced to the public, and new timetables be made available. This made include a publicity campaign, posters, or staff at stations handing out pamphlets to passengers as they go past telling them of any changes to timetables. Perhaps even television or radio advertising can be appropriate.

Managing a Bad Timetable

In rare cases a timetable may be created that is poor, and where trip times are unrealistic, trains may frequently not reach their destination on time. The timetable could be too optimistic, and trains frequently or almost never achieve the times as laid down in a timetable. Whilst this situation is unusual, it has been known to happen. The problem can be fixed with a complete re-write of the timetable, but creating a new timetable can take years, so in the interim an operational railway will need to "do something" to correct the problems with the timetable. Whilst the remedial actions a operational railway make take are outside

the scope of what a rail planner would do, nonetheless, it is important for a rail transport planner to appreciate what happens when a timetable fails. Some of the things an operational railway can do to "fix" a broken timetable include:
- Cancelling services
- Not stopping at stations
- Converting local services into express services
- Overspeeding on some rail services (without telling anyone they are doing it)
- Cancelling services that have long paths and move through many junctions
- Making unofficial changes to timetables

Where a timetable is particularly bad, the entire rail system may degenerate into chaos. Small operational problems become very significant, and small equipment failures can become disastrous problems as the system cannot cope with even minor problems. In very bad cases this situation can represent "railways Armageddon".

For these reasons, and given that for a large rail system a new timetable cannot be created quickly, it is very important to avoid this situation. As a timetable takes a long time to create, when a bad one is built and implemented, a long period of time is needed to undo the changes. Thus a bad timetable can linger in a rail system for years, and cause enormous pain with customers. As a result it is very important, for a complex rail system, for timetables to be simulated before being put into service. It is however very expensive to simulate a timetable, however this normally is not an excuse.

Timetabling Freight

Freight services can also be timetabled. Freight is often much less sensitive to lateness than passenger trains, and small and even moderate delays to a freight service can be tolerated. Some terminals require a freight operator to book a time for loading and unloading of freight, and lateness is penalised with fines and penalties. Other terminals take a much more easy going approach, and allow trains to arrive late with any significant penalty.

Freight trains are not as fast as passenger trains, and cannot brake as quickly. An express passenger train will operate at far higher speeds than almost all freight trains, and so the challenge arises as to how to get passenger trains past slow moving freight trains. This can sometimes be done with passing loops and refuges, and a freight train can be directed to stand there until faster traffic passes the freight train. One of the problems with this strategy is that any passing loop or refuge will need to be longer than the freight train, which can be difficult where freight trains are over 1 kilometre in length.

Another issue with the timetabling of freight is curfews. This concept has been discussed in a number of other chapters, but recall that a rail freight curfew is where freight trains are not permitted into a rail system at certain times. These are common in heavily used rail systems. A curfew will mean that any freight services that are timetabled to enter a busy rail system will need to do so outside the hours of the curfew. Timetabling here for freight services is important, as it is very expensive to have a freight train standing for several hours outside a curfew area.

Problems abound with the scheduling of freight trains, especially where they are scheduled through a network where there are mixed passenger and freight services. If the network is not particularly heavily utilised, then freight and passenger trains may happily co-exist. Where traffic is heavy, then problems will occur.

Freight trains may have particular problems with steep grades. Where a steep grade such as a 1 in 30 runs over a long length such as 1 or 2 kilometres, freight trains may be able to climb the grade if they enter the grade at full speed, but if stopped may have difficultly starting again. This means that freight train cannot be stopped because of signals or another train ahead of them. In rare cases this may require special signalling to allow freight trains a clear run over a long section, such as 10 kilometres of even more. These special signals are called "tonnage signals", and are used to allow freight to pass through long sections unimpeded. Where tonnage signals exist, this needs to be considered and allowed for in any timetables.

Freight trains often accelerate and decelerate more slowly than passenger trains. Reaching speeds of over 70 kms/hr will take longer for freight trains to achieve, and this needs to be included in any timetabling. This is particularly a problem where freight trains are frequently required to start and stop. This will consume a lot of time. Another consideration is that stopping and then restarting a freight train costs money, and the fuel consumption for so doing can be quite large.

Frequent stopping and starting should be avoided in a freight timetable where possible.

Freight trains do not have a dwell time at stations, as no one boards or alights. In some cases where freight trains pass through stations they may be required to slow down for safety reasons.

The time taken to marshal a freight train in a freight yard will depend on a number of factors. These include the design of the freight yard, the number of wagons, and the number of shunting moves needed to build the consist. Where trains are large, and almost all the wagons need to be re-organised, then the time taken to build the freight train may be quite long.

Apart from all the considerations above, there is no real difference between the scheduling of a freight train, and a passenger train. The freight train is allocated a path through the network, with a start and finish time. If a freight train arrives late to its planned path, it may be allowed to travel through the network anyway, or it can be held until there is another path available that does not disrupt any other train.

REFERENCES

1. Landex, A. & Schittenhelm, B. & Kaas A.H. & Schneider-Tilli, J *Capacity measurement with the UIC 406 capacity method*, Computers in Railways XI, 2008

2. Wiggenraad, P. *Alighting and boarding times of passengers at Dutch railway stations, Trail Research School*, Delft, Dec 2001

3. Lam, W. et al *A Study of Train Dwelling Time at Hong Kong Mass Transit Railway System*, Journal of Advanced Transportation, Vol 32, No 3, pp 285 - 296

4. Wardrop, A. & Suess, P. *Strategies to Increase Line Capacity and Reduce Travel Time in a Mixed Passenger and Freight Corridor*, IRSE Australasia Technical Meeting – Sydney, Nov 2009

Choosing Frequencies of Trains and Service Hours

One of the most important decisions for any rail system is the service frequency, and the hours of operations of any new line or rail service, be it for passenger or freight. Service frequency and hours of operation are important variables, and strongly influence the perception of success or failure of a rail system. A railway that has only a small number of rail services per day may be perceived to be a failure. Likewise, where trains are strongly limited on the hours they can operate, again, this may defeat the purpose of the construction of any rail line.

There is rarely any engineering reason why trains cannot run 24 hours a day, 7 days a week, most of the time. There will however need to be times when maintenance is performed, and this will act as a limiter on the maximum possible service hours. In many cases this limit will never reached, as the demand for rail will not require trains to operate at all hours of the day and week. Sometimes, however, high demand rail services will need to be interrupted for essential maintenance to be performed. Otherwise the rail system will degrade and be unable to provide service at all, or under heavily degraded conditions.

Once a rail system or line is constructed the maximum service frequency is limited to what was designed and installed, and without a major project to change it, this is what the rail line can offer. Great care needs to be exercised in determining what the design headways should be for any rail line. In many other cases however, the maximum is never reached, and the total number of services is limited by other factors, such as the number of passengers, or the economic benefit of operating rail services, or the amount of rollingstock available. This is especially the case outside of peak periods, where there may not be enough passengers to run services at a high frequency.

Network design too can play a large role in limiting the number of services. For rail systems where multiple lines combine into one more busy rail line, often in a flat junction, then the limit on the number of services will be the most congested line. Here network design is key, and a poor design will limit the number of services that are needed in busy areas. For the commuter railways in Australia this is often the case, and the limiting factor is the maximum possible frequency of trains through the city centre. Questions about the economic frequency of services rarely arise, but sometimes this question is asked about the number of services away from peak periods. In smaller towns the formulas presented here are very useful.

Recall that many passenger service rail lines have something called a peak period, and road traffic in large cities has peak periods as well. Peak times are when the number of rail services are at a maximum and is at the maximum possible level as per the headway, or sometimes even more. A term that is sometimes used is the "shoulder period", and it represents a time before and after a peak period where service frequency is still high, but not as high as the peak period. Outside of these two times is the off-peak period, where there are limited numbers of services. The last remaining time period is the one where there are no services at all.

For rail systems where passenger services are mixed with freight, they may be a curfew period where freight trains are prohibited from entering the rail system until the peak period has ended. Curfews are extremely irritating for freight companies, and they limit the efficiency of the freight operation. Curfew periods affect the profitability of their rail operations significantly, and a late running freight train can be held in the most awkward position waiting for the curfew to end. Curfews are also sometimes imposed because freight trains are very noisy. In any event, where curfews are imposed then this needs to be clear in the planning stage of any new rail line.

So how to describe the frequency of trains? When the question is asked, how to respond? Well, the type of information that is normally provided is:
- When the peak period is, between what times?
- The number of services per hour, in peak periods. This is also called the frequency
- Any curfews for freight, if there are any
- Service periods, when trains are operational, and when the line is closed.
- The mix of traffic, the number of express services and all stopping services

This is usually enough information to explain how many services will operate and when they will operate.

Choosing a train frequency (and headway)

Setting the frequencies of trains for an already constructed rail line is normally the responsibility of the operational railway, and this decision is made based on operational reasons. Factors affecting this decision include the number of passengers who wish to travel, the number of train sets available, or where to stable these trains, or a number of other reasons. For example, the railway might have only limited number of trains available, or there are limitations to the amount of power that can be provided to move trains around. Rostering of crews and drivers may also be difficult. Other issues such as decanting of toilets on trains, or cleaning of trains, can be important as well.

Passengers always want the maximum service frequency, as this speeds their journey, and is more convenient. Railways often want a low service frequency, requiring a smaller number of trains, fewer staff, more efficient operation, and lower power consumption. Rollingstock wears when it is used, wheels wear down, the carbon strip on the pantograph will wear away, and generally there is a lot more maintenance to do on a train that moves around all the time. So there is a conflict between passengers who want more services, and rail operators who want to be more efficient and provide less. A decision is needed on the number, and it's best to have a clear process to determine how many trains should operate, and some methods to do this are listed below.

Remember that during the design and construction of a rail line that the minimum headway will be determined. Higher headways are much cheaper to build and maintain, and less equipment is needed, so there will be a temptation to increase the headway as much as possible. It would be a terrible shame however for the headway to be too high for what is needed on the line, so some care is needed in choosing what the headway should be. A common headway is about 3 minutes, which is related to the type of signalling equipment installed.

Many rail systems, especially metros, operate without a publicly available timetable, and this is often seen as being an efficient way to operate. The rail operator naturally will have their own internal timetable, called a working timetable, but only the rail operator and staff will be able to view it. So even without a publicly available timetable, the service frequency is still known and controlled. It would be ridiculous for a railway without a timetable to send trains randomly down a rail line, even if passengers cannot check to see what trains should be arriving, a rail operator should know when and where trains are and how many are needed to meet service frequency requirements.

As a general rule trains services need to be very frequent to not have a publicly available timetable. A frequency of one train every ten minutes should be considered the absolute maximum time between trains, to operate without a passenger timetable. Metros operate normally with one train every 3 to 5 minutes, and this is much more appropriate for train services without a timetable.

In comparison bus services can be changed easily, but rail services are much more inflexible. Rail service frequencies often remain unchanged for decades, because the infrastructure and headway places powerful limitations on how many trains can move through the network, and this limit remains in place for a very long time.

The table below has some typical service frequencies. These numbers are really only a very rough guide, and there are many exceptions.

Train Service Frequency - Typical	
Light rail	1 every 10 minutes
Trams	1 every 10 minutes, but can be extremely frequent
Metros	1 every 3 to 5 minutes
Commuter rail	1 every 15 to 30 minutes
Regional rail	1 every 1 to 3 hours, depending on the destination
High speed rail	Huge variety, but 1 every 15 minutes between very large cities
Overnight trains	1 or 2 per night

There are a number of different ways of choosing what the frequency of trains should be, and some of the better known ones are presented below.

1/ Using load factors

Perhaps the best way to plan rail service frequencies is to look at load factors. Load factors are a ratio of the number of passengers on a train, to the total number of seats. Whilst different services will have markedly different load factors, and trains in the peak usually will have much higher load factors, there is enormous variability in the load factors of trains, even ones that operate on the same lines following one another. Despite this, targeting a load factor is often a good and relatively simple way to determine train frequency, as it is clear and easy to apply.

Surveys can be done on the number of passengers on each line, and using the different services throughout the day. Once this is determined, the railway can set the service frequency to target either an average load factor, or a maximum one, depending on which is the most appropriate.

Rail systems with large numbers of people travelling for small numbers of stations are confronted with an interesting problem. The train may operate over a long distance, but between two stops there are large numbers of passengers, perhaps because the stations are large, or are very important interchanges. In this scenario, the train frequency will be chosen on the maximum load factor, and not the average one, because it is this trip between these two stations that is what passengers need and want to do. Setting train frequencies this way may mean that the trains operate for large sections with almost no one on board, which is very unfortunate.

The situation with metros is a little more interesting. Most metros have very few seats, and most passengers stand for most of their trip. The capacity of any metro train is determined based on the available places to stand, and this is a rubbery figure, as in theory a lot of people can stand closely together. A common number is 4 people per square metre, but other railways use 6, especially in Asia in very large cities. A political decision is needed on what exactly the capacity of a metro carriage is. The reader should remember that a small number of railways use 8 people per square metre, and in India it is possible to find trains with up to 14 people per square metre, a very high figure.

2/ Maximising the economic benefit to society

A formula commonly used to maximising the benefit to society for transportation, is given below, and can be used to determine the economic frequency of trains. This equation was first reported from the paper by H Mohring in 1971, and it is sometimes used in different textbooks on urban planning, often related to the frequency of bus services.

This formula works on the basis that the fixed costs of providing the rail service are not relevant, and that the decision on train frequency should be made on the basis of marginal costs. A marginal cost is similar to the direct cost often used in accounting, and represents the cost incurred through operating one additional train. This cost can be thought of as the cost of power, wages for drivers, and direct wear and tear on the train.

So let's define some terms:

EC = economic cost to society

T = Travel time (hours)

C = cost per hour of operating a train

p = number of passengers boarding a train per hour

VPM = value of a passenger minute

The two parameters we are interested in is the waiting time for passengers, and the direct cost of providing the train service. Whilst there are many other factors, it is these two that shall be used to determine the service frequency. We can express this relationship as follows:

Economic cost to society (train frequency)
= marginal cost running trains + cost of passengers waiting for trains

The marginal cost for operating trains on a rail line is:

Marginal cost of running trains =
Cost per hour x train frequency x route length (hours)

The cost of passengers waiting time

$$Passenger\ waiting\ cost = \frac{60 \times p \times VPM}{2f}$$

It's *2f* because on average passengers arrive half way between each train, and not immediately after a train has left. So, combining these terms, we get:

$$EC = TCf + \frac{60pVPM}{2f}$$

And to find the turning point, where the equation is minimised:

$$\frac{dEC}{df} = 0$$

So differentiating the above equation, we get:

$$\frac{dEC}{df} = TC - \frac{60pVPM}{2f^2} = 0$$

We can re-arrange this to obtain:

$$2f^2 = \frac{60pVPM}{TC}$$

And this gives for *f*:

$$f = \sqrt{\frac{60pVPM}{2TC}}$$

To finish this equation, we note that:

Value passenger hour (VPH) = 60 x VPM

So we finally get:

$$f = \sqrt{\frac{pVPH}{2TC}}$$

This is the classic equation for the economic frequency of transport services.

Worked Example

For our example, let's use the following numbers.

The trip length is 45 minutes
The number of passengers per hour = 4000
The cost of operating a train is $150 per hour
The wages per hour in the area is $20 per hour

What is the economic frequency of trains?

T = 45/60 = 0.75 hours
p = 4000
C = $150
VPH = $20 per hour

Substituting into the equation gives:

$$f = \sqrt{\frac{4000 \times 20}{2 \times 0.75 \times 150}}$$

$$f = 18.8 \text{ trains per hour}$$

A frequency of 18.8 trains per hour is quite high, so we can observe that the equation above often provides a high number of trains per hour. The numbers used in the equation above are quite typical.

Something that should be considered is that where a train moves in one direction, typically it needs to move in the other direction as well (but not always). Where this is the case, then the calculation needs to take into account both directions of travel, especially where trains in one direction operate mostly empty.

3/ Community service obligations

Community service obligations refers to the provision of public transport when there are insufficient people to justify the service, but the government wishes the transport provider to provide it anyway. These types of agreements are common in Australia, as there are many places where the population numbers are low, and public transport such as trains run almost empty.

Community service obligations are sometimes abbreviated to CSO. A CSO agreement between the transport provider and government will stipulate the number of services per hour, the capacity, and the times over which this service will run. The areas covered, or a description of the bus or train services, is obviously very important to a CSO. This type of agreement will often also include payments from the government to the transport provider in compensation for providing the service. CSO agreements can be an important source of funding for a transport provider. In Australia most CSO agreements would be with bus companies, but they also exist with rail companies as well.

CSO agreements would be a very unusual thing to implement with a new rail line. CSO's are almost always implemented in areas where the train line has been there for decades, and where population densities are low. It would be unthinkable to build a new expensive rail line, and then have so few people that a CSO was needed. It is conceivable that a new rail freight line may operate with passenger traffic as well, and in this situation small numbers of passengers may be acceptable because the line is there to service the freight, but it is difficult to imagine any other scenario where a rail line would be constructed in parallel with a CSO.

Of course CSO's would rarely provide for a high level of passenger service, such as a train every 3 minutes. Common CSO train frequencies are 2 or 3 trains a day, or potentially 1 train an hour. The frequencies are quite low, but enough for people without a car to get around, should they need to. Trains provided under a CSO agreement are often quite short, only a couple of carriages, and operate at modest speeds. CSO services are often diesel, at least in Australia, as there is often no overhead wiring in areas with very limited traffic.

Looking at CSO's from the perspective of government, they are useful in providing services to places where there would otherwise be no public transport. Passengers who often use CSO services are the elderly, students and young people who are too young to drive, those with disabilities who can't drive, and others who for whatever reason can't buy a car. In car loving Australia, most people have access to cars, CSO services are often almost empty. Where there are lots of people who don't have cars, but not enough to warrant a profitable bus or train service, then a CSO can be a good way to help people with their transport needs. In Australia, in areas where CSO agreements are needed, there are often approaches from local community groups to government, requesting a subsidy for public transport.

4/ Other political reasons

Stations exist where the number of stops at the station is extremely small. In NSW there are some stations where there are only 1 or 2 stops per week. These stations are often only serviced to keep them open, and there may be political pressure to close them. The experience in the UK and Australia is that once a rail line is closed then is can never be returned to service, or it is often very difficult. Later the closure of a rail line is often regretted, and a political decision is sometimes made to keep the line open, and this sometimes means just one train per week.

Choosing Service Hours

Choosing service hours an important decision for any operational railway. Trains cannot run continuously over a stretch of track for 24 hours a day indefinitely, as the track will degrade and its condition will be very poor. Time is needed for maintenance, and this is often a very major factor in determining the hours in which a railway operates. Alternatively, there may not be the demand to operate trains throughout the entire day, and there may be periods where the passenger demand is so low that there is little need for services. Either way, almost all railways are confronted with the decision on what the hours of operation should be.

Many metros, light rail, and tram systems close at night. When they close there are normally maintenance people waiting to jump onto the track to perform maintenance, and this needs to be done. Whilst it is not necessary to perform maintenance every night, most nights something will be done, and this needs to be allowed for. A typical number of hours per night set aside for maintenance is 6 hours, and this seems to be a reasonable compromise. Both the Hong Kong metro and the Shanghai stop operating around 11pm.

The same can be said for commuter systems, and high speed rail. These systems also close at night, and maintenance people enter the rail corridor and start doing work.

It's really important for rail managers to set aside some time for maintenance work to be performed. If there is no time then track conditions will be poor, and any maintenance work that is performed will be hurried and poor quality. Increasing the number of work hours available in a block is a good way to reduce maintenance costs, and blocks of only 2 or 3 hours are difficult to use effectively. It is much better if the maintainers get solid blocks of at least 5 hours.

Of course it is not necessary to make a 6 hour block available every night (in most cases). It is acceptable to have little or no maintenance window for, say, Friday and Saturday nights, as this will give maintenance workers time off and 5 nights per week for maintenance is generally sufficient. Services can operate all night on Fridays and Saturdays, which are nights that are often much more busy than other nights.

Another alternative is to have a longer maintenance window on quiet nights, such as Tuesday and Wednesday nights. This is sometimes done for large work, such as resleepering. Services might end at 9:30 pm, and allow maintenance workers significantly more time to perform whatever work is needed.

Things are a little easier for rail lines with low levels of traffic. Service frequency here is chosen because of the number of people travelling, and where there are large gaps in services, no specific maintenance window is necessary. Maintenance workers can perform maintenance between train services.

High Speed Rail presents some interesting challenges for providing a maintenance window. HSR trips are typically 2 to 4 hours, so a 5 or 6 hour maintenance window means that train services will need to cease around 10pm or even earlier. Whilst in theory it is possible for rail workers to do work on one rail line and not another, having a HSR train pass at 300 kms/hr might be a little disturbing for rail workers and present some real safety risks. Maintenance workers for an HSR rail system will need the entire rail corridor in many cases to perform work, especially where it involves heavy equipment. Having said that, there are maintenance vehicles that allow maintenance workers to work along a rail line alongside a working rail line.

REFERENCES

1. Rietveld, P. et al *Choice of Frequency and Vehicle Size in Rail Transport. Implications for Marginal Costs*, European Journal for Transport and Infrastructure Research, 2, no 2, (2002), pp 95 - 111

2. Wong, R. *Optimising Timetable Synchronisation for Rail Mass Transit*, Transportation Science Vol42, No 1, February 2008, 57 – 69

Index

Access charges, 422
Activity based modelling, 372
Advertising point, 134
Articulation, 29
at grade. *See* Grade separation
Automated People Movers, 41
Automatic Train Protection, 422
Ballast, 73, 74
  Fines, 78
Bangkok Skytrain, 42
Bi-directional track, 418
bi-level. *See* Double decker
Bi-level trains. *See* Double decker
Boardings, 18
Broad gauge, 23
Bulk material freight, 425
Bulk materials, 425
Bus Rapid Transit, 19
Cape gauge, 23
Capping layer, 74
Coaches, 55, 164
Code share. *See*
Codeshare, 57
Community service obligations, 485
Commuter rail, 50
Concourse, 116, 142
Consumer surplus, 342
Contact band, 450, *See* wear band
Control centre, 5
Control system, 101
Cost benefit, 340
Crossover, 206
Curfew, 409, 421
Dangerous goods, 424
Demand elasticity, 347
Demand estimation, 370
Demand inelasticity, 349
Demand supply curve, 341
Derailment, 415
Derived demand, 374
Diamond crossover, 207
Diesel multiple units, 55
Dispatcher. *See* Signaller
Dive, 194
Docklands Light Rail, 39, 41
Double decker, 31
Double slip, 208
Double stacking, 419
Duplication, 417
Dwell time, 45, 49, 265, 287
Dwell times, 464
Dynamic braking, 330
Dynamic gauging, 252
Economic multiplier, 397
Elasticity of demand, 348
Electric multiple units, 55
Electrolysis,, 93
Elevators. *See* Lifts
EMUs, 408
Equilibrium point, 342
Escalators
  Run-off, 286
Externalities, 343
Externality, 356
Fixed costs, 350
Flat car, 430
Flat cars, 413
Fleet utilisation, 451
Flying junction, 29
Flyover, 195
Formation, 74
Freight
  Axle load, 414
  Curfew, 477
  Gross Tonne Kilometres, 414

Million Gross Tonnes, 414
Tank wagons, 413
Weighbridges, 410
Freight corridor, 415
Goods road, 211
Grade separation, 28, 234
Halts, 21, 455
Headway, 84, 275, 287
Heavy haul, 28
Heavy rail, 406
High speed rail, 56
Hikari, 457
Horse crossing, 101
Hot box detector, 410
In-cab signalling, 82
Indirect benefits, 396
Induced benefits, 396
Infrastructure maintainers, 2
Intermodal terminal, 439
International Union of Railways, 8
Kinematic envelope, 251
Kodama, 457
Leakage effect, 397
Lifts, 286
Light metro, 42
Loading factor, 316
Loading gauge, 251
Loop, 228
Maglev, 62
Maintenance centres, 183
Marginal cost, 482
Market equilibrium, 341
Marshalling yards, 410
Mega Joule, 298
Metro, 45
Rubber tyred, 73
Mix of power generation, 296
Mixed system, 21, 28
Modal share, 420
Movement authority, 83
Moving walk, 149
Multiple unit, 164

Narrow gauge, 23
Network statement, 6, 423
Nozomi. *See*
Overhead wiring, 89
Pantograph, 23, 91
Pantograph well, 257
Parallel moves, 192
Passenger information systems, 52, 123
Passing loop, 418
Passing loops, 411
Peak period, 477
Pedestrian crossing, 101
Pendulum line, 231
People per hour, 164
Perway siding, 211
Platform length, 106
Portal, 95
Power
    Electrical power, 298
Producer surplus, 342
Public private partnership, 385
Public private partnerships, 384
Pumping station, 194
Rail
    Tram, 77
Rail cruise, 62
Rail cruises, 11, 69
Rail freight curfew, 474
Rail lubricator,, 332
Rail operators, 2
Rail souvenir shops, 135
RATP, 8
Refuge, 411
Regenerative braking, 330
Regional rail, 54
Reserved seats, 59
Ring network, 246
Road congestion, 360
Road train, 405
Rollingstock
    Double decker, 164
    Pantograph, 89

Set, 163
Route length, 19
Route signalling, 452
Ruling grade, 417
Runaways, 441
Running direction, 205
Russian gauge, 23
Sensitivity analysis, 374
Shinkansen, 57, 318
Shipping container, 426
Short platforms, 151
Shoulder period, 477
Shunter, 441
Shuttle, 200, 238
Sidings, 210
Signal routes, 5
Signaller, 85
Signalling
   Route signalling, 85
   Speed signalling, 85
Single slip, 207
Sketch planning, 370
Sleeper carriage, 62
Sleepers, 74
Social surplus, 343
Speed signalling, 452
Stabling, 19, 183
Stanchions, 90
Standard gauge, 23
Station
   Interchange, 106
Stations
   Concourse, 118
   Halt, 111
   Island platform, 109
   Level of service, 280
   Paid area, 116
   Side platform, 108
   Spanish solution, 117
   Vending machine, 109
Stopping pattern, 52, 454, 470
Streetcars, 30
structure gauge, 251

Structure gauge, 251
sunk costs. *See* Fixed costs
Supercrush loads, 292
Supply and demand, 341
Supply demand model, 341
Switcher, 441
Tank wagon, 426
Terminus, 106, 210, 226
TGV, 57
Third rail, 23
Tilt trains, 67
Timing point, 465
Tonnage signal, 411
Tonnage signals, 474
Tourism economics, 396
Tourist railway, 390
Tourist railways, 448
Tourist Trains, 68
Track
   Dual gauge, 80
Track length, 19
Traction power, 88
   AC, 23
   DC, 23
   Third rail, 89
Tragedy of the commons, 362
Trams
   Powerhouse, 22
Tram-train system, 30
Transport orientated development, 65, 345
Transport Orientated Development, 12
Trip, 449
Tunnels
   Ventilation, 96
Turnback, 227
Turntables, 186
Twenty foot Equivalent Units, 429
Twistlock, 427, 429
Ultra low floor tram, 34
Unit elasticity, 349

Unit trains, 229
Unwired. *See* Traction Power
Utility, 374
Vending machines, 132
Wear band, 75

Well car, 430
Willingness to Pay, 340
Working timetable, 128, 446, 479

www.ingramcontent.com/pod-product-compliance
Lightning Source LLC
Chambersburg PA
CBHW032021290426
44110CB00012B/624